The Faber Book of America

The Faber
Book of America

EDITED BY

Christopher Ricks and William L. Vance

And I ask all to try to forgive me
For being as over-elated
As if I had measured the country
And got the United States stated.

Robert Frost, 'A Record Stride'

Faber and Faber

LONDON • BOSTON

Published in 1992 in the United States by Faber and Faber, Inc., 50 Cross
Street, Winchester, MA 01890 and in the United Kingdom by Faber and
Faber Limited, 3 Queen Square, London WC1N 3AU

Library of Congress Cataloging-in-Publication Data
The Faber book of America / edited by Christopher Ricks
and William L. Vance.
p.   cm.
ISBN 0-571-14405-5
1. American literature.   2. National characteristics. American—Literary
collections.   3. United States—Civilization—Literary collections.
4. America—Literary collections.   I. Ricks, Christopher.
II. Vance, William L.
PS509.U52F3   1992
810.8'03273—dc20   92-20300
CIP

A CIP record for this book is available from the British Library

Photoset by Stanton Publication Services
Printed in the United Kingdom

2   4   6   8   10   9   7   5   3   1

Contents

From Sea to Shining Sea

Union

Beliefs   153

All Men Are Created Equal   187

Character   239

Culture   287

Money and Things

Empire 395

INTRODUCTION

'America'? Don't we mean 'the United States of America'? 'America' is a pair of subcontinents plus an isthmus.

The inhabitants of South America, of Central America and of that part of North America which is not the United States (Mexico and Canada, yes) are on occasion chagrined by the unmisgiving assumption that United States citizens own the words 'America' and 'Americans'. There has to be some political and even imperial pressure exerted by the fact of nomenclature. The Monroe Doctrine (that the Americas are America's 'backyard') may call upon the feeling, though not exactly the thought, that the name vindicates a claim. Citizens of the USA must often sense something odd in there not being a simple name for their citizenship. How cumbrous 'US citizen' feels in comparison with the relation of the French to France, of the Germans to Germany, of the English to England . . . Not that US citizens are alone in this. A world which had got into the way of using the name 'Russians' too loosely is at this very moment having to adapt itself to appreciating that a Russian is not interchangeable with any old citizen of what used to be the USSR. And bona fide Russians would do well to be sensitive to the dangers of imperialistic claim which have lurked in the name. What's in a name? An emanation.

Edgar Allan Poe had his own proposal in the matter:

> It is a thousand pities that the puny witticisms of a few professional objectors should have power to prevent, even for a year, the adoption of a name for our country. At present we have clearly none. There should be no hesitation about 'Appalachia'. In the first place, it is distinctive. 'America' is not and can never be made so.

Footnote by Poe: 'Mr Field, in a meeting of "The New York Historical Society", proposed that we take the name of "America", and bestow "Columbia" upon the Continent.' But it was not for the USA to 'bestow' a name upon a continent which was not its property. So Poe pressed on with his hopeful hopeless case:

> *We* may legislate as much as we please, and assume for our country whatever name we think right – but to us it will be no name, to any purpose for which a name is needed, unless we can take it away from

the regions which employ it at present. South America is 'America', and will insist upon remaining so. In the second place, 'Appalachia' is indigenous, springing from one of the most magnificent and distinctive features of the country itself. Thirdly, in employing this word we do honour to the Aborigines, whom, hitherto, we have at all points unmercifully despoiled, assassinated, and dishonoured. Fourthly, the name is the suggestion of, perhaps, the most deservedly eminent among all the pioneers of American literature. It is but just that Mr Irving should name the land for which, in letters, he first established a name. The last, and by far the most truly important consideration of all, however, is the music of 'Appalachia' itself; nothing could be more sonorous, more liquid, or of fuller volume, while its length is just sufficient for dignity. How the guttural 'Alleghania' could ever have been preferred for a moment is difficult to conceive. I yet hope to find 'Appalachia' assumed.

All such hopes are doomed to be dashed. Formally it will continue to be 'the United States of America', and informally 'America'. The tension between the two is a fact of life and an incitement to the imagination. But at least this application of the word 'American' has been around a long time, and anyway no other nationality (as against continental denizenship) makes any claim to the word. Granted, *The Faber Book of America* is a tendentious title, and politic correctness (or cravenness) did at one stage suggest . . . *of the USA*, but something about the nature of the nation is apprehended in this very tendentiousness.

The closest thing to a neutral dubbing might have been Byron's 'English and Spanish Atlantides', but the phrase was not likely to catch on – despite Byron's acute understanding that what was at issue was the course of empire:

Whenever an American requests to see me (which is *not* uncommon) I comply – firstly because I respect a people who acquired their freedom by firmness without excess – and secondly because these transatlantic visits 'few and far between' make me feel as if talking with posterity from the other side of the Styx. In a century or two the new English and Spanish Atlantides will be masters of the old countries in all probability – as Greece and Rome overcame their mother Asia in the older or earlier ages as they are called.

And now, as a century since Byron turns to two, the empire of the Atlantides faces the Pacific Rim.

'*E pluribus unum*': the aspiration to nationhood asks that from many things there should come forth one. But it asks too the opposite: that from the one thing there come forth many.

This is an anthology of America, not of American literature – our happy brief was to seek and to dispose a range of writings which were not simply (or even necessarily) American but which were *about* America. The distinction is manifest in the contrast between the two great American poets of the nineteenth century: Emily Dickinson and Walt Whitman. Every line of them both is indeflectibly American, and yet whereas almost every poem of Whitman's is in some way about America, to the point at which you find yourself contemplating 'the Whitman Book of America', very few of Dickinson's are, no less American though she is.

The editors of this present book have each of them undertaken separately something like this kind of work before, yet this enterprise has felt very different. It is a different story from an anthology of American literature or one of Victorian verse – not least in that it is not clear what, in the matter of America, could possibly count as a *story*. In the ordinary way, an anthologist is at once aided and circumscribed by the fact that half, say, of what will figure in the final selection was all along sure to figure. But no such confidence, such constraint, for good and ill, could ever be felt with a Book of America. It is clear that there could be a dozen such volumes, each of them knowledgeably unbigoted, in which scarcely a single item would be held in common. Oh, the Declaration of Independence perhaps – but for the rest? It is of the nature of the fecund contrarious history, the cultural dapple and squabble, the sheer scale of America and of its 'collideorscape', that no two anthologies of America need have anything much in common. *Ex uno plures*.

So that such an anthology confronts both its chance and its fate in the fact that America can itself be reasonably considered under the aspect of an anthology.

Philip James Bailey, in *Festus* (a poem which feels twice as big as America and a million times more tedious), took a genially humdrum view of this congeries of a nation:

> America, thou half-brother of the world;
> With something good and bad of every land.

Half-brother perhaps, but often fiercely resistant to any half-and-half-ness, anything which might endanger an entire commitment to union. 'There can be no fifty-fifty Americanism in this country,' insisted Theodore Roosevelt: 'there is room here for only 100 per cent Americanism, only for those who are American and nothing else.'

This is of a piece with religious fervour. The nation which sets itself to separate Church from State, and which commits itself to religious freedom, yet has an oath of allegiance as one nation under God. Its currency has its divine right: In God We Trust. Israel Zangwill was sure that 'God is making the American.' But what about those of us who are atheists or agnostics?

'America is God's Crucible,' Zangwill urged dramatically, 'the great Melting-Pot where all the races of Europe are melting and re-forming.' But since 1909 the Melting-Pot has itself suffered a certain meltdown. Assimilation has felt less and less distinguishable from a simulation. 'I am easily assimilated': so the immigrant sings – winsomely, sardonically – in the new world of Leonard Bernstein's replanting of Voltaire's *Candide*.

The diversity of geography, of climate, of races, nationalities and cultures, and the astonishing changes in political and social conditions in the semi-millennium from 1492 to 1992: these are the stuff of this book and could be the stuff of a score of utterly different books. Our earliest nameable author, the founder of Boston – John Winthrop – was born in 1588, just less than a century after Columbus's voyage. Among our most recent authors are a daughter of Chinese immigrants and a Chicano whose traditions through Mexico connect him with both the native peoples and the first Spanish explorers. The oldest town to appear in these pages – Ácoma – is one that long predates the voyages of Columbus.

We have tried to catch something of these diverse diversities by constituting the book mostly of short or shortish entries, not only because this obviously makes room for a lot more of them but also because of the opportunities for principled disagreement and for the glancing, the oblique and the suggestive in sequence and in perspective.

The ordering within the two sections 'Union' and 'Empire' is straightforward, chronological, since there a history can unfold; in the other sections, we hope to have achieved juxtapositions which are telling. So Henry James's vision of the sheer power of New York, of the abstracted but indubitable energy of its extravagance, is immediately followed by Rudyard Kipling's evocation, a century ago but unchanged today, of the potholes which make you lurch and the squalor which might make you retch. What we hope to gain through these and suchlike counterpointings is not only a sense of how a home-coming American, James, sees and shows different facets from those of the fascinated traveller, Kipling, but also a juxtaposition of the writers themselves – two great men of letters, alert and antagonistic. Or there is W. H. Auden's worldly-wise gratitude to, and dismay at, the poetry-reading round, 'On the Circuit', duly succeeded by Anthony Hecht's 'Application for a Grant', an entirely up-to-the-minute eye-on-the-main-chance plea which nevertheless takes a very long view of these implorings of patronage, since the poem is an adaptation or imitation, 'Freely from Horace'. Freely . . . ? Whereupon we revert for a moment to Auden, on 'The Almighty Dollar'. Almighty enough for us to have glimpsed him just now 'On the Circuit'.

Within our own circuit, most of the items have their headings within quotation marks; this means that the item is excerpted, not complete, its heading being a brief quotation from within it. Headings without quotation marks are their authors' own titles, and the items they precede are complete except in the few cases where 'Excerpt' is noted in the source reference below the item. (These are occasions when an author's title was too good to lose.) Editorial glosses within the items are enclosed in square brackets.

The division of the book into nine sections is provisional, improvisatory – clearly much of what figures in one section, though it may be distinguishable from, is not distinct from much that is elsewhere. Questions of belief are questions of character seen under a different aspect, and both are not just expressed in culture but constitutive of it. A central belief or ideal – that of equality, crucial to a democracy – is of such importance in the contradictions and complexities of American history as to have generated an abundance of record and exhortation: hence a separate section. But a full index (a glossarial index, giving brief notes on persons, places, etc. mentioned in the text) is provided to make possible the reconstitution of different assemblings and of other angles or stories.

Stories: we have included some fiction (Mark Twain, Willa Cather, Sinclair Lewis) when it seized some crucial aspect of American life – the ways of a world, the expanse of a landscape, the contractions of earning a living. But we appreciate that much fiction, because of scale and context, does not lend itself well to our undertaking, and that there is a great deal of unignorable American fiction – such as would be sure to figure in a differently-angled anthology, one of American literature – which we have found ourselves unable to incorporate.

Aware that an anthology like this, being constituted of words, will tend to underrate all those achievements of which the medium is not words, we have tried to do right by such other aspects of American life, culture and history. The art of Whistler, and of Georgia O'Keeffe, though it is not reproduced, is represented here, as are the abstract expressionism of Robert Motherwell and the concrete expressiveness of the great painter-naturalist Audubon. Hollywood is revered and bantered here, and so is Disneyland, and something is heard of jazz, of the blues, of the music of Charles Ives, and of the Big Rock Candy Mountains. Meanwhile, even as someone sings, money talks.

Does all this make for something insufficiently celebratory of America? It is true that much of the writing here is critical – often sharply so – and this even from so great a celebrator of America as Walt Whitman. But criticism does not have to be disrespect and often constitutes an act of deep respect. Great disappointment has to be proportionate to greatness. What America promised, and fulfilled for many people, is implied in what is criticized: its failures to be all it promised. Moreover, critical scrutiny is often more provocative and more penetrating than simple praise can be. Vigilance may be still more necessary today when the unmistakable failure of an alternative ideal on the other side of the world may foster too complacent a view of the American experience, the American model and even the American dream. And though there is much in this book that quizzes, mocks and excoriates some aspects of America, most of the book's items are by Americans themselves (such a tradition of criticism is itself proudly American) and none of them is mere snootiness.

One of Henry James's Americans, Christopher Newman from California, scented just such hauteur in a compatriot of his, back at the time when the United States felt more like a 'them' than an 'it':

He had never been a very systematic patriot, but it vexed him to see the United States treated as little better than a vulgar smell in his friend's nostril, and he finally spoke up for them quite as if it had been Fourth of July, proclaiming that any American who ran them down ought to be carried home in irons and compelled to live in Boston – which for Newman was putting it very vindictively.

The American, 1877, 1907

But then both of this book's editors, though only one of them is an American, live in Boston.

ENCOUNTERS AND POSSESSIONS

October 12, the Discovery. It was wonderful to find America, but it would have been more wonderful to miss it.

Mark Twain, *Pudd'nhead Wilson*, 1894

America was too big to have been discovered all at one time. It would have been better for the graces if it had been discovered in pieces of about the size of France and Germany at a time.

Samuel Butler, *Notebooks*, 1951

America is Hard to See

ROBERT FROST

Columbus may have worked the wind
A new and better way to Ind
And also proved the world a ball,
But how about the wherewithal?
Not just for scientific news
Had the Queen backed him to a cruise.

Remember he had made the test
Finding the East by sailing West.
But had he found it? Here he was
Without one trinket from Ormuz
To save the Queen from family censure
For her investment in his venture.

There had been something strangely wrong
With every coast he tried along.
He could imagine nothing barrener.
The trouble was with him the mariner.
He wasn't off a mere degree;
His reckoning was off a sea.

And to intensify the drama
Another mariner, da Gama,
Came just then sailing into port
From the same general resort,
And with the gold in hand to show for
His claim it was another Ophir.

Had but Columbus known enough
He might have boldly made the bluff
That better than da Gama's gold
He had been given to behold
The race's future trial place,
A fresh start for the human race.

He might have fooled Valladolid.
I was deceived by what he did.
If I had had my chance when young
I should have had Columbus sung

As a god who had given us
A more than Moses' exodus.

But all he did was spread the room
Of our enacting out the doom
Of being in each other's way,
And so put off the weary day
When we would have to put our mind
On how to crowd but still be kind.

For these none-too-apparent gains
He got no more than dungeon chains
And such small posthumous renown
(A country named for him, a town,
A holiday) as, where he is,
He may not recognize for his.

They say his flagship's unlaid ghost
Still probes and dents our rocky coast
With animus approaching hate,
And for not turning out a strait,
He has cursed every river mouth
From fifty North to fifty South.

Someday our navy, I predict,
Will take in tow this derelict
And lock him through Culebra Cut,
His eyes as good (or bad) as shut
To all the modern works of man
And all we call American.

America is hard to see.
Less partial witnesses than he
In book on book have testified
They could not see it from outside –
Or inside either for that matter.
We know the literary chatter.

Columbus, as I say, will miss
All he owes to the artifice
Of tractor-plow and motor-drill.
To naught but his own force of will,
Or at most some Andean quake,
Will he ascribe this lucky break.

High purpose makes the hero rude;
He will not stop for gratitude.
But let him show his haughty stern
To what was never his concern
Except as it denied him way
To fortune-hunting in Cathay.

He will be starting pretty late.
He'll find that Asiatic state
Is about tired of being looted
While having its beliefs disputed.
His can be no such easy raid
As Cortez on the Aztecs made.

In the Clearing, 1962

'One with this world'

[Prayer to the seven deities of the Yokuts tribe, California]

Do you see me!
See me, Tüüshiut!
See me, Pamashiut!
See me, Yuhahait!
See me, Echepat!
See me, Pitsuriut!
See me, Tsuksit!
See me, Ukat!
Do you all help me!
My words are tied in one
With the great mountains,
With the great rocks,
With the great trees,
In one with my body
And my heart.
Do you all help me
With supernatural power
And you, day,
And you, night!

All of you see me
One with this world!

A. L. Kroeber, *Handbook of the Indians of California*, 1925

'Columbus first beheld'

WASHINGTON IRVING

It was on Friday morning, the 12th of October, that Columbus first beheld the New World. As the day dawned he saw before him a level island, several leagues in extent, and covered with trees like a continual orchard. Though apparently uncultivated, it was populous, for the inhabitants were seen issuing from all parts of the woods and running to the shore. They were perfectly naked, and, as they stood gazing at the ships, appeared by their attitudes and gestures to be lost in astonishment. Columbus made signal for the ships to cast anchor, and the boats to be manned and armed. He entered his own boat, richly attired in scarlet, and holding the royal standard; whilst Martin Alonzo Pinzon, and Vincent Jañez his brother, put off in company in their boats; each with a banner of the enterprise emblazoned with a green cross, having on either side the letters F. and Y., the initials of the Castilian monarchs Fernando and Ysabel, surmounted by crowns.

As he approached the shore, Columbus, who was disposed for all kinds of agreeable impressions, was delighted with the purity and suavity of the atmosphere, the crystal transparency of the sea, and the extraordinary beauty of the vegetation. He beheld, also, fruits of an unknown kind upon the trees which overhung the shores. On landing he threw himself on his knees, kissed the earth, and returned thanks to God with tears of joy. His example was followed by the rest, whose hearts indeed overflowed with the same feelings of gratitude. Columbus then rising drew his sword, displayed the royal standard, and assembling round him the two captains, with Rodrigo de Escobedo, notary of the armament, Rodrigo Sanchez, and the rest who had landed, he took solemn possession in the name of the Castilian sovereigns, giving the island the name of San Salvador. Having complied with the requisite forms and ceremonies, he called upon all present to take the oath of obedience to him, as admiral and viceroy, representing the persons of the sovereigns.

The feelings of the crew now burst forth in the most extravagant transports. They had recently considered themselves devoted men, hurrying forward to destruction; they now looked upon themselves as favorites of fortune, and gave themselves up to the most unbounded joy. They thronged

around the admiral with overflowing zeal, some embracing him, others kiss-
ing his hands. Those who had been most mutinous and turbulent during the
voyage, were now most devoted and enthusiastic. Some begged favors of
him, as if he had already wealth and honors in his gift. Many abject spirits,
who had outraged him by their insolence, now crouched at his feet, begging
pardon for all the trouble they had caused him, and promising the blindest
obedience for the future.

The natives of the island, when, at the dawn of day, they had beheld the
ships hovering on their coast, had supposed them monsters which had is-
sued from the deep during the night. They had crowded to the beach, and
watched their movements with awful anxiety. Their veering about, apparently without effort, and the shifting and furling of their sails, resembling
huge wings, filled them with astonishment. When they beheld their boats
approach the shore, and a number of strange beings clad in glittering steel,
or raiment of various colors, landing upon the beach, they fled in affright
to the woods. Finding, however, that there was no attempt to pursue nor
molest them, they gradually recovered from their terror, and approached
the Spaniards with great awe; frequently prostrating themselves on the
earth, and making signs of adoration. During the ceremonies of taking possession, they remained gazing in timid admiration at the complexion, the
beards, the shining armor, and splendid dress of the Spaniards. The admiral
particularly attracted their attention, from his commanding height, his air
of authority, his dress of scarlet, and the deference which was paid him by
his companions; all which pointed him out to be the commander. When
they had still further recovered from their fears, they approached the
Spaniards, touched their beards, and examined their hands and faces, ad-
miring their whiteness. Columbus was pleased with their gentleness and
confiding simplicity, and suffered their scrutiny with perfect acquiescence,
winning them by his benignity. They now supposed that the ships had sailed
out of the crystal firmament which bounded their horizon, or had descended
from above on their ample wings, and that these marvelous beings were inhabitants of the skies.

The natives of the island were no less objects of curiosity to the
Spaniards, differing, as they did, from any race of men they had ever seen.
Their appearance gave no promise of either wealth or civilization, for they
were entirely naked, and painted with a variety of colors. With some it was
confined merely to a part of the face, the nose, or around the eyes; with
others it extended to the whole body, and gave them a wild and fantastic
appearance. Their complexion was of a tawny or copper hue, and they were
entirely destitute of beards. Their hair was not crisped, like the recently-
discovered tribes of the African coast, under the same latitude, but straight
and coarse, partly cut short above the ears, but some locks were left long

behind and falling upon their shoulders. Their features, though obscured and disfigured by paint, were agreeable; they had lofty foreheads and remarkably fine eyes. They were of moderate stature and well-shaped; most of them appeared to be under thirty years of age: there was but one female with them, quite young, naked like her companions, and beautifully formed.

As Columbus supposed himself to have landed on an island at the extremity of India, he called the natives by the general appellation of Indians, which was universally adopted before the true nature of his discovery was known, and has since been extended to all the aboriginals of the New World.

A History of the Life and Voyages of Christopher Columbus, 1828, book 1, ch. 1

Columbus

OGDEN NASH

Once upon a time there was an Italian,
And some people thought he was a rapscallion,
But he wasn't offended,
Because other people thought he was splendid,
And he said the world was round,
And everybody made an uncomplimentary sound,
But his only reply was Pooh,
He replied, Isn't this fourteen ninety-two?
It's time for me to discover America if I know my chronology,
And if I discover America you owe me an apology,
So he went and tried to borrow some money from Ferdinand
But Ferdinand said America was a bird in the bush and he'd rather have
    a berdinand.
But Columbus' brain was fertile, it wasn't arid,
And he remembered that Ferdinand was unhappily married,
And he thought, there is no wife like a misunderstood one,
Because her husband thinks something is a terrible idea she is bound to
    think it a good one,
So he perfumed his handkerchief with bay rum and citronella,
And he went to see Isabella,
And he looked wonderful but he had never felt sillier,
And she said, I can't place the face but the aroma is familiar,
And Columbus didn't say a word,

All he said was, I am Columbus, the fifteenth-century Admiral Byrd,
And just as he thought, her disposition was very malleable,
And she said, Here are my jewels, and she wasn't penurious like Cornelia
    the mother of the Gracchi, she wasn't referring to her children, no, she
    was referring to her jewels, which were very very valuable,
So Columbus said, somebody show me the sunset and somebody did and
    he set sail for it,
And he discovered America and they put him in jail for it,
And the fetters gave him welts,
And they named America after somebody else,
So the sad fate of Columbus ought to be pointed out to every child and every
    voter,
Because it has a very important moral, which is, Don't be a discoverer, be
    a promoter.

I'm a Stranger Here Myself, 1938

'The most distinguished navigators'

HENRY DAVID THOREAU

That Cabot merely landed on the uninhabitable shore of Labrador, gave the
English no just title to New England, or to the United States generally, any
more than to Patagonia. His careful biographer (Biddle) is not certain in
what voyage he ran down the coast of the United States, as is reported, and
no one tells us what he saw. Miller, in the New York Hist. Coll., Vol. I.
p. 28, says he does not appear to have landed anywhere. Contrast with this
Verrazzani's tarrying fifteen days at one place on the New England coast,
and making frequent excursions into the interior thence. It chances that the
latter's letter to Francis I, in 1524, contains 'the earliest original account ex-
tant of the Atlantic coast of the United States'; and even from that time the
northern part of it began to be called *La Terra Francese*, or French Land.
A part of it was called New Holland before it was called New England. The
English were very backward to explore and settle the continent which they
had stumbled upon. The French preceded them both in their attempts to
colonize the continent of North America (Carolina and Florida, 1562–4),
and in their first permanent settlement (Port Royal, 1605); and the right of
possession, naturally enough, was the one which England mainly respected
and recognized in the case of Spain, of Portugal, and also of France, from
the time of Henry VII.

The explorations of the French gave to the world the first valuable maps of these coasts. Denys of Honfleur made a map of the Gulf of St Lawrence in 1506. No sooner had Cartier explored the St Lawrence in 1535, than there began to be published by his countrymen remarkably accurate charts of that river as far up as Montreal. It is almost all of the continent north of Florida that you recognize on charts for more than a generation afterward – though Verrazzani's rude plot (made under French auspices) was regarded by Hackluyt, more than fifty years after his voyage (in 1524), as the most accurate representation of our coast. The French trail is distinct. They went measuring and sounding, and when they got home had something to show for their voyages and explorations. There was no danger of their charts being lost, as Cabot's have been.

The most distinguished navigators of that day were Italians, or of Italian descent, and Portuguese. The French and Spaniards, though less advanced in the science of navigation than the former, possessed more imagination and spirit of adventure than the English, and were better fitted to be the explorers of a new continent even as late as 1751.

This spirit it was which so early carried the French to the Great Lakes and the Mississippi on the north, and the Spaniard to the same river on the south. It was long before our frontiers reached their settlements in the west, and a *voyageur* or *coureur de bois* is still our conductor there. Prairie is a French word, as Sierra is a Spanish one. Augustine in Florida, and Santa Fé in New Mexico [1582], both built by the Spaniards, are considered the oldest towns in the United States. Within the memory of the oldest man, the Anglo-Americans were confined between the Appalachian Mountains and the sea, 'a space not two hundred miles broad', while the Mississippi was by treaty the eastern boundary of New France. (See the pamphlet on settling the Ohio, London, 1763, bound up with the travels of Mr John Bartram.) So far as inland discovery was concerned, the adventurous spirit of the English was that of sailors who land but for a day, and their enterprise the enterprise of traders. Cabot spoke like an Englishman, as he was, if he said, as one reports, in reference to the discovery of the American Continent, when he found it running toward the north, that it was a great disappointment to him, being in his way to India; but we would rather add to than detract from the fame of so great a discoverer.

Samuel Penhallow, in his History (Boston, 1726), p. 51, speaking of 'Port Royal and Nova Scotia', says of the last, that its 'first seizure was by Sir Sebastian Cobbet for the crown of Great Britain, in the reign of King Henry VII; but lay dormant till the year 1621', when Sir William Alexander got a patent of it, and possessed it some years; and afterward Sir David Kirk was proprietor of it, but erelong, 'to the surprise of all thinking men, it was given up unto the French'.

Even as late as 1633 we find Winthrop, the first Governor of the Massachusetts Colony, who was not the most likely to be misinformed, who, moreover, has the *fame*, at least, of having discovered Wachusett Mountain (discerned it forty miles inland), talking about the 'Great Lake' and the 'hideous swamps about it', near which the Connecticut and the 'Patomack' took their rise; and among the memorable events of the year 1642 he chronicles Darby Field, an Irishman's expedition to the 'White hill', from whose top he saw eastward what he 'judged to be the Gulf of Canada', and westward what he 'judged to be the great lake which Canada River comes out of', and where he found much 'Muscovy glass', and 'could rive out pieces of forty feet long and seven or eight broad'. While the very inhabitants of New England were thus fabling about the country a hundred miles inland, which was a *terra incognita* to them – or rather many years before the earliest date referred to – Champlain, the *first Governor of Canada*, not to mention the inland discoveries of Cartier,[1] Roberval, and others, of the preceding century, and his own earlier voyage, had already gone to war against the Iroquois in their forest forts, and penetrated to the Great Lakes and wintered there, before a Pilgrim had heard of New England. In Champlain's 'Voyages', printed in 1613, there is a plate representing a fight in which he aided the Canada Indians against the Iroquois, near the south end of Lake Champlain, in July, 1609, eleven years before the settlement of Plymouth. Bancroft says he joined the Algonquins in an expedition against the Iroquois, or Five Nations, in the northwest of New York. This is that 'Great Lake', which the English, hearing some rumor of from the French, long after, locate in an 'Imaginary Province called Laconia, and spent several years about 1630 in the vain attempt to discover'. (Sir Ferdinand Gorges, in Maine Hist. Coll., Vol. II. p. 68.) Thomas Morton has a chapter on this 'Great Lake'. In the edition of Champlain's map dated 1632, the Falls of Niagara appear; and in a great lake northwest of *Mer Douce* (Lake Huron) there is an island represented, over which is written, '*Isle où il y a une mine de cuivre*', – 'Island where there is a mine of copper'. This will do for an offset to our Governor's 'Muscovy glass'. Of all these adventures and discoveries we have a minute and faithful account, giving facts and dates as well as charts and soundings, all scientific and Frenchman-like, with scarcely one fable or traveller's story.

[1] It is remarkable that the first, if not the only, part of New England which Cartier saw was Vermont (he also saw the mountains of New York), from Montreal Mountain in 1535, sixty-seven years before Gosnold saw Cape Cod. *If seeing is discovering* – and that is *all* that it is proved that Cabot knew of the coast of the United States – then Cartier (to omit Verrazzani and Gomez) was the discoverer of New England rather than Gosnold, who is commonly so styled.

(wr. 1855) *Cape Cod* 1864, ch. 10

'A naked rock in the desert'

WILLA CATHER

[Ácoma is the oldest continuously inhabited site in the United States, having been settled by AD 1100. Spanish explorers reached it in 1540. A church was built by 1629. Cather's novel concerns French missionaries who arrived in the mid-nineteenth century after the area had become the US Territory of New Mexico.]

After early Mass the next morning Father Latour and his guide rode off across the low plain that lies between Laguna and Ácoma. In all his travels the Bishop had seen no country like this. From the flat red sea of sand rose great rock mesas, generally Gothic in outline, resembling vast cathedrals. They were not crowded together in disorder, but placed in wide spaces, long vistas between. This plain might once have been an enormous city, all the smaller quarters destroyed by time, only the public buildings left, – piles of architecture that were like mountains. The sandy soil of the plain had a light sprinkling of junipers, and was splotched with masses of blooming rabbit brush, – that olive-coloured plant that grows in high waves like a tossing sea, at this season covered with a thatch of bloom, yellow as gorse, or orange like marigolds.

This mesa plain had an appearance of great antiquity, and of incompleteness; as if, with all the materials for world-making assembled, the Creator had desisted, gone away and left everything on the point of being brought together, on the eve of being arranged into mountain, plain, plateau. The country was still waiting to be made into a landscape.

*

Jacinto interrupted these reflections by an exclamation.

'Ácoma!' He stopped his mule.

The Bishop, following with his eye the straight, pointing Indian hand, saw, far away, two great mesas. They were almost square in shape, and at this distance seemed close together, though they were really some miles apart.

'The far one' – his guide still pointed.

The Bishop's eyes were not so sharp as Jacinto's, but now, looking down upon the top of the farther mesa from the high land on which they halted, he saw a flat white outline on the grey surface – a white square made up of squares. That, his guide said, was the pueblo of Ácoma.

*

By the time the Bishop and his guide reached the last turn in the trail, and rose through the crack, stepping out on the flat top of the rock, the noontide sun was blazing down upon Ácoma with almost insupportable brightness. The bare stone floor of the town and its deep-worn paths were washed white and clean, and those depressions in the surface which the Ácomas call their cisterns, were full of fresh rain water. Already the women were bringing out their clothes, to begin washing. The drinking water was carried up the stairway in earthen jars on the heads of the women, from a secret spring below; but for all other purposes the people depended on the rainfall held in these cisterns.

The top of the mesa was about ten acres in extent, the Bishop judged, and there was not a tree or a blade of green upon it; not a handful of soil, except the churchyard, held in by an adobe wall, where the earth for burial had been carried up in baskets from the plain below. The white dwellings, two and three storeyed, were not scattered, but huddled together in a close cluster, with no protecting slope of ground or shoulder of rock, lying flat against the flat, bright against the bright, – both the rock and the plastered houses threw off the sun glare blindingly.

At the very edge of the mesa, overhanging the abyss so that its retaining wall was like a part of the cliff itself, was the old warlike church of Ácoma, with its two stone towers. Gaunt, grim, grey, its nave rising some seventy feet to a sagging, half-ruined roof, it was more like a fortress than a place of worship. That spacious interior depressed the Bishop as no other mission church had done. He held a service there before midday, and he had never found it so hard to go through the ceremony of the Mass. Before him, on the grey floor, in the grey light, a group of bright shawls and blankets, some fifty or sixty silent faces; above and behind them the grey walls. He felt as if he were celebrating Mass at the bottom of the sea, for antediluvian creatures; for types of life so old, so hardened, so shut within their shells, that the sacrifice on Calvary could hardly reach back so far. Those shell-like backs behind him might be saved by baptism and divine grace, as undeveloped infants are, but hardly through any experience of their own, he thought. When he blessed them and sent them away, it was with a sense of inadequacy and spiritual defeat.

After he had laid aside his vestments, Father Latour went over the church with Jacinto. As he examined it his wonder grew. What need had there ever been for this great church at Ácoma? It was built early in sixteen hundred, by Fray Juan Ramirez, a great missionary, who laboured on the Rock of Ácoma for twenty years or more. It was Father Ramirez, too, who made the mule trail down the other side, – the only path by which a burro can ascend the mesa, and which is still called 'El Camino del Padre'.

The more Father Latour examined this church, the more he was inclined to think that Fray Ramirez, or some Spanish priest who followed him, was not altogether innocent of worldly ambition, and that they built for their own satisfaction, perhaps, rather than according to the needs of the Indians. The magnificent site, the natural grandeur of this stronghold, might well have turned their heads a little. Powerful men they must have been, those Spanish Fathers, to draft Indian labour for this great work without military support. Every stone in that structure, every handful of earth in those many thousand pounds of adobe, was carried up the trail on the backs of men and boys and women. And the great carved beams of the roof – Father Latour looked at them with amazement. In all the plain through which he had come he had seen no trees but a few stunted piñons. He asked Jacinto where these huge timbers could have been found.

'San Mateo mountain, I guess.'

'But the San Mateo mountains must be forty or fifty miles away. How could they bring such timbers?'

Jacinto shrugged. 'Ácomas carry.' Certainly there was no other explanation.

Besides the church proper there was the cloister, large, thick-walled, which must have required an enormous labour of portage from the plain. The deep cloister corridors were cool when the rock outside was blistering; the low arches opened on an enclosed garden which, judging from its depth of earth, must once have been very verdant. Pacing those shady passages, with four feet of solid, windowless adobe shutting out everything but the green garden and the turquoise sky above, the early missionaries might well have forgotten the poor Ácomas, that tribe of ancient rock-turtles, and believed themselves in some cloister hung on a spur of the Pyrenees.

In the grey dust of the enclosed garden two thin, half-dead peach trees still struggled with the drouth, the kind of unlikely tree that grows up from an old root and never bears. By the wall yellow suckers put out from an old vine stump, very thick and hard, which must once have borne its ripe clusters.

Built upon the north-east corner of the cloister the Bishop found a loggia – roofed, but with open sides, looking down on the white pueblo and the tawny rock, and over the wide plain below. There he decided he would spend the night. From this loggia he watched the sun go down; watched the desert become dark, the shadows creep upward. Abroad in the plain the scattered mesa tops, red with the afterglow, one by one lost their light, like candles going out. He was on a naked rock in the desert, in the stone age, a prey to homesickness for his own kind, his own epoch, for European man and his glorious history of desire and dreams. Through all the centuries that his own part of the world had been changing like the sky at daybreak, this people had been fixed, increasing neither in numbers nor desires, rock-turtles on their rock. Something reptilian he felt here, something that had endured by immobility, a kind of life out of reach, like the crustaceans in their armour.

Death Comes for the Archbishop, 1927, ch. 3

'The first foundation'

WILLIAM BRADFORD

Being thus arrived in good harbour, and brought safe to land, they [the *Mayflower* Pilgrims] fell upon their knees and blessed the God of heaven, who had brought them over the vast and furious ocean, and delivered them from all the perils and miseries thereof, again to set their feet on the firm and stable earth, their proper element.

*

I shall a little turn back and begin with a combination made by them before they came ashore, being the first foundation of their government in this place; occasioned partly by the discontented and mutinous speeches that some of the strangers [non-Pilgrims] amongst them had let fall from them in the ship – That when they came ashore they would use their own liberty; for none had power to command them, the patent they had being for Virginia, and not for New England, which belonged to another government, with which the Virginia Company had nothing to do. And partly that such an act by them done (this their condition considered) might be as firm as any patent, and in some respects more sure.

The form was as followeth:

In the name of God, Amen. We whose names are underwritten, the loyal subjects of our dread sovereign Lord, King James, by the grace of God, of Great Britain, France, and Ireland king, defender of the faith, etc., having undertaken, for the glory of God, and advancement of the Christian faith, and honour of our king and country, a voyage to plant the first colony in the northern parts of Virginia, do by these presents solemnly and mutually in the presence of God and one of another, covenant and combine ourselves together into a civil body politic, for our better ordering and preservation and furtherance of the ends aforesaid; and by virtue hereof to enact, constitute and frame such just and equal laws, ordinances, acts, constitutions and offices, from time to time, as shall be thought most meet and convenient for the general good of the colony, unto which we promise all due submission and obedience. In witness whereof we have hereunder subscribed our names at Cape Cod the 11th of November, in the year of the reign of our sovereign lord, King James, of England, France, and Ireland the eighteenth, and of Scotland the fifty-fourth. Anno Domini 1620.

After this they chose, or rather confirmed, Mr John Carver (a man godly and well approved amongst them) their Governor for that year. And after they had provided a place for their goods, or common store (which were long in unlading for want of boats, foulness of winter weather and sickness of divers) and begun some small cottages for their habitations, as time would admit, they met and consulted of laws and orders, both for their civil and military government, as the necessity of their condition did require, still adding thereunto as urgent occasion in several times, and as cases did require.

In these hard and difficult beginnings they found some discontents and murmurings arise amongst some, and mutinous speeches and carriages in other; but they were soon quelled and overcome by the wisdom, patience, and just and equal carriage of things, by the Governor and better part, which clave faithfully together in the main.

*

[1623] All this while no supply was heard of, neither knew they when they might expect any. So they began to think how they might raise as much corn as they could, and obtain a better crop than they had done, that they might not still thus languish in misery. At length, after much debate of things, the Governor [now Bradford himself] (with the advice of the chiefest among them) gave way that they should set corn every man for his own particular, and in that regard trust to themselves; in all other things to go on in the general way as before. And so assigned to every family a parcel of land, according to the proportion of their number for that end, only for present use (but made no division for inheritance) and ranged all boys and youth under some family. This had very good success; for it made all hands very industrious, so as much more corn was planted than other wise would have been by any means the governor or any other could use, and saved him a great deal of trouble, and gave far better content. The women now went willingly into the field, and took their little ones with them to set corn, which before would allege weakness, and inability; whom to have compelled would have been thought great tyranny and oppression.

The experience that was had in this common course and condition, tried sundry years, and that amongst godly and sober men, may well evince the vanity of that conceit of Plato's and other ancients, applauded by some of later times; – that the taking away of property, and bringing in community into a commonwealth, would make them happy and flourishing; as if they were wiser than God. For this community (so far as it was) was found to breed much confusion and discontent, and retard much employment that would have been to their benefit and comfort. For the young men, that were most able and fit for labour and service, did repine that they should spend their time and strength to work for other men's wives and children, without any recompense. The strong, or man of parts, had no more in division of victuals and clothes than he that was weak and not able to do a quarter the other could; this was thought injustice. The aged and graver men to be ranked and equalized in labours, and victuals, clothes, etc., with the meaner and younger sort, thought it some indignity and disrespect unto them. And for men's wives to be commanded to do service for other men, as dressing their meat, washing their clothes, etc., they deemed it a kind of slavery, neither could many husbands well brook it. Upon the point all being to have alike, and all to do alike, they thought themselves in the like condition, and one as good as another; and so, if it did not cut off those relations that God hath set amongst men, yet it did at least much diminish and take off the mutual respects that should be preserved amongst them. And would have been worse if they had been men of another condition. Let none object this is men's corruption, and nothing to the course itself. I answer, seeing all men have this corruption in them, God in His wisdom saw another course fitter for them.

Bradford's History 'Of Plimouth Plantation' (wr. 1630–51), 1898; book 1, ch. 9; book 2, Anno 1620 and Anno 1623

'That land is ours'

HENRY DAVID THOREAU

When the committee from Plymouth had purchased the territory of Eastham of the Indians, 'it was demanded who laid claim to Billingsgate?' which was understood to be all that part of the Cape north of what they had purchased. 'The answer was, there was not any who owned it. "Then," said the committee, "that land is ours." The Indians answered, that it was.' This was a remarkable assertion and admission. The Pilgrims appear to have regarded themselves as Not Any's representatives. Perhaps this was the first instance of that quiet way of 'speaking for' a place not yet occupied, or at least not improved as much as it may be, which their descendants have practiced, and are still practicing so extensively. Not Any seems to have been the sole proprietor of all America before the Yankees. But history says, that when the Pilgrims had held the lands of Billingsgate many years, at length 'appeared an Indian, who styled himself Lieutenant Anthony', who laid claim to them, and of him they bought them. Who knows but a Lieutenant Anthony may be knocking at the door of the White House some day? At any rate, I know that if you hold a thing unjustly, there will surely be the devil to pay at last.

(wr. 1852) *Cape Cod* 1864, ch. 3

'The Indian was not savage'

FRANÇOIS RENÉ DE CHATEAUBRIAND

Pushed by the European population toward the Northwest of North America, the savage population comes by a singular destiny to expire on the very shore on which they landed in unknown centuries to take possession of America. In the Iroquois language, the Indians give themselves the name 'men of forever' – *Ongoue-onoue*. These 'men of forever' have gone, and the foreigner will soon leave to these legitimate heirs to a whole world, only the earth of their tombs.

The reasons for this depopulation are known: the use of strong liquors, vices, illnesses, and wars, which we have multiplied among the Indians, have precipitated the destruction of these peoples; but it is not entirely true that the social state, coming to be established in the forests, has been a sufficient cause of this destruction.

The Indian was not savage; the European civilization did not act on the pure state of nature; it acted on the rising American civilization; if it had found nothing, it would have created something; but it found manners and destroyed them because it was stronger and did not consider it should mix with those manners.

Asking what would have happened to the inhabitants of America, if America had escaped the sails of navigators, would no doubt be a vain question but still curious to examine. Would they have perished in silence as did those nations more advanced in the arts, which in all probability formerly flourished in the country watered by the Ohio, the Muskingum, the Tennessee, the lower Mississippi, and the Tombigbee?

Putting aside for a moment the great principles of Christianity, as well as the interests of Europe, a philosophical spirit could wish that the people of the New World had had the time to develop outside the circle of our institutions.

We are everywhere reduced to the worn forms of an old civilization (I do not speak of the populations of Asia, fixed for 4,000 years in a despotism which is infantile). There have been found among the savages of Canada, New England, and the Floridas, beginnings of all the customs and all the laws of the Greeks, the Romans and the Hebrews. A civilization of a nature different from ours could have reproduced the men of antiquity or have spread new enlightenment from a still unknown source. Who knows whether we would not have seen one day land on our shores some American Columbus coming to discover the Old World?

'Government among the Indians' in *Travels in America*, 1827;
trans. Richard Switzer, 1969

'United in one family'

THOMAS JEFFERSON

Washington, December 30, 1806
My Children, the Wolf and people of the Mandan nation: – I take you by the hand of friendship and give you a hearty welcome to the seat of the government of the United States. The journey which you have taken to visit your fathers on this side of our island is a long one, and your having under-taken it is a proof that you desired to become acquainted with us. I thank the Great Spirit that he has protected you through the journey and brought you safely to the residence of your friends, and I hope He will have you con-stantly in his safe keeping, and restore you in good health to your nations and families.

My friends and children, we are descended from the old nations which live beyond the great water, but we and our forefathers have been so long here that we seem like you to have grown out of this land. We consider our-selves no longer of the old nations beyond the great water, but as united in one family with our red brethren here. The French, the English, the Spaniards, have now agreed with us to retire from all the country which you and we hold between Canada and Mexico, and never more to return to it. And remember the words I now speak to you, my children, they are never to return again. We are now your fathers; and you shall not lose by the change. As soon as Spain had agreed to withdraw from all the waters of the Missouri and Mississippi, I felt the desire of becoming acquainted with all my red children beyond the Mississippi, and of uniting them with us as we have those on this side of that river, in the bonds of peace and friendship. I wished to learn what we could do to benefit them by furnishing them the necessaries they want in exchange for their furs and peltries. I therefore sent our beloved man, Captain Lewis, one of my own family, to go up the Missouri river to get acquainted with all the Indian nations in its neighborhood, to take them by the hand, deliver my talks to them, and to inform us in what way we could be useful to them. Your nation received him kindly, you have taken him by the hand and been friendly to him. My children, I thank you for the services you rendered him, and for your attention to his words. He will now tell us where we should establish trading houses to be convenient to you all, and what we must send to them.

My friends and children, I have now an important advice to give you. I have already told you that you and all the red men are my children, and I wish you to live in peace and friendship with one another as brethren of the same family ought to do. How much better is it for neighbors to help than to hurt one another; how much happier must it make them. If you will cease to make war on one another, if you will live in friendship with all mankind, you can employ all your time in providing food and clothing for yourselves and your families. Your men will not be destroyed in war, and your women and children will lie down to sleep in their cabins without fear of being surprised by their enemies and killed or carried away. Your numbers will be increased instead of diminishing, and you will live in plenty and in quiet. My children, I have given this advice to all your red brethren on this side of the Mississippi; they are following it, they are increasing in their numbers, are learning to clothe and provide for their families as we do. Remember then my advice, my children, carry it home to your people, and tell them that from the day that they have become all of the same family, from the day that we became father to them all, we wish, as a true father should do, that we may all live together as one household, and that before they strike one another, they should go to their father and let him endeavor to make up the quarrel.

'Address to the Wolf and People of the Mandan Nation', 1806

'These happy people'

GEORGE CATLIN

In traversing the immense regions of the *classic* West, the mind of a philanthropist is filled to the brim with feelings of admiration; but to reach this country, one is obliged to descend from the light and glow of civilized atmosphere, through the different grades of civilization, which gradually sink to the most deplorable condition along the extreme frontier; thence through the most pitiable misery and wretchedness of savage degradation; where the genius of natural liberty and independence have been blasted and destroyed by the contaminating vices and dissipations introduced by the immoral part of *civilized* society. Through this dark and sunken vale of wretchedness one hurries, as through a pestilence, until he gradually rises again into the proud and chivalrous pale of savage society, in its state of original nature, beyond the reach of civilized contamination; here he finds much to fix his enthusiasm upon, and much to admire. Even here, the predominant passions of the savage breast, of ferocity and cruelty, are often found; yet *restrained*, and frequently *subdued*, by the noblest traits of honour and magnanimity, – a race of men who live and enjoy life and its luxuries, and practice its virtues, very far beyond the usual estimation of the world, who are apt to judge the savage and his virtues from the poor, degraded, and humbled specimens which alone can be seen along our frontiers. From the first settlements of our Atlantic coast to the present day, the bane of this *blasting frontier* has regularly crowded upon them, from the northern to the southern extremities of our country; and, like the fire in a prairie, which destroys everything where it passes, it has blasted and sunk them, all but their names, into oblivion, wherever it has travelled. It is to this tainted class alone that the epithet of 'poor, naked, and drunken savage', can be, with propriety, applied; for all those numerous tribes which I have visited, and are yet uncorrupted by the vices of civilized acquaintance, are well clad, in many instances cleanly, and in the full enjoyment of life and its luxuries. It is for the character and preservation of these noble fellows that I am an enthusiast; and it is for these uncontaminated people that I would be willing to devote the energies of my life. It is a sad and melancholy truth to contemplate, that all the numerous tribes who inhabited our vast Atlantic States *have not* 'fled to the West'; – that they are not to be found here – that they have been blasted by the fire which has passed over them – have sunk into their graves, and everything but their names travelled into oblivion.

The distinctive character of all these Western Indians, as well as their traditions relative to their ancient locations, prove beyond a doubt, that they have been for a very long time located on the soil which they now possess; and in most respects, distinct and unlike those nations who formerly inhabited the Atlantic coast, and who (according to the erroneous opinion of a great part of the world), have fled to the West.

It is for these inoffensive and unoffending people, yet unvisited by the vices of civilized society, that I would proclaim to the world, that it is time, for the honour of our country – for the honour of every citizen of the republic – and for the sake of humanity, that our government should raise her strong arm to save the remainder of them from the pestilence which is rapidly advancing upon them. We have gotten from them territory enough, and the country which they now inhabit is most of it too barren of timber for the use of civilized man; it affords them, however, the means and luxuries of savage life; and it is to be hoped that our government will not acquiesce in the continued wilful destruction of these happy people.

Letters and Notes on the Manners, Customs, and
Condition of the North American Indians, 1841, letter 10

'The White Man will never be alone'

CHIEF SEATTLE

[Translated and transcribed on the occasion of its delivery as an oration in reply to the governor of the newly organized Washington Territory in 1853]

Yonder sky that has wept tears of compassion upon my people for centuries untold, and which to us appears changeless and eternal, may change. Today is fair. Tomorrow it may be overcast with clouds. My words are like the stars that never change. Whatever Seattle says the great chief at Washington can rely upon with as much certainty as he can upon the return of the sun or the seasons. The White Chief says that Big Chief at Washington sends us greetings of friendship and goodwill. This is kind of him for we know he has little need of our friendship in return. His people are many. They are like the grass that covers vast prairies. My people are few. They resemble the scattering trees of a storm-swept plain. The great – and I presume – good White Chief sends us word that he wishes to buy our lands but is willing to allow us enough to live comfortably. This indeed appears just, even generous, for the Red Man no longer has rights that he need respect, and the offer may be wise also, as we are no longer in need of an extensive country.

There was a time when our people covered the land as the waves of a wind-ruffled sea cover its shell paved floor, but that time long since passed away with the greatness of tribes that are now but a mournful memory. I will not dwell on, nor mourn over, our untimely decay, nor reproach my paleface brothers with hastening it as we too may have been somewhat to blame.

*

Day and night cannot dwell together. The Red Man has ever fled the approach of the White Man, as the morning mist flees before the morning sun.

However, your proposition seems fair and I think that my people will accept it and will retire to the reservation you offer them. Then we will dwell in peace, for the words of the Great White Chief seem to be the words of nature speaking to my people out of dense darkness.

It matters little where we pass the remnant of our days. They will not be many. The Indians' night promises to be dark. Not a single star of hope hovers above his horizon. Sad-voiced winds moan in the distance. Grim fate seems to be on the Red Man's trail, and wherever he goes he will hear the approaching footsteps of his fell destroyer and prepare stolidly to meet his doom, as does the wounded doe that hears the approaching footsteps of the hunter.

A few more moons. A few more winters – and not one of the descendants of the mighty hosts that once moved over this land or lived in happy homes, protected by the Great Spirit, will remain to mourn over the graves of a people – once more powerful and hopeful than yours. But why should I mourn at the untimely fate of my people? Tribe follows tribe, and nation follows nation, like the waves of the sea. It is the order of nature, and regret is useless. Your time of decay may be distant, but it will surely come, for even the White Man whose God walked and talked with him as friend with friend, cannot be exempt from the common destiny. We may be brothers after all. We will see.

We will ponder your proposition and when we decide will let you know. But should we accept it, I here and now make this condition that we will not be denied the privilege without molestation of visiting at any time the tombs of our ancestors, friends and children. Every part of this soil is sacred in the estimation of my people. Every hillside, every valley, every plain and grove, has been hallowed by some sad or happy event in days long vanished. Even the rocks, which seem to be dumb and dead as they swelter in the sun along the silent shore, thrill with memories of stirring events connected with the lives of my people, and the very dust upon which you now stand responds more lovingly to their footsteps than to yours, because it is rich with the blood of our ancestors and our bare feet are conscious of the sympathetic touch. Our departed braves, fond mothers, glad, happy-hearted maidens, and even our little children who lived here and rejoiced here for a brief season, will love these somber solitudes and at eventide they greet shadowy returning spirits. And when the last Red Man shall have perished, and the memory of my tribe shall have become a myth among the White Men, these shores will swarm with the invisible dead of my tribe, and when your children's children think themselves alone in the field, the store, the shop, upon the highway, or in the silence of the pathless woods, they will not be alone. In all the earth there is no place dedicated to solitude. At night when the streets of your cities and villages are silent and you think them deserted, they will throng with the returning hosts that once filled them and still love this beautiful land. The White Man will never be alone.

Let him be just and deal kindly with my people, for the dead are not powerless. Dead, did I say? There is no death, only a change of worlds.

Indian Oratory: Famous Speeches by Noted Indian Chieftains,
ed. W. C. Vanderwerth, 1971

The Gift Outright

ROBERT FROST

The land was ours before we were the land's.
She was our land more than a hundred years
Before we were her people. She was ours
In Massachusetts, in Virginia,
But we were England's, still colonials,
Possessing what we still were unpossessed by,
Possessed by what we now no more possessed.
Something we were withholding made us weak
Until we found out that it was ourselves
We were withholding from our land of living,
And forthwith found salvation in surrender.
Such as we were we gave ourselves outright
(The deed of gift was many deeds of war)
To the land vaguely realizing westward,
But still unstoried, artless, unenhanced,
Such as she was, such as she would become.

A Witness Tree, 1942

'Emigration to America'

BENJAMIN FRANKLIN

Who then are the kind of persons to whom an emigration to America may be advantageous? And what are the advantages they may reasonably expect?

Land being cheap in that country, from the vast forests still void of inhabitants, and not likely to be occupied in an age to come, insomuch that the propriety of an hundred acres of fertile soil full of wood may be obtained near the frontiers, in many places, for eight or ten guineas, hearty young laboring men, who understand the husbandry of corn and cattle, which is nearly the same in that country as in Europe, may easily establish themselves there. A little money saved of the good wages they receive there, while they work for others, enables them to buy the land and begin their plantation, in which they are assisted by the good-will of their neighbors, and some credit. Multitudes of poor people from England, Ireland, Scotland, and Germany, have by this means in a few years become wealthy farmers, who, in their own countries, where all the lands are fully occupied, and the wages of labor low, could never have emerged from the poor condition wherein they were born.

From the salubrity of the air, the healthiness of the climate, the plenty of good provisions, and the encouragement to early marriages by the certainty of subsistence in cultivating the earth, the increase of inhabitants by natural generation is very rapid in America, and becomes still more so by the accession of strangers; hence there is a continual demand for more artisans of all the necessary and useful kinds, to supply those cultivators of the earth with houses, and with furniture and utensils of the grosser sorts, which cannot so well be brought from Europe. Tolerably good workmen in any of these mechanic arts are sure to find employ, and to be well paid for their work, there being no restraints preventing strangers from exercising any art they understand, nor any permission necessary. If they are poor, they begin first as servants or journeymen; and if they are sober, industrious, and frugal, they soon become masters, establish themselves in business, marry, raise families, and become respectable citizens.

Also, persons of moderate fortunes and capitals, who, having a number of children to provide for, are desirous of bringing them up to industry, and to secure estates for their posterity, have opportunities of doing it in America, which Europe does not afford. There they may be taught and practice profitable mechanic arts, without incurring disgrace on that account, but on the contrary acquiring respect by such abilities. There small capitals laid out in lands, which daily become more valuable by the increase of people, afford a solid prospect of ample fortunes thereafter for those children. The writer of this has known several instances of large tracts of land, bought, on what was then the frontier of Pennsylvania, for ten pounds per hundred acres, which after 20 years, when the settlements had been extended far beyond them, sold readily, without any improvement made upon them, for three pounds per acre. The acre in America is the same with the English acre, or the acre of Normandy.

*

The almost general mediocrity of fortune that prevails in America obliging its people to follow some business for subsistence, those vices, that arise usually from idleness, are in great measure prevented. Industry and constant employment are great preservatives of the morals and virtue of a nation. Hence bad examples to youth are more rare in America, which must be a comfortable consideration to parents. To this may be truly added, that serious religion, under its various denominations, is not only tolerated, but respected and practiced. Atheism is unknown there; infidelity rare and secret; so that persons may live to a great age in that country, without having their piety shocked by meeting with either an atheist or an infidel. And the Divine Being seems to have manifested his approbation of the mutual forbearance and kindness with which the different sects treat each other, by the remarkable prosperity with which He has been pleased to favour the whole country.

Information for Those Who Would Remove to America, 1782

'As for Emigration'

SYDNEY SMITH

As for Emigration, every man, of course, must determine for himself. A carpenter under 30 years of age, who finds himself at Cincinnati with an axe over his shoulder, and ten pounds in his pocket, will get rich in America, if the change of climate does not kill him. So will a farmer who emigrates early with some capital. But any person with tolerable prosperity here had better remain where he is. There are considerable evils, no doubt, in England: but it would be madness not to admit, that it is, upon the whole, a very happy country, – and we are much mistaken if the next 20 years will not bring with it a great deal of internal improvement. The country has long been groaning under the evils of the greatest foreign war we were ever engaged in; and we are just beginning to look again into our home affairs. Political economy has made an astonishing progress since they were last investigated; and every session of Parliament brushes off some of the cobwebs and dust of our ancestors. The Apprentice Laws have been swept away; the absurd nonsense of the Usury Laws will probably soon follow; Public Education and Savings Banks have been the invention of these last ten years; and the strong fortress of Bigotry has been rudely assailed. Then, with all its defects, we have a Parliament of inestimable value. If there be a place in any country where 500 well educated men can meet together and talk with impunity of public affairs, and if what they say is published, that country must improve. It is not pleasant to emigrate into a country of changes and revolution, the size and integrity of whose empire no man can predict. The Americans are a very sensible, reflecting people, and have conducted their affairs extremely well; but it is scarcely possible to conceive that such an empire should very long remain undivided, or that the dwellers on the Columbia should have common interest with the navigators of the Hudson and the Delaware.

England is, to be sure, a very expensive country; but a million of millions has been expended in making it habitable and comfortable; and this is a constant source of revenue, or, what is the same thing, a constant diminution of expense to every man living in it. The price an Englishman pays for a turnpike road is not equal to the tenth part of what the delay would cost him without a turnpike. The New River Company brings water to every inhabitant of London at an infinitely less price than he could dip for it out of the Thames. No country, in fact, is so expensive as one which human beings are just beginning to inhabit; – where there are no roads, no bridges, no skill, no help, no combination of powers, and no force of capital.

How, too, can any man take upon himself to say, that he is so indifferent to his country that he will not begin to love it intensely, when he is 5000 or 6000 miles from it? And what a dreadful disease Nostalgia must be on the banks of the Missouri! Severe and painful poverty will drive us all anywhere: but a wise man should be quite sure he has so irresistible a plea, before he ventures on the Great or the Little Wabash. He should be quite sure that he does not go there from ill temper – or to be pitied – or to be regretted – or from ignorance of what is to happen to him – or because he is a poet – but because he has not enough to eat here, and is sure of abundance where he is going.

Edinburgh Review, December 1818

'The progress of society'

THOMAS JEFFERSON

Monticello, September 6, 1824

Sir, – the idea which you present in your letter of July 30th, of the progress of society from its rudest state to that it has now attained, seems conformable to what may be probably conjectured. Indeed, we have under our eyes tolerable proofs of it. Let a philosophic observer commence a journey from the savages of the Rocky Mountains, eastwardly towards our sea-coast. These he would observe in the earliest stage of association living under no law but that of nature, subscribing and covering themselves with the flesh and skins of wild beasts. He would next find those on our frontiers in the pastoral state, raising domestic animals to supply the defects of hunting.

Then succeed our own semi-barbarous citizens, the pioneers of the advance of civilization, and so in his progress he would meet the gradual shades of improving man until he would reach his, as yet, most improved state in our seaport towns. This, in fact, is equivalent to a survey, in time, of the progress of man from the infancy of creation to the present day. I am eighty-one years of age, born where I now live, in the first range of mountains in the interior of our country. And I have observed this march of civilization advancing from the sea coast, passing over us like a cloud of light, increasing our knowledge and improving our condition, insomuch as that we are at this time more advanced in civilization here than the seaports were when I was a boy. And where this progress will stop no one can say. Barbarism has, in the meantime, been receding before the steady step of amelioration; and will in time, I trust, disappear from the earth.

To William Ludlow, 6 September 1824

'A highly civilized being'

ALEXIS DE TOCQUEVILLE

The Americans never use the word 'peasant', because they have no idea of the class which that term denotes; the ignorance of more remote ages, the simplicity of rural life, and the rusticity of the villager, have not been preserved amongst them; and they are alike unacquainted with the virtues, the vices, the coarse habits, and the simple graces of an early stage of civilization. At the extreme borders of the Confederate States, upon the confines of society and the wilderness, a population of bold adventurers have taken up their abode, who pierce the solitudes of the American woods, and seek a country there, in order to escape the poverty which awaited them in their native home. As soon as the pioneer reaches the place which is to serve him for a retreat, he fells a few trees and builds a log-house. Nothing can offer a more miserable aspect than these isolated dwellings. The traveller who approaches one of them towards nightfall sees the flicker of the hearth-flame through the chinks in the walls; and at night, if the wind rises, he hears the roof of boughs shake to and fro in the midst of the great forest-trees. Who would not suppose that this poor hut is the asylum of rudeness and ignorance? Yet no sort of comparison can be drawn between the pioneer and the dwelling which shelters him. Everything about him is primitive and wild, but he is himself the result of the labor and experience of eighteen centuries. He wears the dress and speaks the language of cities; he is acquainted with the past, curious about the future, and ready for argument upon the present; he is, in short, a highly civilized being, who consents for a time to inhabit the backwoods, and who penetrates into the wilds of the New World with the Bible, an axe, and some newspapers. It is difficult to imagine the incredible rapidity with which thought circulates in the midst of these deserts.[1] I do not think that so much intellectual activity exists in the most enlightened and populous districts of France.

[1] I travelled along a portion of the frontier of the United States in a sort of cart, which was termed the mail. We passed, day and night, with great rapidity, along the roads, which were scarcely marked out through immense forests. When the gloom of the woods became impenetrable, the driver lighted branches of pine, and we journeyed along by the light they cast. From time to time, we came to a hut in the midst of the forest; this was a post-office. The mail dropped an enormous bundle of letters at the door of this isolated dwelling, and we pursued our way at full gallop, leaving the inhabitants of the neighboring log-houses to send for their share of the treasure.

Democracy in America, vol. 1, ch. 17, 1835, trans. Henry Reeve;
rev. Francis Bowen, 1862

'The shores of America'

HENRY DAVID THOREAU

I am reminded by my journey how exceedingly new this country still is. You have only to travel for a few days into the interior and back parts even of many of the old States, to come to that very America which the Northmen, and Cabot, and Gosnold, and Smith, and Raleigh visited. If Columbus was the first to discover the islands, Americus Vespucius, and Cabot, and the Puritans, and we their descendants, have discovered only the shores of America. While the republic has already acquired a history world-wide, America is still unsettled and unexplored. Like the English in New Holland, we live only on the shores of a continent even yet, and hardly know where the rivers come from which float our navy. The very timber and boards and shingles of which our houses are made, grew but yesterday in a wilderness where the Indian still hunts and the moose runs wild. New York has her wilderness within her own borders; and though the sailors of Europe are familiar with the soundings of her Hudson, and Fulton long since invented the steamboat on its waters, an Indian is still necessary to guide her scientific men to its head-waters in the Adirondac country.

Have we even so much as discovered and settled the shores? Let a man travel on foot along the coast, from the Passamaquoddy to the Sabine, or to the Rio Bravo, or to wherever the end is now, if he is swift enough to overtake it, faithfully following the windings of every inlet and of every cape, and stepping to the music of the surf – with a desolate fishing-town once a week, and a city's port once a month to cheer him, and putting up at the light-houses, when there are any, and tell me if it looks like a discovered and settled country, and not rather, for the most part, like a desolate island, and No-man's Land.

We have advanced by leaps to the Pacific, and left many a lesser Oregon and California unexplored behind us. Though the railroad and the telegraph have been established on the shores of Maine, the Indian still looks out from her interior mountains over all these to the sea. There stands the city of Bangor, fifty miles up the Penobscot, at the head of navigation for vessels of the largest class, the principal lumber depot on this continent, with a population of twelve thousand, like a star on the edge of night, still hewing at the forests of which it is built, already overflowing with the luxuries and refinement of Europe, and sending its vessels to Spain, to England, and to the West Indies for its groceries, – and yet only a few axemen have gone 'up river', into the howling wilderness which feeds it. The bear and deer are still found within its limits; and the moose, as he swims the Penobscot, is entangled amid its shipping, and taken by foreign sailors in its harbor. Twelve miles in the rear, twelve miles of railroad, are Orono and the Indian Island, the home of the Penobscot tribe, and then commence the batteau and the canoe, and the military road; and sixty miles above, the country is virtually unmapped and unexplored, and there still waves the virgin forest of the New World.

'Ktaadn' (wr. 1848) in *The Maine Woods*, 1864

Shenandoah

ANONYMOUS

Oh, Missouri, she's a mighty river,
    Away you rolling river.
The Red-skins' camp lies on its borders,
    Ah-ha, I'm bound away 'cross the wide Missouri.

The white man loved the Indian maiden,
    Away you rolling river.
With notions sweet his canoe was laden.
    Ah-ha, I'm bound away 'cross the wide Missouri.

'O Shenandoah, I love your daughter,
    Away you rolling river.

I'll take her 'cross yon rolling water.'
    Ah-ha, I'm bound away 'cross the wide Missouri.

The chief disdained the trader's dollars:
    Away you rolling river.
'My daughter never you shall follow.'
    Ah-ha, I'm bound away 'cross the wide Missouri.

At last there came a Yankee skipper,
    Away you rolling river.
He winked his eye, and he tipped his flipper.
    Ah-ha, I'm bound away 'cross the wide Missouri.

He sold the chief that fire-water,
    Away you rolling river.
And 'cross the river he stole his daughter,
    Ah-ha, I'm bound away 'cross the wide Missouri.

'O Shenandoah, I long to hear you,
    Away you rolling river.
Across that wide and rolling river.'
    Ah-ha, I'm bound away 'cross the wide Missouri.

Early nineteenth century

As I Walked Out in the Streets of Laredo

ANONYMOUS

As I walked out in the streets of Laredo,
As I walked out in Laredo one day,
I spied a poor cowboy wrapped up in white linen,
Wrapped up in white linen and cold as the clay.

'I see by your outfit that you are a cowboy,'
These words he did say as I boldly stepped by.
'Come sit down beside me and hear my sad story;
I was shot in the breast and I know I must die.

'Let sixteen gamblers come handle my coffin,
Let sixteen cowboys come sing me a song,
Take me to the graveyard and lay the sod o'er me,
For I'm a poor cowboy and I know I've done wrong.

'It was once in the saddle I used to go dashing,
It was once in the saddle I used to go gay.
'Twas first to drinking and then to card playing,
Got shot in the breast, I am dying today.

'Get six jolly cowboys to carry my coffin,
Get six pretty girls to carry my pall;
Put bunches of roses all over my coffin,
Put roses to deaden the clods as they fall.

'O beat the drum slowly and play the fife lowly
And play the dead march as you carry me along,
Take me to the green valley and lay the sod o'er me,
For I'm a young cowboy and I know I've done wrong.'

We beat the drum slowly and played the fife lowly,
And bitterly wept as we bore him along;
For we all loved our comrade, so brave, young, and handsome,
We all loved our comrade although he'd done wrong.

c. 1860

The Big Rock Candy Mountains

ANONYMOUS

INTRODUCTION

On a summer day in the month of May,
A burly little bum come a-hikin',
He was travelin' down that lonesome road,
A-lookin' for his likin'.
He was headed for a land that's far away,
Beside those crystal fountains,
'I'll see you all, this comin' fall
In the Big Rock Candy Mountains.'

I

In the Big Rock Candy Mountains
You never change your socks,
And the little streams of alkyhol
Come a-tricklin' down the rocks.
Where the shacks all have to tip their hats,
And the railroad bulls are blind,

There's a lake of stew, and whiskey, too,
And you can paddle all around 'em in your big canoe,
In the Big Rock Candy Mountains.

CHORUS
O . . . the . . . buzzin' of the bees
In the cigarette trees,
Round the sodawater fountains,
Near the lemonade springs,
Where the whangdoodle sings
In the Big Rock Candy Mountains.

2

In the Big Rock Candy Mountains,
There's a land that's fair and bright,
Where the handouts grow on bushes,
And you sleep out every night.
Where the box cars are all empty
And the sun shines every day,
O I'm bound to go, where there ain't no snow,
Where the rain don't fall and the wind don't blow,
In the Big Rock Candy Mountains.

3

In the Big Rock Candy Mountains,
The jails are made of tin,
And you can bust right out again
As soon as they put you in.
The farmers' trees are full of fruit,
The barns are full of hay,
I'm goin' to stay where you sleep all day,
Where they boiled in oil the inventor of toil,
In the Big Rock Candy Mountains.

c. 1885

'Beneath the sunset'

HAMLIN GARLAND

Green's Coulee [Wisconsin] was a delightful place for boys. It offered hunting and coasting and many other engrossing sports, but my father, as the

seasons went by, became thoroughly dissatisfied with its disadvantages. More and more he resented the stumps and ridges which interrupted his plow. Much of his quarter-section remained unbroken. There were ditches to be dug in the marsh and young oaks to be uprooted from the forest, and he was obliged to toil with unremitting severity. There were times, of course, when field duties did not press, but never a day came when the necessity for twelve hours' labor did not exist.

Furthermore, as he grubbed or reaped he remembered the glorious prairies he had crossed on his exploring trip into Minnesota before the war, and the oftener he thought of them the more bitterly he resented his up-tilted, horse-killing fields, and his complaining words sank so deep into the minds of his sons that for years thereafter they were unable to look upon any rise of ground as an object to be admired.

It irked him beyond measure to force his reaper along a steep slope, and he loathed the irregular little patches running up the ravines behind the timbered knolls, and so at last like many another of his neighbors he began to look away to the west as a fairer field for conquest. He no more thought of going east than a liberated eagle dreams of returning to its narrow cage. He loved to talk of Boston, to boast of its splendor, but to live there, to earn his bread there, was unthinkable. Beneath the sunset lay the enchanted land of opportunity and his liberation came unexpectedly.

Sometime in the spring of 1868, a merchant from LaCrosse, a plump man who brought us candy and was very cordial and condescending, began negotiations for our farm, and in the discussion of plans which followed, my conception of the universe expanded. I began to understand that 'Minnesota' was not a bluff but a wide land of romance, a prairie, peopled with red men, which lay far beyond the big river. And then, one day, I heard my father read to my mother a paragraph from the county paper which ran like this, 'It is reported that Richard Garland has sold his farm in Green's Coulee to our popular grocer, Mr Speer. Mr Speer intends to make of it a model dairy farm.'

This intention seemed somehow to reflect a ray of glory upon us, though I fear it did not solace my mother, as she contemplated the loss of home and kindred. She was not by nature an emigrant – few women are. She was content with the pleasant slopes, the kindly neighbors of Green's Coulee. Furthermore, most of her brothers and sisters still lived just across the ridge in the valley of the Neshonoc, and the thought of leaving them for a wild and unknown region was not pleasant.

To my father, on the contrary, change was alluring. Iowa was now the place of the rainbow, and the pot of gold. He was eager to push on toward it, confident of the outcome. His spirit was reflected in one of the songs which we children particularly enjoyed hearing our mother sing, a ballad

which consisted of a dialogue between a husband and wife on this very subject of emigration. The words as well as its wailing melody still stir me
deeply, for they lay hold of my subconscious memory – embodying admirably the debate which went on in our home as well as in the homes of other
farmers in the valley – only, alas! our mothers did not prevail.

It begins with a statement of unrest on the part of the husband who con-
fesses that he is about to give up his plow and his cart –

> Away to Colorado a journey I'll go,
> For to double my fortune as other men do,
> *While here I must labor each day in the field*
> *And the winter consumes all the summer doth yield.*

To this the wife replies:

> Dear husband, I've noticed with a sorrowful heart
> That you long have neglected your plow and your cart,
> Your horses, sheep, cattle at random do run,
> And your new Sunday jacket goes every day on.
> *Oh, stay on your farm and you'll suffer no loss,*
> *For the stone that keeps rolling will gather no moss.*

But the husband insists:

> Oh, wife, let us go; Oh don't let us wait;
> I long to be there, and I long to be great,
> While you some fair lady and who knows but l
> May be some rich governor long 'fore I die,
> *Whilst here I must labor each day in the field,*
> *And the winter consumes all the summer doth yield.*

But wife shrewdly retorts:

> Dear husband, remember those lands are so dear
> They will cost you the labor of many a year.
> Your horses, sheep, cattle will all be to buy,
> You will hardly get settled before you must die.
> *Oh, stay on the farm, etc.*

The husband then argues that as in that country the lands are all cleared
to the plow, and horses and cattle not very dear, they would soon be rich.

Indeed, 'we will feast on fat venison one-half of the year.' Thereupon the wife brings in her final argument:

Oh, husband, remember those lands of delight
Are surrounded by Indians who murder by night.
Your house will be plundered and burnt to the ground
While your wife and your children lie mangled around.

This fetches the husband up with a round turn:

Oh, wife, you've convinced me, I'll argue no more,
I never once thought of your dying before.
I love my dear children although they are small
And you, my dear wife, I love greatest of all.
Refrain (both together)
We'll stay on the farm and we'll suffer no loss
For the stone that keeps rolling will gather no moss.

This song has not an especial favorite of my father. Its minor strains and its expressions of womanly doubts and fears were antipathetic to his sanguine, buoyant, self-confident nature. He was inclined to ridicule the conclusions of its last verse and to say that the man was a mollycoddle – or whatever the word of contempt was in those days. As an antidote he usually called for 'O'er the hills in legions, boys,' which exactly expressed his love of exploration and adventure.

This ballad which dates back to the conquest of the Allegheny mountains opens with a fine uplifting note.

Cheer up, brothers, as we go
O'er the mountains, westward ho,
Where herds of deer and buffalo
Furnish the fare.

and the refrain is at once a bugle call and a vision:

Then o'er the hills in legions, boys,
Fair freedom's star
Points to the sunset regions, boys,
Ha, ha, ha-ha!

and when my mother's clear voice rose on the notes of that exultant chorus, our hearts responded with a surge of emotion akin to that which sent the followers of Daniel Boone across the Blue Ridge, and lined the trails of Kentucky and Ohio with the canvas-covered wagons of the pioneers.

A little farther on in the song came these words,

> When we've wood and prairie land,
> Won by our toil,
> We'll reign like kings in fairy land,
> Lords of the soil!

which always produced in my mind the picture of a noble farmhouse in a parklike valley, just as the line, 'We'll have our rifles ready, boys,' expressed the boldness and self-reliance of an armed horseman.

The significance of this song in the lives of the McClintocks and the Garlands cannot be measured. It was the marching song of my Grandfather's generation and undoubtedly profoundly influenced my father and my uncles in all that they did. It suggested shining mountains, and grassy vales, swarming with bear and elk. It called to green savannahs and endless flowery glades. It voiced as no other song did, the pioneer impulse throbbing deep in my father's blood. That its words will not bear close inspection today takes little from its power. Unquestionably it was a directing force in the lives of at least three generations of my pioneering race.

A Son of the Middle Border, 1917, ch. 4

The Butchering at Wounded Knee

BLACK ELK

[The incident described occurred at Wounded Knee Creek on the Pine Ridge Reservation in South Dakota on 29 December 1890 during the last major armed conflict between Indians and whites. 153 Sioux were killed and 44 wounded.]

That evening before it happened, I went in to Pine Ridge and heard these things, and while I was there, soldiers started for where the Big Foots were. These made about five hundred soldiers that were there next morning. When I saw them starting I felt that something terrible was going to happen. That night I could hardly sleep at all. I walked around most of the night.

In the morning I went out after my horses, and while I was out I heard shooting off toward the east, and I knew from the sound that it must be wagon-guns (cannon) going off. The sounds went right through my body, and I felt that something terrible would happen.

When I reached camp with the horses, a man rode up to me and said: 'Hey-hey-hey! The people that are coming are fired on! I know it!'

I saddled up my buckskin and put on my sacred shirt. It was one I had made to be worn by no one but myself. It had a spotted eagle outstretched on the back of it, and the daybreak star was on the left shoulder, because when facing south that shoulder is toward the east. Across the breast, from the left shoulder to the right hip, was the flaming rainbow, and there was another rainbow around the neck, like a necklace, with a star at the bottom. At each shoulder, elbow, and wrist was an eagle feather; and over the whole shirt were red streaks of lightning. You will see that this was from my great vision, and you will know how it protected me that day.

I painted my face all red, and in my hair I put one eagle feather for the One Above.

It did not take me long to get ready, for I could still hear the shooting over there.

I started out alone on the old road that ran across the hills to Wounded Knee. I had no gun. I carried only the sacred bow of the west that I had seen in my great vision. I had gone only a little way when a band of young men came galloping after me. The first two who came up were Loves War and Iron Wasichu. I asked what they were going to do, and they said they were just going to see where the shooting was. Then others were coming up, and some older men.

We rode fast, and there were about twenty of us now. The shooting was getting louder. A horseback from over there came galloping very fast toward us, and he said: 'Hey-hey-hey! They have murdered them!' Then he whipped his horse and rode away faster toward Pine Ridge.

In a little while we had come to the top of the ridge where, looking to the east, you can see for the first time the monument and the burying ground on the little hill where the church is. That is where the terrible thing started. Just south of the burying ground on the little hill a deep dry gulch runs about east and west, very crooked, and it rises westward to nearly the top of the ridge where we were. It had no name, but the Wasichus [white men], sometimes call it Battle Creek now. We stopped on the ridge not far from the head of the dry gulch. Wagon-guns were still going off over there on the little hill, and they were going off again where they hit along the gulch. There was much shooting down yonder, and there were many cries, and we could see cavalrymen scattered over the hills ahead of us. Cavalrymen were riding along the gulch and shooting into it, where the women and children were running away and trying to hide in the gullies and the stunted pines.

A little way ahead of us, just below the head of the dry gulch, there were some women and children who were huddled under a clay bank, and some cavalrymen were there pointing guns at them.

We stopped back behind the ridge, and I said to the others: 'Take courage. These are our relatives. We will try to get them back.' Then we all sang a song which went like this:

> A thunder being nation I am, I have said.
> A thunder being nation I am, I have said.
> You shall live.
> You shall live.
> You shall live.
> You shall live.

Then I rode over the ridge and the others after me, and we were crying: 'Take courage! It is time to fight!' The soldiers who were guarding our relatives shot at us and then ran away fast, and some more cavalrymen on the other side of the gulch did too. We got our relatives and sent them across the ridge to the northwest where they would be safe.

I had no gun, and when we were charging, I just held the sacred bow out in front of me with my right hand. The bullets did not hit us at all.

We found a little baby lying all alone near the head of the gulch. I could not pick her up just then, but I got her later and some of my people adopted her. I just wrapped her up tighter in a shawl that was around her and left her there. It was a safe place, and I had other work to do.

The soldiers had run eastward over the hills where there were some more soldiers, and they were off their horses and lying down. I told the others to stay back, and I charged upon them holding the sacred bow out toward them with my right hand. They all shot at me, and I could hear bullets all around me, but I ran my horse right close to them, and then swung around. Some soldiers across the gulch began shooting at me too, but I got back to the others and was not hurt at all.

By now many other Lakotas, who had heard the shooting, were coming up from Pine Ridge, and we all charged on the soldiers. They ran eastward toward where the trouble began. We followed down along the dry gulch, and what we saw was terrible. Dead and wounded women and children and little babies were scattered all along there where they had been trying to run away. The soldiers had followed along the gulch, as they ran, and murdered them in there. Sometimes they were in heaps because they had huddled together, and some were scattered all along. Sometimes bunches of them had been killed and torn to pieces where the wagon-guns hit them. I saw a little baby trying to suck its mother, but she was bloody and dead.

There were two little boys at one place in this gulch. They had guns and they had been killing soldiers all by themselves. We could see the soldiers they had killed. The boys were all alone there, and they were not hurt. These were very brave little boys.

When we drove the soldiers back, they dug themselves in, and we were not enough people to drive them out from there. In the evening they marched off up Wounded Knee Creek, and then we saw all that they had done there.

Men and women and children were heaped and scattered all over the flat at the bottom of the little hill where the soldiers had their wagon-guns, and westward up the dry gulch all the way to the high ridge, the dead women and children and babies were scattered.

When I saw this I wished that I had died too, but I was not sorry for the women and children. It was better for them to be happy in the other world, and I wanted to be there too. But before I went there I wanted to have revenge. I thought there might be a day, and we should have revenge.

After the soldiers marched away, I heard from my friend, Dog Chief, how the trouble started, and he was right there by Yellow Bird when it happened. This is the way it was:

In the morning the soldiers began to take all the guns away from the Big Foots, who were camped in the flat below the little hill where the monument and burying ground are now. The people had stacked most of their guns, and even their knives, by the tepee where Big Foot was lying sick. Soldiers were on the little hill and all around, and there were soldiers across the dry gulch to the south and over east along Wounded Knee Creek too. The people were nearly surrounded, and the wagon-guns were pointing at them.

Some had not yet given up their guns, and so the soldiers were searching all the tepees, throwing things around and poking into everything. There was a man called Yellow Bird, and he and another man were standing in front of the tepee where Big Foot was lying sick. They had white sheets around and over them, with eyeholes to look through, and they had guns under these. An officer came to search them. He took the other man's gun, and then started to take Yellow Bird's. But Yellow Bird would not let go. He wrestled with the officer, and while they were wrestling, the gun went off and killed the officer. Wasichus and some others have said he meant to do this, but Dog Chief was standing right there, and he told me it was not so. As soon as the gun went off, Dog Chief told me, an officer shot and killed Big Foot who was lying sick inside the tepee.

Then suddenly nobody knew what was happening, except that the soldiers were all shooting and the wagon-guns began going off right in among the people.

Many were shot down right there. The women and children ran into the gulch and up west, dropping all the time, for the soldiers shot them as they ran. There were only about a hundred warriors and there were nearly five hundred soldiers. The warriors rushed to where they had piled their guns and knives. They fought soldiers with only their hands until they got their guns.

Dog Chief saw Yellow Bird run into a tepee with his gun, and from there he killed soldiers until the tepee caught fire. Then he died full of bullets.

It was a good winter day when all this happened. The sun was shining. But after the soldiers marched away from their dirty work, a heavy snow began to fall. The wind came up in the night. There was a big blizzard, and it grew very cold. The snow drifted deep in the crooked gulch, and it was one long grave of butchered women and children and babies, who had never done any harm and were only trying to run away.

Black Elk Speaks, as told through John G. Neihardt, 1932, ch. 24

The Jewish Cemetery at Newport

HENRY WADSWORTH LONGFELLOW

How strange it seems! These Hebrews in their graves,
    Close by the street of this fair seaport town,
Silent beside the never-silent waves,
    At rest in all this moving up and down!

The trees are white with dust, that o'er their sleep
    Wave their broad curtains in the southwind's breath,
While underneath these leafy tents they keep
    The long, mysterious Exodus of Death.

And these sepulchral stones, so old and brown,
    That pave with level flags their burial-place,
Seem like the tablets of the Law, thrown down
    And broken by Moses at the mountain's base.

The very names recorded here are strange,
    Of foreign accent, and of different climes;
Alvares and Rivera interchange
    With Abraham and Jacob of old times.

'Blessed be God, for he created Death!'
    The mourners said, 'and Death is rest and peace';

Then added, in the certainty of faith,
    'And giveth Life that nevermore shall cease.'

Closed are the portals of their Synagogue,
    No Psalms of David now the silence break,
No Rabbi reads the ancient Decalogue
    In the grand dialect the Prophets spake.

Anathema maranatha! was the cry
    That rang from town to town, from street to street:
At every gate the accursed Mordecai
    Was mocked and jeered, and spurned by Christian feet.

Pride and humiliation hand in hand
    Walked with them through the world where'er they went;
Trampled and beaten were they as the sand,
    And yet unshaken as the continent.

For in the background figures vague and vast
    Of patriarchs and of prophets rose sublime,
And all the great traditions of the Past
    They saw reflected in the coming time.

And thus forever with reverted look
    The mystic volume of the world they read,
Spelling it backward, like a Hebrew book,
    Till life became a Legend of the Dead.

Gone are the living, but the dead remain,
    And not neglected; for a hand unseen,
Scattering its bounty, like a summer rain,
    Still keeps their graves and their remembrance green.

How came they here? What burst of Christian hate,
    What persecution, merciless and blind,
Drove o'er the sea — that desert desolate —
    These Ishmaels and Hagars of mankind?

They lived in narrow streets and lanes obscure,
    Ghetto and Judenstrass, in mirk and mire;
Taught in the school of patience to endure
    The life of anguish and the death of fire.

All their lives long, with the unleavened bread
    And bitter herbs of exile and its fears,

The wasting famine of the heart they fed,
      And slaked its thirst with marah of their tears.

But ah! what once has been shall be no more!
      The groaning earth in travail and in pain
Brings forth its races, but does not restore,
      And the dead nations never rise again.

1852

The New Colossus

EMMA LAZARUS

[This sonnet is carved on the base of the Statue of Liberty.]

Not like the brazen giant of Greek fame,
With conquering limbs astride from land to land;
Here at our sea-washed, sunset gates shall stand
A mighty woman with a torch, whose flame
Is the imprisoned lightning, and her name
Mother of Exiles. From her beacon-hand
Glows world-wide welcome; her mild eyes command
The air-bridged harbor that twice cities frame.
'Keep, ancient lands, your storied pomp!' cries she
With silent lips. 'Give me your tired, your poor,
Your huddled masses yearning to breathe free,
The wretched refuse of your teeming shore.
Send these, the homeless, tempest-tossed to me:
I lift my lamp beside the golden door!'

1883

'The inconceivable alien'

HENRY JAMES

In the Bay, the rest of the morning, the dense raw fog that delayed the big boat, allowing sight but of the immediate ice-masses through which it thumped its way, was not less of the essence. Anything blander, as a medium, would have seemed a mockery of the facts of the terrible little Ellis

Island, the first harbour of refuge and stage of patience for the million or so of immigrants annually knocking at our official door. Before this door, which opens to them there only with a hundred forms and ceremonies, grindings and grumblings of the key, they stand appealing and waiting, marshalled, herded, divided, subdivided, sorted, sifted, searched, fumigated, for longer or shorter periods – the effect of all which prodigious process, an intendedly 'scientific' feeding of the mill, is again to give the earnest observer a thousand more things to think of than he can pretend to retail. The impression of Ellis Island, in fine, would be – as I was to find throughout that so many of my impressions would be – a chapter by itself; and with a particular page for recognition of the degree in which the liberal hospitality of the eminent Commissioner of this wonderful service, to whom I had been introduced, helped to make the interest of the whole watched drama poignant and unforgettable. It is a drama that goes on, without a pause, day by day and year by year, this visible act of ingurgitation on the part of our body politic and social, and constituting really an appeal to amazement beyond that of any sword-swallowing or fire-swallowing of the circus. The wonder that one couldn't keep down was the thought that these two or three hours of one's own chance vision of the business were but as a tick or two of the mighty clock, the clock that never, never stops – least of all when it strikes, for a sign of so much winding-up, some louder hour of our national fate than usual. I think indeed that the simplest account of the action of Ellis Island on the spirit of any sensitive citizen who may have happened to 'look in' is that he comes back from his visit not at all the same person that he went. He has eaten of the tree of knowledge, and the taste will be for ever in his mouth. He had thought he knew before, thought he had the sense of the degree in which it is his American fate to share the sanctity of his American consciousness, the intimacy of his American patriotism, with the inconceivable alien; but the truth had never come home to him with any such force. In the lurid light projected upon it by those courts of dismay it shakes him – or I like at least to imagine it shakes him – to the depths of his being; I like to think of him, I positively *have* to think of him, as going about ever afterwards with a new look, for those who can see it, in his face, the outward sign of the new chill in his heart. So is stamped, for detection, the questionably privileged person who has had an apparition, seen a ghost in his supposedly safe old house. Let not the unwary, therefore, visit Ellis Island.

The after-sense of that acute experience, however, I myself found, was by no means to be brushed away; I felt it grow and grow, on the contrary, wherever I turned: other impressions might come and go, but this affirmed claim of the alien, however immeasurably alien, to share in one's supreme relation was everywhere the fixed element, the reminder not to be dodged.

One's supreme relation, as one had always put it, was one's relation to one's country – a conception made up so largely of one's countrymen and one's countrywomen. Thus it was as if, all the while, with such a fond tradition of what these products predominantly were, the idea of the country itself underwent something of that profane overhauling through which it appears to suffer the indignity of change. Is not our instinct in this matter, in general, essentially the safe one – that of keeping the idea simple and strong and continuous, so that it shall be perfectly sound? To touch it overmuch, to pull it about, is to put it in peril of weakening; yet on this free assault upon it, this readjustment of it in *their* monstrous, presumptuous interest, the aliens, in New York, seemed perpetually to insist. The combination there of their quantity and their quality – that loud primary stage of alienism which New York most offers to sight – operates, for the native, as their note of settled possession, something they have nobody to thank for; so that *un*settled possession is what we, on our side, seem reduced to – the implication of which, in its turn, is that, to recover confidence and regain lost ground, we, not they, must make the surrender and accept the orientation. We must go, in other words, *more* than half-way to meet them; which is all the difference, for us, between possession and dispossession. This sense of dispossession, to be brief about it, haunted me so, I was to feel, in the New York streets and in the packed trajectiles to which one clingingly appeals from the streets, just as one tumbles back into the streets in appalled reaction from *them*, that the art of beguiling or duping it became an art to be cultivated – though the fond alternative vision was never long to be obscured, the imagination, exasperated to envy, of the ideal, in the order in question; of the luxury of some such close and sweet and *whole* national consciousness as that of the Switzer and the Scot.

The American Scene, 1907, ch. 2

'Let them all come'

H. G. WELLS

Every American above forty, and most of those below that limit, seem to be enthusiastic advocates of unrestricted immigration. I could not make them understand the apprehension with which this huge dilution of the American people with profoundly ignorant foreign peasants filled me. I rode out on an automobile into the pretty New York country beyond Yonkers with that finely typical American, Mr Z – he wanted to show me the pleasantness of the land – and he sang the song of American confidence, I think, more clearly and loudly than any one else. He told me how everybody had hope, how everybody had incentive, how magnificently it was all going on. He told me – what is, I am afraid, a widely-spread delusion – that elementary education stands on a higher level of efficiency in the States than in England. He had no doubt whatever of the national powers of assimilation.

'Let them all come,' he said cheerfully.

'The Chinese?' said I.

'We can do with them all . . . '

He was exceptional in that extension. Most Americans stop at the Ural mountains and refuse the 'Asiatic'. It was not a matter for discussion with him, but a question of belief. He had ceased to reason about immigration long ago. He was a man in the fine autumn of life, abounding in honours, wrapped in furs, and we drove swiftly in his automobile through the spring sunshine. ('By Jove,' thought I, 'you talk like Pippa's rich uncle!') By some half-brother of a coincidence we happened first upon this monument commemorating a memorable incident of the War of Independence, and then upon that. He recalled details of that great campaign as Washington was fought out of Manhattan northward. I remember one stone among the shooting trees that indicated where, in the Hudson River near by, a British sloop had fired the first salute in honour of the American flag. That salute was vividly present still to him; it echoed among the woods, it filled him with a sense of personal triumph, it seemed halfway back to Agincourt to me. All that bright morning the stars and stripes made an almost luminous, visible presence about us. Openhanded hospitality and confidence in God so swayed me, that it is indeed only now, as I put this book together, I see this shining buoyancy, this bunting patriotism in its direct relation to the Italian babies in the cotton-mills, to the sinister crowd that stands in the saloon, smoking and drinking beer, an accumulating reserve of unintelligent force behind the manoeuvres of the professional politicians . . .

I tried my views upon Commissioner Watchorn as we leant together over the gallery railing and surveyed that bundle-carrying crowd creeping step by step through the wire filter of the central hall of Ellis Island – into America.

'You don't think they'll swamp you?' I said.

'Now, look here,' said the Commissioner, 'I'm English-born – Derbyshire. I came into America when I was a lad. I had fifteen dollars. And here I am! Well, do you expect me, now I'm here, to shut the door on any other poor chaps who want a start – a start with hope in it – in the new world?'

A pleasant-mannered, fair-haired young man, speaking excellent English, had joined us as we went round, and nodded approval.

I asked him for his opinion, and gathered he was from Milwaukee, and the son of a Scandinavian immigrant. He too was for 'fair play' and an open door for every one. 'Except', he added, 'Asiatics.' So also, I remember, was a very New England lady I met at Hull House, who wasn't, as a matter of fact, a New Englander at all, but the daughter of a German settler in the middle west. They all seemed to think I was inspired by hostility to the immigrant and Anglomania in breathing any doubt about the desirability of this immense process . . .

I tried in each case to point out that this idea of not being churlishly exclusive did not exhaust the subject, that the present immigration is a different thing entirely from the immigration of half a century ago, that in the interest of the immigrant and his offspring, more than any one, is the protest to be made. Fifty years ago more than half of the torrent was English-speaking, and the rest mostly from the Teutonic and Scandinavian north-west of Europe, an influx of people closely akin to the native Americans in temperament and social tradition. They were able to hold their own and mix perfectly. Even then the quantity of illiterate Irish produced a marked degradation of political life. The earlier immigration was an influx of energetic people who wanted to come, and who had put themselves to considerable exertion to get here; it was higher in character and in social quality than the present flood. The immigration of today is largely the result of energetic canvassing by the steamship companies; it is, in the main, an importation of labourers, and not of economically independent settlers, and it is increasingly alien to the native tradition. The bulk of it now is Italian, Russian Jewish, Russian, Hungarian, Croatian, Roumanian, and Eastern European generally.

'The children learn English, and become more American and better patriots than the Americans,' Commissioner Watchorn – echoing everybody in that – told me . . .

(In Boston one optimistic lady looked to the Calabrian and Sicilian peasants to introduce an artistic element into the population – no doubt because they come from the same peninsula that produced the Florentines.)

(Ellipses are Wells's.) *The Future in America*, 1906, ch. 9

'An American among Americans'

MARY ANTIN

I was about ten years old when my father emigrated. I was used to his going away from home, and 'America' did not mean much more to me than 'Kherson', or 'Odessa', or any other names of distant places. I understood vaguely, from the gravity with which his plans were discussed, and from references to ships, societies, and other unfamiliar things, that this enterprise was different from previous ones; but my excitement and emotion on the morning of my father's departure were mainly vicarious.

I know the day when 'America' as a world entirely unlike Polotzk lodged in my brain, to become the centre of all my dreams and speculations. Well I know the day. I was in bed, sharing the measles with some of the other children. Mother brought us a thick letter from father, written just before boarding the ship. The letter was full of excitement. There was something in it besides the description of travel, something besides the pictures of crowds of people, of foreign cities, of a ship ready to put out to sea. My father was travelling at the expense of a charitable organization, without means of his own, without plans, to a strange world where he had no friends; and yet he wrote with the confidence of a well-equipped soldier going into battle. The rhetoric is mine. Father simply wrote that the emigration committee was taking good care of everybody, that the weather was fine, and the ship comfortable. But I heard something, as we read the letter together in the darkened room, that was more than the words seemed to say. There was an elation, a hint of triumph, such as had never been in my father's letters before. I cannot tell how I knew it. I felt a stirring, a straining in my father's letter. It was there, even though my mother stumbled over strange words, even though she cried, as women will when somebody is going away. My father was inspired by a vision. He saw something – he promised us something. It was this 'America'. And 'America' became my dream.

*

In after years, when I passed as an American among Americans, if I was suddenly made aware of the past that lay forgotten, – if a letter from Russia, or a paragraph in the newspaper, or a conversation overheard in the street-car, suddenly reminded me of what I might have been, – I thought it miracle enough that I, Mashke, the granddaughter of Raphael the Russian, born to a humble destiny, should be at home in an American metropolis, be free to fashion my own life, and should dream my dreams in English phrases. But in the beginning my admiration was spent on more concrete embodiments of the splendors of America; such as fine houses, gay shops, electric engines and apparatus, public buildings, illuminations, and parades. My early letters to my Russian friends were filled with boastful descriptions of these glories of my new country. No native citizen of Chelsea [Massachusetts] took such pride and delight in its institutions as I did. It required no fife and drum corps, no Fourth of July procession, to set me tingling with patriotism. Even the common agents and instruments of municipal life, such as the letter carrier and the fire engine, I regarded with a measure of respect. I know what I thought of people who said that Chelsea was a very small, dull, unaspiring town, with no discernible excuse for a separate name or existence.

The apex of my civic pride and personal contentment was reached on the bright September morning when I entered the public school. That day I must always remember, even if I live to be so old that I cannot tell my name. To most people their first day at school is a memorable occasion. In my case the importance of the day was a hundred times magnified, on account of the years I had waited, the road I had come, and the conscious ambitions I entertained.

I am wearily aware that I am speaking in extreme figures, in superlatives. I wish I knew some other way to render the mental life of the immigrant child of reasoning age. I may have been ever so much an exception in acuteness of observation, powers of comparison, and abnormal self-consciousness; none the less were my thoughts and conduct typical of the attitude of the intelligent immigrant child toward American institutions. And what the child thinks and feels is a reflection of the hopes, desires, and purposes of the parents who brought him overseas, no matter how precocious and independent the child may be. Your immigrant inspectors will tell you what poverty the foreigner brings in his baggage, what want in his pockets. Let the overgrown boy of twelve, reverently drawing his letters in the baby class, testify to the noble dreams and high ideals that may be hidden beneath the greasy caftan of the immigrant. Speaking for the Jews, at least, I know I am safe in inviting such an investigation.

*

It was characteristic of the looseness of our family discipline at this time that nobody was seriously interested in our visits to Morgan Chapel. Our time was our own, after school duties and household tasks were done. Joseph sold newspapers after school; I swept and washed dishes; Dora minded the baby. For the rest, we amused ourselves as best we could. Father and mother were preoccupied with the store day and night; and not so much with weighing and measuring and making change as with figuring out how long it would take the outstanding accounts to ruin the business entirely. If my mother had scruples against her children resorting to a building with a cross on it, she did not have time to formulate them. If my father heard us talking about Morgan Chapel, he dismissed the subject with a sarcastic characterization, and wanted to know if we were going to join the Salvation Army next; but he did not seriously care, and he was willing that the children should have a good time. And if my parents had objected to Morgan Chapel, was the sidewalk in front of the saloon a better place for us children to spend the evening? They could not have argued with us very long, so they hardly argued at all.

In Polotzk we had been trained and watched, our days had been regulated, our conduct prescribed. In America, suddenly, we were let loose on the street. Why? Because my father having renounced his faith, and my mother being uncertain of hers, they had no particular creed to hold us to. The conception of a system of ethics independent of religion could not at once enter as an active principle in their life; so that they could give a child no reason why to be truthful or kind. And as with religion, so it fared with other branches of our domestic education. Chaos took the place of system; uncertainty, inconsistency undermined discipline. My parents knew only that they desired us to be like American children; and seeing how their neighbors gave their children boundless liberty, they turned us also loose, never doubting but that the American way was the best way. In public deportment, in etiquette, in all matters of social intercourse, they had no standards to go by, seeing that America was not Polotzk. In their bewilderment and uncertainty they needs must trust us children to learn from such models as the tenements afforded. More than this, they must step down from their throne of parental authority, and take the law from their children's mouths; for they had no other means of finding out what was good American form. The result was that laxity of domestic organization, that inversion of normal relations which makes for friction, and which sometimes ends in breaking up a family that was formerly united and happy.

This sad process of disintegration of home life may be observed in almost any immigrant family of our class and with our traditions and aspirations. It is part of the process of Americanization; an upheaval preceding the state of repose. It is the cross that the first and second generations must bear, an involuntary sacrifice for the sake of the future generations. These are the pains of adjustment, as racking as the pains of birth. And as the mother forgets her agonies in the bliss of clasping her babe to her breast, so the bent and heart-sore immigrant forgets exile and homesickness and ridicule and loss and estrangement, when he beholds his sons and daughters moving as Americans among Americans.

The Promised Land, 1912, chs. 7, 9, 14

Compson: 1699–1945

WILLIAM FAULKNER

IKKEMOTUBBE. A dispossessed American king called 'l'Homme' (and sometimes 'de l'homme') by his fosterbrother, a Chevalier of France, who had he not been born too late could have been among the brightest in that glittering galaxy of knightly blackguards who were Napoleon's marshals, who thus translated the Chickasaw title meaning 'The Man'; which translation Ikkemotubbe, himself a man of wit and imagination as well as a shrewd judge of character, including his own, carried one step further and anglicised it to 'Doom'. Who granted out of his vast lost domain a solid square mile of virgin North Mississippi dirt as truly angled as the four corners of a cardtable top (forested then because these were the old days before 1833 when the stars fell and Jefferson Mississippi was one long rambling onestorey mudchinked log building housing the Chickasaw Agent and his tradingpost store) to the grandson of a Scottish refugee who had lost his own birthright by casting his lot with a king who himself had been dispossessed. This in partial return for the right to proceed in peace, by whatever means he and his people saw fit, afoot or ahorse provided they were Chickasaw horses, to the wild western land presently to be called Oklahoma: not knowing then about the oil.

JACKSON. A Great White Father with a sword (An old duellist, a brawling lean fierce mangy durable imperishable old lion who set the wellbeing of the nation above the White House and the health of his new political party above either and above them all set not his wife's honor but the principle that honor must be defended whether it was or not because defended it was whether or not) who patented sealed and countersigned the grant with his own hand in his gold tepee in Wassi Town, not knowing about the oil either: so that one day the homeless descendants of the dispossessed would ride supine with drink and splendidly comatose above the dusty allotted harborage of their bones in speciallybuilt scarletpainted hearses and fireengines.

These were Compsons:

QUENTIN MACLACHAN. Son of a Glasgow printer, orphaned and raised by his mother's people in the Perth highlands. Fled to Carolina from Culloden Moor with a claymore and the tartan he wore by day and slept under by night, and little else. At eighty, having fought once against an English king and lost, he would not make that mistake twice and so fled again one night in 1779, with his infant grandson and the tartan (the claymore had vanished, along with his son, the grandson's father, from one of Tarleton's regiments on a Georgia battlefield about a year ago) into Kentucky, where a neighbor named Boon or Boone had already established a settlement.

CHARLES STUART. Attainted and proscribed by name and grade in his British regiment. Left for dead in a Georgia swamp by his own retreating army and then by the advancing American one, both of which were wrong. He still had the claymore even when on his homemade wooden leg he finally overtook his father and son four years later at Harrodsburg, Kentucky, just in time to bury the father and enter upon a long period of being a split personality while still trying to be the schoolteacher which he believed he wanted to be, until he gave up at last and became the gambler he actually was and which no Compson seemed to realize they all were provided the gambit was desperate and the odds long enough. Succeeded at last in risking not only his neck but the security of his family and the very integrity of the name he would leave behind him, by joining the confederation headed by an acquaintance named Wilkinson (a man of considerable talent and influence and intellect and power) in a plot to secede the whole Mississippi Valley from the United States and join it to Spain. Fled in his turn when the bubble burst (as anyone except a Compson schoolteacher should have known it would), himself unique in being the only one of the plotters who had to flee the country: this not from the vengeance and retribution of the government which he had attempted to dismember, but from the furious revulsion of his late confederates now frantic for their own safety. He was not expelled from the United States, he talked himself countryless, his expulsion due not to the treason but to his having been so vocal and vociferant in the conduct of it, burning each bridge vocally behind him before he had even reached the place to build the next one: so that it was no provost marshal nor even a civic agency but his late coplotters themselves who put afoot the movement to evict him from Kentucky and the United States and, if they had caught him, probably from the world too. Fled by night, running true to family tradition, with his son and old claymore and the tartan.

JASON LYCURGUS. Who, driven perhaps by the compulsion of the flamboyant name given him by the sardonic embittered woodenlegged indomitable father who perhaps still believed with his heart that what he wanted to be was a classicist schoolteacher, rode up the Natchez Trace one day in 1811 with a pair of fine pistols and one meagre saddlebag on a small lightwaisted but stronghocked mare which could do the first two furlongs in definitely under the halfminute and the next two in not appreciably more, though that was all. But it was enough: who reached the Chickasaw Agency at Okatoba (which in 1860 was still called Old Jefferson) and went no further. Who within six months was the Agent's clerk and within twelve his partner, officially still the clerk though actually halfowner of what was now a considerable store stocked with the mare's winnings in races against the horses of Ikkemotubbe's young men which he, Compson, was always careful to limit to a quarter or at most three furlongs; and in the next year it was Ikkemotubbe who owned the little mare and Compson owned the solid square mile of land which someday would be almost in the center of the town of Jefferson, forested then and still forested twenty years later though rather a park than a forest by that time, with its slavequarters and stables and kitchengardens and the formal lawns and promenades and pavilions laid out by the same architect who built the columned porticoed house furnished by steamboat from France and New Orleans, and still the square intact mile in 1840 (with not only the little white village called Jefferson beginning to enclose it but an entire white county about to surround it because in a few years now Ikkemotubbe's descendants and people would be gone, those remaining living not as warriors and hunters but as white men – as shiftless farmers or, here and there, the masters of what they too called plantations and the owners of shiftless slaves, a little dirtier than the white man, a little lazier, a little crueller – until at last even the wild blood itself would have vanished, to be seen only occasionally in the noseshape of a Negro on a cottonwagon or a white sawmill hand or trapper or locomotive fireman), known as the Compson Domain then, since now it was fit to breed princes, statesmen and generals and bishops, to avenge the dispossessed Compsons from Culloden and Carolina and Kentucky, then known as the Governor's house because sure enough in time it did produce or at least spawn a governor – Quentin MacLachan again, after the Culloden grandfather – and still known as the Old Governor's even after it had spawned (1861) a general – (called so by predetermined accord and agreement by the whole town and county, as though they knew even then and beforehand that the old governor was the last Compson who would not fail at everything he touched save longevity or suicide) – the Brigadier Jason Lycurgus II who failed at Shiloh in '62 and failed again though not so badly at Resaca in '64, who put the first mortgage on the still intact square mile to a New England carpetbagger in '66, after the old town had been burned by the Federal General Smith and the new little town, in time to be populated mainly by the descendants not of Compsons but of Snopeses, had begun to encroach and then nibble at and into it as the failed brigadier spent the next forty years selling fragments of it off to keep up the mortgage on the remainder: until one day in 1900 he died quietly on an army cot in the hunting and fishing camp in the Tallahatchie River bottom where he passed most of the end of his days.

And even the old governor was forgotten now; what was left of the old square mile was now known merely as the Compson place – the weedchoked traces of the old ruined lawns and promenades, the house which had needed painting too long already, the scaling columns of the portico where

Jason III (bred for a lawyer and indeed he kept an office upstairs above the Square, where entombed in dusty filingcases some of the oldest names in the county – Holston and Sutpen, Grenier and Beauchamp and Coldfield – faded year by year among the bottomless labyrinths of chancery: and who knows what dream in the perennial heart of his father, now completing the third of his three avatars – the one as son of a brilliant and gallant states-man, the second as battleleader of brave and gallant men, the third as a sort of privileged pseudo-Daniel Boone-Robinson Crusoe, who had not returned to juvenility because actually he had never left it – that that lawyer's office might again be the anteroom to the governor's mansion and the old splen-dor) sat all day long with a decanter of whiskey and a litter of dogeared Horaces and Livys and Catulluses, composing (it was said) caustic and sa-tiric eulogies on both his dead and his living fellowtownsmen, who sold the last of the property, except that fragment containing the house and the kitchengarden and the collapsing stables and one servant's cabin in which Dilsey's family lived, to a golfclub for the ready money with which his daughter Candace could have her fine wedding in April and his son Quentin could finish one year at Harvard and commit suicide in the following June of 1910; already known as the Old Compson place even while Compsons were still living in it on the spring dusk in 1928 when the old governor's doomed lost nameless seventeen-year-old greatgreatgranddaughter robbed her last remaining sane male relative (her uncle Jason IV) of his secret hoard of money and climbed down a rainpipe and ran off with a pitchman in a travelling streetshow, and still known as the Old Compson place long after all traces of Compsons were gone from it; after the widowed mother died and Jason IV, no longer needing to fear Dilsey now, committed his idiot brother Benjamin, to the State Asylum in Jackson and sold the house to a countryman who operated it as a boarding house for juries and horse- and muletraders, and still known as the Old Compson place even after the boardinghouse (and presently the golfcourse too) had vanished and the old square mile was even intact again in row after row of small crowded jer-rybuilt individuallyowned demiurban bungalows.

Excerpt from the 'Appendix' (1946) to *The Sound and the Fury*, 1929

FROM SEA TO SHINING SEA

In the United States there is more space where nobody is than where anybody is. That is what makes America what it is.

Gertrude Stein, *The Geographical History of America*, 1936

And, at this day, though I have kind invitations enough to visit America, I could not, even for a couple of months, live in a country so miserable as to possess no castles.

John Ruskin, *Fors Clavigera*, vol. 1, letter 10, 1871

'All America behind'

HENRY DAVID THOREAU

We went to see the Ocean, and that is probably the best place of all our coast to go to. If you go by water, you may experience what it is to leave and to approach these shores; you may see the Stormy Petrel by the way, ϑαλασσοδρομα, running over the sea, and if the weather is but a little thick, may lose sight of the land in mid-passage. I do not know where there is another beach in the Atlantic States, attached to the mainland, so long, and at the same time so straight, and completely uninterrupted by creeks or coves or freshwater rivers or marshes; for though there may be clear places on the map, they would probably be found by the foot traveller to be intersected by creeks and marshes; certainly there is none where there is a double way, such as I have described, a beach and a bank, which at the same time shows you the land and the sea, and part of the time two seas. The Great South Beach of Long Island, which I have since visited, is longer still without an inlet, but it is literally a mere sand-bar, exposed, several miles from the Island, and not the edge of a continent wasting before the assaults of the ocean. Though wild and desolate, as it wants the bold bank, it possesses but half the grandeur of Cape Cod in my eyes, nor is the imagination contented with its southern aspect. The only other beaches of great length on our Atlantic coast, which I have heard sailors speak of, are those of Barnegat on the Jersey shore, and Currituck between Virginia and North Carolina; but these, like the last, are low and narrow sand-bars, lying off the coast, and separated from the mainland by lagoons. Besides, as you go farther south the tides are feebler, and cease to add variety and grandeur to the shore. On the Pacific side of our country also no doubt there is good walking to be found; a recent writer and dweller there tells us that 'the coast from Cape Disappointment (or the Columbia River) to Cape Flattery (at the Strait of Juan de Fuca) is nearly north and south, and can be travelled almost its entire length on a beautiful sand-beach,' with the exception of two bays, four or five rivers, and a few points jutting into the sea. The common shell-fish found there seem to be often of corresponding types, if not identical species, with those of Cape Cod. The beach which I have described, however, is not hard enough for carriages, but must be explored on foot. When one carriage has passed along, a following one sinks deeper still in its rut. It has at present no name any more than fame.

*

Most persons visit the sea-side in warm weather, when fogs are frequent, and the atmosphere is wont to be thick, and the charm of the sea is to some extent lost. But I *suspect* that the fall is the best season, for then the atmosphere is more transparent, and it is a greater pleasure to look out over the sea. The clear and bracing air, and the storms of autumn and winter even, are necessary in order that we may get the impression which the sea is calculated to make. In October, when the weather is not intolerably cold, and the landscape wears its autumnal tints, such as, methinks, only a Cape Cod landscape ever wears, especially if you have a storm during your stay, – that I am convinced is the best time to visit this shore. In autumn, even in August, the thoughtful days begin, and we can walk anywhere with profit. Beside, an outward cold and dreariness, which make it necessary to seek shelter at night, lend a spirit of adventure to a walk.

The time must come when this coast will be a place of resort for those New-Englanders who really wish to visit the sea-side. At present it is wholly unknown to the fashionable world, and probably it will never be agreeable to them. If it is merely a ten-pin alley, or a circular railway, or an ocean of mint-julep, that the visitor is in search of, – if he thinks more of the wine than the brine, as I suspect some do at Newport – I trust that for a long time he will be disappointed here. But this shore will never be more attractive than it is now. Such beaches as are fashionable are here made and unmade in a day, I may almost say, by the sea shifting its sands. Lynn and Nantasket! this bare and bended arm it is that makes the bay in which they lie so snugly. What are springs and waterfalls? Here is the spring of springs, the waterfall of waterfalls. A storm in the fall or winter is the time to visit it; a light-house or a fisherman's hut the true hotel. A man may stand there and put all America behind him.

(wr. 1855?) *Cape Cod*, 1864, ch. 10

American Names

STEPHEN VINCENT BENÉT

I have fallen in love with American names,
The sharp names that never get fat.
The snakeskin-titles of mining-claims,
The plumed war-bonnet of Medicine Hat,
Tucson and Deadwood and Lost Mule Flat.

Seine and Piave are silver spoons,
But the spoonbowl-metal is thin and worn,
There are English counties like hunting-tunes

Played on the keys of a postboy's horn,
But I will remember where I was born.

I will remember Carquinez Straits,
Little French Lick and Lundy's Lane,
The Yankee ships and the Yankee dates
And the bullet-towns of Calamity Jane.
I will remember Skunktown Plain.

I will fall in love with a Salem tree
And a rawhide quirt from Santa Cruz,
I will get me a bottle of Boston sea
And a blue-gum nigger to sing me blues.
I am tired of loving a foreign muse.

Rue des Martyrs and Bleeding-Heart-Yard,
Senlis, Pisa, and Blindman's Oast,
It is a magic ghost you guard
But I am sick for a newer ghost,
Harrisburg, Spartanburg, Painted Post.

Henry and John were never so
And Henry and John were always right?
Granted, but when it was time to go
And the tea and the laurels had stood all night,
Did they never watch for Nantucket Light?

I shall not rest quiet in Montparnasse.
I shall not lie easy at Winchelsea.
You may bury my body in Sussex grass,
You may bury my tongue at Champmédy.
I shall not be there. I shall rise and pass.
Bury my heart at Wounded Knee.

(1927) *Ballads and Poems*, 1931

'The biggest little place in America'

HENRY JAMES

I felt myself, on the spot, cast about a little for the right expression of it, and then lost any hesitation to say that, putting the three or four biggest cities aside, Concord, Massachusetts, had an identity more palpable to the mind, had nestled in other words more successfully beneath her narrow fold of the mantle of history, than any other American town. 'Compare me with places of my size, you know,' one seemed to hear her plead, with the modesty that, under the mild autumn sun, so well became her russet beauty; and this exactly it was that prompted the emphasis of one's reply, or, as it may even be called, of one's declaration.

'Ah, my dear, it isn't a question of places of your "size", since among places of your size you're too obviously and easily first: it's a question of places, so many of them, of fifty times your size, and which yet don't begin to have a fraction of your weight, or your character, or your intensity of presence and sweetness of tone, or your moral charm, or your pleasant appreciability, or, in short, of anything that is yours. Your "size"? Why, you're the biggest little place in America – with only New York and Boston and Chicago, by what I make out, to surpass you; and the country is lucky indeed to have you, in your sole and single felicity, for if it hadn't, where in the world should we go, inane and unappeased, for the particular communication of which you have the secret? The country is colossal, and you but a microscopic speck on the hem of its garment; yet there's nothing else like you, take you all round, for we *see* you complacently, with the naked eye, whereas there are vast sprawling, bristling areas, great grey "centres of population" that spread, on the map, like irremediable grease-spots, which fail utterly of any appeal to our vision or any control of it, leaving it to pass them by as if they were not. If you are so thoroughly the opposite of one of these I don't say it's all your superlative merit; it's rather, as I have put it, your felicity, your good fortune, the result of the half-dozen happy turns of the wheel in your favour. Half-a-dozen such turns, you see, are, for any mortal career, a handsome allowance; and your merit is that, recognizing this, you have not fallen below your estate. But it's your fortune, above all, that's your charm. One doesn't want to be patronizing, but you didn't, thank goodness, make yours. That's what the other places, the big ones that are as nothing to you, are trying to do, the country over – to make theirs; and, from the point of view of these remarks, all in vain. Your luck is that you didn't have to; yours had been, just as it shows in you to-day, made *for* you, and you at the most but gratefully submitted to it. It must be said for you, however, that you keep it; and it isn't every place that would have been capable – ! You keep the look, you keep the feeling, you keep the air. Your great trees arch over these possessions more protectingly, covering them in as a cherished presence; and you have settled to your tone and your type as to treasures that can now never be taken. Show me the other places in America (of the few that have *had* anything) from which the best hasn't mainly been taken, or isn't in imminent danger of being. There is old Salem, there is old Newport, which I am on my way to see again, and which, if you will, are, by what I hear, still comparatively intact; but their having was never a having like yours, and they adorn, precisely, my little tale of your supremacy. No, I don't want to be patronizing, but your only fault is your tendency to improve — I mean just by your duration as you *are*; which indeed is the only sort of improvement that is not questionable.'

Such was the drift of the warm flood of appreciation, of reflection, that Concord revisited could set rolling over the field of a prepared sensibility; and I feel as if I had quite made my point, such as it is, in asking what other American village could have done anything of the sort I should have been at fault perhaps only in speaking of the interest in question as visible, on that large scale, to the 'naked eye'; the truth being perhaps that one wouldn't have been so met half-way by one's impression unless one had rather particularly *known*, and that knowledge, in such a case, amounts to a pair of magnifying spectacles. I remember indeed putting it to myself on the November Sunday morning, tepid and bright and perfect for its use, through which I walked from the station under the constant archway of the elms, as yet but indulgently thinned: would one know, for one's self, what had formerly been the matter here, if one hadn't happened to be able to get round behind, in the past, as it were, and more or less understand? Would the operative elements of the past – little old Concord Fight, essentially, and Emerson and Hawthorne and Thoreau, with the rest of the historic animation and the rest of the figured and shifting 'transcendental' company, to its last and loosest ramifications – would even these handsome quantities have so lingered to one's intelligent after-sense, if one had not brought with one some sign by which they too would know; dim, shy spectralities as, for themselves, they must, at the best, have become? Idle, however, such questions when, by the chance of the admirable day, everything, in its own way and order, unmistakably came *out* – every string sounded as if, for all the world, the loose New England town (and I apply the expression but to the relations of objects and places), were a lyre swept by the hand of Apollo.

The American Scene, 1907, ch. 8

The River of Rivers in Connecticut

WALLACE STEVENS

There is a great river this side of Stygia,
Before one comes to the first black cataracts
And trees that lack the intelligence of trees.

In that river, far this side of Stygia,
The mere flowing of the water is a gayety,
Flashing and flashing in the sun. On its banks,

No shadow walks. The river is fateful,
Like the last one. But there is no ferryman.
He could not bend against its propelling force.

It is not to be seen beneath the appearances
That tell of it. The steeple at Farmington
Stands glistening and Haddam shines and sways.

It is the third commonness with light and air,
A curriculum, a vigor, a local abstraction . . .
Call it, once more, a river, an unnamed flowing,

Space-filled, reflecting the seasons, the folk-lore
Of each of the senses; call it, again and again,
The river that flows nowhere, like a sea.

(1953) *Collected Poems*, 1955

Crossing Brooklyn Ferry

WALT WHITMAN

1

Flood-Tide below me! I see you face to face!
Clouds of the west – sun there half an hour high – I see you also face to
　face.

Crowds of men and women attired in the usual costumes, how curious
　you are to me!
On the ferry-boats the hundreds and hundreds that cross, returning
　home, are more curious to me than you suppose,
And you that shall cross from shore to shore years hence are more to
　me, and more in my meditations, than you might suppose.

2

The impalpable sustenance of me from all things at all hours of the day,
The simple, compact, well-join'd scheme, myself disintegrated, every one
　disintegrated yet part of the scheme,
The similitudes of the past and those of the future,

The glories strung like beads on my smallest sights and hearings, on the
walk in the street and the passage over the river,
The current rushing so swiftly and swimming with me far away,
The others that are to follow me, the ties between me and them,
The certainty of others, the life, love, sight, hearing of others.

Others will enter the gates of the ferry and cross from shore to shore,
Others will watch the run of the flood-tide,
Others will see the shipping of Manhattan north and west, and the heights
of Brooklyn to the south and east,
Others will see the islands large and small;
Fifty years hence, others will see them as they cross, the sun half an hour
high,
A hundred years hence, or ever so many hundred years hence, others will
see them,
Will enjoy the sunset, the pouring-in of the flood-tide, the falling-back to
the sea of the ebb-tide.

3

It avails not, time nor place – distance avails not,
I am with you, you men and women of a generation, or ever so many
generations hence,
Just as you feel when you look on the river and sky, so I felt,
Just as any of you is one of a living crowd, I was one of a crowd,
Just as you are refresh'd by the gladness of the river and the bright flow,
I was refresh'd,
Just as you stand and lean on the rail, yet hurry with the swift current, I
stood yet was hurried,
Just as you look on the numberless masts of ships and the thick-stemm'd
pipes of steamboats, I look'd.

I too many and many a time cross'd the river of old,
Watched the Twelfth-month sea-gulls, saw them high in the air floating
with motionless wings, oscillating their bodies,
Saw how the glistening yellow lit up parts of their bodies and left the rest
in strong shadow,
Saw the slow-wheeling circles and the gradual edging toward the south,
Saw the reflection of the summer sky in the water,
Had my eyes dazzled by the shimmering track of beams,
Look'd at the fine centrifugal spokes of light round the shape of my head
in the sunlit water,
Look'd on the haze on the hills southward and southwestward,
Look'd on the vapor as it flew in fleeces tinged with violet,

Look'd toward the lower bay to notice the vessels arriving,
Saw their approach, saw aboard those that were near me,
Saw the white sails of schooners and sloops, saw the ships at anchor,
The sailors at work in the rigging or out astride the spars,
The round masts, the swinging motion of the hulls, the slender serpentine
    pennants,
The large and small steamers in motion, the pilots in their pilot-houses,
The white wake left by the passage, the quick tremulous whirl of the
    wheels,
The flags of all nations, the falling of them at sunset,
The scallop-edged waves in the twilight, the ladled cups, the frolicsome
    crests and glistening,
The stretch afar growing dimmer and dimmer, the gray walls of the granite
    storehouses by the docks,
On the river the shadowy group, the big steam-tug closely flank'd on each
    side by the barges, the hay-boat, the belated lighter,
On the neighboring shore the fires from the foundry chimneys burning high
    and glaringly into the night,
Casting their flicker of black contrasted with wild red and yellow light over
    the tops of houses, and down into the clefts of streets.

4

These and all else were to me the same as they are to you,
I loved well those cities, loved well the stately and rapid river,
The men and women I saw were all near to me,
Others the same – others who look back on me because I look'd forward
    to them,
(The time will come, though I stop here to-day and to-night.)

5

What is it then between us?
What is the count of the scores or hundreds of years between us?
Whatever it is, it avails not – distance avails not, and place avails not,
I too lived, Brooklyn of ample hills was mine,
I too walk'd the streets of Manhattan island, and bathed in the waters
    around it,
I too felt the curious abrupt questionings stir within me,
In the day among crowds of people sometimes they came upon me,
In my walks home late at night or as I lay in my bed they came upon me,
I too had been struck from the float forever held in solution,
I too had receiv'd identity by my body,
That I was I knew was of my body, and what I should be I knew I should
    be of my body.

6

It is not upon you alone the dark patches fall,
The dark threw its patches down upon me also,
The best I had done seem'd to me blank and suspicious,
My great thoughts as I supposed them, were they not in reality meagre?
Nor is it you alone who know what it is to be evil,
I am he who knew what it was to be evil,
I too knotted the old knot of contrariety,
Blabb'd, blush'd, resented, lied, stole, grudg'd,
Had guile, anger, lust, hot wishes I dared not speak,
Was wayward, vain, greedy, shallow, sly, cowardly, malignant,
The wolf, the snake, the hog, not wanting in me,
The cheating look, the frivolous word, the adulterous wish, not wanting,
Refusals, hates, postponements, meanness, laziness, none of these wanting,
Was one with the rest, the days and haps of the rest,
Was call'd by my nighest name by clear loud voices of young men as they
    saw me approaching or passing,
Felt their arms on my neck as I stood, or the negligent leaning of their flesh
    against me as I sat,
Saw many I loved in the street or ferry-boat or public assembly, yet never
    told them a word,
Lived the same life with the rest, the same old laughing, gnawing, sleeping,
Play'd the part that still looks back on the actor or actress,
The same old role, the role that is what we make it, as great as we like,
Or as small as we like, or both great and small.

7

Closer yet I approach you,
What thought you have of me now, I had as much of you – I laid in my
    stores in advance,
I consider'd long and seriously of you before you were born.

Who was to know what should come home to me?
Who knows but I am enjoying this?
Who knows, for all the distance, but I am as good as looking at you now,
    for all you cannot see me?

8

Ah, what can ever be more stately and admirable to me than mast-hemm'd
    Manhattan?
River and sunset and scallop-edg'd waves of flood-tide?
The sea-gulls oscillating their bodies, the hay-boat in the twilight, and the
    belated lighter?

What gods can exceed these that clasp me by the hand, and with voices I
  love call me promptly and loudly by my nighest name as I approach?
What is more subtle than this which ties me to the woman or man that looks
  in my face?
Which fuses me into you now, and pours my meaning into you?

We understand then do we not?
What I promis'd without mentioning it, have you not accepted?
What the study could not teach – what the preaching could not accomplish
  is accomplish'd, is it not?

9

Flow on, river! flow with the flood-tide, and ebb with the ebb-tide!
Frolic on, crested and scallop-edg'd waves!
Gorgeous clouds of the sunset! drench with your splendor me, or the men
  and women generations after me!
Cross from shore to shore, countless crowds of passengers!
Stand up, tall masts of Mannahatta! stand up, beautiful hills of Brooklyn!
Throb, baffled and curious brain! throw out questions and answers!
Suspend here and everywhere, eternal float of solution!
Gaze, loving and thirsting eyes, in the house or street or public assembly!
Sound out, voices of young men! loudly and musically call me by my nighest
  name!
Live, old life! play the part that looks back on the actor or actress!
Play the old role, the role that is great or small according as one makes it!
Consider, you who peruse me, whether I may not in unknown ways be
  looking upon you;
Be firm, rail over the river, to support those who lean idly, yet haste with
  the hasting current;
Fly on, sea-birds! fly sideways, or wheel in large circles high in the air;
Receive the summer sky, you water, and faithfully hold it till all downcast
  eyes have time to take it from you!
Diverge, fine spokes of light, from the shape of my head, or any one's head,
  in the sunlit water!
Come on, ships from the lower bay! pass up or down, white-sail'd
  schooners, sloops, lighters!
Flaunt away, flags of all nations! be duly lower'd at sunset!
Burn high your fires, foundry chimneys! cast black shadows at nightfall!
  cast red and yellow light over the tops of the houses!
Appearances, now or henceforth, indicate what you are,
You necessary film, continue to envelop the soul,
About my body for me, and your body for you, be hung out divinest
  aromas,

Thrive, cities – bring your freight, bring your shows, ample and sufficient rivers,
Expand, being than which none else is perhaps more spiritual,
Keep your places, objects than which none else is more lasting.

You have waited, you always wait, you dumb, beautiful ministers,
We receive you with free sense at last, and are insatiate henceforward,
Not you any more shall be able to foil us, or withhold yourselves from us,
We use you, and do not cast you aside – we plant you permanently within us,
We fathom you not – we love you – there is perfection in you also,
You furnish your parts toward eternity,
Great or small, you furnish your parts toward the soul.

Leaves of Grass, 1856

'Most extravagant of cities'

HENRY JAMES

It is indubitably a 'great' bay, a great harbour, but no one item of the romantic, or even of the picturesque, as commonly understood, contributes to its effect. The shores are low and for the most part depressingly furnished and prosaically peopled; the islands, though numerous, have not a grace to exhibit, and one thinks of the other, the real flowers of geography in this order, of Naples, of Capetown, of Sydney, of Seattle, of San Francisco, of Rio, asking how if *they* justify a reputation, New York should seem to justify one. Then, after all, we remember that there are reputations and reputations; we remember above all that the imaginative response to the conditions here presented may just happen to proceed from the intellectual extravagance of the given observer. When this personage is open to corruption by almost any large view of an intensity of life, his vibrations tend to become a matter difficult even for *him* to explain. He may have to confess that the group of evident facts fails to account by itself for the complacency of his appreciation. Therefore it is that I find myself rather backward with a perceived sanction, of an at all proportionate kind, for the fine exhilaration with which, in this free wayfaring relation to them, the wide waters of New York inspire me. There is the beauty of light and air, the great scale of space, and, seen far away to the west, the open gates of the Hudson, majestic in their degree, even at a distance, and announcing still nobler things. But the real appeal, unmistakably, is in that note of vehemence in the local life of which I have spoken, for it is the appeal of a particular type of dauntless power.

The aspect the power wears then is indescribable; it is the power of the most extravagant of cities, rejoicing, as with the voice of the morning, in its might, its fortune, its unsurpassable conditions, and imparting to every object and element, to the motion and expression of every floating, hurrying, panting thing, to the throb of ferries and tugs, to the plash of waves and the play of winds and the glint of lights and the shrill of whistles and the quality and authority of breeze-borne cries – all, practically, a diffused, wasted clamour of *detonations* – something of its sharp free accent and, above all, of its sovereign sense of being 'backed' and able to back. The universal *applied* passion struck me as shining unprecedentedly out of the composition; in the bigness and bravery and insolence, especially, of everything that rushed and shrieked; in the air as of a great intricate frenzied dance, half merry, half desperate, or at least half defiant, performed on the huge watery floor. This appearance of the bold lacing-together, across the waters, of the scattered members of the monstrous organism – lacing as by the ceaseless play of an enormous system of steam-shuttles or electric bobbins (I scarce know what to call them), commensurate in form with their infinite work – does perhaps more than anything else to give the pitch of the vision of energy. One has the sense that the monster grows and grows, flinging abroad its loose limbs even as some unmannered young giant at his 'larks', and that the binding stitches must for ever fly further and faster and draw harder; the future complexity of the web, all under the sky and over the sea, becoming thus that of some colossal set of clockworks, some steel-souled machine-room of brandished arms and hammering fists and opening and closing jaws. The immeasurable bridges are but as the horizontal sheaths of pistons working at high pressure, day and night, and subject, one apprehends with perhaps inconsistent gloom, to certain, to fantastic, to merciless multiplication. In the light of this apprehension indeed the breezy brightness of the Bay puts on the semblance of the vast white page that awaits beyond any other perhaps the black overscoring of science.

Let me hasten to add that its present whiteness is precisely its charming note, the frankest of the signs you recognize and remember it by. That is the distinction I was just feeling my way to name as the main ground of its doing so well, for effect, without technical scenery. There are great imposing ports – Glasgow and Liverpool and London – that have already their page blackened almost beyond redemption from any such light of the picturesque as can hope to irradiate fog and grime, and there are others, Marseilles and Constantinople say, or, for all I know to the contrary, New Orleans, that contrive to abound before everything else in colour, and so to make a rich and instant and obvious show. But memory and the actual impression keep investing New York with the tone, predominantly, of summer dawns and winter frosts, of sea-foam, of bleached sails and stretched awnings, of blanched hulls, of scoured decks, of new ropes, of polished brasses, of streamers clear in the blue air; and it is by this harmony, doubtless, that the projection of the individual character of the place, of the candour of its avidity and the freshness of its audacity, is most conveyed. The 'tall buildings', which have so promptly usurped a glory that affects you as rather surprised, as yet, at itself, the multitudinous sky-scrapers standing up to the view, from the water, like extravagant pins in a cushion already overplanted, and stuck in as in the dark, anywhere and anyhow, have at least the felicity of carrying out the fairness of tone, of taking the sun and the shade in the manner of towers of marble. They are not all of marble, I believe, by any means, even if some may be, but they are impudently new and still more impudently 'novel' – this in common with so many other terrible things in America – and they are triumphant payers of dividends; all of which uncontested and unabashed pride, with flash of innumerable windows and flicker of subordinate gilt attributions, is like the flare, up and down their long, narrow faces, of the lamps of some general permanent 'celebration'.

The American Scene, 1907, ch. 2

'The outcome of squalid barbarism'

RUDYARD KIPLING

It is not easy to escape from a big city. An entire continent was waiting to be traversed, and, for that reason, we lingered in New York till the city felt so homelike that it seemed wrong to leave it. And further, the more one studied it, the more grotesquely bad it grew – bad in its paving, bad in its streets, bad in its street-police, and but for the kindness of the tides would be worse than bad in its sanitary arrangements. No one as yet has approached the management of New York in a proper spirit; that is to say, regarding it as the shiftless outcome of squalid barbarism and reckless extravagance. No one is likely to do so, because reflections on the long, narrow pig-trough are construed as malevolent attacks against the spirit and majesty of the Great American People, and lead to angry comparisons. Yet, if all the streets of London were permanently up and all the lamps permanently down, this would not prevent the New York streets taken in a lump from being first cousins to a Zanzibar foreshore, or kin to the approaches of a Zulu kraal. Gullies, holes, ruts, cobble-stones awry, kerbstones rising from two to six inches above the level of the slatternly pavement; tram-lines from two to three inches above street level; building materials scattered half across the street; lime, boards, cut stone, and ash-barrels generally and generously everywhere; wheeled traffic taking its chances, dray *versus* brougham, at cross roads; sway-backed poles whittled and unpainted; drunken lamp-posts with twisted irons; and, lastly, a generous scatter of filth and more mixed stinks than the winter wind can carry away, are matters which can be considered quite apart from the 'Spirit of Democracy' or 'the future of this great and growing country'. In any other land they would be held to represent slovenliness, sordidness, and want of capacity. Here it is explained, not once but many times, that they show the speed at which the city has grown and the enviable indifference of her citizens to matters of detail. One of these days, you are told, everything will be taken in hand and put straight. The unvirtuous rulers of the city will be swept away by a cyclone, or a tornado, or something big and booming, of popular indignation; everybody will unanimously elect the right man, who will justly earn the enormous salaries that are at present being paid to inadequate aliens for road sweepings, and all will be well. At the same time the lawlessness ingrained by governors among the governed during the last thirty, forty, or it may be fifty years; the brutal levity of the public conscience in regard to public duty; the toughening and suppling of public morals, and the reckless disregard for human life, bred by impotent laws and fostered by familiarity with needless accidents and criminal neglect, will miraculously disappear. If the laws of cause and effect that control even the freest people in the world say otherwise, so much the worse for the laws. America makes her own. Behind her stands the ghost of the most bloody war of the century caused in a peaceful land by long temporising with lawlessness, by letting things slide, by shiftlessness and blind disregard for all save the material need of the hour, till the hour, long conceived and let alone, stood up full-armed, and men said, 'Here is an unforeseen crisis,' and killed each other in the name of God for four years.

In a heathen land the three things that are supposed to be the pillars of moderately decent government are regard for human life, justice, criminal and civil, as far as it lies in man to do justice, and good roads. In this Christian city they think lightly of the first – their own papers, their own speech, and their own actions prove it; buy and sell the second at a price openly and without shame; and are, apparently, content to do without the third. One would almost expect racial sense of humour would stay them from expecting only praise – slab, lavish, and slavish – from the stranger within their gates. But they do not. If he holds his peace, they forge tributes to their own excellence which they put into his mouth, thereby treating their own land which they profess to honour as a quack treats his pills. If he speaks – but you shall see for yourselves what happens then. And they cannot see that by untruth and invective it is themselves alone that they injure.

The blame of their city evils is not altogether with the gentlemen, chiefly of foreign extraction, who control the city. These find a people made to their hand – a lawless breed ready to wink at one evasion of the law if they themselves may profit by another, and in their rare leisure hours content to smile over the details of a clever fraud. Then, says the cultured American, 'Give us time. Give us time, and we shall arrive.' The otherwise American, who is aggressive, straightway proceeds to thrust a piece of half-hanged municipal botchwork under the nose of the alien as a sample of perfected effort. There is nothing more delightful than to sit for a strictly limited time with a child who tells you what he means to do when he is a man; but when that same child, loud-voiced, insistent, unblushingly eager for praise, but thin-skinned as the most morbid of hobbledehoys, stands about all your ways telling you the same story in the same voice, you begin to yearn for something made and finished – say Egypt and a completely dead mummy. It is neither seemly nor safe to hint that the government of the largest city in the States is a despotism of the alien by the alien for the alien, tempered with occasional insurrections of the decent folk. Only the Chinaman washes the dirty linen of other lands.

'Across a Continent' in *From Tideway to Tideway*, 1892

New York

MARIANNE MOORE

the savage's romance,
accreted where we need the space for commerce –
the center of the wholesale fur trade,
starred with tepees of ermine and peopled with foxes,
the long guard-hairs waving two inches beyond the body of the pelt;
the ground dotted with deer-skins – white with white spots,
'as satin needlework in a single color may carry a varied pattern',
and wilting eagle's-down compacted by the wind;
and picardels of beaver-skin; white ones alert with snow.
It is a far cry from the 'queen full of jewels'
and the beau with the muff,
from the gilt coach shaped like a perfume-bottle,
to the conjunction of the Monongahela and the Allegheny,
and the scholastic philosophy of the wilderness.

It is not the dime-novel exterior,
Niagara Falls, the calico horses and the war-canoe;
it is not that 'if the fur is not finer than such as one sees others wear,
one would rather be without it' –
that estimated in raw meat and berries, we could feed the universe;
it is not the atmosphere of ingenuity,
the otter, the beaver, the puma skins
without shooting-irons or dogs;
it is not the plunder,
but 'accessibility to experience'.

(1921) *Selected Poems*, 1935

'Harlem was Seventh Heaven'

MALCOLM X

I went along with the railroad job for my own reasons. For a long time I'd wanted to visit New York City. Since I had been in Roxbury, I had heard a lot about 'the Big Apple', as it was called by the well-traveled musicians, merchant mariners, salesmen, chauffeurs for white families, and various kinds of hustlers I ran into. Even as far back as Lansing, I had been hearing about how fabulous New York was, and especially Harlem. In fact, my father had described Harlem with pride, and showed us pictures of the huge parades by the Harlem followers of Marcus Garvey. And every time Joe Louis won a fight against a white opponent, big front-page pictures in the Negro newspapers such as the *Chicago Defender*, the *Pittsburgh Courier* and the *Afro-American* showed a sea of Harlem Negroes cheering and waving and the Brown Bomber waving back at them from the balcony of Harlem's Theresa Hotel. Everything I'd ever heard about New York City was exciting – things like Broadway's bright lights and the Savoy Ballroom and Apollo Theater in Harlem, where great bands played and famous songs and dance steps and Negro stars originated.

*

After a few of the Washington runs, I snatched the chance when one day personnel said I could temporarily replace a sandwich man on the 'Yankee Clipper' to New York. I was into my zoot suit before the first passenger got off.

The cooks took me up to Harlem in a cab. White New York passed by like a movie set, then abruptly, when we left Central Park at the upper end, at 110th Street, the people's complexion began to change.

Busy Seventh Avenue ran along in front of a place called Small's Paradise. The crew had told me before we left Boston that it was their favorite night spot in Harlem, and not to miss it. No Negro place of business had ever impressed me so much. Around the big, luxurious-looking, circular bar were thirty or forty Negroes, mostly men, drinking and talking.

I was hit first, I think, by their conservative clothes and manners. Wherever I'd seen as many as ten Boston Negroes – let alone Lansing Negroes – drinking, there had been a big noise. But with all of these Harlemites drinking and talking, there was just a low murmur of sound. Customers came and went. The bartenders knew what most of them drank and automatically fixed it. A bottle was set on the bar before some.

Every Negro I'd ever known had made a point of flashing whatever money he had. But these Harlem Negroes quietly laid a bill on the bar. They drank. They nonchalantly nodded to the bartender to pour a drink, for some friend, while the bartenders, smooth as any of the customers, kept making change from the money on the bar.

Their manners seemed natural; they were not putting on any airs. I was awed. Within the first five minutes in Small's, I had left Boston and Roxbury forever.

I didn't yet know that these weren't what you might call everyday or average Harlem Negroes. Later on, even later that night, I would find out that Harlem contained hundreds of thousands of my people who were just as loud and gaudy as Negroes anywhere else. But these were the cream of the older, more mature operators in Harlem. The day's 'numbers' business was done. The night's gambling and other forms of hustling hadn't yet begun. The usual night-life crowd, who worked on regular jobs all day, were at home eating their dinners. The hustlers at this time were in the daily six o'clock congregation, their favorite bars all over Harlem largely to themselves.

From Small's, I taxied over to the Apollo Theater. (I remember so well that Jay McShann's band was playing, because his vocalist was later my close friend, Walter Brown, the one who used to sing 'Hooty Hooty Blues'.) From there, on the other side of 125th Street, at Seventh Avenue, I saw the big, tall, gray Theresa Hotel. It was the finest in New York City where Negroes could then stay, years before the downtown hotels would accept the black man. (The Theresa is now best known as the place where Fidel Castro went during his UN visit, and achieved a psychological coup over the US State Department when it confined him to Manhattan, never dreaming that he'd stay uptown in Harlem and make such an impression among the Negroes.)

The Braddock Hotel was just up 126th Street, near the Apollo's backstage entrance. I knew its bar was famous as a Negro celebrity hang-out. I walked in and saw, along that jam-packed bar, such famous stars as Dizzy Gillespie, Billy Eckstine, Billie Holiday, Ella Fitzgerald, and Dinah Washington.

As Dinah Washington was leaving with some friends, I overheard someone say she was on her way to the Savoy Ballroom where Lionel Hampton was appearing that night – she was then Hamp's vocalist. The ballroom made the Roseland in Boston look small and shabby by comparison. And the lindy-hopping there matched the size and elegance of the place. Hampton's hard-driving outfit kept a red-hot pace with his greats such as Arnett Cobb, Illinois Jacquet, Dexter Gordon, Alvin Hayse, Joe Newman, and George Jenkins. I went a couple of rounds on the floor with girls from the sidelines.

Probably a third of the sideline booths were filled with white people, mostly just watching the Negroes dance; but some of them danced together, and, as in Boston, a few white women were with Negroes. The people kept shouting for Hamp's 'Flyin' Home', and finally he did it. (I could believe the story I'd heard in Boston about this number – that once in the Apollo, Hamp's 'Flyin' Home' had made some reefer-smoking Negro in the second balcony believe he could fly, so he tried – and jumped – and broke his leg, an event later immortalized in song when Earl Hines wrote a hit tune called 'Second Balcony Jump'.) I had never seen such fever-heat dancing. After a couple of slow numbers cooled the place off, they brought on Dinah Washington. When she did her 'Salty Papa Blues', those people just about tore the Savoy roof off. (Poor Dinah's funeral was held not long ago in Chicago. I read that over 20,000 people viewed her body, and I should have been there myself. Poor Dinah! We became great friends, back in those days.)

But this night of my first visit was Kitchen Mechanics' Night at the Savoy, the traditional Thursday night off for domestics. I'd say there were twice as many women as men in there, not only kitchen workers and maids, but also war wives and defense-worker women, lonely and looking. Out in the street, when I left the ballroom, I heard a prostitute cursing bitterly that the professionals couldn't do any business because of the amateurs.

Up and down along and between Lenox and Seventh and Eighth Avenues, Harlem was like some technicolor bazaar. Hundreds of Negro soldiers and sailors, gawking and young like me, passed by. Harlem by now was officially off limits to white servicemen. There had already been some muggings and robberies, and several white servicemen had been found murdered. The police were also trying to discourage white civilians from coming uptown, but those who wanted to still did. Every man without a woman on his arm was being 'worked' by the prostitutes. 'Baby, wanna have some fun?' The pimps would sidle up close, stage-whispering, 'All kinds of women, Jack – want a white woman?' And the hustlers were merchandising: 'Hundred dollar ring, man, diamond; ninety-dollar watch, too – look at 'em. Take 'em both for twenty-five.'

In another two years, I could have given them all lessons. But that night, I was mesmerized. This world was where I belonged. On that night I had started on my way to becoming a Harlemite. I was going to become one of the most depraved parasitical hustlers among New York's eight million people – four million of whom work, and the other four million of whom live off them.

*

Every layover night in Harlem, I ran and explored new places. I first got a room at the Harlem YMCA, because it was less than a block from Small's Paradise. Then, I got a cheaper room at Mrs Fisher's rooming house which was close to the YMCA. Most of the railroad men stayed at Mrs Fisher's. I combed not only the bright-light areas, but Harlem's residential areas from best to worst, from Sugar Hill up near the Polo Grounds, where many famous celebrities lived, down to the slum blocks of old rat-trap apartment houses, just crawling with everything you could mention that was illegal and immoral. Dirt, garbage cans overflowing or kicked over; drunks, dope addicts, beggars. Sleazy bars, storefront churches with gospels being shouted inside, 'bargain' stores, hockshops, undertaking parlours. Greasy 'home-cooking' restaurants, beauty shops smoky inside from Negro women's hair getting fried, barberships advertising conk experts. Cadillacs, secondhand and new, conspicuous among the cars on the streets.

All of it was Lansing's West Side or Roxbury's South End magnified a thousand times. Little basement dance halls with 'For Rent' signs on them. People offering you little cards advertising 'rent-raising parties'. I went to one of these – thirty or forty Negroes sweating, eating, drinking, dancing, and gambling in a jammed, beat-up apartment, the record player going full blast, the fried chicken or chitlins with potato salad and collard greens for a dollar a plate, and cans of beer or shots of liquor for fifty cents. Negro and white canvassers sidled up alongside you, talking fast as they tried to get you to buy a copy of the *Daily Worker:* 'This paper's trying to keep your rent controlled . . . Make that greedy landlord kill them rats in your apartment . . . This paper represents the only political party that ever ran a black man for the Vice Presidency of the United States . . . Just want you to read, won't take but a little of your time . . . Who do you think fought the hardest to help free those Scottsboro boys?' Things I overheard among

Negroes when the salesmen were around let me know that the paper somehow was tied in with the Russians, but to my sterile mind in those early
days, it didn't mean much; the radio broadcasts and the newspapers were
then full of our-ally-Russia, a strong, muscular people, peasants, with their
backs to the wall helping America to fight Hitler and Mussolini.

But New York was heaven to me. And Harlem was Seventh Heaven!

The Autobiography of Malcolm X, 1965, ch. 5

Iron Landscapes
(and the Statue of Liberty)

THOM GUNN

No trellisses, no vines
           a fire escape
Repeats a bare black Z from tier to tier
Hard flower, tin scroll embellish this landscape.
Between iron columns I walk toward the pier.

And stand a long time at the end of it
Gazing at iron on the New Jersey side.
A girdered ferry-building opposite,
Displaying the name LACKAWANNA, seems to ride

The turbulent brown-grey waters that intervene:
Cool seething incompletion that I love.
The zigzags come and go, sheen tracking sheen;
And water wrestles with the air above.

But I'm at peace with the iron landscape too,
Hard because buildings must be hard to last
– Block, cylinder, cube, built with their angles true,
A dream of righteous permanence, from the past.

In Nixon's era, decades after the ferry,
The copper embodiment of the pieties
Seems hard, but hard like a revolutionary
With indignation, constant as she is.

From here you can glimpse her downstream, her far charm,
Liberty, tiny woman in the mist

– You cannot see the torch – raising her arm
Lorn, bold, as if saluting with her fist.

Barrow Street Pier, New York
May 1973

Jack Straw's Castle, 1976

'A bragging boast'

FRANCES ANNE KEMBLE

I confess the sight of it [Niagara] reminded me, with additional admiration,
of Sir Charles Bagot's daring denial of its existence; having failed to make
his pilgrimage thither during his stay in the United States, he declared on
his return to England that he had never been able to find it, that he didn't
believe there was any such thing, and that it was nothing but a bragging
boast of the Americans.

(1833) *Records of a Girlhood*, 1878

Dixie's Land

DANIEL DECATUR EMMETT

I wish I was in de land ob cotton,
Old times dar am not forgotten,
    Look away! look away! look away! Dixie land.
In Dixie land, whar I was born in,
Early on one frosty mornin',
    Look away! look away! look away! Dixie land.

CHORUS
Den I wish I was in Dixie,
Horray! Horray!
In Dixie land I'll take my stand,
To lib and die in Dixie!
Away, away, away down South in Dixie!
Away, away, away down South in Dixie!

Old Missus marry Will de weaber,
William was a gay deceaber,
    Look away! look away! look away! Dixie land.

But when he put his arm around 'er
He smiled as fierce as a forty-pounder,
   Look away! look away! look away! Dixie land.

His face was sharp as a butcher's cleaber,
But dat did not seem to greab 'er
   Look away! look away! look away! Dixie land.
Old Missus acted the foolish part,
And died for a man dat broke her heart,
   Look away! look away! look away! Dixie land.

Now here's a health to the next old Missus,
And all de gals dat want to kiss us,
   Look away! look away! look away! Dixie land.
But if you want to drive 'way sorrow,
Come and hear dis song tomorrow,
   Look away! look away! look away! Dixie land.

Dar's buckwheat cakes an' Ingen batter,
Makes you fat, or a little fatter,
   Look away! look away! look away! Dixie land.
Den hoe it down an' scratch your grabble.
To Dixie's land I'm bound to trabble,
   Look away! look away! look away! Dixie land.

1859

'Virginia, equal to any land'

ROBERT BEVERLEY

78. The country is in a very happy situation, between the extremes of heat
and cold, but inclining rather to the first. Certainly it must be a happy climate, since it is very near the same latitude with the Land of Promise. Besides, as Judaea was full of rivers, and branches of rivers, so is Virginia. As
that was seated upon a great bay and sea, wherein were all the conveniences
for shipping and trade, so is Virginia. Had that fertility of soil? So has Virginia, equal to any land in the known world. In fine, if anyone impartially
considers all the advantages of this country, as Nature made it, he must allow it to be as fine a place as any in the universe. But I confess I am ashamed
to say anything of its improvements, because I must at the same time reproach my countrymen with a laziness that is unpardonable. If there be any
excuse for them in this matter, 'tis the exceeding plenty of good things with

which Nature has blessed them; for where God Almighty is so merciful as to work for people, they never work for themselves.

*

79. That which makes this country most unfortunate is that it must submit to receive its character from the mouths not only of unfit, but very unequal judges. For all its reproaches happen after this manner.

Many of the old merchants and others that go thither from England make no distinction between a cold and a hot country, but wisely go sweltering about in their thick clothes all the summer because they used to do so in their northern climate, and then unfairly complain of the heat of the country. They greedily surfeit with their delicious fruits and are guilty of great intemperance through the exceeding generosity of the inhabitants, by which means they fall sick, and then unjustly complain of the unhealthiness of the country. In the next place, the sailors, for want of towns there, are put to the hardship of rolling most of the tobacco a mile or more to the waterside. This splinters their hands sometimes and provokes 'em to curse the country. Such exercise, and a bright sun, makes them hot, and then they imprudently fall to drinking cold water or perhaps new cider, which in its season they find at every planter's house. Or else they greedily devour all the green fruit and unripe trash they meet with, and so fall into fluxes, fevers, and belly-ache. And then, to spare their own indiscretion, they in their tarpaulin language cry 'God D – ' the country. This is the true state of the case, as to the complaints of its being sickly. For by the impartial observation I can make, if people will be persuaded to be temperate and take due care of themselves, I believe it is as healthy a country as any under Heaven. But the extraordinary pleasantness of the weather and the goodness of the fruit lead people into many temptations.

The clearness and brightness of the sky add new vigour to their spirits and perfectly remove all splenetic and sullen thoughts. Here they enjoy all the benefits of a warm sun, and by the shady groves are protected from its inconvenience. Here all their senses are entertained with an endless succession of native pleasures. Their eyes are ravished with the beauties of naked Nature. Their ears are serenaded with the perpetual murmur of brooks and the thorough-bass which the wind plays when it wantons through the trees. The merry birds, too, join their pleasing notes to this rural consort, especially the mock-birds, who love society so well that whenever they see mankind, they will perch upon a twig very near them and sing the sweetest airs in the world. But what is most remarkable in these melodious animals, they will frequently fly at small distances before a traveller, warbling their notes several miles on end, and by their music make a man forget the fatigues of his journey. Their taste is regaled with the most delicious fruits, which without art they have in great variety and perfection. And then their smell is refreshed with an eternal fragrancy of flowers and sweets with which Nature perfumes and adorns the woods almost the whole year round.

The History and Present State of Virginia, 1705, ch. 19

Virginia

T. S. ELIOT

Red river, red river,
Slow flow heat is silence
No will is still as a river
Still. Will heat move
Only through the mocking-bird
Heard once? Still hills
Wait. Gates wait. Purple trees,
White trees, wait, wait,
Delay, decay. Living, living,
Never moving. Ever moving
Iron thoughts came with me
And go with me:
Red river, river, river.

(1934) *Collected Poems 1909–1935*, 1936

Anecdote of the Jar

WALLACE STEVENS

I placed a jar in Tennessee,
And round it was, upon a hill.
It made the slovenly wilderness
Surround that hill.

The wilderness rose up to it,
And sprawled around, no longer wild.
The jar was round upon the ground
And tall and of a port in air.

It took dominion everywhere.
The jar was gray and bare.
It did not give of bird or bush,
Like nothing else in Tennessee.

Harmonium, 1923

Wild Turkey

JOHN JAMES AUDUBON

The great size and beauty of the Wild Turkey, its value as a delicate and highly prized article of food, and the circumstance of its being the origin of the domestic race now generally dispersed over both continents, render it one of the most interesting of the birds indigenous to the United States of America.

The unsettled parts of the States of Ohio, Kentucky, Illinois, and Indiana, an immense extent of country to the north-west of these districts, upon the Mississippi and Missouri, and the vast regions drained by these rivers from their confluence to Louisiana, including the wooded parts of Arkansas, Tennessee, and Alabama, are the most abundantly supplied with this magnificent bird. It is less plentiful in Georgia and the Carolinas, becomes still scarcer in Virginia and Pennsylvania, and is now very rarely seen to the eastward of the last mentioned States. In the course of my rambles through Long Island, the State of New York, and the country around the Lakes, I did not meet with a single individual, although I was informed that some exist in those parts. Turkeys are still to be found along the whole line of the Alleghany Mountains, where they have become so wary as to be approached only with extreme difficulty. While, in the Great Pine Forest, in 1829, I found a single feather that had been dropped from the tail of a female, but saw no bird of the kind. Farther eastward, I do not think they are now to be found.

*

About the beginning of October, when scarcely any of the seeds and fruits have yet fallen from the trees, these birds assemble in flocks, and gradually move towards the rich bottom lands of the Ohio and Mississippi. The males, or, as they are more commonly called, the *gobblers*, associate in parties of from ten to a hundred, and search for food apart from the females; while the latter are seen either advancing singly, each with its brood of young, then about two-thirds grown, or in connexion with other families, forming parties often amounting to seventy or eighty individuals, all intent on shunning the old cocks, which, even when the young birds have attained this size, will fight with, and often destroy them by repeated blows on the head. Old and young, however, all move in the same course, and on foot, unless their progress be interrupted by a river, or the hunter's dog force them to take wing. When they come upon a river, they betake themselves to the highest eminences, and there often remain a whole day, or sometimes two, as if for the purpose of consultation. During this time, the males are heard *gobbling*, calling, and making much ado, and are seen strutting about, as if to raise their courage to a pitch befitting the emergency. Even the females and young assume something of the same pompous demeanour, spread out their tails, and run round each other, *purring* loudly, and performing extravagant leaps. At length, when the weather appears settled, and all around is quiet, the whole party mounts to the tops of the highest trees, whence, at a signal, consisting of a single *cluck*, given by a leader, the flock takes flight for the opposite shore. The old and fat birds easily get over, even should the river be a mile in breadth; but the younger and less robust frequently fall into the water, – not to be drowned, however, as might be imagined. They bring their wings close to their body, spread out their tail as a support, stretch forward their neck, and, striking out their legs with great vigour, proceed rapidly towards the shore; on approaching which, should they find it too steep for landing, they cease their exertions for a few moments, float down the stream until they come to an accessible part, and by a violent effort generally extricate themselves from the water. It is remarkable, that immediately after thus crossing a large stream, they ramble about for some time, as if bewildered. In this state, they fall an easy prey to the hunter.

When the Turkeys arrive in parts where the mast is abundant, they separate into smaller flocks, composed of birds of all ages and both sexes, promiscuously mingled, and devour all before them. This happens about the middle of November. So gentle do they sometimes become after these long journeys, that they have been seen to approach the farmhouses, associate with the domestic fowls, and enter the stables and corncribs in quest of food. In this way, roaming about the forests, and feeding chiefly on mast, they pass the autumn and part of the winter.

As early as the middle of February, they begin to experience the impulse of propagation. The females separate, and fly from the males. The latter strenuously pursue, and begin to gobble or to utter the notes of exultation. The sexes roost apart, but at no great distance from each other. When a female utters a call-note, all the gobblers within hearing return the sound, return rolling note after note with as much rapidity as if they intended to emit the last and the first together, not with spread tail, as when fluttering round the females on the ground, or practising on the branches of the trees on which they have roosted for the night, but much in the manner of the domestic turkey, when an unusual or unexpected noise elicits its singular hubbub. If the call of the female comes from the ground, all the males immediately fly towards the spot, and the moment they reach it, whether the hen be in sight or not, spread out and erect their tail, draw the head back on the shoulders, depress their wings with a quivering motion, and strut pompously about, emitting at the same time a succession of puffs from the lungs, and stopping now and then to listen and look. But whether they spy the female or not, they continue to puff and strut, moving with as much celerity as their ideas of ceremony seem to admit. While thus occupied, the males often encounter each other, in which case desperate battles take place, ending in bloodshed, and often in the loss of many lives, the weaker falling under the repeated blows inflicted upon their head by the stronger.

I have often been much diverted, while watching two males in fierce conflict, by seeing them move alternately backwards and forwards, as either had obtained a better hold, their wings drooping, their tails partly raised, their body-feathers ruffled, and their heads covered with blood. If, as they thus struggle, and gasp for breath, one of them should lose his hold, his chance is over, for the other, still holding fast, hits him violently with spurs and wings, and in a few minutes brings him to the ground. The moment he is dead, the conqueror treads him under foot, but, what is strange, not with hatred, but with all the motions which he employs in caressing the female.

When the male has discovered and made up to the female (whether such a combat has previously taken place or not), if she be more than one year old, she also struts and gobbles, turns round him as he continues strutting, suddenly opens her wings, throws herself towards him, as if to put a stop to his idle delay, lays herself down, and receives his dilatory caresses. If the cock meet a young hen, he alters his mode of procedure. He struts in a different manner, less pompously and more energetically, moves with rapidity, sometimes rises from the ground, taking a short flight around the hen, as is the manner of some Pigeons, the Red-breasted Thrush, and many other birds, and on alighting, runs with all his might, at the same time rubbing his tail and wings along the ground, for the space of perhaps ten yards. He then draws near the timorous female, allays her fears by purring, and when she at length assents, caresses her.

When a male and a female have thus come together, I believe the connexion continues for that season, although the former by no means confines his attention to one female, as I have seen a cock caress several hens, when he happened to fall in with them in the same place, for the first time. After this the hens follow their favourite cock, roosting in his immediate neighbourhood, if not on the same tree, until they begin to lay, when they separate themselves, in order to save their eggs from the male, who would break them all, for the purpose of protracting his sexual enjoyments. The females then carefully avoid him, excepting during a short period each day. After this the males become clumsy and slovenly, if one may say so, cease to fight with each other, give up gobbling or calling so frequently, and assume so careless a habit, that the hens are obliged to make all the advances themselves. They *yelp* loudly and almost continually for the cocks, run up to them, caress them, and employ various means to rekindle their expiring ardour.

Ornithological Biography, vol. I, 1831

My Old Kentucky Home

STEPHEN COLLINS FOSTER

The sun shines bright in the old Kentucky home,
    'T is summer, the darkies are gay;
The corn top's ripe and the meadow's in the bloom,
    While the birds make music all the day.
The young folks roll on the little cabin floor,
    All merry, all happy and bright;
By'm by hard times come a-knocking at the door,
    Then my old Kentucky home, good night.

CHORUS
Weep no more, my lady,
O weep no more today!
We will sing one song
For the old Kentucky home,
For the old Kentucky home,
Far away.

They hunt no more for the possum and the coon,
    On the meadow, the hill, and the shore;
They sing no more by the glimmer of the moon,
    On the bench by the old cabin door.
The day goes by like a shadow o'er the heart,
    With sorrow where all was delight;
The time has come when the darkies have to part,
    Then my old Kentucky home, good night.

The head must bow and the back will have to bend,
　　Wherever the darkey may go;
A few more days, and the trouble all will end,
　　In the field where the sugar canes grow.
A few more days for to tote the weary load,
　　No matter 't will never be light;
A few more days til we totter on the road,
　　Then my old Kentucky home, good night.

1853

'Southern Georgia in July'

W. E. B. DU BOIS

It gets pretty hot in Southern Georgia in July, – a sort of dull, determined heat that seems quite independent of the sun; so it took us some days to muster courage enough to leave the porch and venture out on the long country roads, that we might see this unknown world. Finally we started. It was about ten in the morning, bright with a faint breeze, and we jogged leisurely southward in the valley of the Flint. We passed the scattered box-like cabins of the brick-yard hands, and the long tenement-row facetiously called 'The Ark', and were soon in the open country, and on the confines of the great plantations of other days. There is the 'Joe Fields place'; a rough old fellow was he, and had killed many a 'nigger' in his day. Twelve miles his plantation used to run, – a regular barony. It is nearly all gone now; only straggling bits belong to the family, and the rest has passed to Jews and Negroes. Even the bits which are left are heavily mortgaged, and, like the rest of the land, tilled by tenants. Here is one of them now, – a tall brown man, a hard worker and a hard drinker, illiterate, but versed in farmlore, as his nodding crops declare. This distressingly new board house is his, and he has just moved out of yonder moss-grown cabin with its one square room.

From the curtains in Benton's house, down the road, a dark comely face is staring at the strangers; for passing carriages are not every-day occurrences here. Benton is an intelligent yellow man with a good-sized family, and manages a plantation blasted by the war and now the broken staff of the widow. He might be well-to-do, they say; but he carouses too much in Albany. And the half-desolate spirit of neglect born of the very soil seems to have settled on these acres. In times past there were cotton-gins and machinery here; but they have rotted away.

The whole land seems forlorn and forsaken. Here are the remnants of the vast plantations of the Sheldons, the Pellots, and the Rensons; but the souls of them are passed. The houses lie in half ruin, or have wholly disappeared; the fences have flown, and the families are wandering in the world. Strange vicissitudes have met these whilom masters. Yonder stretch the wide acres of Bildad Reasor; he died in war-time, but the upstart overseer hastened to wed the widow. Then he went, and his neighbors too, and now only the black tenant remains; but the shadow-hand of the master's grand-nephew or cousin or creditor stretches out of the gray distance to collect the rack-rent remorselessly, and so the land is uncared-for and poor. Only black tenants can stand such a system, and they only because they must. Ten miles we have ridden to-day and have seen no white face.

A resistless feeling of depression falls slowly upon us, despite the gaudy sunshine and the green cotton-fields. This, then, is the Cotton Kingdom, – the shadow of a marvellous dream.

The Souls of Black Folk, 1903, ch. 7

Daybreak in Alabama

LANGSTON HUGHES

When I get to be a composer
I'm gonna write me some music about
Daybreak in Alabama.
And I'm gonna put the purtiest songs in it
Rising out of the ground like a swamp mist
And falling out of heaven like soft dew.
I'm gonna put some tall tall trees in it
And the scent of pine needles
And the smell of red clay after rain
And long red necks
And poppy colored faces
And big brown arms
And the field daisy eyes
Of black and white black white black people
And I'm gonna put white hands
And black hands and brown and yellow hands
And red clay earth hands in it
Touching everybody with kind fingers
And touching each other natural as dew
In that dawn of music when I

Get to be a composer
And write about daybreak
In Alabama.

(1940) *Selected Poems*, 1959

Florida

ELIZABETH BISHOP

The state with the prettiest name,
the state that floats in brackish water,
held together by mangrove roots
that bear while living oysters in clusters,
and when dead strew white swamps with skeletons,
dotted as if bombarded, with green hummocks
like ancient cannon-balls sprouting grass.
The state full of long S-shaped birds, blue and white,
and unseen hysterical birds who rush up the scale
every time in a tantrum.
Tanagers embarrassed by their flashiness,
and pelicans whose delight it is to clown;
who coast for fun on the strong tidal currents
in and out among the mangrove islands
and stand on the sand-bars drying their damp gold wings
on sun-lit evenings.
Enormous turtles, helpless and mild,
die and leave their barnacled shells on the beaches,
and their large white skulls with round eye-sockets
twice the size of a man's.
The palm trees clatter in the stiff breeze
like the bills of the pelicans. The tropical rain comes down
to freshen the tide-looped strings of fading shells:
Job's Tear, the Chinese Alphabet, the scarce Junonia,
parti-colored pectins and Ladies' Ears,
arranged as on a gray rag of rotted calico,
the buried Indian Princess's skirt;
with these the monotonous, endless, sagging coast-line
is delicately ornamented.

Thirty or more buzzards are drifting down, down, down,
over something they have spotted in the swamp,

in circles like stirred-up flakes of sediment
sinking through water.
Smoke from woods-fires filters fine blue solvents.
On stumps and dead trees the charring is like black velvet.
The mosquitoes
go hunting to the tune of their ferocious obbligatos.
After dark, the fireflies map the heavens in the marsh
until the moon rises.
Cold white, not bright, the moonlight is coarse-meshed,
and the careless, corrupt state is all black specks
too far apart, and ugly whites; the poorest
post-card of itself.
After dark, the pools seem to have slipped away.
The alligator, who has five distinct calls:
friendliness, love, mating, war, and a warning –
whimpers and speaks in the throat
of the Indian Princess.

(1939) *North and South*, 1946

'An enormous ditch'

CHARLES DICKENS

At length, upon the morning of the third day, we arrived at a spot so much
more desolate than any we had yet beheld, that the forlornest places we had
passed were, in comparison with it, full of interest. At the junction of the
two rivers, on ground so flat and low and marshy, that at certain seasons
of the year it is inundated to the housetops, lies a breeding-place of fever,
ague, and death; vaunted in England as a mine of Golden Hope, and specu-
lated in, on the faith of monstrous representations, to many people's ruin.
A dismal swamp, on which the half-built houses rot away: cleared here and
there for the space of a few yards; and teeming, then, with rank, unwhole-
some vegetation, in whose baleful shade the wretched wanderers who are
tempted hither droop, and die, and lay their bones; the hateful Mississippi
circling and eddying before it, and turning off upon its southern course, a
slimy monster hideous to behold; a hotbed of disease, an ugly sepulchre, a
grave uncheered by any gleam of promise: a place without one single quality, in earth or air or water, to commend it: such is this dismal Cairo.

But what words shall describe the Mississippi, great father of rivers, who
(praise be to Heaven!) has no young children like him? An enormous ditch,

sometimes two or three miles wide, running liquid mud, six miles an hour: its strong and frothy current choked and obstructed everywhere by huge logs and whole forest trees: now twining themselves together in great rafts, from the interstices of which a sedgy, lazy foam works up, to float upon the water's top: now rolling past like monstrous bodies, their tangled roots showing like matted hair; now glancing singly by like giant leeches; and now writhing round and round in the vortex of some small whirlpool like wounded snakes. The banks low, the trees dwarfish, the marshes swarming with frogs, the wretched cabins few and far apart, their inmates hollow-cheeked and pale, the weather very hot, mosquitoes penetrating into every crack and crevice of the boat, mud and slime on everything: nothing pleasant in its aspect, but the harmless lightning which flickers every night upon the dark horizon.

For two days we toiled up this foul stream, striking constantly against the floating timber, or stopping to avoid those more dangerous obstacles, the snags, or sawyers, which are the hidden trunks of trees that have their roots below the tide. When the nights are very dark, the look-out stationed in the head of the boat knows, by the ripple of the water, if any great impediment be near at hand, and rings a bell beside him, which is the signal for the engine to be stopped; but always in the night this bell has work to do, and, after every ring, there comes a blow which renders it no easy matter to remain in bed.

American Notes, 1842, ch. 12

'The majestic, the magnificent Mississippi'

MARK TWAIN

When I was a boy, there was but one permanent ambition among my comrades in our village [Hannibal, Missouri] on the west bank of the Mississippi River. That was, to be a steamboatman. We had transient ambitions of other sorts, but they were only transient. When a circus came and went, it left us all burning to become clowns; the first negro minstrel show that came to our section left us all suffering to try that kind of life; now and then we had a hope that if we lived and were good, God would permit us to be pirates. These ambitions faded out, each in its turn; but the ambition to be a steamboatman always remained.

Once a day a cheap, gaudy packet arrived upward from St Louis, and another downward from Keokuk. Before these events, the day was glorious with expectancy; after them, the day was a dead and empty thing. Not only the boys, but the whole village, felt this. After all these years I can picture that old time to myself now, just as it was then: the white town drowsing in the sunshine of a summer's morning; the streets empty, or pretty nearly so; one or two clerks sitting in front of the Water Street stores, with their splint-bottomed chairs tilted back against the wall, chins on breasts, hats slouched over their faces, asleep – with shingle-shavings enough around to show what broke them down; a sow and a litter of pigs loafing along the sidewalk, doing a good business in watermelon rinds and seeds; two or three lonely little freight piles scattered about the 'levee'; a pile of 'skids' on the slope of the stone-paved wharf, and the fragrant town drunkard asleep in the shadow of them; two or three wood flats at the head of the wharf, but nobody to listen to the peaceful lapping of the wavelets against them; the great Mississippi, the majestic, the magnificent Mississippi, rolling its mile-wide tide along, shining in the sun; the dense forest away on the other side; the 'point' above the town, and the 'point' below, bounding the river-glimpse and turning it into a sort of sea, and withal a very still and brilliant and lonely one. Presently a film of dark smoke appears above one of those remote 'points'; instantly a negro drayman, famous for his quick eye and prodigious voice, lifts up the cry, 'S-t-e-a-m-boat a-comin'!' and the scene changes! The town drunkard stirs, the clerks wake up, a furious clatter of drays follows, every house and store pours out a human contribution, and all in a twinkling the dead town is alive and moving. Drays, carts, men, boys, all go hurrying from many quarters to a common centre, the wharf. Assembled there, the people fasten their eyes upon the coming boat as upon a wonder they are seeing for the first time. And the boat *is* rather a handsome sight, too. She is long and sharp and trim and pretty; she has two tall, fancy-topped chimneys, with a gilded device of some kind swung between them; a fanciful pilot-house, all glass and 'gingerbread', perched on top of the 'texas' deck behind them; the paddle-boxes are gorgeous with a picture or with gilded rays above the boat's name; the boiler deck, the hurricane deck, and the texas deck are fenced and ornamented with clean white railings; there is a flag gallantly flying from the jack-staff; the furnace doors are open and the fires glaring bravely; the upper decks are black with passengers; the captain stands by the big bell, calm, imposing, the envy of all; great volumes of the blackest smoke are rolling and tumbling out of the chimneys – a husbanded grandeur created with a bit of pitch pine just before arriving at a town; the crew are grouped on the forecastle; the broad stage is run far out over the port bow, and an envied deck-hand stands picturesquely on the end of it with a coil of rope in his hand; the pent steam is screaming through the gauge-cocks, the captain lifts his hand, a bell rings, the wheels stop; then they turn back, churning the water to foam, and the steamer is at rest. Then such a scramble as there is to get aboard, and to get ashore, and to take in freight and to discharge freight, all at one and the same time; and such a yelling and cursing as the mates facilitate it all with! Ten minutes later the steamer is under way again, with no flag on the jack-staff and no black smoke issuing from the chimneys. After ten more minutes the town is dead again, and the town drunkard asleep by the skids once more.

(1875) Life on the Mississippi, 1883, ch. 4

America's Characteristic Landscape

WALT WHITMAN

Speaking generally as to the capacity and sure future destiny of that plain and prairie area (larger than any European kingdom) it is the inexhaustible land of wheat, maize, wool, flax, coal, iron, beef and pork, butter and cheese, apples and grapes – land of ten million virgin farms – to the eye at present wild and unproductive – yet experts say that upon it when irrigated may easily be grown enough wheat to feed the world. Then as to scenery (giving my own thought and feeling,) while I know the standard claim is that Yosemite, Niagara falls, the upper Yellowstone and the like, afford the greatest natural shows, I am not so sure but the Prairies and Plains, while less stunning at first sight, last longer, fill the esthetic sense fuller, precede all the rest, and make North America's characteristic landscape.

Indeed through the whole of this journey, with all its shows and varieties, what most impress'd me, and will longest remain with me, are these same prairies. Day after day, and night after night, to my eyes, to all my senses – the esthetic one most of all – they silently and broadly unfolded. Even their simplest statistics are sublime.

Specimen Days, 1882

'The world's cornfields'

WILLA CATHER

July came on with that breathless, brilliant heat which makes the plains of Kansas and Nebraska the best corn country in the world. It seemed as if we could hear the corn growing in the night; under the stars one caught a faint crackling in the dewy, heavy-odoured cornfields where the feathered stalks stood so juicy and green. If all the great plain from the Missouri to the

Rocky Mountains had been under glass, and the heat regulated by a thermometer, it could not have been better for the yellow tassels that were
ripening and fertilizing the silk day by day. The cornfields were far apart
in those times, with miles of wild grazing land between. It took a clear,
meditative eye like my grandfather's to foresee that they would enlarge and
multiply until they would be, not the Shimerdas' cornfields, or Mr Bushy's,
but the world's cornfields; that their yield would be one of the great economic facts, like the wheat crop of Russia, which underlie all the activities
of men, in peace or war.

My Ántonia, 1918, ch. 19

'Quarter sections make a picture'

GERTRUDE STEIN

It was then in a kind of way that I really began to know what the ground
looked like. Quarter sections make a picture and going over America like
that made any one know why the post-cubist painting was what it was. The
wandering line of Masson was there the mixed line of Picasso coming and
coming again and following itself into a beginning was there, the simple solution of Braque was there and I suppose Leger might be there but I did not
see it not over there. Particularly the track of a wagon making a perfect circle and then going back to the corner from where they had come and later
in the South as finally we went everywhere by air and always wanted the
front seat so I could look down and what is the use, the earth does look
like that and even if none of them had seen it and they had not very likely
had not but since every one was going to see it they had to see it like that.

Everybody's Autobiography, 1937, ch. 4

'The raw body of America'

JACK KEROUAC

It was an ordinary bus trip with crying babies and hot sun, and countryfolk
getting on at one Penn town after another, till we got on the plain of Ohio
and really rolled, up by Ashtabula and straight across Indiana in the night.
I arrived in Chi quite early in the morning, got a room in the Y, and went
to bed with a very few dollars in my pocket. I dug Chicago after a good
day's sleep.

The wind from Lake Michigan, bop at the Loop, long walks around South Halsted and North Clark, and one long walk after midnight into the jungles, where a cruising car followed me as a suspicious character. At this time, 1947, bop was going like mad all over America. The fellows at the Loop blew, but with a tired air, because bop was somewhere between its Charlie Parker Ornithology period and another period that began with Miles Davis. And as I sat there listening to that sound of the night which bop has come to represent for all of us, I thought of all my friends from one end of the country to the other and how they were really all in the same vast backyard doing something so frantic and rushing-about. And for the first time in my life, the following afternoon, I went into the West. It was a warm and beautiful day for hitchhiking. To get out of the impossible complexities of Chicago traffic I took a bus to Joliet, Illinois, went by the Joliet pen, stationed myself just outside town after a walk through its leafy rickety streets behind, and pointed my way. All the way from New York to Joliet by bus, and I had spent more than half my money.

My first ride was a dynamite truck with a red flag, about thirty miles into great green Illinois, the truckdriver pointing out the place where Route 6, which we were on, intersects Route 66 before they both shoot west for incredible distances. Along about three in the afternoon, after an apple pie and ice cream in a roadside stand, a woman stopped for me in a little coupe. I had a twinge of hard joy as I ran after the car. But she was a middle-aged woman, actually the mother of sons my age, and wanted somebody to help her drive to Iowa. I was all for it. Iowa! Not so far from Denver, and once I got to Denver I could relax. She drove the first few hours, at one point insisted on visiting an old church somewhere, as if we were tourists, and then I took over the wheel and, though I'm not much of a driver, drove clear through the rest of Illinois to Davenport, Iowa, via Rock Island. And here for the first time in my life I saw my beloved Mississippi River, dry in the summer haze, low water, with its big rank smell that smells like the raw body of America itself because it washes it up. Rock Island – railroad tracks, shacks, small downtown section; and over the bridge to Davenport, same kind of town, all smelling of sawdust in the warm midwest sun. Here the lady had to go on to her Iowa hometown by another route, and I got out.

The sun was going down. I walked, after a few cold beers, to the edge of town, and it was a long walk. All the men were driving home from work, wearing railroad hats, baseball hats, all kinds of hats, just like after work in any town anywhere. One of them gave me a ride up the hill and left me at a lonely crossroads on the edge of the prairie. It was beautiful there. The only cars that came by were farmer-cars; they gave me suspicious looks, they clanked along, the cows were coming home. Not a truck. A few cars zipped by. A hotrod kid came by with this scarf flying. The sun went all the way down and I was standing in the purple darkness. Now I was scared. There weren't even any lights in the Iowa countryside; in a minute nobody would be able to see me. Luckily a man going back to Davenport gave me a lift downtown. But I was right where I started from.

I went to sit in the bus station and think this over. I ate another apple pie and ice cream; that's practically all I ate all the way across the country, I knew it was nutritious and it was delicious, of course. I decided to gamble. I took a bus in downtown Davenport, after spending a half-hour watching a waitress in the bus-station café, and rode to the city limits, but this time near the gas stations. Here the big trucks roared, wham, and inside two minutes one of them cranked to a stop for me. I ran for it with my soul whoopeeing. And what a driver – a great big tough truckdriver with popping eyes and a hoarse raspy voice who just slammed and kicked at everything and got his rig under way and paid hardly any attention to me. So I could rest my tired soul a little, for one of the biggest troubles hitchhiking is having to talk to innumerable people, make them feel that they didn't make a mistake picking you up, even entertain them almost, all of which is a great strain when you're going all the way and don't plan to sleep in hotels. The guy just yelled above the roar, and all I had to do was yell back, and we relaxed. And he balled that thing clear to Iowa City and yelled me the funniest stories about how he got around the law in every town that had an unfair speed limit, saying over and over again, 'Them goddam cops can't put no flies on *my* ass!' Just as we rolled into Iowa City he saw another truck coming behind us, and because he had to turn off at Iowa City he blinked his tail lights at the other guy and slowed down for me to jump out, which I did with my bag, and the other truck, acknowledging this exchange, stopped for me, and once again, in the twink of nothing, I was in another big high cab, all set to go hundreds of miles across the night, and was I happy! And the new truckdriver was as crazy as the other and yelled just as much, and all I had to do was lean back and roll on. Now I could see Denver looming ahead of me like the Promised Land, way out there beneath the stars, across the prairie of Iowa and the plains of Nebraska, and I could see the greater vision of San Francisco beyond, like jewels in the night. He balled the jack and told stories for a couple of hours, then, at a town in Iowa where years later Dean and I were stopped on suspicion in what looked like a stolen Cadillac, he slept a few hours in the seat. I slept too, and took one little walk along the lonely brick walls illuminated by one lamp, with the prairie brooding at the end of each little street and the smell of the corn like dew in the night.

He woke up with a start at dawn. Off we roared, and an hour later the smoke of Des Moines appeared ahead over the green cornfields. He had to eat his breakfast now and wanted to take it easy, so I went right on into

Des Moines, about four miles, hitching a ride with two boys from the University of Iowa; and it was strange sitting in their brand-new comfortable car and hearing them talk of exams as we zoomed smoothly into town. Now I wanted to sleep a whole day. So I went to the Y to get a room; they didn't have any, and by instinct I wandered down to the railroad tracks – and there're a lot of them in Des Moines – and wound up in a gloomy old Plains inn of a hotel by the locomotive roundhouse, and spent a long day sleeping on a big clean hard white bed with dirty remarks carved in the wall beside my pillow and the beat yellow windowshades pulled over the smoky scene of the railyards. I woke up as the sun was reddening; and that was the one distinct time in my life, the strangest moment of all, when I didn't know who I was – I was far away from home, haunted and tired with travel, in a cheap hotel room I'd never seen, hearing the hiss of steam outside, and the creak of the old wood of the hotel, and footsteps upstairs, and all the sad sounds, and I looked at the cracked high ceiling and really didn't know who I was for about fifteen strange seconds. I wasn't scared; I was just somebody else, some stranger, and my whole life was a haunted life, the life of a ghost. I was halfway across America, at the dividing line between the East of my youth and the West of my future, and maybe that's why it happened right there and then, that strange red afternoon.

On the Road, 1957, part 1, ch. 3

'Slow movement is the country'

GERTRUDE STEIN

Then we flew to Oklahoma, of course we had been over the bad lands, they come in nicely in every Western story and I never did think that I would ever see them certainly not fly over them, and they were just as bad as they had been called with nothing growing and a very strange color and not hills or flat land either they certainly were bad lands and they made reading the stories more real than ever. I like Western stories of Texas bad lands.

When I first heard about Oklahoma I always thought it was in the northwest, until I really saw it and saw it so close to Texas did I really believe that it is where it does exist. Oklahoma City with its towers that is its skyscrapers coming right up out of the flat oil country was as exciting as when going to Alsace just after the armistice we first saw the Strasbourg Cathedral. They do come up wonderfully out of that flat country and it was exciting and seeing the oil wells and the funny shapes they made the round things as well as the Eiffel Tower ones gave me a feeling like I have in going to Marseilles and seeing the chimneys come out of the earth and there are no houses or anything near them, it always is a strange-looking country that produces that kind of thing, of course Alice Toklas' father had once almost had an oil well they dug and dug but naturally the oil did not gush, naturally not these things never do happen to any one one knows, if it could happen to them you would not be very likely to know them most naturally not. We did later see in California some small oil fields and the slow movement of the oil wells make it perfectly all right that in America the prehistoric beasts moved slowly. America is funny that way everything is quick but really everybody does move slowly, and the movement of the oil well that slow movement very well that slow movement is the country and it makes it pre-historic and large shapes and moving slowly very very slowly so slowly that they do almost stand still. I do think Americans are slow minded, it seems quick but they are slow minded yes they are.

Everybody's Autobiography, 1937, ch. 4

'The triple nationalities'

FREDERICK LAW OLMSTED

The principal part of the town [San Antonio, Texas] lies within a sweep of the river upon the other side. We descend to the bridge, which is close down upon the water, as the river, owing to its peculiar source, never varies in height or temperature. We irresistibly stop to examine it, we are so struck with its beauty. It is of a rich blue and pure as crystal, flowing rapidly but noiselessly over pebbles and between reedy banks. One could lean for hours over the bridge-rail.

From the bridge we enter Commerce street, the narrow principal thoroughfare, and here are American houses, and the triple nationalities break out into the most amusing display, till we reach the main plaza. The sauntering Mexicans prevail on the pavements, but the bearded Germans and the sallow Yankees furnish their proportion. The signs are German by all odds, and perhaps the houses, trim-built, with pink window-blinds. The American dwellings stand back, with galleries and jalousies and a garden picket-fence against the walk, or rise, next door, in three-story brick to re-spectable city fronts. The Mexican buildings are stronger than those we saw before but still of all sorts, and now put to all sorts of new uses. They are all low, of adobe or stone, washed blue and yellow, with flat roofs close down upon their single story. Windows have been knocked in their blank walls, letting the sun into their dismal vaults, and most of them are stored with dry goods and groceries, which overflow around the door. Around the plaza are American hotels, and new glass-fronted stores, alternating with sturdy battlemented Spanish walls, and [these are] confronted by the dirty, grim, old stuccoed stone cathedral, whose cracked bell is now clunking for vespers in a tone that bids us no welcome, as more of the intruding race who have caused all this progress on which its traditions, like its imperturbable dome, frown down.

We have no city except perhaps New Orleans that can vie, in point of the picturesque interest that attaches to odd and antiquated foreignness, with San Antonio. Its jumble of races, costumes, languages and buildings; its religious ruins, holding to an antiquity for us indistinct enough to breed an unaccustomed solemnity; its remote, isolated, outposted situation, and the vague conviction that it is the first of a new class of conquered cities into whose decaying streets our rattling life is to be infused, combine with the heroic touches in its history to enliven and satisfy your traveler's curiosity.

Not suspecting the leisure we were to have to examine it at our ease, we set out to receive its impressions while we had the opportunity.

After drawing, at the Post-office window, our personal share of the dear income of happiness divided by that department, we strolled, by moonlight, about the streets. They are laid out with tolerable regularity, parallel with the sides of the main plaza, and are pretty distinctly shared among the nations that use them. On the plaza and the busiest streets, a surprising number of old Mexican buildings are converted, by trowel, paintbrush, and gaudy carpentry, into drinking-places, always labeled 'Exchange', and conducted on the New Orleans model. About these loitered a set of customers, sometimes rough, sometimes affecting an 'exquisite' dress, by no means attracting to a nearer acquaintance with themselves or their haunts. Here and there was a restaurant of a quieter look, where the traditions of Paris are preserved under difficulties by the exiled Gaul.

The doors of the cabins of the real natives stood open wide, if indeed they exist at all, and many were the family pictures of jollity or sleepy comfort they displayed to us as we sauntered curious about. The favorite dress appeared to be a dishabille, and a free-and-easy, loloppy sort of life generally seemed to have been adopted as possessing, on the whole, the greatest advantages for a reasonable being. The larger part of each family appeared to be made up of black-eyed, olive girls, full of animation of tongue and glance, but sunk in a soft embonpoint, which added a somewhat extreme good-nature to their charms. Their dresses seemed lazily reluctant to cover their plump persons, and their attitudes were always expressive of the influences of a Southern sun upon national manners. The matrons, dark and wrinkled, formed a strong contrast to their daughters, though, here and there, a fine cast of feature and a figure erect with dignity, attracted the eye.

The men lounged in roundabouts and cigaritos, as was to be expected, and in fact the whole picture lacked nothing that is Mexican.

*

The street-life of San Antonio is more varied than might be supposed. Hardly a day passes without some noise. If there be no personal affray to arouse talk, there is some Government train to be seen, with its hundred of mules, on its way from the coast to a fort above; or a Mexican ox-train from the coast, with an interesting supply of ice, or flour, or matches, or of whatever the shops find themselves short. A Government express clatters off, or news arrives from some exposed outpost, or from New Mexico. An Indian in his finery appears on a shaggy horse, in search of blankets, powder and ball. Or at the least, a stagecoach with the 'States', or the Austin, mail, rolls into the plaza and discharges its load of passengers and newspapers.

The street affrays are numerous and characteristic. I have seen for a year or more a San Antonio weekly, and hardly a number fails to have its fight or its murder. More often than otherwise, the parties meet upon the plaza by chance, and each, on catching sight of his enemy, draws a revolver and fires away. As the actors are under more or less excitement, their aim is not apt to be of the most careful and sure; consequently it is, not seldom, the passers-by who suffer. Sometimes it is a young man at a quiet dinner in a restaurant who receives a ball in the head, sometimes an old negro woman returning from market who gets winged. After disposing of all their lead, the parties close to try their steel, but as this species of metallic amusement is less popular, they generally contrive to be separated ('Hold me! Hold me!') by friends before the wounds are mortal. If neither is seriously injured, they are brought to drink together on the following day, and the town waits for the next excitement.

Where borderers and idle soldiers are hanging about drinking-places, and where different races mingle on unequal terms, assassinations must be expected. Murders, from avarice or revenge, are common here. Most are charged upon the Mexicans, whose passionate motives are not rare, and to whom escape over the border is easiest and most natural.

The town amusements of a less exciting character are not many. There is a permanent company of Mexican mountebanks, who give performances of agility and buffoonery two or three times a week, parading before night in their spangled tights with drum and trombone through the principal streets. They draw a crowd of whatever little Mexicans can get adrift, and this attracts a few sellers of whisky, *tortillas* and *tamaules* (corn, slap-jacks and hashed meat in corn-shucks), all by the light of torches making a ruddily picturesque evening group.

The more grave Americans are served with tragedy by a thin local company, who are death on horrors and despair, long rapiers and well oiled hair, and for lack of a better place to flirt with passing officers, the city belles may sometimes be seen looking on. The national background of peanuts and yells is not, of course, wanting.

A day or two after our arrival, there was the hanging of a Mexican. The whole population left the town to see. Family parties, including the grandmother and the little negroes, came from all the plantations and farms within reach, and little ones were held up high to get their share of warning. The Mexicans looked on imperturbable.

A Journey Through Texas, 1857, ch. 3

'The "livest" town'

MARK TWAIN

Six months after my entry into journalism the grand 'flush times' of Silverland began, and they continued with unabated splendor for three years. All difficulty about filling up the 'local department' ceased, and the only trouble now was how to make the lengthened columns hold the world of incidents and happenings that came to our literary net every day. Virginia [Virginia City, Nevada] had grown to be the 'livest' town, for its age and population, that America had ever produced. The sidewalks swarmed with people – to such an extent, indeed, that it was generally no easy matter to stem the human tide. The streets themselves were just as crowded with quartz wagons, freight teams, and other vehicles. The procession was endless. So great was the pack, that buggies frequently had to wait half an hour for an opportunity to cross the principal street. Joy sat on every countenance, and there was a glad, almost fierce, intensity in every eye, that told of the money-getting schemes that were seething in every brain and the high hope that held sway in every heart. Money was as plenty as dust; every individual considered himself wealthy, and a melancholy countenance was nowhere to be seen. There were military companies, fire companies, brass bands, banks, hotels, theaters, 'hurdy-gurdy houses', wide-open gambling palaces, political pow-wows, civic processions, street fights, murders, inquests, riots, a whisky mill every fifteen steps, a Board of Aldermen, a Mayor, a City Surveyor, a City Engineer, a Chief of the Fire Department, with First, Second and Third Assistants, a Chief of Police, City Marshal, and a large police force, two Boards of Mining Brokers, a dozen breweries, and half a dozen jails and station-houses in full operation, and some talk of building a church. The 'flush times' were in magnificent flower! Large fire-proof brick buildings were going up in the principal streets, and the wooden suburbs were spreading out in all directions. Town lots soared up to prices that were amazing.

The great 'Comstock lode' stretched its opulent length straight through the town from north to south, and every mine on it was in diligent process of development. One of these mines alone employed six hundred and seventy-five men, and in the matter of elections the adage was, 'as the "Gould & Curry" goes, so goes the city.' Laboring men's wages were four and six dollars a day, and they worked in three 'shifts' or gangs, and the blasting and picking and shoveling went on without ceasing, night and day.

The 'city' of Virginia roosted royally midway up the steep side of Mount Davidson, seven thousand two hundred feet above the level of the sea, and in the clear Nevada atmosphere was visible from a distance of fifty miles! It claimed a population of fifteen thousand to eighteen thousand, and all day long half of this little army swarmed the streets like bees and the other half swarmed among the drifts and tunnels of the 'Comstock', hundreds of feet down in the earth directly under those same streets. Often we felt our chairs jar, and heard the faint boom of a blast down in the bowels of the earth under the office.

The mountain side was so steep that the entire town had a slant to it like a roof. Each street was a terrace, and from each to the next street below the descent was forty or fifty feet. The fronts of the houses were level with the street they faced, but their rear first floors were propped on lofty stilts; a man could stand at a rear first-floor window of a C street house and look down the chimneys of the row of houses below him facing D street. It was a laborious climb, in that thin atmosphere, to ascend from D to A street, and you were panting and out of breath when you got there; but you could turn around and go down again like a house a-fire – so to speak. The atmosphere was so rarefied, on account of the great altitude, that one's blood lay near the surface always, and the scratch of a pin was a disaster worth worrying about, for the chances were that a grievous erysipelas would ensue. But to offset this, the thin atmosphere seemed to carry healing to gunshot wounds, and, therefore, to simply shoot your adversary through both lungs was a thing not likely to afford you any permanent satisfaction, for he would be nearly certain to be around looking for you within the month, and not with an opera glass, either.

Roughing It, 1872, ch. 43

A Trip Through the Mind Jail

RAÚL SALINAS

[This poem first appeared in the Leavenworth (Kansas) Federal Penitentiary newspaper, which Salinas edited. La Loma is a section of Austin, Texas.]

LA LOMA

Neighborhood of my youth
    demolished, erased forever from
    the universe.
    You live on, captive, in the lonely
    cellblocks of my mind.

Neighborhood of endless hills
    muddied streets – all chuckhole lined –
    that never drank of asphalt.
    Kids barefoot/snotty-nosed
    playing marbles/munching on bean tacos
    (the kind you'll never find in a café)
    2 peaceful generations removed from
    their abuelos' revolution.

Neighborhood of dilapidated community hall
    – Salón Cinco de Mayo –
    yearly (May 5/Sept. 16) gathering
    of the familias. Re-asserting pride
    on those two significant days.
    Speeches by the elders,
    patriarchs with evidence of oppression
    distinctly etched upon mestizo faces.
    'Sons of Independence!'
    Emphasis on allegiance to the tri-color
    obscure names: JUAREZ & HIDALGO
    their heroic deeds. Nostalgic tales of war
    years under VILLA'S command. No one listened,
    no one seemed to really care.
    Afterwards, the dance. Modest Mexican
    maidens dancing polkas together
    across splintered wooden floor.
    They never deigned to dance with boys!
    The careful scrutiny by curbstone sex-perts

8 & 9 years old. 'Minga's bow-legged,
so we know she's done it, huh?'

Neighborhood of Sunday night jamaicas
    at Guadalupe Church.
    Fiestas for any occasion
    holidays holy days happy days
    'round and 'round the promenade
    eating snowcones – raspas – & tamales
    the games – bingo cakewalk spin-the-wheel
    making eyes at girls from cleaner neighborhoods
    the unobtainables
    who responded all giggles and excitement.

Neighborhood of forays down to Buena Vista –
    Santa Rita Courts – Los Projects – friendly neighborhood
    cops n' robbers on the rooftops, sneaking peeks
    in people's private night-time bedrooms
    bearing gifts of Juicy Fruit gum for
    the Project girls/chasing them in adolescent heat
    causing skinned knees & being run off for the night
    disenchanted walking home affections spurned
    stopping stay-out-late chicks in search of
    Modern Romance lovers, who always stood them up
    unable to leave their world in the magazines' pages.
    Angry fingers grabbing, squeezing, feeling,
    french kisses imposed; close bodily contact, thigh &
    belly rubbings under shadows of Cristo Rey Church.

Neighborhood that never saw a school-bus
    the cross-town walks were much more fun
    embarrassed when acquaintances or friends or relatives
    were sent home excused from class
    for having cooties in their hair!
    Did only Mexicans have cooties in their hair?
                    ¡Qué gacho!

Neighborhood of Zaragoza Park
    where scary stories interspersed with
    inherited superstitions were exchanged
    waiting for midnight and the haunting
    lament of La Llorona – the weeping lady
    of our myths & folklore – who wept nightly
    along the banks of Boggy Creek

for the children she'd lost or drowned
in some river (depending on the version).
i think i heard her once
and cried
out of sadness and fear
running all the way home nape hairs at attention
swallow a pinch of table salt and
make the sign of the cross
sure cure for frightened Mexican boys.

Neighborhood of Spanish Town Café
first grown-up (13) hangout
Andrés,
tolerant manager, proprietor, cook
victim of bungling baby burglars
your loss: Fritos n' Pepsi Colas – was our gain
you put up with us and still survived!
You too, are granted immortality.

Neighborhood of groups and clusters
sniffing gas, drinking muscatel
solidarity   cement hardening
the clan   the family   the neighborhood   the gang
NOMAS!
Restless innocents tattoo'd crosses on their hands
'just doing things different'
'From now on, all troublemaking mex kids will be
sent to Gatesville for 9 months.'
Henry home from La Corre
khakis worn too low – below the waist
the stomps, the greña with duck-tail
– Pachuco Yo –

Neighborhood of could-be artists
who plied their talents on the pool's
bath-house walls/intricately adorned
with esoteric symbols of their cult:

the art form of our slums
more meaningful & significant
than Egypt's finest hieroglyphics.

Neighborhood where purple clouds of Yesca
smoke one day descended & embraced us all.
Skulls uncapped – Rhythm n' Blues
                    Chalie's 7th St Club
loud funky music/wine spodee-odees/barbecue & grass
our very own connection man: big black Johnny B——.

Neighborhood of Reyes' Bar
where Lalo shotgunned
Pete Evans to death because of
an unintentional stare
and because he was escuadra,
only to end his life neatly sliced
by prison barber's razor.
Durán's grocery & gas station
Güero drunkenly stabbed Julio
arguing over who'd drive home
and got 55 years for his crime.
Ratón: 20 years for a matchbox of weed. Is that cold?
No lawyer   no jury   no trial   i'm guilty
                    Aren't we all guilty?
Indian mothers, too unaware
of courtroom tragi-comedies
folded arms across their bosoms
saying, 'Sea por Dios.'

Neighborhood of my childhood
neighborhood that no longer exists
some died young – fortunate – some rot in prisons
the rest drifted away to be conjured up
in minds of others like them.
For me: only the NOW of THIS journey is REAL!

Neighborhood of my adolescence
neighborhood that is no more
YOU ARE TORN PIECES OF MY FLESH!!!!
Therefore, you ARE.
LA LOMA – AUSTIN – MI BARRIO –
                    i bear you no grudge
i needed you then . . . identity . . . a sense of belonging

i need you now.
so essential to adult days of imprisonment,
you keep me away from INSANITY'S hungry jaws;
    Smiling/Laughing/Crying.

i respect your having been:
my Loma of Austin
my Rose Hill of Los Angeles
my Westside of San Anto
my Quinto of Houston
my Jackson of San Jo
my Segundo of El Paso
my Barelas of Alburqueque
my Westside of Denver
Flats, Los Marcos, Maravilla, Calle Guadalupe,
Magnolia, Buena Vista, Mateo, La Seís, Chíquis,
El Sur, and all Chicano neighborhoods that
now exist and once existed;
   somewhere . . . , someone remembers . . . . .

14 Sept. '69
Leavenworth

Un Trip Through the Mind Jail y Otras Excursions, 1980

'California is a tragic country'

CHRISTOPHER ISHERWOOD

California is a tragic country – like Palestine, like every Promised Land. Its short history is a fever-chart of migrations – the land rush, the gold rush, the oil rush, the movie rush, the Okie fruit-picking rush, the wartime rush to the aircraft factories – followed, in each instance, by counter-migrations of the disappointed and unsuccessful, moving sorrowfully homeward. You will find plenty of people in the Middle West and in the East who are very bitter against California in general and Los Angeles in particular. They complain that the life there is heartless, materialistic, selfish. But emigrants to Eldorado have really no right to grumble. Most of us come to the Far West with somewhat cynical intentions. Privately, we hope to get something for nothing – or, at any rate, for very little. Well, perhaps we shall. But if we don't, we have no one to blame but ourselves.

The movie industry – to take the most obvious example – is still very like a goldmining camp slowly and painfully engaged in transforming itself into a respectable, ordered community. Inevitably, the process is violent. The anarchy of the old days, with every man for himself and winner take the jackpot, still exercises an insidious appeal. It is not easy for the writer who earns 3,000 dollars a week to make common cause with his colleague who only gets 250. The original tycoons were not monsters; they were merely adventurers, in the best and worst sense of the word. They had risked everything and won – often after an epic and ruthless struggle – and they thought themselves entitled to every cent of their winnings. Their attitude toward their employees, from stars down to stagehands, was possessive and paternalistic. Knowing nothing about art and very little about technique, they did not hesitate to interfere in every stage of film production – blue-pencilling scripts, dictating casting, bothering directors and criticizing camera-angles. The spectre of the Box Office haunted them night and day. This was their own money, and they were madly afraid of losing it. 'There's nothing so cowardly', a producer once told me, 'as a million dollars.' The paternalist is a sentimentalist at heart, and the sentimentalist is always potentially cruel. When the studio operatives ceased to rely upon their bosses' benevolence and organized themselves into unions, the tycoon became an injured papa, hurt and enraged by their ingratitude. If the boys did not trust him – well, that was just too bad. He knew what was good for them, and to prove it he was ready to use strike-breakers and uniformed thugs masquerading as special police. But the epoch of the tycoons is now, happily, almost over. The financier of today has learnt that it pays better to give his artists and technicians a free hand, and to concentrate his own energies on the business he really understands; the promotion and distribution of the finished product. The formation of independent units within the major studios is making possible a much greater degree of co-operation between directors, writers, actors, composers and art-directors. Without being childishly optimistic, one can foresee a time when quite a large proportion of Hollywood's films will be entertainment fit for adults, and when men and women of talent will come to the movie colony not as absurdly overpaid secretaries resigned to humouring their employers but as responsible artists free and eager to do their best. Greed is, however, only one of two disintegrating forces which threaten the immigrant's character: the other, far more terrible, is sloth. Out there, in the eternal lazy morning of the Pacific, days slip away into months, months into years; the seasons are reduced to the faintest nuance by the great central fact of the sunshine; one might pass a lifetime, it seems, between two yawns, lying bronzed and naked on the sand. The trees keep their green, the flowers perpetually bloom, beautiful girls and superb boys ride the foaming breakers. They are not always the same boys, girls, flowers and trees; but that you scarcely notice. Age and death are very discreet there; they seem as improbable as the Japanese submarines which used to lurk up and down the coast during the war and sometimes sink ships within actual sight of the land. I need not describe the de luxe, parklike cemeteries which so hospitably invite you to the final act of relaxation: Aldous Huxley has done this classically already in *After Many a Summer*. But it is worth recalling one of their advertisements, in which a charming, well-groomed elderly lady (presumably risen from the dead) assured the public: 'It's better at Forest Lawn. *I speak from experience.*'

To live sanely in Los Angeles (or, I suppose, in any other large American city) you have to cultivate the art of staying awake. You must learn to resist (firmly but not tensely) the unceasing hypnotic suggestions of the radio, the billboards, the movies and the newspapers; those demon voices which are forever whispering in your ear what you should desire, what you should fear, what you should wear and eat and drink and enjoy, what you should think and do and be. They have planned a life for you – from the cradle to the grave and beyond – which it would be easy, fatally easy, to accept. The least wandering of the attention, the least relaxation of your awareness, and already the eyelids begin to droop, the eyes grow vacant, the body starts to move in obedience to the hypnotist's command. Wake up, wake up – before you sign that seven-year contract, buy that house you don't really want, marry that girl you secretly despise. Don't reach for the whisky, that won't help you. You've got to think, to discriminate, to exercise your own free will and judgment. And you must do this, I repeat, without tension, quite rationally and calmly. For if you give way to fury against the hypnotists, if you smash the radio and tear the newspapers to shreds, you will only rush to the other extreme and fossilize into defiant eccentricity. Hollywood's two polar types are the cynically drunken writer aggressively nursing a ten-year-old reputation and the theatrically self-conscious hermit who strides the boulevard in sandals, home-made shorts and a prophetic beard, muttering against the Age of the Machines.

An afternoon drive from Los Angeles will take you up into the high mountains, where eagles circle above the forests and the cold blue lakes, or out over the Mojave Desert, with its weird vegetation and immense vistas. Not very far away are Death Valley, and Yosemite, and the Sequoia Forest with its giant trees which were growing long before the Parthenon was built; they are the oldest living things in the world. One should visit such places often, and be conscious, in the midst of the city, of their surrounding presence. For this is the real nature of California and the secret of its fascination; this untamed, undomesticated, aloof, prehistoric landscape which relentlessly reminds the traveller of his human condition and the circumstances of his tenure upon the earth. 'You are perfectly welcome', it tells him, 'during your short visit. Everything is at your disposal. Only, I must warn you, if things go wrong, don't blame me. I accept no responsibility. I am not part of your neurosis. Don't cry to me for safety. There is no home here. There is no security in your mansions or your fortresses, your family vaults or your banks or your double beds. Understand this fact, and you will be free. Accept it, and you will be happy.'

'Los Angeles' (1947) in *Exhumations*, 1966

'Ocean people'

MAXINE HONG KINGSTON

I have gone east, that is, west, as far as Hawai'i, where I have stood along-side the highway at the edge of the sugarcane and listened for the voices of the great grandfathers. But the cane is merely green in the sunlight; the tassels waving in the wind make no blurry fuzzy outlines that I can construe as a message from them. The dirt and sun are red and not aglitter with gold motes like in California. Red and green do not readily blend, nothing lurking in the overlaps to bend the eyes. The winds blowing in the long leaves do not whisper words I hear. Yet the rows and fields, organized like conveyor belts, hide murdered and raped bodies; this is a dumping ground. Old Filipino men die in abandoned sheds. Mushrooms and marijuana grow amidst the cane, irrigated by the arches of vaulting water. People with friends on the mainland steal long-distance calls on the field telephones.

Driving along O'ahu's windward side, where sugarcane grew in my great grandfathers' day, I like looking out at the ocean and seeing the pointed island offshore, not much bigger than a couple of houses, nothing else out in that ocean to catch the eye – Mokoli'i Island, but nobody calls it that. I had a shock when I heard it's also named Chinaman's Hat. I had only encountered that slurred-together word in taunts when walking past racists. (They would be the ones loafing on a fence, and they said the Chinaman was sitting on a fence ' . . . trying to make a dollar out of fifty cents.') But Hawai'i people call us Paké, which is their way of pronouncing Bak-ah, Uncle. They even call Chinese women Paké.

When driving south, clockwise, there is an interesting optical illusion. At a certain point in the road, the sky is covered with Chinaman's Hat, which bulges huge, near. The closer you drive toward what seems like a mountain, the farther it shrinks away until there it is, quite far off, an island, a brim and crown on the water.

At first, I did not say Chinaman's Hat; I didn't call the island anything.

'You see the island that looks like a Chinaman's hat?' locals ask, and visitors know right away which one they mean.

I swam out to Chinaman's Hat. We walked partway in low tide, then put on face masks. Once you open your eyes in the water, you become a flying creature. Schools of fish – zebra fish, rainbow fish, red fish – curve with the currents, swim alongside and away; balloon fish puff out their porcupine quills. How unlike a dead fish a live fish is. We swam through spangles of silver-white fish, their scales like sequins. Sometimes we entered cold spots, deserts, darkness under clouds, where the sand churned like gray fog, and sometimes we entered golden chambers. There are summer forests and winter forests down there. Sea cucumbers, holothurians, rocked side to side. A sea turtle glided by and that big shell is no encumbrance in the water. We saw no sharks, though they spawn in that area, and pilot fish swam ahead in front of our faces. The shores behind and ahead kept me unafraid.

Approaching Chinaman's Hat, we flew around and between a group of tall black stones like Stonehenge underwater, and through there, came up onto the land, where we rested with arms out holding on to the island. We walked among the palm trees and bushes that we had seen from the other shore. Large white birds were nesting on the ground under these bushes. We hurried to the unseen side of the island. Even such a tiny island has its windward and leeward. On the ocean side, we found a cave, a miniature pirate's cove with a finger of ocean for its river, a beach of fine yellow sand, a blowhole, brown and lavender cowry shells, not broken, black live crabs sidestepping and red dead crabs drying in the red sun, a lava rock shelf with tide pools as warm as baths and each one with its ecology. A brown fish with a face like a cartoon cow's mugged at me. A white globule quivered, swelled, flipped over or inside out, stretched and turned like a human being getting out of bed, opened and opened; two arms and two legs flexed, and feathery wings, webbing the arms and the legs to the body, unfolded and flared; its thighs tapered to a graceful tail, and its ankles had tiny wings on them – like Mercury; its back was muscled like a comic book superhero's – blue and silver metallic leotards outlined with black racing stripes. It's a spaceman, I thought. A tiny spaceman in a spacesuit. Scooping these critters into another tide pool, I got into theirs, and lying in it, saw nothing but sky and black rock, the ocean occasionally flicking cold spit.

At sunset we built a campfire and sat around it inside a cleft in the hillside. We cooked and ate the fish we caught. We were climbing along a ledge down to the shore, holding on to the face of the island in the twilight, when a howling like wolves, like singing, came rising out of the island. 'Birds,' somebody said. 'The wind,' said someone else. But the air was still, and the high clear sound wound through the trees. It continued until we departed.

It was, I know it, the island, the voice of the island singing, the sirens Odysseus heard.

The Navy continues to bomb Kaho'olawe and the Army blasts the green skin off the red mountains of O'ahu. But the land sings. We heard something.

It's a tribute to the pioneers to have a living island named after their work hat.

I have heard the land sing. I have seen the bright blue streaks of spirits whisking through the air. I again search for my American ancestors by listening in the cane.

Ocean people are different from land people. The ocean never stops saying and asking into ears, which don't sleep like eyes. Those who live by the sea examine the driftwood and glass balls that float from foreign ships. They let scores of invisible imps loose out of found bottles. In a scoop of salt water, they revive the dead blobs that have been beached in storms and tides: fins, whiskers, and gills unfold; mouths, eyes, and colors bloom and spread. Sometimes ocean people are given to understand the newness and oldness of the world; then all morning they try to keep that boundless joy like a little sun inside their chests. The ocean also makes its people know immensity.

They wonder what continents contain the ocean on its other side, what people live there. Hong Kong off the coast tugged like a moon at the Cantonese; curiosity had a land mass to fasten upon, and beyond Hong Kong, Taiwan, step by step a leading out. Cantonese travel and gamble.

But China has a long round coastline, and the northern people enclosed Peiping, only one hundred miles from the sea, with walls and made roads westward across the loess. The Gulf of Chihli has arms, and beyond, Korea, and beyond that, Japan. So the ocean and hunger and some other urge made the Cantonese people explorers and Americans.

'The Great Grandfathers of the Sandlewood Mountains' in *China Men*, 1980

UNION

My country need not change her gown,
Her triple suit as sweet
As when 'twas cut at Lexington,
And first pronounced 'a fit'.

Great Britain disapproves, 'the stars';
Disparagement discreet, –
There's something in their attitude
That taunts her bayonet.

Emily Dickinson (wr. c. 1881) 1891

'A Seal or Medal'

JOHN ADAMS

I am put upon a committee to prepare a device for a golden Medal to commemorate the surrender of Boston to the American arms, and upon another to prepare devices for a Great Seal for the confederated States. There is a gentleman here of French extraction, whose name is Du Simitiere, a painter by profession whose designs are very ingenuous, and his drawings well esteemed. He has been applied to for his advice. I waited on him yesterday, and saw his sketches. For the Medal he proposes Liberty with her spear and pileus, leaning on General Washington. The British fleet in Boston Harbour, with all their sterns towards the town, the American troops marching in. For the Seal he proposes: The Arms of the several nations from whence America has been peopled, as English, Scotch, Irish, Dutch, German, etc. each in a shield. On one side of them Liberty, with her pileus, on the other a rifler, in his uniform, with his rifled gun in one hand, and his tomahawk in the other. This dress and these troops with this kind of armour, being peculiar to America – unless the dress was known to the Romans. Dr Franklin showed me, yesterday, a book, containing an account of the dresses of all the Roman soldiers, one of which appeared exactly like it.

This Mr Du Simitiere is a very curious man. He has begun a collection of materials for an History of this Revolution. He begins with the first advices of the tea ships. He cuts out of the newspapers every scrap of intelligence, and every piece of speculation, and pastes it upon clean paper, arranging them under the head of the State to which they belong, and intends to bind them up in volumes. He has a list of every speculation and pamphlet concerning Independence, and another of those concerning forms of government.

Dr Franklin proposes a device for a Seal: Moses lifting up his wand, and dividing the Red Sea, and Pharaoh in his chariot overwhelmed with the waters. This motto: Rebellion to Tyrants is Obedience to God.

Mr Jefferson proposed: The Children of Israel in the wilderness, led by a cloud by day, and pillar of fire by night, and on the other side Hengist and Horsa, the Saxon chiefs, from whom we claim the honour of being descended and whose political principles and forms of government we have assumed.

I proposed the Choice of Hercules, as engraved by Gribeline in some editions of Lord Shaftesbury's Works. The hero resting on his club. Virtue pointing to her rugged mountain, on one hand, and persuading him to ascend. Sloth, glancing at her flowery paths of pleasure, wantonly reclining on the ground, displaying the charms both of her eloquence and person, to seduce him into vice. But this is too complicated a group for a Seal or Medal, and it is not original.

To Abigail Adams, 14 August 1776

'The American governments'

JOHN ADAMS

The United States of America have exhibited, perhaps, the first example of governments erected on the simple principles of nature; and if men are now sufficiently enlightened to disabuse themselves of artifice, imposture, hypocrisy, and superstition, they will consider this event as an era in their history. Although the detail of the formation of the American governments is at present little known or regarded either in Europe or in America, it may hereafter become an object of curiosity. It will never be pretended that any persons employed in that service had interviews with the gods, or were in any degree under the inspiration of Heaven, more than those at work upon ships or houses, or laboring in merchandise or agriculture; it will forever be acknowledged that these governments were contrived merely by the use of reason and the senses, as Copley painted Chatham; West, Wolf; and Trumbull, Warren and Montgomery; as Dwight, Barlow, Trumbull, and Humphries composed their verse, and Belknap and Ramsay history; as Godfrey invented his quadrant, and Rittenhouse his planetarium; as Boylston practised inoculation, and Franklin electricity; as Paine exposed the mistakes of Raynal, and Jefferson those of Buffon, so unphilosophically borrowed from the despicable dreams of De Pau. Neither the people, nor their conventions, committees, or sub-committees, considered legislation in any other light than as ordinary arts and sciences, only more important. Called without expectation, and compelled without previous inclination, though undoubtedly at the best period of time, both for England and America, suddenly to erect new systems of laws for their future government, they adopted the method of a wise architect, in erecting a new palace for the residence of his sovereign. They determined to consult Vitruvius, Palladio, and all other writers of reputation in the art; to examine the most celebrated buildings, whether they remain entire or in ruins; to compare these with the principles of writers; and to inquire how far both the theories and models were founded in nature, or created by fancy; and when this was done, so far as their circumstances would allow, to adopt the advantages and reject the inconveniences of all. Unembarrassed by attachments to noble families, hereditary lines and successions, or any considerations of royal blood, even the pious mystery of holy oil had no more influence than that other one of holy water. The people were universally too enlightened to be imposed on by artifice; and their leaders, or more properly followers, were men of too much honor to attempt it. Thirteen governments thus founded on the natural authority of the people alone, without a pretence of miracle or mystery, and which are destined to spread over the northern part of that whole quarter of the globe, are a great point gained in favor of the rights of mankind. The experiment is made, and has completely succeeded; it can no longer be called in question, whether authority in magistrates and obedience of citizens can be grounded on reason, morality, and the Christian religion, without the monkery of priests, or the knavery of politicians.

Defense of the Constitutions of the United States, 1787, Preface

'The constitutions of America'

THOMAS PAINE

As soon as nine states had concurred, (and the rest followed in the order their conventions were elected), the old fabric of the federal government was taken down, and the new one erected, of which General Washington is President. – In this place I cannot help remarking, that the character and services of this gentleman are sufficient to put all those men called kings to shame. While they are receiving from the sweat and labours of mankind, a prodigality of pay, to which neither their abilities nor their services can entitle them, he is rendering every service in his power, and refusing every pecuniary reward. He accepted no pay as commander in chief; he accepts none as President of the United States.

After the new federal constitution was established, the state of Pennsylvania, conceiving that some parts of its own constitution required to be altered, elected a convention for that purpose. The proposed alterations were published, and the people concurring therein, they were established.

In forming those constitutions, or in altering them, little or no inconvenience took place. The ordinary course of things was not interrupted, and the advantages have been much. It is always the interest of a far greater number of people in a nation to have things right, than to let them remain wrong; and when public matters are open to debate, and the public judgement free, it will not decide wrong, unless it decides too hastily.

In the two instances of changing the constitutions, the governments then in being were not actors either way. Government has no right to make itself a party in any debate respecting the principles or modes of forming, or of changing, constitutions. It is not for the benefit of those who exercise the powers of government, that constitutions, and the governments issuing from them, are established. In all those matters, the right of judging and acting are in those who pay, and not in those who receive.

A constitution is the property of a nation, and not of those who exercise the government. All the constitutions of America are declared to be established on the authority of the people. In France, the word nation is used instead of the people; but in both cases, a constitution is a thing antecedent to the government, and always distinct therefrom.

In England, it is not difficult to perceive that everything has a constitution, except the nation. Every society and association that is established, first agreed upon a number of original articles, digested into form, which are its constitution. It then appointed its officers, whose powers and authorities are described in that constitution, and the government of that society then commenced. Those officers, by whatever name they are called, have no authority to add to, alter, or abridge the original articles. It is only to the constituting power that this right belongs.

From the want of understanding the difference between a constitution and a government, Dr Johnson, and all writers of his description, have always bewildered themselves. They could not but perceive, that there must necessarily be a *controlling* power existing somewhere, and they placed this power in the discretion of the persons exercising the government, instead of placing it in a constitution formed by the nation. When it is in a constitution, it has the nation for its support, and the natural and the political controlling powers are together. The laws which are enacted by governments, control men only as individuals, but the nation, through its constitution, controls the whole government, and has a natural ability so to do. The final controlling power, therefore, and the original constituting power, are one and the same power.

The Rights of Man, part 2, 1792, ch. 4

'I knew General Washington'

THOMAS JEFFERSON

You say that in taking General Washington on your shoulders, to bear him harmless through the federal coalition, you encounter a perilous topic. I do not think so. You have given the genuine history of the course of his mind through the trying scenes in which it was engaged, and of the seductions by which it was deceived, but not depraved. I think I knew General Washington intimately and thoroughly; and were I called on to delineate his character, it would be in terms like these.

His mind was great and powerful, without being of the very first order; his penetration strong, though not so acute as that of a Newton, Bacon, or Locke; and as far as he saw, no judgment was ever sounder. It was slow in operation, being little aided by invention or imagination, but sure in conclusion. Hence the common remark of his officers, of the advantage he derived from councils of war, where hearing all suggestions, he selected whatever was best; and certainly no General ever planned his battles more judiciously. But if deranged during the course of the action, if any member of his plan was dislocated by sudden circumstances, he was slow in readjustment. The consequence was, that he often failed in the field, and rarely against an enemy in station, as at Boston and York. He was incapable of fear, meeting personal dangers with the calmest unconcern. Perhaps the strongest feature in his character was prudence, never acting until every circumstance, every consideration, was maturely weighed; refraining if he saw a doubt, but, when once decided, going through with his purpose, whatever obstacles opposed. His integrity was most pure, his justice the most inflexible I have ever known, no motives of interest or consanguinity, of friendship or hatred, being able to bias his decision. He was, indeed, in every sense of the words, a wise, a good, and a great man. His temper was naturally high toned; but reflection and resolution had obtained a firm and habitual ascendency over it. If ever, however, it broke its bonds, he was most tremendous in his wrath. In his expenses he was honorable, but exact; liberal in contributions to whatever promised utility; but frowning and unyielding on all visionary projects and all unworthy calls on his charity. His heart was not warm in its affections; but he exactly calculated every man's value, and gave him a solid esteem proportioned to it. His person, you know, was fine, his stature exactly what one would wish, his deportment easy, erect and noble; the best horseman of his age, and the most graceful figure that could be seen on horseback. Although in the circle of his friends, where he might be unreserved with safety, he took a free share in conversation, his colloquial talents were not above mediocrity, possessing neither copiousness of ideas, nor fluency of words. In public, when called on for a sudden opinion, he was unready, short and embarrassed. Yet he wrote readily, rather diffusely, in an easy and correct style. This he had acquired by conversation with the world, for his education was merely reading, writing and common arithmetic, to which he added surveying at a later day. His time was employed in action chiefly, reading little, and that only in agriculture and English history. His correspondence became necessarily extensive, and, with journalizing his agricultural proceedings, occupied most of his leisure hours within doors. On the whole, his character was, in its mass, perfect, in nothing bad, in few points indifferent; and it may truly be said, that never did nature and fortune combine more perfectly to make a man great, and to place him in the same constellation with whatever worthies have merited from man an everlasting remembrance. For his was the singular destiny and merit, of leading the armies of his country successfully through an arduous war, for the establishment of its independence; of conducting its councils through the birth of a government, new in its forms and principles, until it had settled down into a quiet and orderly train; and of scrupulously obeying the laws through the whole of his career, civil and military, of which the history of the world furnishes no other example.

How, then, can it be perilous for you to take such a man on your shoulders? I am satisfied the great body of republicans think of him as I do. We were, indeed, dissatisfied with him on his ratification of the British treaty. But this was short lived. We knew his honesty, the wiles with which he was encompassed, and that age had already begun to relax the firmness of his purposes; and I am convinced he is more deeply seated in the love and gratitude of the republicans, than in the Pharisaical homage of the federal monarchists. For he was no monarchist from preference of his judgment. The soundness of that gave him correct views of the rights of man, and his severe justice devoted him to them. He has often declared to me that he considered our new constitution as an experiment on the practicability of republican government, and with what dose of liberty man could be trusted for his own good; that he was determined the experiment should have a fair trial, and would lose the last drop of his blood in support of it. And these declarations he repeated to me the oftener and more pointedly, because he knew my suspicions of Colonel Hamilton's views, and probably had heard from him the same declarations which I had, to wit, 'that the British constitution, with its unequal representation, corruption and other existing abuses, was the most perfect government which had ever been established on earth, and that a reformation of those abuses would make it an impracticable government.' I do believe that General Washington had not a firm confidence in the durability of our government. He was naturally distrustful of men, and inclined to gloomy apprehensions; and I was ever persuaded that a belief that we must at length end in something like a British constitution, had some weight in his adoption of the ceremonies of levees, birthdays, pompous meetings with Congress, and other forms of the same character, calculated to prepare us gradually for a change which he believed possible, and to let it come on with as little shock as might be to the public mind.

These are my opinions of General Washington, which I would vouch at the judgment seat of God, having been formed on an acquaintance of thirty years. I served with him in the Virginia legislature from 1769 to the Revolutionary war, and again, a short time in Congress, until he left us to take command of the army. During the war and after it we corresponded occasionally, and in the four years of my continuance in the office of Secretary of State, our intercourse was daily, confidential and cordial. After I retired from that office, great and malignant pains were taken by our federal monarchists, and not entirely without effect, to make him view me as a theorist, holding French principles of government, which would lead infallibly to licentiousness and anarchy. And to this he listened the more easily, from my known disapprobation of the British treaty. I never saw him afterwards, or these malignant insinuations should have been dissipated before his just judgment, as mists before the sun. I felt on his death, with my countrymen, that 'verily a great man hath fallen this day in Israel.'

To Walter Jones, 2 January 1814

'The 4th of July'

FRANCES TROLLOPE

And now arrived the 4th of July, that greatest of all American festivals. On the 4th of July, 1776, the declaration of their independence was signed, at the State-house in Philadelphia.

To me, the dreary coldness and want of enthusiasm in American manners is one of their greatest defects, and I therefore hailed the demonstrations of general feeling which this day elicits with real pleasure. On the 4th of July the hearts of the people seem to awaken from a three hundred and sixty-four days' sleep; they appear high-spirited, gay, animated, social, generous, or at least liberal in expense; and would they but refrain from spitting on that hallowed day, I should say, that on the 4th of July, at least, they appeared to be an amiable people. It is true that the women have but little to do with the pageantry, the splendour, or the gaiety of the day; but, setting this defect aside, it was indeed a glorious sight to behold a jubilee so heartfelt as this; and had they not the bad taste and bad feeling to utter an annual oration, with unvarying abuse of the mother country, to say nothing of the warlike manifesto called the Declaration of Independence, our gracious king himself might look upon the scene and say that it was good; nay, even rejoice, that twelve millions of bustling bodies, at four thousand miles distance from his throne and his altars, should make their own laws, and drink their own tea, after the fashion that pleased them best.

Domestic Manners of the Americans, 1832, ch. 2

Concord Hymn

RALPH WALDO EMERSON

[Sung at the completion of the Battle Monument, July 4, 1837]

By the rude bridge that arched the flood,
　　Their flag to April's breeze unfurled,
Here once the embattled farmers stood
　　And fired the shot heard round the world.

The foe long since in silence slept;
　　Alike the conqueror silent sleeps;
And Time the ruined bridge has swept
　　Down the dark stream which seaward creeps.

On this green bank, by this soft stream,
　　We set to-day a votive stone;
That memory may their dead redeem,
　　When, like our sires, our sons are gone.

Spirit, that made those heroes dare
　　To die, and leave their children free,
Bid Time and Nature gently spare
　　The shaft we raise to them and thee.

1837, rev. 1876

'Universal suffrage'

ALEXIS DE TOCQUEVILLE

Many people in Europe are apt to believe without saying it, or to say without believing it, that one of the great advantages of universal suffrage is, that it intrusts the direction of affairs to men who are worthy of the public confidence. They admit that the people are unable to govern of themselves, but they aver that the people always wish the welfare of the state, and instinctively designate those who are animated by the same good wishes, and who are the most fit to wield the supreme authority. I confess that the observations I made in America by no means coincide with these opinions. On my arrival in the United States, I was surprised to find so much distinguished talent among the subjects, and so little among the heads of the government. It is a constant fact, that, at the present day, the ablest men in the United States are rarely placed at the head of affairs; and it must be acknowledged that such has been the result, in proportion as democracy has outstepped all its former limits. The race of American statesmen has evidently dwindled most remarkably in the course of the last fifty years.

Several causes may be assigned for this phenomenon. It is impossible, after the most strenuous exertions, to raise the intelligence of the people above a certain level. Whatever may be the facilities of acquiring information, whatever may be the profusion of easy methods and cheap science, the human mind can never be instructed and developed without devoting considerable time to these objects.

The greater or the less possibility of subsisting without labor is therefore the necessary boundary of intellectual improvement. This boundary is more remote in some countries, and more restricted in others; but it must exist somewhere, as long as the people are constrained to work in order to procure the means of subsistence, that is to say, as long as they continue to be the people. It is therefore quite as difficult to imagine a state in which all the citizens should be very well informed, as a state in which they should all be wealthy; these two difficulties are correlative. I readily admit that the mass of the citizens sincerely wish to promote the welfare of the country; nay, more, I even allow that the lower classes mix fewer considerations of personal interest with their patriotism than the higher orders; but it is always more or less difficult for them to discern the best means of attaining the end which they sincerely desire. Long and patient observation and much acquired knowledge are requisite to form a just estimate of the character of a single individual. Men of the greatest genius often fail to do it, and can it be supposed that the vulgar will always succeed? The people have neither the time nor the means for an investigation of this kind. Their conclusions are hastily formed from a superficial inspection of the more prominent features of a question. Hence it often happens that mountebanks of all sorts are able to please the people, whilst their truest friends frequently fail to gain their confidence.

Moreover, the democracy not only lack that soundness of judgment which is necessary to select men really deserving of their confidence, but often have not the desire or the inclination to find them out. It cannot be denied that democratic institutions strongly tend to promote the feeling of envy in the human heart; not so much because they afford to every one the means of rising to the same level with others, as because those means perpetually disappoint the persons who employ them. Democratic institutions awaken and foster a passion for equality which they can never entirely satisfy. This complete equality eludes the grasp of the people at the very moment when they think they have grasped it, and 'flies', as Pascal says, 'with an eternal flight'; the people are excited in the pursuit of an advantage, which is more precious because it is not sufficiently remote to be unknown, or sufficiently near to be enjoyed. The lower orders are agitated by the chance of success, they are irritated by its uncertainty; and they pass from the enthusiasm of pursuit to the exhaustion of ill-success, and lastly to the acrimony of disappointment. Whatever transcends their own limits appears to be an obstacle to their desires, and there is no superiority, however legitimate it may be, which is not irksome in their sight.

It has been supposed that the secret instinct, which leads the lower orders to remove their superiors as much as possible from the direction of public affairs, is peculiar to France. This, however, is an error; the instinct to which I allude is not French, it is democratic; it may have been heightened by peculiar political circumstances, but it owes its origin to a higher cause.

In the United States, the people do not hate the higher classes of society, but are not favorably inclined towards them, and carefully exclude them from the exercise of authority. They do not dread distinguished talents, but are rarely fond of them. In general, every one who rises without their aid seldom obtains their favor.

Whilst the natural instincts of democracy induce the people to reject distinguished citizens as their rulers, an instinct not less strong induces able men to retire from the political arena, in which it is so difficult to retain their independence, or to advance without becoming servile. This opinion has been candidly expressed by Chancellor Kent, who says, in speaking with high praise of that part of the Constitution which empowers the executive to nominate the judges: 'It is indeed probable that the men who are best fitted to discharge the duties of this high office would have too much reserve in their manners, and too much austerity in their principles, for them to be returned by the majority at an election where universal suffrage is adopted.' Such were the opinions which were printed without contradiction in America in the year 1830!

I hold it to be sufficiently demonstrated, that universal suffrage is by no means a guaranty of the wisdom of the popular choice. Whatever its advantages may be, this is not one of them.

Democracy in America, vol. 1, ch. 13, 1835, trans. Henry Reeve;
rev. Francis Bowen, 1862

'The City of Magnificent Intentions'

CHARLES DICKENS

It [Washington] is sometimes called the City of Magnificent Distances, but it might with greater propriety be termed the City of Magnificent Intentions; for it is only on taking a bird's-eye view of it from the top of the Capitol that one can at all comprehend the vast designs of its projector, an aspiring Frenchman. Spacious avenues that begin in nothing, and lead nowhere; streets, mile-long, that only want houses, roads, and inhabitants; public buildings that need but a public to be complete; and ornaments of great thoroughfares, which only lack great thoroughfares to ornament – are its leading features. One might fancy the season over, and most of the houses gone out of town for ever with their masters. To the admirers of cities it is a Barmecide Feast; a pleasant field for the imagination to rove in; a monument raised to a deceased project, with not even a legible inscription to record its departed greatness.

Such as it is, it is likely to remain. It was originally chosen for the seat of Government as a means of averting the conflicting jealousies and interests of the different States; and very probably, too, as being remote from mobs: a consideration not to be slighted, even in America. It has no trade or commerce of its own: having little or no population beyond the President and his establishment: the members of the legislature, who reside there during the session; the Government clerks and officers employed in the various departments; the keepers of the hotels and boarding-houses; and the tradesmen who supply their tables. It is very unhealthy. Few people would live in Washington, I take it, who were not obliged to reside there; and the tides of emigration and speculation, those rapid and regardless currents, are little likely to flow at any time towards such dull and sluggish water.

The principal features of the Capitol are, of course, the two Houses of Assembly. But there is, besides, in the centre of the building, a fine rotunda, ninety-six feet in diameter, and ninety-six high, whose circular wall is divided into compartments, ornamented by historical pictures. Four of these have for their subjects prominent events in the revolutionary struggle. They were painted by Colonel Trumbull, himself a member of Washington's staff at the time of their occurrence; from which circumstance they derive a peculiar interest of their own. In this same hall Mr Greenough's large statue of Washington has been lately placed. It has great merits, of course, but it struck me as being rather strained and violent for its subject. I could wish, however, to have seen it in a better light than it can ever be viewed in where it stands.

There is a very pleasant and commodious library in the Capitol; and from

a balcony in front, the bird's-eye view, of which I have just spoken, may
be had, together with a beautiful prospect of the adjacent country. In one
of the ornamented portions of the building there is a figure of Justice;
whereunto, the Guide Book says, 'the artist at first contemplated giving
more of nudity, but he was warned that the public sentiment in this country
would not admit of it, and in his caution he has gone, perhaps, to the opposite extreme.' Poor Justice! she has been made to wear much stranger gar-
ments in America than those she pines in in the Capitol. Let us hope that
she has changed her dressmaker since they were fashioned, and that the
public sentiment of the country did not cut out the clothes she hides her
lovely figure in just now.

American Notes, 1842, ch. 8

What *may* be in America

WALTER BAGEHOT

It is especially important for merchants, the success or failure of whose commercial enterprises so much depends on the correctness of the estimate they
form of future contingencies, to consider and be prepared for *any* contin-
gency which is not absolutely improbable. Now, in such a case as America
presents to us at this moment, no result that is not impossible can be said
to be improbable. There, perhaps, never was conjuncture of such magnitude in which it was so hopeless to predict the direction which events are
likely to take. The materials on which to form a rational guess are extraordinarily scanty and uncertain. It is not so much that *we* do not know the
Americans, as that the Americans do not know themselves. From first to last
in this matter, they have been singularly at fault in their conjectures and
prophecies: we, on this side of the water, have, hitherto at least, been much
nearer the truth in the expectations which we entertained.

There is nothing that should surprise us in this uncertainty, when we give
the matter a little dispassionate consideration. The fact is, the Americans are
a wholly untried people; – and till people have been tried, no one can pretend
to say what they are, or what under any given circumstances they will do.
They have never been *tested* by any great difficulty, any great danger, any
great calamity: they have never been called upon for any sustained effort, any
serious sacrifices, any prolonged endurance. They do not know, therefore, – nor do we – the possible reach of their virtues and their powers, nor
the possible range of their vices and their weaknesses. They have never yet
faced a really formidable foe. It will astonish and disgust them to be told this;

but it is the simple truth. No one who reads the details of the revolution by which they won their independence, while full of admiration for their pluck and energy, fails to be utterly amazed at their success. The indescribable imbecility of their enemies was yet more wonderful than their own vigour. Against any English army and any English ministry that have existed since the days of Lord North, they would not have had the shadow of a chance – as every one except themselves is now perfectly aware. And, moreover (be it said in passing), they are not what they were then; both their institutions and their men have degenerated frightfully; their *morale* has gone down almost as fast and as far as their power and prosperity have increased. In the short war of 1812, they fought bravely – behind walls and at sea; but the great feat of Andrew Jackson – for which they made him a hero and a president – was defending a walled city, made almost impregnable by cotton bags and riflemen, against an inadequately-provided invading force lodged in an unhealthy swamp. All their other contests have been against naked Indians and degenerate and undisciplined Mexicans: these were *raids* rather than wars, and though accompanied by individual risk, never involved any serious danger of discomfiture. Therefore we are undoubtedly warranted in saying – and we say it without wishing to throw the slightest slur on American prowess and courage – that till now neither Northerners nor Southerners have ever encountered a capable enemy or a real peril; and how they will behave in the face of such no man can foresee. They have gained their ends hitherto not by fighting but by bullying; they have bullied every nation in turn; – and their success in this sort of warfare has not only enormously enhanced their own conceptions of their military prowess, but has entirely blinded them as to the flimsy and *unproved* foundation upon which these conceptions rest. No one doubts that a regular army of Americans, well disciplined and well officered, would fight as bravely and as skilfully as any in the world; but how American volunteers will fight, hastily got together, utterly unaccustomed to obedience, without experience, and without confidence either in their officers or in each other, no one can venture to predict; – and the panic at Manassas Gap, and the subsequent behaviour of the defeated troops, warrant the very worst and most disrespectful misgivings on this head.

We are in equal uncertainty as to American statesmen and American institutions. They have never been tried in a storm before, and no one can tell how they will stand the strain. The leaders in Washington's time were gentlemen and men of education. The institutions in Washington's time were free, but not democratic. Since that time the country has gone through a course of unexampled and uninterrupted prosperity – demoralising assuredly, though not enervating. Laws and manners have changed to a degree which few persons have yet fully realised. The constitution has become an almost unmitigated *ochlocracy*. The masses are everywhere omnipotent; and the masses in most parts are only half educated, and in many parts are as ignorant as those of Europe and far more ruffianly. The men of thoughtful minds and lofty purpose, the men of noble sentiments and stainless honour, have retired from public life; and, naturally enough, as the work of politics became dirtier and rougher, have left it to dirtier and rougher men. The consequence, as every one is too well aware, and as even Americans themselves have repeated *usque ad nauseam*, has been that the rulers and legislators of the United States are, almost without exception, either the vulgarer and shallower men of the nation who share the popular faults and passions, or cleverer minds who flatter and obey them without sharing them – unworthy in the one case intellectually, unworthier still, in the other, from voluntary moral degradation. Now, how can such men be expected to meet a crisis like the present – a crisis which might try the ablest and the noblest spirits that ever directed the fortunes of a great country? How can men who have risen to power by low means be expected to use power for lofty purposes? How can men who are where they are because they have truckled and temporised and cajoled and cringed and fawned upon the mob, now coerce that mob to its duty, or overawe it into obedience and order? Or how can men who are corrupt, or are believed to be so – or both – preach patriotism and purity and patient endurance and the noble spirit of self-sacrifice to a sneering and unbelieving crowd? – or expect a hearing if they do? Moral courage is more needed at Washington now than any other political virtue – the moral courage to speak unpopular truths, to face popular rage, and to resist popular delusions; – and when was such courage the common virtue of democracies? – and where, in this wide world, has this virtue, rare everywhere, been so utterly trampled out as in America?

Lastly, we know the real qualities of the American people as imperfectly as those of their army and their statesmen. That is, we do not know how they will come out under trial. There is plenty of sterling stuff in them, we may be sure, for they come of a good stock; but, on the other hand, their career has not been of a nature to develop the virtues most needed on an occasion like the present, – *viz.*, fortitude under reverses, submission to needful discipline, and loyal trust in the men who are to lead them; and their whole history as well as their recent conduct has displayed the very opposite characteristics. It would be idle to deny that the behaviour of the people on the occasion of the defeat at Manassas Junction, and since that discreditable occurrence, has given a great shock to the confidence of those who had formed high expectations of Northern capacity and vigour. There has been apparently an entire absence of all sense of shame and mortification, which is absolutely incomprehensible, – a sort of perverse pride in the very magnitude of their disaster and disgrace, combined with the usual and very ominous disposition to lay all the blame on their chiefs and their officers, and to take none upon themselves. The patriotism of the volunteers seems to bear an inverse ratio to their bluster. Without in any way wishing to detract from the extraordinary faculty which the Northern Americans have always shown for recovering and retrieving misfortune, for prompt and energetic organisation, and for ready lavishing of their immense resources, – the events of the last few weeks have begot a fear that the rottenness of the country in all that relates to administration and to political virtue has spread deeper and wider than has yet been believed. So much so that a doubt is beginning to be generally expressed whether there is confidence enough left in the heart of the people to induce them to trust sufficient power in the hands of any public man or of any administration; – whether even in the gravest crisis a dictator could be found, or would be appointed, or would be obeyed if appointed; – whether the political corruption of which every one is conscious in himself, and which every one attributes to his neighbour, has not utterly destroyed the very sources of that mutual faith and loyalty without which the vastest resources are unavailing because no one will be suffered to wield them; and finally, whether the habit of what is there called self-government, but what we should call Lynch law, mob interference, lawless wilfulness, and reckless self-assertion, has not incapacitated the people for that generous, rational, legitimate obedience which is the saving virtue of armies and of nations in the hour of crisis.

Considering all these things, we are strongly impressed with the conviction that there is no degree of incapacity, confusion, feebleness, mismanagement, and thorough imbecility on the part of the Government at Washington, which is not *upon the cards*. We do not say it is probable. We should deeply grieve, for the honour of our common ancestry, to see it. But it would not surprise us; and we think that all men practically concerned ought to be prepared for it as one of the not improbable eventualities of the conjuncture.

Excerpt, *The Economist*, 7 August 1861

The Battle Hymn of the Republic

JULIA WARD HOWE

Mine eyes have seen the glory of the coming of the Lord:
He is trampling out the vintage where the grapes of wrath are stored;
He hath loosed the fatal lightning of His terrible swift sword:
  His truth is marching on.

I have seen Him in the watch-fires of a hundred circling camps,
They have builded Him an altar in the evening dews and damps;

I can read His righteous sentence by the dim and flaring lamps:
    His day is marching on.

I have read a fiery gospel writ in burnished rows of steel:
'As ye deal with my contemners, so with you my grace shall deal;
Let the Hero, born of woman, crush the serpent with his heel,
    Since God is marching on.'

He has sounded forth the trumpet that shall never call retreat;
He is sifting out the hearts of men before His judgement seat:
Oh, be swift, my soul, to answer Him! Be jubilant, my feet!
    Our God is marching on.

In the beauty of the lilies Christ was born across the sea,
With a glory in his bosom that transfigures you and me:
As he died to make men holy, let us die to make men free,
    While God is marching on.

                                                              1861

Address Delivered at the Dedication of the Cemetery at Gettysburg

ABRAHAM LINCOLN

Four score and seven years ago our fathers brought forth on this continent,
a new nation, conceived in Liberty, and dedicated to the proposition that
all men are created equal.

Now we are engaged in a great civil war, testing whether that nation, or
any nation so conceived and so dedicated, can long endure. We are met on
a great battle-field of that war. We have come to dedicate a portion of that
field, as a final resting place for those who here gave their lives that that nation might live. It is altogether fitting and proper that we should do this.

But, in a larger sense, we can not dedicate – we can not consecrate – we
can not hallow – this ground. The brave men, living and dead, who struggled here, have consecrated it, far above our poor power to add or detract.
The world will little note, nor long remember what we say here, but it can
never forget what they did here. It is for us the living, rather, to be dedicated
here to the unfinished work which they who fought here have thus far so
nobly advanced. It is rather for us to be here dedicated to the great task
remaining before us – that from these honored dead we take increased devotion to that cause for which they gave the last full measure of devo-

tion – that we here highly resolve that these dead shall not have died in vain – that this nation, under God, shall have a new birth of freedom – and that government of the people, by the people, for the people, shall not perish from the earth.

19 November 1863

Cavalry Crossing a Ford

WALT WHITMAN

A line in long array where they wind betwixt green islands,
They take a serpentine course, their arms flash in the sun – hark to the
   musical clank,
Behold the silvery river, in it the splashing horses loitering stop to
   drink,
Behold the brown-faced men, each group, each person a picture, the
   negligent rest on the saddles,
Some emerge on the opposite bank, others are just entering the
   ford – while,
Scarlet and blue and snowy white,
The guidon flags flutter gayly in the wind.

Drum-Taps, 1865

'Seeing a battle'

WILLIAM HOWARD RUSSELL

It was a strange scene before us. From the hill a densely wooded country dotted at intervals with green fields and cleared lands, spread five or six miles in front, bounded by a line of blue and purple ridges, terminating abruptly in escarpment towards the left front, and swelling gradually towards the right into the lower spines of an offshoot from the Blue Ridge Mountains. On our left the view was circumscribed by a forest which clothed the side of the ridge on which we stood, and covered its shoulder far down into the plain. A gap in the nearest chain of the hills in our front was pointed out by the by-standers as the Pass of Manassas, by which the railway from the West is carried into the plain, and still nearer at hand, before us, is the junction of that rail with the line from Alexandria, and with the railway leading southwards to Richmond. The intervening space was not a deal level; undulating lines of forest marked the course of the streams which intersected it, and gave, by their variety of color and shading an additional charm to the landscape which, enclosed in a framework of blue and purple hills, softened into violet in the extreme distance, presented one of the most agreeable displays of simple pastoral woodland scenery that could be conceived.

But the sounds which came upon the breeze, and the sights which met our eyes, were in terrible variance with the tranquil character of the landscape. The woods far and near echoed to the roar of cannon, and thin frayed lines of blue smoke marked the spots whence came the muttering sound of rolling musketry; the white puffs of smoke burst high above the tree-tops, and the gunners' rings from shell and howitzer marked the fire of the artillery.

Clouds of dust shifted and moved through the forest; and through the wavering mists of light-blue smoke, and the thicker masses which rose commingling from the feet of men and the mouths of cannon, I could see the gleam of arms and the twinkling of bayonets.

On the hill beside me there was a crowd of civilians on horseback, and in all sorts of vehicles, with a few of the fairer, if not gentler sex. A few officers and some soldiers, who had straggled from the regiments in reserve, moved about among the spectators, and pretended to explain the movements of the troops below, of which they were profoundly ignorant.

The cannonade and musketry had been exaggerated by the distance and by the rolling echoes of the hills; and sweeping the position narrowly with my glass from point to point, I failed to discover any traces of close encounter or very severe fighting. The spectators were all excited, and a lady with an opera-glass who was near me, was quite beside herself when an unusually heavy discharge roused the current of her blood – 'That is splendid. Oh, my! Is not that first-rate? I guess we will be in Richmond this time tomorrow.' These, mingled with coarser exclamations, burst from the politicians who had come out to see the triumph of the Union arms. I was particularly irritated by constant applications for the loan of my glass. One broken-down looking soldier observing my flask, asked me for a drink, and took a startling pull, which left but little between the bottom and utter vacuity.

'Stranger, that's good stuff and no mistake. I have not had such a drink since I come South. I feel now as if I'd like to whip ten Seceshers.'

From the line of the smoke it appeared to me that the action was in an oblique line from our left, extending farther outwards towards the right, bisected by a road from Centreville, which descended the hill close at hand and ran right across the undulating plain, its course being marked by the white covers of the baggage and commissariat wagons as far as a turn of the road, where the trees closed in upon them. Beyond the right of the curling smoke clouds of dust appeared from time to time in the distance, as if bodies of cavalry were moving over a sandy plain.

Notwithstanding all the exultation and boastings of the people at Centreville, I was well convinced no advance of any importance or any great success had been achieved, because the ammunition and baggage wagons had never moved, nor had the reserves received any orders to follow in the line of the army.

The clouds of dust on the right were quite inexplicable. As we were looking, my philosophic companion asked me in perfect seriousness, 'Are we really seeing a battle now? Are they supposed to be fighting where all that smoke is going on? This is rather interesting, you know.'

My Diary North and South, 1863, ch. 50

Second Inaugural Address

ABRAHAM LINCOLN

At this second appearing to take the oath of the presidential office, there is less occasion for an extended address than there was at the first. Then a statement, somewhat in detail, of a course to be pursued, seemed fitting and proper. Now, at the expiration of four years, during which public declarations have been constantly called forth on every point and phase of the great contest which still absorbs the attention, and engrosses the energies of the nation, little that is new could be presented. The progress of our arms, upon which all else chiefly depends, is as well known to the public as to myself; and it is, I trust, reasonably satisfactory and encouraging to all. With high hope for the future, no prediction in regard to it is ventured.

On the occasion corresponding to this four years ago, all thoughts were anxiously directed to an impending civil war. All dreaded it – all sought to avert it. While the inaugural address was being delivered from this place, devoted altogether to *saving* the Union without war, insurgent agents were in the city seeking to *destroy* it without war – seeking to dissol[v]e the Union, and divide effects, by negotiation. Both parties deprecated war; but one of them would *make* war rather than let the nation survive; and the other would *accept* war rather than let it perish. And the war came.

One eighth of the whole population were colored slaves, not distributed generally over the Union, but localized in the Southern part of it. These slaves constituted a peculiar and powerful interest. All knew that this interest was, somehow, the cause of the war. To strengthen, perpetuate, and extend this interest was the object for which the insurgents would rend the

Union, even by war; while the government claimed no right to do more than to restrict the territorial enlargement of it. Neither party expected for the war, the magnitude, or the duration, which it has already attained. Neither anticipated that the *cause* of the conflict might cease with, or even before, the conflict itself should cease. Each looked for an easier triumph, and a result less fundamental and astounding. Both read the same Bible, and pray to the same God; and each invokes His aid against the other. It may seem strange that any men should dare to ask a just God's assistance in wringing their bread from the sweat of other men's faces; but let us judge not that we be not judged. The prayers of both could not be answered; that of neither has been answered fully. The Almighty has his own purposes. 'Woe unto the world because of offences! for it must needs be that offences come; but woe to that man by whom the offence cometh!' If we shall suppose that American Slavery is one of those offences which, in the providence of God, must needs come, but which, having continued through His appointed time, He now wills to remove, and that He gives to both North and South, this terrible war, as the woe due to those by whom the offence came, shall we discern therein any departure from those divine attributes which the believers in a Living God always ascribe to Him? Fondly do we hope – fervently do we pray – that this mighty scourge of war may speedily pass away. Yet, if God wills that it continue, until all the wealth piled by the bond-man's two hundred and fifty years of unrequited toil shall be sunk, and until every drop of blood drawn with the lash, shall be paid by another drawn with the sword, as was said three thousand years ago, so still it must be said 'the judgments of the Lord, are true and righteous altogether.'

With malice toward none; with charity for all; with firmness in the right, as God gives us to see the right, let us strive on to finish the work we are in; to bind up the nation's wounds; to care for him who shall have borne the battle, and for his widow, and his orphan – to do all which may achieve and cherish a just and lasting peace, among ourselves, and with all nations.

4 March 1865

Battle of Murfreesboro
1862–1922

ALLEN TATE

He shakes the dust from off his feet
And shambles down the dirty street –

The last man in the town, they said,
Who'd shot a hundred Yankees dead.

At every door he looks inside
Where pansies bloom and violets hide;
Some little boys offer him a cheer,
And only the town-dog seems to leer.

What does he seek with watery eyes?
A face or two, perhaps, or lies
That tell him Genevieve is there,
Behind the trellis, just as fair.

I cannot say he walks in vain,
Nor back of his leather-lips is pain –
Only no bottle yields its cork
And skyscrapers tower in far New York.

(1922) *Collected Poems*, 1977

'That Civil War'

GERTRUDE STEIN

So I went on walking around Richmond and seeing the statues there are a great many of them, and I meditated as I always had meditated about the Civil War. It was one of the interesting wars in the world the Civil War, the French revolutionary fighting before Napoleon took charge of it had been the first one of one crowd against another crowd of people just that, and the Civil War was completely that. The 1914–1918 war was bigger and had different arms but eventually it added nothing to what had been imagined in the Civil War and naturally I always thought about that. And here I was in Richmond and I had always thought about General Lee and I did think about that. I had always thought not thought but felt that Lee was a man who knew that the South could not win of course he knew that thing how could a man who was destined by General Scott to succeed him in command of the American armies who knew that war was dependent upon arms and resources and who knew all that how could he not know that the South could not win and he did know it of that I am completely certain, he did know it, he acted he always acted like a man leading a country in defeat, he always knew it but and that is why I think him a weak man he did not have the courage to say it, if he had had that courage well perhaps there would have been not just then and so not likely later that Civil War but if there had not been would America have been as interesting. Very likely not very likely not. But the man who could knowing it lead his people to defeat it well any way I could never feel that any one could make a hero of him. I could not. I said this one day down in Charleston, I was talking to some man who had a Southern wife and a Southern father-in-law, who was an important Southern newspaper editor and he said that is interesting because my father-in-law one day it was a rainy Sunday and some body said something about Lee and my father-in-law said yes he was a great man a great great man and we all love him and I sometimes think that if he had been here of a rainy Sunday well yes I would not want him here all day of a rainy Sunday.

No, leading his fellow citizens to defeat did not excite him it did not exalt him it did not depress him, he did it because he could not say no to it and that does not make him interesting all day of a rainy Sunday.

So I was interested in being in Richmond and in Virginia and I was interested in hearing what they were all saying and I was interested, after all there never will be anything more interesting in America than that Civil War never.

Everybody's Autobiography, 1937

'Federal city'

HENRY JAMES

One might have been sure in advance that the character of a democracy would nowhere more sharply mark itself than in the democratic substitute for a court city, and Washington is cast in the mould that expresses most the absence of salient social landmarks and constituted features. Here it is that conversation, as the only invoked presence, betrays a little its inadequacy to the furnishing forth, all by itself, of an outward view. It tells us it must be there, since in all the wide empty vistas nothing else is, and the general elimination *can* but have left it. A pleading, touching effect, indeed, lurks in this sense of it as seated, at receipt of custom, by any decent door of any decent domicile and watching the vacancy for reminder and appeal. It is left to conversation alone to people the scene with accents; putting aside two or three objects to be specified, there is *never* an accent in it, up and down, far and wide, save such as fall rather on the ear of the mind: those projected by the social spirit starved for the sense of an occasional emphasis. The White House is an accent – one of the lightest, sharpest possible; and the Capitol, of course, immensely, another; though the latter falls on the exclusively political page, as to which I have been waiting to say a word. It should meanwhile be mentioned that we are promised these enhancements, these illustrations, of the great general text, on the most magnificent scale; a splendid projected and announced Washington of the future, with approaches even now grandly outlined and massively marked; in face of which one should perhaps confess to the futility of any current estimate. If I speak thus of the Capitol, however, let me not merely brush past the White House to get to it – any more than feel free to pass into it without some preliminary stare at that wondrous Library of Congress which glitters in fresh and almost unmannerly emulation, almost frivolous irrelevance of form, in the neighbourhood of the greater building. About the ingenuities and splendours of this last costly structure, a riot of rare material and rich ornament, there would doubtless be much to say – did not one everywhere, on all such ground, meet the open eye of criticism simply to establish with it a private intelligence, simply to respond to it by a deprecating wink. The guardian of that altar, I think, is but too willing, on such a hint, to let one pass without the sacrifice.

It is a case again here, as on fifty other occasions, of the tribute instantly paid by the revisiting spirit; but paid, all without question, to the general *kind* of presence for which the noisy air, over the land, feels so sensibly an inward ache – the presence that corresponds there, no matter how loosely, to that of the housing and harbouring European Church in the ages of great disorder. The Universities and the greater Libraries (the smaller, for a hundred good democratic reasons, are another question), repeat, in their manner, to the imagination, East and West, the note of the old thick-walled convents and quiet cloisters: they are large and charitable, they are sturdy, often proud and often rich, and they have the incalculable value that they represent the only intermission to inordinate rapacious traffic that the scene offers to view. With this suggestion of sacred ground they play even upon the most restless of analysts as they will, making him face about, with ecstasy, any way they seem to point; so that he feels it his business much less to count over their shortcomings than to proclaim them places of enchantment. They are better at their worst than anything else at its best, and the comparatively sweet sounds that stir their theoretic stillness are for him as echoes of the lyre of Apollo. The Congressional Library is magnificent, and would become thus a supreme sanctuary even were it ten times more so: there would seem to be nothing then but to pronounce it a delight and have done with it – or let the appalled imagination, in other words, slink into it and stay there. But here is pressed precisely, with particular force, the spring of the question that takes but a touch to sound: is the case of this remarkable creation, by exception, a case in which the violent waving of the pecuniary wand *has* incontinently produced interest? The answer can only be, I feel, a shy assent – though shy indeed only till the logic of the matter is apparent. This logic is that, though money alone can gather in on such a scale the treasures of knowledge, these treasures, in the form of books and documents, themselves organize and furnish their world. They appoint and settle the proportions, they thicken the air, they people the space, they create and consecrate all their relations, and no one shall say that, where they scatter life, which they themselves in fact *are*, history does not promptly attend. Emphatically yes, therefore, the great domed and tiered, galleried and statued central hall of the Congressional, the last word of current constructional science and artistic resource, already crowns itself with that grace.

The graceful thing in Washington beyond any other, none the less, is the so happily placed and featured White House, the late excellent extensions and embellishments of which have of course represented expenditure – but only of the refined sort imposed by some mature portionless gentlewoman on relatives who have accepted the principle of making her, at a time of life, more honourably comfortable. The whole ample precinct and margin formed by the virtual continuity of its grounds with those expanses in which the effect of the fine Washington Obelisk rather spends or wastes itself (not a little as if some loud monosyllable had been uttered, in a preoccupied company, without a due production of sympathy or sense) – the fortunate isolation of the White House, I say, intensifies its power to appeal to that musing and mooning visitor whose perceptions alone, in all the conditions, I hold worthy of account. Hereabouts, beyond doubt, history had from of old seemed to me insistently seated, and I remember a short spring-time of years ago when Lafayette Square itself, contiguous to the Executive Mansion, could create a rich sense of the past by the use of scarce other witchcraft than its command of that pleasant perspective and its possession of the most prodigious of all Presidential effigies, Andrew Jackson, as archaic as a Ninevite king, prancing and rocking through the ages. If that atmosphere, moreover, in the fragrance of the Washington April, was even a quarter of a century since as a liquor of bitter-sweet taste, overflowing its cup, what was the ineffable mixture now, with all the elements further distilled, all the life further sacrificed, to make it potent? One circled about the place as for meeting the ghosts, and one paused, under the same impulse, before the high palings of the White House drive, as if wondering at haunted ground. There the ghosts stood in their public array, spectral enough and clarified; yet scarce making it easier to 'place' the strange, incongruous blood-drops, as one looked through the rails, on that revised and freshened page. But one fortunately has one's choice, in all these connections, as one turns away; the mixture, as I have called it, is really here so fine. General Jackson, in the centre of the Square, still rocks his hobby and the earth; but the fruit of the interval, to my actual eyes, hangs nowhere brighter than in the brilliant memorials lately erected to Lafayette and to Rochambeau. Artful, genial, expressive, the tribute of French talent, these happy images supply, on the spot, the note without which even the most fantasticating sense of our national past would feel itself rub forever against mere brown homespun. Everything else gives way, for me, I confess, as I again stand before them; everything, whether as historic fact, or present *agrément*, or future possibility, yields to this one high luxury of our old friendship with France.

The 'artistic' Federal city already announced spreads itself then before us, in plans elaborated even to the finer details, a city of palaces and monuments and gardens, symmetries and circles and far radiations, with the big Potomac for water-power and water-effect and the recurrent Maryland spring, so prompt and so full-handed, for a perpetual benediction. This imagery has, above all, the value, for the considering mind, that it presents itself as under the wide-spread wings of the general Government, which fairly make it figure to the rapt vision as the object caught up in eagle claws and lifted into fields of air that even the high brows of the municipal boss fail to sweep. The wide-spread wings affect us, in the prospect, as great fans that, by their mere tremor, will blow the work, at all steps and stages, clean and clear, disinfect it quite ideally of any germ of the job, and prepare thereby for the American voter, on the spot and in the pride of possession, quite a new kind of civic consciousness. The scheme looms largest, surely, as a demonstration of the possibilities of that service to him, and nothing about it will be more interesting than to measure – though this may take time – the nature and degree of his alleviation. Will the new pride I speak of sufficiently inflame him? Will the taste of the new consciousness, finding him so fresh to it, prove the right medicine? One can only regret that we must still rather indefinitely wait to see – and regret it all the more that there is always, in America, yet another lively source of interest involved in the execution of such designs, and closely involved just in proportion as the high intention, the formal majesty, of the thing seems assured. It comes back to what we constantly feel, throughout the country, to what the American scene everywhere depends on for half its appeal or its effect; to the fact that the social conditions, the material, pressing and pervasive, make the particular experiment or demonstration, whatever it may pretend to, practically a new and incalculable thing. This general Americanism is often the one tag of character attaching to the case after every other appears to have abandoned it. The thing is happening, or will have to happen, in the American way – that American way which is more different from all other native ways, taking country with country, than any of these latter are different from each other; and the question is of how, each time, the American way will see it through.

The American Scene, 1907, ch. 11

The Happy Warrior

JOHN DOS PASSOS

The Roosevelts had lived for seven righteous generations on Manhattan Island; they owned a big brick house on Twentieth Street, an estate up at Dobbs Ferry, lots in the city, a pew in the Dutch Reformed Church, interests, stocks and bonds, they felt Manhattan was theirs, they felt America was theirs. Their son,

Theodore,

was a sickly youngster, suffered asthma, was very nearsighted; his hands and feet were so small it was hard for him to learn to box; his arms were very short;

his father was something of a humanitarian, gave Christmas dinners to newsboys, deplored conditions, slums, the East Side, Hell's Kitchen.

Young Theodore had ponies, was encouraged to walk in the woods, to go camping, was instructed in boxing and fencing (an American gentleman should know how to defend himself), taught Bible Class, did mission work (an American gentleman should do his best to uplift those not so fortunately situated);

righteousness was his by birth;

he had a passion for nature study, for reading about birds and wild animals, for going hunting; he got to be a good shot in spite of his glasses, a good walker in spite of his tiny feet and short legs, a fair horseman, an aggressive scrapper in spite of his short reach, a crack politician in spite of being the son of one of the owning Dutch families of New York.

In 1876 he went up to Cambridge to study at Harvard, a wealthy talkative erratic young man with sidewhiskers and definite ideas about everything under the sun;

at Harvard he drove around in a dogcart, collected stuffed birds, mounted specimens he'd shot on his trips in the Adirondacks; in spite of not drinking and being somewhat of a christer, having odd ideas about reform and remedying abuses, he made Porcellian and the Dickey and the clubs that were his right as the son of one of the owning Dutch families of New York.

He told his friends he was going to devote his life to social service: *I wish to preach not the doctrine of ignoble ease, but the doctrine of the strenuous life, the life of toil and effort, of labor and strife.*

From the time he was eleven years old he wrote copiously, filled diaries, notebooks, loose leaves, with a big impulsive scrawl about everything he did and thought and said;

naturally he studied law.

He married young and went to Switzerland to climb the Matterhorn; his first wife's early death broke him all up. He went out to the badlands of western Dakota to become a rancher on the Little Missouri River;

when he came back to Manhattan he was Teddy, the straight shooter from the West, the elkhunter, the man in the Stetson hat, who'd roped steers, fought a grizzly hand to hand, acted as Deputy Sheriff

(a Roosevelt has a duty to his country; the duty of a Roosevelt is to uplift those not so fortunately situated, those who have come more recently to our shores);

in the West, Deputy Sheriff Roosevelt felt the white man's burden, helped to arrest malefactors, badmen; service was bully.

All this time he'd been writing, filling the magazines with stories of his hunts and adventures, filling political meetings with his opinions, his denunciations, his pat phrases: Strenuous Life, Realizable Ideals, Just Government, *when men fear work or fear righteous war, when women fear motherhood, they tremble on the brink of doom, and well it is that they should vanish from the earth, where they are fit subjects for the scorn of all men and women who are themselves strong and brave and highminded.*

T. R. married a wealthy woman and righteously raised a family at Sagamore Hill.

He served a term in the New York Legislature, was appointed by Grover Cleveland to the unremunerative job of Commissioner for Civil Service Reform,

was Reform Police Commissioner of New York, pursued malefactors, stoutly maintained that white was white and black was black,

wrote the Naval History of the War of 1812,

was appointed Assistant Secretary of the Navy,

and when the *Maine* blew up resigned to lead the Rough Riders, Lieutenant-Colonel.

This was the Rubicon, the Fight, the Old Glory, the Just Cause. The American public was not kept in ignorance of the Colonel's bravery when the bullets sang, how he charged without his men up San Juan Hill and had to go back to fetch them, how he shot a running Spaniard in the tail.

It was too bad that the regulars had gotten up San Juan Hill first from the other side, that there was no need to get up San Juan Hill at all. Santiago was surrendered. It was a successful campaign. T. R. charged up San Juan Hill into the governorship of the Empire State;

but after the fighting, volunteers warcorrespondents magazinewriters began to want to go home;

it wasn't bully huddling under puptents in the tropical rain or scorching in the morning sun of the seared Cuban hills with malaria mowing them down and dysentery and always yellowjack to be afraid of.

T. R. got up a roundrobin to the President and asked for the amateur warriors to be sent home and leave the dirtywork to the regulars

who were digging trenches and shovelling crap and fighting malaria and dysentery and yellowjack

to make Cuba cozy for the Sugar Trust

and the National City Bank.

When he landed at home, one of his first interviews was with Lemuel Quigg, emissary of Boss Platt who had the votes of upstate New York sewed into the lining of his vest;

he saw Boss Platt too, but he forgot about that afterwards. Things were bully. He wrote a life of Oliver Cromwell whom people said he resembled. As Governor he doublecrossed the Platt machine (a righteous man may have a short memory); Boss Platt thought he'd shelved him by nominating him for the Vice-Presidency in 1900;

Czolgocz made him President.

T. R. drove like a fiend in a buckboard over the muddy roads through the driving rain from Mount Marcy in the Adirondacks to catch the train to Buffalo where McKinley was dying.

As President

he moved Sagamore Hill, the healthy happy normal American home, to the White House, took foreign diplomats and fat army officers out walking in Rock Creek Park, where he led them a terrible dance through brambles, hopping across the creek on steppingstones, wading the fords, scrambling up the shaly banks,

and shook the Big Stick at malefactors of great wealth.

Things were bully.

He engineered the Panama revolution under the shadow of which took place the famous hocuspocus of juggling the old and new canal companies by which forty million dollars vanished into the pockets of the international bankers,

but Old Glory floated over the Canal Zone

and the canal was cut through.

He busted a few trusts,

had Booker Washington to lunch at the White House,
and urged the conservation of wild life.

He got the Nobel Peace Prize for patching up the Peace of Portsmouth
that ended the Russo-Japanese War,

and sent the Atlantic Fleet around the world for everybody to see that
America was a firstclass power. He left the presidency to Taft after his second term leaving to that elephantine lawyer the congenial task of pouring
judicial oil on the hurt feelings of the moneymasters

and went to Africa to hunt big game.

Biggame hunting was bully.

Every time a lion or an elephant went crashing down into the jungle un-
derbrush, under the impact of a wellplaced mushroom bullet,

the papers lit up with headlines;

when he talked with the Kaiser on horseback

the world was not ignorant of what he said, or when he lectured the Na-
tionalists at Cairo telling them that this was a white man's world.

He went to Brazil where he traveled through the Matto Grosso in a dugout over waters infested with the tiny maneating fish, the piranha,

shot tapirs,

jaguars,

specimens of the whitelipped peccary.

He ran the rapids of the River of Doubt

down to the Amazon frontiers where he arrived sick, an infected abscess
in his leg, stretched out under an awning in a dugout with a tame trumpeter-
bird beside him.

Back in the States he fought his last fight when he came out for the Republican nomination in 1912 a Progressive, champion of the Square Deal, cru-
sader for the Plain People; the Bull Moose bolted out from under the Taft
steamroller and formed the Progressive Party for righteousness' sake at the
Chicago Colosseum while the delegates who were going to restore democratic government rocked with tears in their eyes as they sang

> *On   ward Christian so   old   gers*
> *March   ing   as   to   war*

Perhaps the River of Doubt had been too much for a man of his age; perhaps things weren't so bully any more; T. R. lost his voice during the triangular campaign. In Duluth a maniac shot him in the chest, his life was saved
only by the thick bundle of manuscript of the speech he was going to deliver. T. R. delivered the speech with the bullet still in him, heard the scared

applause, felt the plain people praying for his recovery, but the spell was broken somehow.

The Democrats swept in, the World War drowned out the righteous voice of the Happy Warrior in the roar of exploding lyddite.

Wilson wouldn't let T. R. lead a division, this was no amateur's war (perhaps the regulars remembered the roundrobin at Santiago). All he could do was write magazine articles against the Huns, send his sons; Quentin was killed.

It wasn't the bully amateur's world any more. Nobody knew that on Armistice Day, Theodore Roosevelt, happy amateur warrior with the grinning teeth, the shaking forefinger, naturalist, explorer, magazinewriter, Sundayschool teacher, cowpuncher, moralist, politician, righteous orator with a short memory, fond of denouncing liars (the Ananias Club) and having pillowfights with his children, was taken to the Roosevelt Hospital gravely ill with inflammatory rheumatism.

Things weren't bully any more;

T. R. had grit;

he bore the pain, the obscurity, the sense of being forgotten as he had borne the grilling portages when he was exploring the River of Doubt, the heat, the fetid jungle mud, the infected abscess in his leg,

and died quietly in his sleep

at Sagamore Hill

on January 6, 1919

and left on the shoulders of his sons

the white man's burden.

1919, 1932

Vive le Roi!

H. L. MENCKEN

The abdication of Congress is certainly not as overt and abject as that of the German Reichstag or the Italian Parliamento; nevertheless, it has gone so far that the constitutional potency of the legislative arm is reduced to what the lawyers call a nuisance value. The two Houses can still make faces at Dr Roosevelt, and when a strong body of public opinion happens to stand behind them they can even force him, in this detail or that, into a kind of accounting, but it must be manifest that if they tried to impose their will upon him in any major matter he could beat them easily. The only will left in the national government is his will. To all intents and purposes he is the state.

We have thus come to a sort of antithesis of the English system, under which Parliament is omnipotent and the King is only a falseface. It would be rather absurd to call the change revolutionary, for it has been under way for more than a hundred years. Since Jackson's first election, in fact, Congress has always knuckled down to the President in times of national emergency. After 1863 Lincoln ruled like an oriental despot, and after 1917 Wilson set himself up, not only as Emperor, but also as Pope. In 1864, as antiquaries familiar with *Ex parte* Merryman will recall, the Supreme Court undertook to bring old Abe to book, but as the same antiquaries know, it had to confess in the end that it could do nothing.

There is no likehood that it will intervene in the present situation. For one thing, there seems to be no public demand that it do so. For another thing, judges as a class are naturally sympathetic toward arbitrary power, for their own authority rests upon it. Thus there seems to be every probability that Dr Roosevelt will continue to operate as an absolute monarch, at least for some time to come. If the schemes of salvation concocted by his Brain Trust, *i.e.*, by the King in Council, appear to be working, then no one save a few touchy Senators will want to depose him. And if we continue wandering in the wilderness, with our shirttails out and the hot sun scorching our necks, then most Americans will probably hold that it is better to go on following one leader, however bad, than to start scrambling after a couple of hundred of them, each with a different compass.

My gifts as a constructive critic are of low visibility, but the state of affairs thus confronting the country prompts me to make a simple suggestion. It is that a convention be called under Article V of the Constitution, and that it consider the desirability of making Dr Roosevelt King in name as well as in fact. There is no Constitutional impediment to such a change, and it would thus not amount to a revolution. The people of the United States are quite as free, under Article V, to establish a monarchy as they were to give the vote to women. Even if it be held, as some argue, that the Bill of Rights is inviolable and cannot be changed by constitutional amendment, it may be answered that there is nothing in the Bill of Rights requiring that the national government shall be republican in form.

The advantages that would lie in making Dr Roosevelt King must be plain to everyone. His great difficulty today is that he is candidate for reëlection in 1936, and must shape all his acts with that embarrassing fact in mind. Even with a docile Congress awaiting his orders he cannot carry on with a really free hand, for there remains a minority in that Congress which may, soon or late, by the arts of the demagogue, convince the public, or a large part of it, that what he is doing is dangerous, and so his reëlection may be imperiled. To meet and circumvent this peril he must play the demagogue himself, which is to say, he must only too often subordinate what he believes to be wise to what he believes to be popular.

It is a cruel burden to lay upon a man facing a multitude of appalling problems, some of them probably next door to insoluble. No other man of genuine responsibility under our system of government is called upon to bear it. It lies, to be sure, upon Congressmen, but Congressmen, after all, are minor functionaries, and no one has expected them, these hundred years past, to be wise. We try to lighten it for Senators, who are a cut higher, by giving them six-year terms and so postponing their ordeal by ballot, and we remove it altogether for Federal judges by letting them sit during good behavior. But the President has to go on the auction block every four years, and the fact fills his mind and limits his freedom of action from the moment he takes the oath of office.

I am not a Roosevelt fanatic, certainly, though I voted for the right hon. gentleman last November, and even printed a few discreet pieces arguing that he might be worse. But it must be manifest that, in any situation as full of dynamite as the present one, it is a great advantage to have a leader who can devote his whole time and thought to the problems before him, without any consideration of extraneous matters. Yet that is precisely what, under our present system, a President cannot do. He is forced, at every moment of his first term, to remember that he may be thrown out at the end of it, and it is thus no wonder that his concern often wobbles him, and makes him a too easy mark for the political blackmailers who constantly threaten him.

If his term were unlimited, or limited only by his good behavior – in brief, if he were in the position of an elected King – he would get rid of all this nuisance, and be free to apply himself to his business. I believe that any man, under such circumstances, would do immensely better than he could possibly do under the present system. And I believe that Dr Roosevelt, in particular, would be worth at least ten times what he is worth now, for he is a good enough politician to know that his current high and feverish popularity cannot last, democracy being what it is, and that the only way he can save himself in 1936 is by forgetting the Depression once or twice a day, and applying himself to very practical politics.

What this division of aim and interest amounts to is shown brilliantly by some of his appointments. He has made a plain effort to surround himself with men in whose competence and good faith he can put his trust, but he has been forced by the exigencies of his uncomfortable situation to give a number of important posts to political plugs of the most depressing sort. These plugs were too powerful to be flouted, and now that they are in office they are even more powerful than before. If they remain they will disgrace the administration soon or late, and if they are turned out they will imperil it in 1936. An elected King could rid himself of them at once, and they could do him no damage, now or hereafter.

The objections to monarchy are mainly sentimental, and do not bear up well under inspection. I shall rehearse some of them at length in a future article, and try to show how hollow they are. Suffice it for the moment to glance at a few of them. One is the objection that a King, once in office, can't be got rid of. The answer is that Kings are got rid of very often, and usually very easily, and that the same constitutional convention which provided one for the United States might also provide for his ready impeachment and removal, and even for his lawful and Christian execution.

Another objection is that the problem of the succession is hard to solve, and that any King that we set up would probably want his son to succeed him, and would root for that son exactly as a President in his first term now roots for himself, and in his second term for some favorite in his entourage. Well, why not? I believe that a Crown Prince, brought up in his father's office, is likely to make at least as good a King as any other fellow. Moreover, is it so soon forgotten that Dr Roosevelt himself came in as a sort of Crown Prince? – though I should add that he was challenged by a Legitimist party led *de jure* by the Young Pretender, Prince Theodore Minor, and *de facto* by Princess Alice. If His Excellency's name were Kelly, Kraus or Kaminsky would he be in the White House today? To ask the question is to answer it. Despite the theory that Americans fear and abhor the hereditary principle they have elected one President's son to the Presidency, one President's grandson and one President's cousin, and in at least two other instances they have made motions in the same direction. This is five times in thirty-one times at the bat, or nearly one in six.

But the succession is really a minor matter. I see no objection to letting the sitting King nominate three candidates, and then choosing between them, by plebiscite, at his death. His nominations, at worst, would be far better than any that professional politicians could or would make, and three nominees would give the voters sufficient choice. There remains the problem of starting the ball rolling. But that problem, as I have sought to show, is already solved. We have a King in the White House at this minute, and he is quite as much of the Blood Royal as George V. All that remains is to call a constitutional convention, and, as it were, make an honest woman of him.

Baltimore Evening Sun, 1 May 1933

'Four essential freedoms'

FRANKLIN DELANO ROOSEVELT

In the future days, which we seek to make secure, we look forward to a world founded upon four essential human freedoms.

The first is freedom of speech and expression – everywhere in the world.

The second is freedom of every person to worship God in his own way – everywhere in the world.

The third is freedom from want – which, translated into world terms, means economic understandings which will secure to every nation a healthy peacetime life for its inhabitants – everywhere in the world.

The fourth is freedom from fear – which, translated into world terms, means a world-wide reduction of armaments to such a point and in such a thorough fashion that no nation will be in a position to commit an act of physical aggression against any neighbor – anywhere in the world.

That is no vision of a distant millennium. It is a definite basis for a kind of world attainable in our own time and generation. That kind of world is the very antithesis of the so-called new order of tyranny which the dictators seek to create with the crash of a bomb.

To that new order we oppose the greater conception – the moral order. A good society is able to face schemes of world domination and foreign revolutions alike without fear.

Since the beginning of our American history, we have been engaged in change – in a perpetual peaceful revolution – a revolution which goes on steadily, quietly adjusting itself to changing conditions – without the concentration camp or the quick-lime in the ditch. The world order which we seek is the cooperation of free countries, working together in a friendly, civilized society.

This nation has placed its destiny in the hands and heads and hearts of its millions of free men and women; and its faith in freedom under the guidance of God. Freedom means the supremacy of human rights everywhere. Our support goes to those who struggle to gain those rights or keep them. Our strength is our unity of purpose.

To that high concept there can be no end save victory.

Message to Congress, 6 January 1941

For the Union Dead

ROBERT LOWELL

'Relinquunt Omnia Servare Rem Publicam.'

The old South Boston Aquarium stands
in a Sahara of snow now. Its broken windows are boarded.
The bronze weathervane cod has lost half its scales.
The airy tanks are dry.

Once my nose crawled like a snail on the glass;
my hand tingled
to burst the bubbles
drifting from the noses of the cowed, compliant fish.

My hand draws back. I often sigh still
for the dark downward and vegetating kingdom
of the fish and reptile. One morning last March,
I pressed against the new barbed and galvanized

fence on the Boston Common. Behind their cage,
yellow dinosaur steamshovels were grunting
as they cropped up tons of mush and grass
to gouge their underworld garage.

Parking spaces luxuriate like civic
sandpiles in the heart of Boston.
A girdle of orange, Puritan-pumpkin colored girders
braces the tingling Statehouse,

shaking over the excavations, as it faces Colonel Shaw
and his bell-cheeked Negro infantry
on St Gaudens' shaking Civil War relief,
propped by a plank splint against the garage's earthquake.

Two months after marching through Boston,
half the regiment was dead;
at the dedication,
William James could almost hear the bronze Negroes breathe.

Their monument sticks like a fishbone
in the city's throat.
Its Colonel is as lean
as a compass-needle.

He has an angry wrenlike vigilance,
a greyhound's gentle tautness;
he seems to wince at pleasure,
and suffocate for privacy.

He is out of bounds now. He rejoices in man's lovely,
peculiar power to choose life and die –
when he leads his black soldiers to death,
he cannot bend his back.

On a thousand small town New England greens,
the old white churches hold their air
of sparse, sincere rebellion; frayed flags
quilt the graveyards of the Grand Army of the Republic.

The stone statues of the abstract Union Soldier
grow slimmer and younger each year –
wasp-wasted, they doze over muskets
and muse through their sideburns . . .

Shaw's father wanted no monument
except the ditch,
where his son's body was thrown
and lost with his 'niggers'.

The ditch is nearer.
There are no statues for the last war here;
on Boylston Street, a commercial photograph
shows Hiroshima boiling

over a Mosler Safe, the 'Rock of Ages'
that survived the blast. Space is nearer.
When I crouch to my television set,
the drained faces of Negro school-children rise like balloons.

Colonel Shaw
is riding on his bubble,
he waits
for the blessèd break.

The Aquarium is gone. Everywhere,
giant finned cars nose forward like fish;
a savage servility
slides by on grease.

For the Union Dead, 1964

'The black man'

MALCOLM X

I felt a challenge to plan, and build, an organization that could help to cure the black man in North America of the sickness which has kept him under the white man's heel.

The black man in North America was mentally sick in his cooperative, sheeplike acceptance of the white man's culture.

The black man in North America was spiritually sick because for centuries he had accepted the white man's Christianity – which asked the black so-called Christian to expect no true Brotherhood of Man, but to endure the cruelties of the white so-called Christians. Christianity had made black men fuzzy, nebulous, confused in their thinking. It had taught the black man to think if he had no shoes, and was hungry, 'we gonna get shoes and milk and honey and fish fries in Heaven.'

The black man in North America was economically sick and that was evident in one simple fact: as a consumer, he got less than his share, and as a producer gave *least*. The black American today shows us the perfect parasite image – the black tick under the delusion that he is progressing because he rides on the udder of the fat, three-stomached cow that is white America. For instance, annually, the black man spends over $3 billion for automobiles, but America contains hardly any franchised black automobile dealers. For instance, forty per cent of the expensive imported Scotch whisky consumed in America goes down the throats of the status-sick black man; but the only black-owned distilleries are in bathtubs, or in the woods somewhere. Or for instance – a scandalous shame – in New York City, with over a million Negroes, there aren't twenty black-owned businesses employing over ten people. It's because black men don't own and control their own community's retail establishments that they can't stabilize their own community.

The black man in North America was sickest of all politically. He let the white man divide him into such foolishness as considering himself a black 'Democrat', a black 'Republican', a black 'Conservative', or a black 'Liberal' . . . when a ten-million black vote bloc could be the deciding balance of power in American politics, because the white man's vote is almost always evenly divided. The polls are one place where every black man could fight the black man's cause with dignity, and with the power and the tools that the white man understands, and respects, and fears, and cooperates with. Listen, let me tell you something! If a black bloc committee told Washington's worst 'nigger-hater', 'We represent ten million votes,' why, that 'nigger-hater' would leap up: 'Well, how *are* you? Come on *in* here!'

Why, if the Mississippi black man voted in a bloc, Eastland would pretend to be more liberal than Jacob Javits – or Eastland would not survive in his office. Why else is it that racist politicians fight to keep black men from the polls?

Whenever any group can vote in a bloc, and decide the outcome of elections, and it *fails* to do this, then that group is politically sick. Immigrants once made Tammany Hall the most powerful single force in American politics. In 1880, New York City's first Irish Catholic Mayor was elected and by 1960 America had its first Irish Catholic President. America's black man, voting as a bloc, could wield an even more powerful force.

US politics is ruled by special-interest blocs and lobbies. What group has a more urgent special interest, what group needs a bloc, a lobby, more than the black man? Labor owns one of Washington's largest non-government buildings – situated where they can literally watch the White House – and no political move is made that doesn't involve how Labor feels about it. A lobby got Big Oil its depletion allowance. The farmer, through his lobby, is the most government-subsidized special-interest group in America today, because a million farmers vote, not as Democrats, or Republicans, liberals, conservatives, but as farmers.

Doctors have the best lobby in Washington. Their special-interest influence successfully fights the Medicare program that's wanted, and needed, by millions of other people. Why, there's a Beet Growers' Lobby! A Wheat Lobby! A Cattle Lobby! A China Lobby! Little countries no one ever heard of have their Washington lobbies, representing their special interests.

The government has departments to deal with the special-interest groups that make themselves heard and felt. A Department of Agriculture cares for the farmers' needs. There is a Department of Health, Education and Welfare. There is a Department of the Interior – in which the Indians are included. Is the farmer, the doctor, the Indian, the greatest problem in America today? No – it is the black man! There ought to be a Pentagon-sized Washington department dealing with every segment of the black man's problems.

Twenty-two million black men! They have given America four hundred years of toil; they have bled and died in every battle since the Revolution; they were in America before the Pilgrims, and long before the mass immigrations – and they are still today at the bottom of everything!

Why, twenty-two million black people should tomorrow give a dollar apiece to build a skyscraper lobby building in Washington, D.C. Every morning, every legislator should receive a communication about what the black man in America expects and wants and needs. The demanding voice of the black lobby should be in the ears of every legislator who votes on any issue.

The cornerstones of this country's operation are economic and political strength and power. The black man doesn't have the economic strength – and it will take time for him to build it. But right now the American black man has the political strength and power to change his destiny overnight.

The Autobiography of Malcom X, 1965, ch. 16

BELIEFS

Congress shall make no law respecting an establishment of religion, or prohibiting the free exercise thereof; or abridging the freedom of speech, or of the press; or the right of the people peaceably to assemble, and to petition the Government for a redress of grievances.

First Amendment to the Constitution, 1791

There is nothing wrong with Americans except their ideals. The real American is all right; it is the ideal American who is all wrong.

G. K. Chesterton, *New York Times*, 1 February 1931

America the Beautiful

KATHERINE LEE BATES

O beautiful for spacious skies,
    For amber waves of grain,
For purple mountain majesties
    Above the fruited plain!
      America! America!
    God shed His grace on thee
And crown thy good with brotherhood
    From sea to shining sea!

O beautiful for pilgrim feet,
    Whose stern, impassioned stress
A thoroughfare for freedom beat
    Across the wilderness!
      America! America!
    God mend thine every flaw,
Confirm thy soul in self-control,
    Thy liberty in law!

O beautiful for heroes proved
    In liberating strife,
Who more than self their country loved,
    And mercy more than life!
      America! America!
    May God thy gold refine
Till all success be nobleness
    And every gain divine!

O beautiful for patriot dream
    That sees beyond the years
Thine alabaster cities gleam
    Undimmed by human tears!
      America! America!
    God shed His grace on thee
And crown thy good with brotherhood
    From sea to shining sea!

1893

'The source from which they came'

NATIVE AMERICAN (OSAGE)

Way beyond, a part of the Osage lived in the sky. They desired to know their origin, the source from which they came into existence. They went to the sun. He told them that they were his children. Then they wandered still farther and came to the moon. She told them that she gave birth to them, and that the sun was their father. She told them that they must leave their present abode and go down to the earth and dwell there. They came to the earth, but found it covered with water. They could not return to the place they had left, so they wept, but no answer came to them from anywhere. They floated about in the air, seeking in every direction for help from some god; but they found none. The animals were with them, and of all these the elk was the finest and most stately, and inspired all the creatures with confidence; so they appealed to the elk for help. He dropped into the water and began to sink. Then he called to the winds, and the winds came from all quarters and blew until the waters went upward as in a mist.

At first rocks only were exposed, and the people traveled on the rocky places that produced no plants, and there was nothing to eat. Then the waters began to go down until the soft earth was exposed. When this happened, the elk in his joy rolled over and over on the soft earth, and all his loose hairs clung to the soil. The hairs grew, and from them sprang beans, corns, potatoes, and wild turnips, and then all the grasses and trees.

The Omaha Tribe, trans. Alice Fletcher and Francis La Flesche, 1905–6

'As a City upon a hill'

JOHN WINTHROP

[Written on board the Arbella *before the landing of the Puritans in New England]*

Now the only way to avoid this shipwreck, and to provide for our posterity, is to follow the counsel of Micah, *to do justly, to love mercy, to walk humbly with our God.* For this end we must be knit together in this work as one man. We must entertain each other in brotherly affection. We must be willing to abridge ourselves of our superfluities, for the supply of others' necessities. We must uphold a familiar commerce together in all meekness, gentleness, patience, and liberality. We must delight in each other; make other's condition our own; rejoice together, mourn together, labor and suffer together, always having before our eyes our commission and community in the work, as members of the same body. So shall we *keep the unity of the spirit in the bond of peace.* The Lord will be our God, and delight to dwell among us, as his own people, and will command a blessing upon us in all our ways. So that we shall see much more of his wisdom, power, goodness and truth, than formerly we have been acquainted with. We shall find that the God of Israel is among us, when ten of us shall be able to resist a thousand of our enemies; when he shall make us a praise and glory that men shall say of succeeding plantations, 'The Lord make it likely that of *New England.*' For we must consider that we shall be as a City upon a hill. The eyes of all people are upon us. So that if we shall deal falsely with our God in this work we have undertaken, and so cause him to withdraw his present help from us, we shall be made a story and a by-word through the world. We shall open the mouths of enemies to speak evil of the ways of God and all professors for God's sake. We shall shame the faces of many of God's worthy servants, and cause their prayers to be turned into curses upon us till we be consumed out of the good land whither we are a-going.

'A Model of Christian Charity' (wr. 1630), 1792

On Being Brought from Africa to America

PHILLIS WHEATLEY

'Twas mercy brought me from my *Pagan* land,
Taught my benighted soul to understand
That there's a God, that there's a *Saviour* too:
Once I redemption neither sought nor knew.
Some view our sable race with scornful eye,
'Their colour is a diabolic die.'
Remember, *Christians*, *Negroes*, black as *Cain*,
May be refin'd, and join th' angelic train.

1773

'Back to Nature'

THOMAS PAINE

What Archimedes said of the mechanical powers, may be applied to Reason and Liberty: '*Had we*', said he, '*a place to stand upon, we might raise the world.*'

The revolution of America presented in politics what was only theory in mechanics. So deeply rooted were all the governments of the old world, and so effectually had the tyranny and the antiquity of habit established itself over the mind, that no beginning could be made in Asia, Africa, or Europe, to reform the political condition of man. Freedom had been hunted round the globe; reason was considered as rebellion; and the slavery of fear had made men afraid to think.

But such is the irresistible nature of truth, that all it asks, and all it wants, is the liberty of appearing. The sun needs no inscription to distinguish him from darkness; and no sooner did the American governments display themselves to the world, than despotism felt a shock, and man began to contemplate redress.

The independence of America, considered merely as a separation from England, would have been a matter but of little importance, had it not been accompanied by a revolution in the principles and practice of governments. She made a stand, not for herself only, but for the world, and looked beyond the advantages herself could receive. Even the Hessian, though hired to fight against her, may live to bless his defeat; and England, condemning the viciousness of its government, rejoice in its miscarriage.

As America was the only spot in the political world, where the principles of universal reformation could begin, so also was it the best in the natural world. An assemblage of circumstances conspired, not only to give birth, but to add gigantic maturity to its principles. The scene which that country presents to the eye of a spectator, has something in it which generates and encourages great ideas. Nature appears to him in magnitude. The mighty objects he beholds, act upon his mind by enlarging it, and he partakes of the greatness he contemplates. – Its first settlers were emigrants from different European nations, and of diversified professions of religion, retiring from the governmental persecutions of the old world, and meeting in the new, not as enemies, but as brothers. The wants which necessarily accompany the cultivation of a wilderness produced among them a state of society, which countries, long harassed by the quarrels and intrigues of governments, had neglected to cherish. In such a situation man becomes what he ought. He sees his species, not with the inhuman idea of a natural enemy, but as kindred; and the example shows to the artificial world, that man must go back to Nature for information.

Introduction to The Rights of Man, *1792, part 2*

'A different religion'

SA-GO-YE-WAT-HA (RED JACKET)

[Response of the Seneca chief to a missionary at Buffalo Creek, New York in 1805]

BROTHER: Listen to what we say. There was a time when our forefathers owned this great island. Their seats extended from the rising to the setting sun. The Great Spirit had made it for the use of Indians. He had created the buffalo, the deer, and other animals for food. He had made the bear and the beaver. Their skins served us for clothing. He had scattered them over the country, and taught us how to take them. He had caused the earth to produce corn for bread. All this He had done for his red children, because He loved them. If we had some disputes about our hunting ground, they were generally settled without the shedding of much blood. But an evil day came upon us. Your forefathers crossed the great water and landed on this island. Their numbers were small. They found friends and not enemies. They told us they had fled from their own country for fear of wicked men, and had come here to enjoy their religion. They asked for a small seat. We took pity on them, granted their request; and they sat down amongst us. We gave them corn and meat; they gave us poison [rum] in return.

The white people, BROTHER, had now found our country. Tidings were carried back, and more came amongst us. Yet we did not fear them. We took them to be friends. They called us brothers. We believed them and gave them a larger seat. At length their numbers had greatly increased. They wanted more land; they wanted our country. Our eyes were opened, and our minds became uneasy. Wars took place. Indians were hired to fight against Indians, and many of our people were destroyed. They also brought strong liquor amongst us. It was strong and powerful, and has slain thousands.

BROTHER: Our seats were once large and yours were small. You have now become a great people, and we have scarcely a place left to spread our blankets. You have got our country, but are not satisfied; you want to force your religion upon us.

BROTHER: Continue to listen. You say that you are sent to instruct us how to worship the Great Spirit agreeably to his mind, and, if we do not take hold of the religion which you white people teach, we shall be unhappy hereafter. You say that you are right and we are lost. How do we know this to be true? We understand that your religion is written in a book. If it was intended for us as well as you, why has not the Great Spirit given to us, and not only to us, but why did he not give to our forefathers, the knowledge of that book, with the means of understanding it rightly? We only know what you tell us about it. How shall we know when to believe, being so often deceived by the white people?

BROTHER: You say there is but one way to worship and serve the Great Spirit. If there is but one religion, why do you white people differ so much about it? Why not all agreed, as you can all read the book?

BROTHER: We do not understand these things. We are told that your religion was given to your forefathers, and has been handed down from father to son. We also have a religion, which was given to our forefathers, and has been handed down to us their children. We worship in that way. It teaches us to be thankful for all the favors we receive; to love each other, and to be united. We never quarrel about religion.

BROTHER: The Great Spirit has made us all, but He has made a great difference between his white and red children. He has given us different complexions and different customs. To you He has given the arts. To these He has not opened our eyes. We know these things to be true. Since He has made so great a difference between us in other things, why may we not conclude that He has given us a different religion according to our understanding? The Great Spirit does right. He knows what is best for his children; we are satisfied.

BROTHER: We do not wish to destroy your religion, or take it from you. We only want to enjoy our own.

BROTHER: You say you have not come to get our land or our money, but to enlighten our minds. I will now tell you that I have been at your meetings, and saw you collect money from the meeting. I cannot tell what this money was intended for, but suppose that it was for your minister, and if we should conform to your way of thinking, perhaps you may want some from us.

BROTHER: We are told that you have been preaching to the white people in this place. These people are our neighbors. We are acquainted with them. We will wait a little while, and see what effect your preaching has upon them. If we find it does them good, makes them honest and less disposed to cheat Indians, we will then consider again of what you have said.

BROTHER: You have now heard our answer to your talk, and this is all we have to say at present. As we are going to part, we will come and take

you by the hand, and hope the Great Spirit will protect you on your journey, and return you safe to your friends.

William L. Stone, *Life and Times*, 1841

'Devout without being unjust'

SYDNEY SMITH

A lesson upon the importance of Religious Toleration, we are determined,
it would seem, *not* to learn, – either from America or from any other quarter of the globe. The High Sheriff of New York, last year, was a Jew. It was
with the utmost difficulty that a bill was carried this year to allow the first
Duke of England to carry a gold stick before the King – because he was a
Catholic! – and yet we think ourselves entitled to indulge in impertinent
sneers at America, – as if civilisation did not depend more upon making
wise laws for the promotion of human happiness, than in having good inns,
and post-horses, and civil waiters.

*

In fact, it is hardly possible for any nation to show a greater superiority
over another than the Americans, in this particular, have done over this
country. They have fairly and completely, and probably for ever, extin-
guished that spirit of religious persecution which has been the employment
and the curse of mankind for four or five centuries, – not only that persecution which imprisons and scourges for religious opinions, but the tyranny
of incapacitation, which, by disqualifying from civil offices, and cutting a
man off from the lawful objects of ambition, endeavours to strangle religious freedom in silence, and to enjoy all the advantages, without the blood,
and noise, and fire of persecution. What passes in the mind of one mean
blockhead is the general history of all persecution. 'This man pretends to
know better than me – I cannot subdue him by argument; but I will take
care he shall never be major or alderman of the town in which he lives; I
will never consent to the repeal of the Test Act or to Catholic emancipation;
I will teach the fellow to differ from me in religious opinions!' So says the
Episcopalian to the Catholic – and so the Catholic says to the Protestant.
But the wisdom of America keeps them all down – secures to them all their
just rights – gives to each of them their separate pews, and bells, and stee-
ples – makes them all aldermen in their turns – and quietly extinguishes the
faggots which each is preparing for the combustion of the other. Nor is this
indifference to religious subjects in the American people, but pure civilisa-

tion – a thorough comprehension of what is best calculated to secure the public happiness and peace – and a determination that this happiness and peace shall not be violated by the insolence of any human being, in the garb, and under the sanction, of religion. In this particular, the Americans are at the head of all the nations of the world: and at the same time they are, especially in the Eastern and Midland States, so far from being indifferent on subjects of religion, that they may be most justly characterised as a very religious people: but they are devout without being unjust (the great problem in religion); an higher proof of civilisation than painted tea-cups, waterproof leather, or broad cloth at two guineas a yard.

Edinburgh Review, July 1824

'Liberty, daughter of enlightenment'

FRANÇOIS RENÉ DE CHATEAUBRIAND

The Abbé Raynal had proposed a prize for the solution to this question: 'What will be the influence of the discovery of the New World on the Old World?'

The writers lost themselves in calculations relative to the exportation and importation of metals, the depopulation of Spain, the growth of commerce, the perfecting of navies: no one, as far as I know, sought the influence of the discovery of America on Europe in the establishment of the American republics. They still saw only the old monarchies just about as they were, society stationary, human spirit neither advancing nor retreating; they had not the least idea of the revolution which in the space of forty years took place in men's minds.

The most precious of the treasures that America held in her breast was liberty; each people is called upon to draw from this inexhaustible mine. The discovery of the representative republic in the United States is one of the greatest political events in the world. That event has proved, as I have said elsewhere, that there are two types of practical liberty. One belongs to the infancy of nations; it is the daughter of manners and virtue – it is that of the first Greeks, the first Romans, and that of the savages of America. The other is born out of the old age of nations; it is the daughter of enlightenment and reason – it is this liberty of the United States which replaces the liberty of the Indian. Happy land which in the space of less than three centuries has passed from the one liberty to the other almost without effort, and that by a battle lasting no more than eight years!

Will America preserve her second kind of liberty? Will not the United

States divide? Can we not see already the seeds of that division? Has not a representative of Virginia already defended the thesis of the old Greek and Roman liberty with the system of slavery, against a representative of Massachusetts who defended the cause of modern liberty without slaves, such as Christianity has made it?

The western states, extending more and more, too far away from the Atlantic states, will they not want a separate government?

Finally, are Americans perfect men? Do they not have their vices as do other men? Are they morally superior to the English from whom they draw their origin? This foreign immigration that constantly flows into their population from all parts of Europe, will it not at length destroy the homogeneity of their race? Will not the mercantile spirit dominate them? Will not self-interest begin to be the dominant national fault?

*

Whatever the future, liberty will never entirely disappear from America; and it is here that we must point out one of the great advantages of liberty, daughter of enlightenment, over liberty, daughter of manners.

Liberty, daughter of manners, disappears where her principle is altered, and it is of the nature of manners to deteriorate with time. Liberty, daughter of manners, begins before despotism in the days of obscurity and poverty; she finally is lost in the centuries of brilliance and luxury. Liberty, daughter of enlightenment, shines after the ages of oppression and corruption; she walks with the principle that preserves and renews her; the enlightenment of which she is the effect, far from weakening with time, as do the manners that give birth to the first liberty, the enlightenment, I say, fortifies itself rather with time; thus it does not abandon the liberty it has produced; always in the company of that liberty, it is at the same time the generative virtue and the inexhaustible source of liberty.

Finally, the United States has another safeguard: its population occupies only an eighteenth of its territory. America still inhabits solitude; for a long time yet her wilderness will be her manners, and her enlightenment will be her liberty.

'The United States Today' in *Travels in America*, 1827;
trans. Richard Switzer, 1969

'Forever untamable *Nature*'

HENRY DAVID THOREAU

Perhaps I most fully realized that this was primeval, untamed, and forever untamable *Nature*, or whatever else men call it, while coming down this part of the mountain. We were passing over 'Burnt Lands', burnt by lightning, perchance, though they showed no recent marks of fire, hardly so much as a charred stump, but looked rather like a natural pasture for the moose and deer, exceedingly wild and desolate, with occasional strips of timber crossing them, and low poplars springing up, and patches of blueberries here and there. I found myself traversing them familiarly, like some pasture run to waste, or partially reclaimed by man; but when I reflected what man, what brother or sister or kinsman of our race made it and claimed it, I expected the proprietor to rise up and dispute my passage. It is difficult to conceive of a region uninhabited by man. We habitually presume his presence and influence everywhere. And yet we have not seen pure Nature, unless we have seen her thus vast and drear and unhuman, though in the midst of cities. Nature was here something savage and awful, though beautiful. I looked with awe at the ground I trod on, to see what the Powers had made there, the form and fashion and material of their work. This was that Earth of which we have heard, made out of Chaos and Old Night. Here was no man's garden, but the unhandselled globe. It was not lawn, nor pasture, nor mead, nor woodland, nor lea, nor arable, nor waste land. It was the fresh and natural surface of the planet Earth, as it was made forever and ever – to be the dwelling of man, we say – so Nature made it, and man may use it if he can. Man was not to be associated with it. It was Matter, vast, terrific – not his Mother Earth that we have heard of, not for him to tread on, or be buried in – no, it were being too familiar even to let his bones lie there – the home, this, of Necessity and Fate. There was man nearer of kin to the rocks and to wild animals than we. We walked over it with a certain awe, stopping, from time to time, to pick the blueberries which grew there, and had a smart and spicy taste. Perchance where *our* wild pines stand, and leaves lie on their forest floor, in Concord, there were once reapers, and husbandmen planted grain; but here not even the surface had been scarred by man, but it was a specimen of what God saw fit to make this world. What is it to be admitted to a museum, to see a myriad of particular things, compared with being shown some star's surface, some hard matter in its home! I stand in awe of my body, this matter to which I am bound has become so strange to me. I fear not spirits, ghosts, of which I am one – *that* my body might – but I fear bodies, I tremble to meet them. What is this Titan that has possession of me? Talk of mysteries! Think of our life in nature – daily to be shown matter, to come in contact with it – rocks, trees, wind on our cheeks! the *solid* earth! the *actual* world! the *common sense*! *Contact! Contact! Who* are we? *where* are we?

'Ktaadn' (wr. 1848) in *The Maine Woods*, 1864

'A night in the back woods'

FRANCES TROLLOPE

It was in the course of this summer that I found the opportunity I had long wished for, of attending a camp-meeting, and I gladly accepted the invitation of an English lady and gentleman to accompany them in their carriage to the spot where it is held; this was in a wild district in the confines of Indiana.

The prospect of passing a night in the back woods of Indiana was by no means agreeable, but I screwed my courage to the proper pitch, and set forth determined to see with my own eyes, and hear with my own ears, what a camp-meeting really was. I had heard it said that being at a camp-meeting was like standing at the gate of heaven, and seeing it opening before you; I had heard it said, that being at a camp-meeting was like finding yourself within the gates of hell; in either case there must be something to gratify curiosity, and compensate one for the fatigue of a long rumbling ride and a sleepless night.

We reached the ground about an hour before midnight, and the approach to it was highly picturesque. The spot chosen was the verge of an unbroken forest, where a space of about twenty acres appeared to have been partially cleared for the purpose. Tents of different sizes were pitched very near together in a circle round the cleared space; behind them were ranged an exterior circle of carriages of every description, and at the back of each were fastened the horses which had drawn them hither. Through this triple circle of defence we distinguished numerous fires burning brightly within it; and still more numerous lights flickering from the trees that were left in the enclosure. The moon was in meridian splendour above our heads.

We left the carriage to the care of a servant, who was to prepare a bed in it for Mrs B and me, and entered the inner circle. The first glance reminded me of Vauxhall, from the effect of the lights among the trees, and the moving crowd below them; but the second shewed a scene totally unlike any thing I had ever witnessed. Four high frames, constructed in the form of altars, were placed at the four corners of the enclosure; on these were supported layers of earth and sod, on which burned immense fires of blazing pine-wood. On one side a rude platform was erected to accommodate the preachers, fifteen of whom attended this meeting, and with very short intervals for necessary refreshment and private devotion, preached in rotation, day and night, from Tuesday to Saturday.

When we arrived, the preachers were silent; but we heard issuing from nearly every tent mingled sounds of praying, preaching, singing, and lamentation. The curtains in front of each tent were dropped, and the faint light that gleamed through the white drapery, backed as it was by the dark forest, had a beautiful and mysterious effect, that set the imagination at work; and had the sounds which vibrated around us been less discordant, harsh, and unnatural, I should have enjoyed it; but listening at the corner of a tent, which poured forth more than its proportion of clamour, in a few moments chased every feeling derived from imagination, and furnished realities that could neither be mistaken or forgotten.

Great numbers of persons were walking about the ground, who appeared like ourselves to be present only as spectators; some of these very unceremoniously contrived to raise the drapery of this tent, at one corner, so as to afford us a perfect view of the interior.

The floor was covered with straw, which round the sides was heaped in masses, that might serve as seats, but which at that moment were used to support the heads and the arms of the close-packed circle of men and women who kneeled on the floor.

Out of about thirty persons thus placed, perhaps half a dozen were men. One of these, a handsome looking youth of eighteen or twenty, kneeled just below the opening through which I looked. His arm was encircling the neck of a young girl who knelt beside him, with her hair hanging dishevelled upon her shoulders, and her features working with the most violent agitation; soon after they both fell forward on the straw, as if unable to endure in any other attitude the burning eloquence of a tall grim figure in black, who, standing erect in the centre, was uttering with incredible vehemence an oration that seemed to hover between praying and preaching; his arms hung stiff and immoveable by his side, and he looked like an ill-constructed machine, set in action by a movement so violent, as to threaten its own destruction, so jerkingly, painfully, yet rapidly, did his words tumble out; the kneeling circle ceasing not to call in every variety of tone, on the name of Jesus; accompanied with sobs, groans, and a sort of low howling inexpressibly painful to listen to. But my attention was speedily withdrawn from the preacher, and the circle round him, by a figure which knelt alone at some distance; it was a living image of Scott's Macbriar, as young, as wild, and as terrible. His thin arms tossed above his head, had forced themselves so far out of his sleeves, that they were bare to the elbow; his large eyes glared frightfully, and he continued to scream without an instant's intermission the word 'Glory!' with a violence that seemed to swell every vein to bursting. It was too dreadful to look upon long, and we turned away shuddering.

We made the circuit of the tents, pausing where attention was particularly excited by sounds more vehement than ordinary. We contrived to look into many; all were strewed with straw, and the distorted figures that we saw kneeling, sitting, and lying amongst it, joined to the woeful and convulsive cries, gave to each, the air of a cell in Bedlam.

One tent was occupied exclusively by Negroes. They were all full-dressed, and looked exactly as if they were performing a scene on the stage. One woman wore a dress of pink gauze trimmed with silver lace; another was dressed in pale yellow silk; one or two had splendid turbans; and all wore a profusion of ornaments. The men were in snow white pantaloons, with gay coloured linen jackets. One of these, a youth of coal-black comeliness, was preaching with the most violent gesticulations, frequently springing high from the ground, and clapping his hands over his head. Could our missionary societies have heard the trash he uttered, by way of an address to the Deity, they might perhaps have doubted whether his conversion had much enlightened his mind.

At midnight a horn sounded through the camp, which, we were told, was to call the people from private to public worship; and we presently saw them flocking from all sides to the front of the preachers' stand. Mrs B and I contrived to place ourselves with our backs supported against the lower part of this structure, and we were thus enabled to witness the scene which followed without personal danger. There were about two thousand persons assembled.

One of the preachers began in a low nasal tone, and, like all other Methodist preachers, assured us of the enormous depravity of man as he comes from the hands of his Maker, and of his perfect sanctification after he had wrestled sufficiently with the Lord to get hold of him, *et cætera*. The admiration of the crowd was evinced by almost constant cries of 'Amen! Amen!' 'Jesus! Jesus!' 'Glory! Glory!' and the like. But this comparative tranquillity did not last long: the preacher told them that 'this night was the time fixed upon for anxious sinners to wrestle with the Lord'; that he and his brethren 'were at hand to help them', and that such as needed their help were to come forward into 'the pen'.

*

The crowd fell back at the mention of the *pen*, and for some minutes there was a vacant space before us. The preachers came down from their stand and placed themselves in the midst of it, beginning to sing a hymn, calling upon the penitents to come forth. As they sung they kept turning themselves round to every part of the crowd, and, by degrees, the voices of the whole multitude joined in chorus. This was the only moment at which I perceived any thing like the solemn and beautiful effect, which I had heard ascribed to this woodland worship. It is certain that the combined voices of such a multitude, heard at dead of night, from the depths of their eternal forests, the many fair young faces turned upward, and looking paler and lovelier as they met the moon-beams, the dark figures of the officials in the middle of the circle, the lurid glare thrown by the altar-fires on the woods beyond, did altogether produce a fine and solemn effect, that I shall not easily forget; but ere I had well enjoyed it, the scene changed, and sublimity gave place to horror and disgust.

The exhortation nearly resembled that which I had heard at 'the Revival', but the result was very different; for, instead of the few hysterical women who had distinguished themselves on that occasion, above a hundred persons, nearly all females, came forward, uttering howlings and groans, so terrible that I shall never cease to shudder when I recall them. They appeared to drag each other forward, and on the word being given, 'let us pray,' they all fell on their knees; but this posture was soon changed for others that permitted greater scope for the convulsive movements of their limbs; and they were soon all lying on the ground in an indescribable confusion of heads and legs. They threw about their limbs with such incessant and violent motion, that I was every instant expecting some serious accident to occur.

But how am I to describe the sounds that proceeded from this strange mass of human beings? I know no words which can convey an idea of it. Hysterical sobbings, convulsive groans, shrieks and screams the most appalling, burst forth on all sides. I felt sick with horror.

*

The stunning noise was sometimes varied by the preachers beginning to sing; but the convulsive movements of the poor maniacs only became more violent. At length the atrocious wickedness of this horrible scene increased to a degree of grossness, that drove us from our station; we returned to the carriage at about three o'clock in the morning, and passed the remainder of the night in listening to the ever increasing tumult at the pen. To sleep was impossible. At day-break the horn again sounded, to send them to private devotion; and in about an hour afterward, I saw the whole camp as joyously and eagerly employed in preparing and devouring their most substantial breakfasts as if the night had been passed in dancing; and I marked many a fair but pale face, that I recognised as a demoniac of the night, simpering beside a swain, to whom she carefully administered hot coffee and eggs. The preaching saint and the howling sinner seemed alike to relish this mode of recruiting their strength.

After enjoying abundance of strong tea, which proved a delightful restorative after a night so strangely spent, I wandered alone into the forest, and I never remember to have found perfect quiet more delightful.

We soon after left the ground; but before our departure we learnt that a very *satisfactory* collection had been made by the preachers, for Bibles, Tracts, and *all other religious purposes*.

Domestic Manners of the Americans, 1832, ch. 15

'The most remarkable man in the world'

RICHARD F. BURTON

The 'President of the Church of Jesus Christ of Latter-Day Saints all over the World' is obliged to use caution in admitting strangers, not only for personal safety, but also to defend his dignity from the rude and unfeeling remarks of visitors, who seem to think themselves entitled, in the case of a Mormon, to transgress every rule of civility.

About noon, after a preliminary visit to Mr Gilbert – and a visit in these lands always entails a certain amount of smiling – I met Governor Cumming in Main Street, and we proceeded together to our visit. After a slight scrutiny we passed the guard – which is dressed in plain clothes and to the eye unarmed – and walking down the verandah, entered the Prophet's private office. Several people who were sitting there rose at Mr Cumming's entrance. At a few words of introduction, Mr Brigham Young advanced, shook hands with complete simplicity of manner, asked me to be seated on a sofa at one side of the room, and presented me to those present.

Under ordinary circumstances it would be unfair in a visitor to draw the portrait of one visited. But this is no common case. I have violated no rites of hospitality. Mr Brigham Young is a 'seer, revelator, and prophet, having all the gifts of God which He bestows upon the Head of the Church': his memoirs, lithographs, photographs, and portraits have been published again and again; I add but one more likeness; and, finally, I have nothing to say except in his favour.

The Prophet was born at Whittingham, Vermont, on the 1st of June, 1801; he was consequently, in 1860, fifty-nine years of age: he looks about forty-five. *La célébrité vieillit* – I had expected to see a venerable-looking old man. Scarcely a grey thread appears in his hair, which is parted on the side, light coloured, rather thick, and reaches below the ears with a half curl. He formerly wore it long after the Western style, now it is cut level with the ear lobes. The forehead is somewhat narrow, the eyebrows are thin, the eyes between grey and blue, with a calm, composed, and somewhat reserved expression: a slight droop in the left lid made me think that he had suffered from paralysis, I afterwards heard that the ptosis is the result of a neuralgia which has long tormented him. For this reason he usually covers his head – except in his own house or in the tabernacle. Mrs Ward, who is followed by the 'Revue des deux Mondes', therefore errs again in asserting that 'his Mormon majesty never removes his hat in public.' The nose, which is fine and somewhat sharp pointed, is bent a little to the left. The lips are close like the New Englander's, and the teeth, especially those of the under jaw, are imperfect. The cheeks are rather fleshy, and the line between the alæ of the nose and the mouth is broken; the chin is somewhat peaked, and the face clean shaven, except under the jaws, where the beard is allowed to grow. The hands are well made, and not disfigured by rings. The figure is somewhat large, broad-shouldered, and stooping a little when standing.

The Prophet's dress was neat and plain as a Quaker's, all grey homespun, except the cravat and waistcoat. His coat was of antique cut, and, like the pantaloons, baggy, and the buttons were black. A necktie of dark silk, with a large bow, was loosely passed round a starchless collar, which turned down of its own accord. The waistcoat was of black satin – once an article of almost national dress – single-breasted and buttoned nearly to the neck, and a plain gold chain was passed into the pocket. The boots were Wellingtons, apparently of American make.

Altogether the Prophet's appearance was that of a gentleman farmer in New England – in fact such as he is: his father was an agriculturist and revolutionary soldier, who settled 'down East'. He is a well-preserved man; a fact which some attribute to his habit of sleeping, as the Citizen Proudhon so strongly advises, in solitude. His manner is at once affable and impressive, simple and courteous: his want of pretension contrasts favourably with certain pseudo-prophets that I have seen, each and every one of whom holds himself to be a 'Logos' without other claim save a semi-maniacal self-esteem. He shows no signs of dogmatism, bigotry, or fanaticism, and never once entered – with me at least – upon the subject of religion. He impresses a stranger with a certain sense of power: his followers are, of course, wholly fascinated by his superior strength of brain. It is commonly said there is only one chief in G[reat] S[alt] L[ake] City, and that is 'Brigham'. His temper is even and placid, his manner is cold, in fact, like his face, somewhat bloodless, but he is neither morose nor methodistic, and where occasion requires he can use all the weapons of ridicule to direful effect, and 'speak a bit of his mind' in a style which no one forgets. He often reproves his erring followers in purposely violent language, making the terrors of a scolding the punishment in lieu of hanging for a stolen horse or cow. His powers of observation are intuitively strong, and his friends declare him to be gifted with an excellent memory and a perfect judgment of character. If he dislikes a stranger at the first interview, he never sees him again. Of his temperance and sobriety there is but one opinion. His life is ascetic: his favourite food is baked potatoes with a little butter-milk, and his drink water: he disapproves, as do all strict Mormons, of spirituous liquors, and never touches anything stronger than a glass of thin Lager-bier; moreover, he abstains from tobacco. Mr Hyde has accused him of habitual intemperance: he is, as his appearance shows, rather disposed to abstinence than to the reverse. Of his education I cannot speak: 'men not books, deeds not words', has ever been his motto: he probably has, as Mr Randolph said of Mr Johnston, 'a mind uncorrupted by books'. In the only discourse which I heard him deliver, he pronounced impĕtus, impētus. Yet he converses with ease and correctness, has neither snuffle nor pompousness, and speaks as an authority upon certain subjects, such as agriculture and stock-breeding. He assumes no airs of extra sanctimoniousness, and has the plain, simple manners of honesty. His followers deem him an angel of light, his foes, a goblin damned: he is, I presume, neither one nor the other. I cannot pronounce about his scrupulousness: all the world over, the sincerest religious belief, and the practice of devotion, are sometimes compatible not only with the most disorderly life but also with the most terrible crimes; for mankind mostly believes that –

'Il est avec le ciel des accommodements.'

He has been called hypocrite, swindler, forger, murderer. – No one looks it less. The best authorities – from those who accuse Mr Joseph Smith of the most heartless deception, to those who believe that he began as an impostor and ended as a prophet – find in Mr Brigham Young 'an earnest, obstinate egotistic enthusiasm, fanned by persecution and inflamed by bloodshed'. He is the St Paul of the New Dispensation: true and sincere, he gave point, and energy, and consistency to the somewhat disjointed, turbulent, and unforeseeing fanaticism of Mr Joseph Smith; and if he has not been able to create, he has shown himself great in controlling, circumstances. Finally, there is a total absence of pretension in his manner, and he has been so long used to power that he cares nothing for its display. The arts by which he rules the heterogeneous mass of conflicting elements are indomitable will, profound secrecy, and uncommon astuteness.

Such is His Excellency President Brigham Young, 'painter and glazier', – his earliest craft – prophet, revelator, translator and seer; the man who is revered as king or kaiser, pope or pontiff never was; who, like the Old Man of the Mountain, by holding up his hand could cause the death of any one within his reach; who, governing as well as reigning, long stood up to fight with the sword of the Lord, and with his few hundred guerillas, against the then mighty power of the United States; who has outwitted all diplomacy opposed to him; and finally, who made a treaty of peace with the President of the Great Republic as though he had wielded the combined power of France, Russia, and England.

*

It is observable that, although every Gentile writer has represented Mr Joseph Smith as an heartless impostor, few have ventured to apply the term to Mr Brigham Young. I also remarked an instance of the veneration shown by his followers, whose affection for him is equalled only by the confidence with which they entrust to him their dearest interests in this world and in the next. After my visit many congratulated me, as would the followers of the Tien Wong or Heavenly King, upon having at last seen what they consider 'a per se' the most remarkable man in the world.

The City of the Saints, 1861, ch. 5

Mount Lebanon

E. M. FORSTER

Two hundred years ago, Anne Lee, a Quaker of Manchester, England, went to New England and became a Shaker. She founded a sect. The early records of the Shakers are curious and show fantastic elements which have disappeared. There was an attempt to rectify Christianity in the interests of the female – an attempt also made by Mariolatry in the Middle Ages. Mother Anne made a half-hearted bid for equality with Christ, and there are hymns – not sung today – in which homage is paid to them both as the co-regents of the universe, and Adam celebrated as bisexual. This had to be dropped. The sect did not take the intransigent route of Mormonism, it dug up no plates of gold, and commended itself to its neighbours by hard work, good if dull craftsmanship, satisfactory bank-balances, honesty, and celibacy – recruiting its ranks from orphanages. It became a quiet community of men and women – simple folk who liked to feel a little different: even the simplest have this weakness. Meetings were held where sometimes they were seized by the Spirit and shook: otherwise nothing remarkable occurred.

The sect today has almost died out, for its industry has been superseded by industrialism, and orphans have something better to do. But a few settle-

ments of aged people survive or recently survived, and the friends with
whom I was stopping in Massachusetts in 1947 were in touch with the most
considerable of these settlements: Mount Lebanon, where Mother Anne
herself had once dwelt. It was arranged that we should call at Mount Lebanon. We had with us a pleasant journalist from the *New Yorker* who had
been commissioned to write the Shakers up, though I never saw his article – only what he wrote up on me. It was a twelve hours' expedition. The
month was April but the weather wintry and myriads of birch trees were
bare and sharp against the sky. We ascended to a broad pass with a view
over sub-Alpine scenery, half covered with snow. The settlement was down
hill, below the high-raised modern road. Life had shrunk into one enormous
house, a huge wooden box measuring a hundred and eighty feet long and
fifty feet thick, and it was five or six storeys high. We knocked at the door
and an old lady peeped out and greeted us in a dazed fashion. This was Elderess Theresa. Farther down the box another door opened and another old
lady peeped out. This was Sister Susan and she was bidden to retire. They
seemed a bit dishevelled, and it was agreed we should go away for lunch
and come back again: they wished they could have entertained us. My
friends were in great excitement. The experience was more romantic for
them than it was for me, and the idea of home-made chairs hanging from
pegs on a wall filled them with nostalgia. It was part of the 'dream that got
bogged', the dream of an America which should be in direct touch with the
elemental and the simple. America has chosen the power that comes
through machinery but she never forgets her dream. I have seen several instances of it. The most grotesque was the handicraft fair in Greenwich Village, where pieces of copper, wood and wool, which had been bothered into
ugly shapes at home, were offered for sale at high prices. Another instance
is the yearning for Mexico, whose peasants were drunk and dirty, but they
did sing. And another instance was these Shakers, to whom, having had our
lunch at a drug store, we returned.

They had smartened themselves up no end. Elderess Theresa wore a
dove-coloured cape and Sister Susan's hair had been combed. Sisters Ellen,
Ada, Maimie and Ruth also appeared – the first-named sensible and com-
panionable and evidently running the place. Each had plenty of room in the
vast building since the community had shrunk: it was like an almshouse
where the inmates are not crowded and need not quarrel, and they seemed
happy. I had a touching talk with the Elderess, now ninety-one, who had
come from England, and dimly remembered a baker's shop in the Waterloo
Road, and the voyage in a sailing ship away from it. She did not regret the
days when Mount Lebanon had eighty inmates. 'It is much better like this,'
she said. Her room was full of mess and mementoes, all of which she mis-
described as Shaker-made. It was nothing to the mess in the apartment of

Sisters Ada and Maimie, who kept kneeling without obvious reason on the carpet and crackling toilet paper at the parrot to make him dance. On their wall ticked a clock which had the face of a cat, and a cat's tail for pendulum. Up and down the enormous passages Sister Susan stalked, her raven locks flying, and gesticulating with approval on the presence of so many men. We saw the dining-room, where a place was laid, a little humorously, for Christ. We saw the communal meeting-room. Did they – er – shake ever? No – nobody shook now. Did they – er – meet here for prayer? No, said the Elderess complacently. We used to meet once a month. Now we never meet. They were in fact bone idle and did not even know it. I found myself wishing that other groups, the Oxford for instance, would imitate them.

While the New Yorker questioned them, I went out and looked at the five or six other houses which completed the original Mount Lebanon colony (Shaker houses are always in little colonies). They were empty except for ponderous wooden machinery. The ground still sloped into a view, and bright streams and pools of water twinkled at every corner. The sun shone, the snow melted, the planks steamed. The simplicity of the buildings was impressive but not interesting. I went back into the main building to meet Brother Curtis. For the sisters above described only occupied half the huge house. On each floor in the longitudinal central passage was a door, which was locked or supposed to be locked, and beyond the doors, all alone in the other half, dwelt the enigmatical brother Curtis. He could also be reached by walking along outside. He was a healthy elderly man in overalls, very stupid from the New Yorker point of view, though probably not from his own. Much time was spent in trying to make him say something characteristic: he was understood to have different ideas on carrying in logs from the Sisters' ideas, but since he carried in the logs his ideas prevailed. Perhaps he had been interviewed before. He had a roguish twinkle. Then we took our leave. One of our party found a tin dust-pan in the attic, and was allowed to purchase it; and I myself became an object of envy because the Elderess presented me with a ruler. It is an ordinary wooden ruler, it is eighteen inches long, it rules, but little more can be said of it. We waved good-bye – Sister Susan again bursting out of her special door – and that is the last I saw of these gentle harmless people, though the New Yorker returned on the following day to consolidate his investigations. To me, the Shakers were interesting because they interested. My companions were moved by them to a degree which I could not share; they were a symbol of something which America supposes herself to have missed, they were the dream that got bogged. Mount Lebanon has, I believe, now been closed down.

(1951) *Two Cheers for Democracy*, 1951

'How *not* to worship'

JOHN RUSKIN

You have felt, doubtless, at least those of you who have been brought up in any habit of reverence, that every time when in this letter I have used an American expression, or aught like one, there came upon you a sense of sudden wrong – the darting through you of acute cold. I meant you to feel that: for it is the essential function of America to make us all feel that. It is the new skill they have found there; – this skill of degradation; others they have, which other nations had before them, from whom they have learned all they know, and among whom they must travel, still, to see any human work worth seeing. But this is their speciality, this their one gift to their race, – to show men how *not* to worship, – how never to be ashamed in the presence of anything.

Fors Clavigera, vol. 1, 1871, letter 12

'Spoiled by prosperity'

MARGARET FULLER

My friends write to urge my return; they talk of our country as the land of the future. It is so, but that spirit which made it all it is of value in my eyes, which gave all hope with which I can sympathize for that future, is more alive here [Rome] at present than in America. My country is at present spoiled by prosperity, stupid with the lust of gain, soiled by crime in its willing perpetuation of slavery, shamed by an unjust war, noble sentiment much forgotten even by individuals, the aims of politicians selfish or petty, the literature frivolous and venal. In Europe, amid the teachings of adversity, a nobler spirit is struggling, – a spirit which cheers and animates mine. I hear earnest words of pure faith and love. I see deeds of brotherhood. This is what makes *my* America. I do not deeply distrust my country. She is not dead, but in my time she sleepeth, and the spirit of our fathers flames no more, but lies hid beneath the ashes. It will not be so long; bodies cannot live when the soul gets too overgrown with gluttony and falsehood. But it is not the making of a President out of the Mexican war that would make me wish to come back.

(wr. 1848) *Writings*, 1941

'As to a Model Republic'

THOMAS CARLYLE

Of the various French Republics that have been tried, or that are still on trial, – of these also it is not needful to say any word. But there is one modern instance of Democracy nearly perfect, the Republic of the United States, which has actually subsisted for threescore years or more, with immense success as is affirmed; to which many still appeal, as to a sign of hope for all nations, and a 'Model Republic'. Is not America an instance in point? Why should not all Nations subsist and flourish on Democracy, as America does?

Of America it would ill beseem any Englishman, and me perhaps as little as another, to speak unkindly, to speak *unpatriotically*, if any of us even felt so. Sure enough, America is a great, and in many respects a blessed and hopeful phenomenon. Sure enough, these hardy millions of Anglo-saxon men prove themselves worthy of their genealogy; and, with the axe and plough and hammer, if not yet with any much finer kind of implements, are triumphantly clearing-out wide spaces, seedfields for the sustenance and refuge of mankind, arenas for the future history of the world; doing, in their day and generation, a creditable and cheering feat under the sun. But as to a Model Republic, or a model anything, the wise among themselves know too well that there is nothing to be said. Nay, the title hitherto to be a Commonwealth or Nation at all, among the ε'θνη of the world, is, strictly considered, still a thing they are but striving for, and indeed have not yet done much towards attaining. Their Constitution, such as it may be, was made here, not there; went over with them from the Old-Puritan English workshop ready-made. Deduct what they carried with them from England readymade, – their common English Language, and that same Constitution, or rather elixir of constitutions, their inveterate and now, as it were, inborn reverence for the Constable's Staff; two quite immense attainments, which England had to spend much blood, and valiant sweat of brow and brain, for centuries long, in achieving; – and what new elements of polity or nationhood, what noble new phasis of human arrangement, or social device worthy of Prometheus or of Epimetheus, yet comes to light in America? Cotton-crops and Indian-corn and dollars come to light; and half a world of untilled land, where populations that respect the constable can live, for the present *without* Government: this comes to light; and the profound sorrow of all nobler hearts, here uttering itself as silent patient unspeakable ennui, there coming out as vague elegiac wailings, that there is still next to nothing more. 'Anarchy *plus* a street-constable': that also is anarchic to me, and other than quite lovely!

I foresee, too, that, long before the waste lands are full, the very street-constable, on these poor terms, will have become impossible: without the waste lands, as here in our Europe, I do not see how he could continue possible many weeks. Cease to brag to me of America, and its model institutions and constitutions. To men in their sleep there is nothing granted in this world: nothing, or as good as nothing, to men that sit idly *caucusing* and ballot-boxing on the graves of their heroic ancestors, saying, 'It is well, it is well!' Corn and bacon are granted: not a very sublime boon, on such conditions; a boon moreover which, on such conditions, cannot last! No: America too will have to strain its energies, in quite other fashion than this; to crack its sinews, and all-but break its heart, as the rest of us have had to do, in thousandfold wrestle with the Pythons and mud-demons, before it can become a habitation for the gods. America's battle is yet to fight; and we, sorrowful though nothing doubting, will wish her strength for it. New Spiritual Pythons, plenty of them; enormous Megatherions, as ugly as were ever born of mud, loom huge and hideous out of the twilight Future on America; and she will have her own agony, and her own victory, but on other terms than she is yet quite aware of. Hitherto she but ploughs and hammers, in a very successful manner; hitherto, in spite of her 'roast-goose with apple-sauce', she is not much. 'Roast-goose with apple-sauce for the poorest working-man': well, surely that is something, – thanks to your respect for the street-constable, and to your continents of fertile waste land; – but that, even if it could continue, is by no means enough; that is not even an instalment towards what will be required of you. My friend, brag not yet of our American cousins! Their quantity of cotton, dollars, industry and resources, I believe to be almost unspeakable; but I can by no means worship the like of these. What great human soul, what great thought, what great noble thing that one could worship, or loyally admire, has yet been produced there? None: the American cousins have yet done none of these things. 'What they have done?' growls Smelfungus, tired of the subject: 'They have doubled their population every twenty years. They have begotten, with a rapidity beyond recorded example, Eighteen Millions of the greatest *bores* ever seen in this world before, – that hitherto is their feat in History!' – And so we leave them, for the present; and cannot predict the success of Democracy, on this side of the Atlantic, from their example.

Alas, on this side of the Atlantic and on that, Democracy, we apprehend, is forever impossible!

'The Present Time' in *Latter-Day Pamphlets*, 1850

'The last franchise'

OLIVER WENDELL HOLMES

Never, since man came into this atmosphere of oxygen and azote, was there anything like the condition of the young American of the nineteenth century. Having in possession or in prospect the best part of half a world, with all its climates and soils to choose from; equipped with wings of fire and smoke that fly with him day and night, so that he counts his journey not in miles, but in degrees, and sees the seasons change as the wild fowl sees them in his annual flights; with huge leviathans always ready to take him on their broad backs and push behind them with their pectoral or caudal fins the waters that seam the continent or separate the hemispheres; heir of all old civilizations, founder of that new one which, if all the prophecies of the human heart are not lies, is to be the noblest, as it is the last; isolated in space from the races that are governed by dynasties whose divine right grows out of human wrong, yet knit into the most absolute solidarity with mankind of all times and places by the one great thought he inherits as his national birthright; free to form and express his opinions on almost every subject, and assured that he will soon acquire the last franchise which men withhold from man, – that of stating the laws of his spiritual being and the beliefs he accepts without hindrance except from clearer views of truth, – he seems to want nothing for a large, wholesome, noble, beneficent life. In fact, the chief danger is that he will think the whole planet is made for him, and forget that there are some possibilities left in the *débris* of the old-world civilization which deserve a certain respectful consideration at his hands.

The combing and clipping of this shaggy wild continent are in some measure done for him by those who have gone before. Society has subdivided itself enough to have a place for every form of talent. Thus, if a man show the least sign of ability as a sculptor or a painter, for instance, he finds the means of education and a demand for his services. Even a man who knows nothing but science will be provided for, if he does not think it necessary to hang about his birthplace all his days, – which is a most unAmerican weakness. The apron-strings of an American mother are made of India-rubber. Her boy belongs where he is wanted; and that young Marylander of ours spoke for all our young men, when he said that his home was wherever the stars and stripes blew over his head.

The Professor at the Breakfast Table, 1860, ch. 12

'Results to come'

WALT WHITMAN

America, filling the present with greatest deeds and problems, cheerfully accepting the past, including feudalism, (as, indeed, the present is but the legitimate birth of the past, including feudalism,) counts, as I reckon, for her justification and success, (for who, as yet, dare claim success?) almost entirely on the future. Nor is that hope unwarranted. To-day, ahead, though dimly yet, we see, in vistas, a copious, sane, gigantic offspring. For our New World I consider far less important for what it has done, or what it is, than for results to come. Sole among nationalities, these States have assumed the task to put in forms of lasting power and practicality, on areas of amplitude rivaling the operations of the physical kosmos, the moral political speculations of ages, long, long deferr'd, the democratic republican principle, and the theory of development and perfection by voluntary standards, and self-reliance. Who else, indeed, except the United States, in history, so far, have accepted in unwitting faith, and, as we now see, stand, act upon, and go security for, these things?

*

I say we had best look our times and lands searchingly in the face, like a physician diagnosing some deep disease. Never was there, perhaps, more hollowness at heart than at present, and here in the United States. Genuine belief seems to have left us. The underlying principles of the States are not honestly believ'd in, (for all this hectic glow, and these melo-dramatic screamings,) nor is humanity itself believ'd in. What penetrating eye does not everywhere see through the mask? The spectacle is appalling. We live in an atmosphere of hypocrisy throughout. The men believe not in the women, nor the women in the men. A scornful superciliousness rules in literature. The aim of all the *littérateurs* is to find something to make fun of. A lot of churches, sects, &c., the most dismal phantasms I know, usurp the name of religion. Conversation is a mass of badinage. From deceit in the spirit, the mother of all false deeds, the offspring is already incalculable. An acute and candid person, in the revenue department in Washington, who is led by the course of his employment to regularly visit the cities, north, south and west, to investigate frauds, has talk'd much with me about his discoveries. The depravity of the business classes of our country is not less than has been supposed, but infinitely greater. The official services of America, national, state, and municipal, in all their branches and departments, except the judiciary, are saturated in corruption, bribery, falsehood, mal-administration; and the judiciary is tainted. The great cities reek with respectable as much as non-respectable robbery and scoundrelism. In fashionable life, flippancy, tepid amours, weak infidelism, small aims, or no aims at all, only to kill time. In business, (this all-devouring modern word, business,) the one sole object is, by any means, pecuniary gain. The magician's serpent in the fable ate up all the other serpents; and money-making is our magician's serpent, remaining to-day sole master of the field. The best class we show, is but a mob of fashionably dress'd speculators and vulgarians. True, indeed, behind this fantastic farce, enacted on the visible stage of society, solid things and stupendous labors are to be discover'd, existing crudely and going on in the background, to advance and tell themselves in time. Yet the truths are none the less terrible. I say that our New World democracy, however great a success in uplifting the masses out of their sloughs, in materialistic development, products, and in a certain highly-deceptive superficial popular intellectuality, is, so far, an almost complete failure in its social aspects, and in really grand religious, moral, literary, and esthetic results. In vain do we march with unprecedented strides to empire so colossal, outvying the antique, beyond Alexander's, beyond the proudest sway of Rome. In vain have we annex'd Texas, California, Alaska, and reach north for Canada and south for Cuba. It is as if we were somehow being endow'd with a vast and more and more thoroughly-appointed body, and then left with little or no soul.

Democratic Vistas, 1871

'The most generous people'

EZRA POUND

So far as I can make out, there is no morality in England which is not in one way or another a manifestation of the sense of property.

A thing is right if it tends to conserve an estate, or to maintain a succession, no matter what servitude or oppression this inflict.

Our presumption is that those things are right which give the greatest freedom, the greatest opportunity for individual development to the individual, of whatever age or sex or condition.

We are, I believe, the most generous people in the world, or, at least, the most catholic in our generosity.

William Blake has written: 'The only evils are cruelties and repressions', and there is in the 'Book of the Dead', in the negative confession a clause: 'I have not repulsed God in his manifestations'.

I think we, in America, hold by these elements – whether consciously or unconsciously.

It is certain that we 'get the horrors' when we first come to know certain phases of English life and to understand them. They seem sordid, animal, and in the worst sense 'mediaeval'.

To return to America is like going through some very invigorating, very cleansing sort of bath. At least, we feel it so. There may be evil in the country, but the odour of the rottenness is not continually obtruded upon one. You meet so many people who are innocent and unconscious of its existence – so many naïve grown children who miss a double entente.

Patria Mia (wr. 1911–13), 1950

next to of course god america i

e. e. cummings

"next to of course god america i
love you land of the pilgrims' and so forth oh
say can you see by the dawn's early my
country 'tis of centuries come and go
and are no more what of it we should worry
in every language even deafanddumb
thy sons acclaim your glorious name by gorry
by jingo by gee by gosh by gum
why talk of beauty what could be more beautiful than these heroic happy dead
who rushed like lions to the roaring slaughter
they did not stop to think they died instead
then shall the voice of liberty be mute?"

He spoke. And drank rapidly a glass of water

is 5, 1926

'My creed as an American Catholic'

ALFRED E. SMITH

I summarize my creed as an American Catholic. I believe in the worship of God according to the faith and practice of the Roman Catholic Church. I recognize no power in the institutions of my Church to interfere with the operations of the Constitutions of the United States or the enforcement of the law of the land. I believe in absolute freedom of conscience for all men and in equality of all churches, all sects, and all beliefs before the law as a matter of right and not as a matter of favor. I believe in the absolute separation of Church and State and in the strict enforcement of the provisions of the Constitution that Congress shall make no law respecting an establishment of religion or prohibiting the free exercise thereof. I believe that no tribunal of any church has any power to make any decree of any force in the law of the land, other than to establish the status of its own communicants within its own church. I believe in the support of the public school as one of the corner stones of American liberty. I believe in the right of every parent to choose whether his child shall be educated in the public school or in a religious school supported by those of his own faith. I believe in the principle of noninterference by this country in the internal affairs of other nations and that we should stand steadfastly against any such interference by whomsoever it may be urged. And I believe in the common brotherhood of man under the common fatherhood of God.

In this spirit I join with fellow Americans of all creeds in a fervent prayer that never again in this land will any public servant be challenged because of the faith in which he has tried to walk humbly with his God.

'Catholic and Patriot: Governor Smith Replies' in *Atlantic Monthly*, May 1927

To Brooklyn Bridge

HART CRANE

How many dawns, chill from his rippling rest
The seagull's wings shall dip and pivot him,
Shedding white rings of tumult, building high
Over the chained bay waters Liberty –

Then, with inviolate curve, forsake our eyes
As apparitional as sails that cross
Some page of figures to be filed away;
– Till elevators drop us from our day . . .

I think of cinemas, panoramic sleights
With multitudes bent toward some flashing scene
Never disclosed, but hastened to again,
Foretold to other eyes on the same screen;

And Thee, across the harbor, silver-paced
As though the sun took step of thee, yet left
Some motion ever unspent in thy stride, –
Implicitly thy freedom staying thee!

Out of some subway scuttle, cell or loft
A bedlamite speeds to thy parapets,
Tilting there momently, shrill shirt ballooning,
A jest falls from the speechless caravan.

Down Wall, from girder into street noon leaks,
A rip-tooth of the sky's acetylene;
All afternoon the cloud-flown derricks turn . . .
Thy cables breathe the North Atlantic still.

As obscure as the heaven of the Jews,
Thy guerdon . . . Accolade thou dost bestow
Of anonymity time cannot raise:
Vibrant reprieve and pardon thou dost show.

O harp and altar, of the fury fused,
(How could mere toil align thy choiring strings!)
Terrific threshold of the prophet's pledge,
Prayer of pariah, and the lover's cry, –

Again the traffic lights that skim thy swift
Unfractioned idiom, immaculate sigh of stars,
Beading thy path – condense eternity:
And we have seen night lifted in thine arms.

Under thy shadow by the piers I waited;
Only in darkness is thy shadow clear.
The City's fiery parcels all undone,
Already snow submerges an iron year . . .

O Sleepless as the river under thee,
Vaulting the sea, the prairies' dreaming sod,
Unto us lowliest sometime sweep, descend
And of the curveship lend a myth to God.

The Bridge, 1930

'Building the Just City'

W. H. AUDEN

A long time since it seems today
The Saints in Massachusetts Bay
Heard theocratic COTTON preach
And legal WINTHROP's Little Speech;
Since MISTRESS HUTCHINSON was tried
By those her Inner Light defied,
And WILLIAMS questioned Moses' law
But in Rhode Island waited for
The Voice of the Beloved to free
Himself and the Democracy;
Long since inventive JEFFERSON
Fought realistic HAMILTON,
Pelagian versus Jansenist;
But the same heresies exist.
Time makes old formulas look strange,
Our properties and symbols change,
But round the freedom of the Will
Our disagreements centre still,
And now as then the voter hears
The battle cries of two ideas.
Here, as in Europe, is dissent,
This raw untidy continent
Where the Commuter can't forget
The Pioneer; and even yet
A *Völkerwanderung* occurs:
Resourceful manufacturers
Trek southward by progressive stages
For sites with no floor under wages,
No ceiling over hours; and by
Artistic souls in towns that lie
Out in the weed and pollen belt
The need for sympathy is felt,
And east to hard New York they come;
And self-respect drives Negroes from
The one-crop and race-hating delta
To northern cities helter-skelter;
And in jalopies there migrates
A rootless tribe from windblown states

To suffer further westward where
The tolerant Pacific air
Makes logic seem so silly, pain
Subjective, what he seeks so vain.
The wanderer may die; and kids,
When their imagination bids,
Hitch-hike a thousand miles to find
The Hesperides that's on their mind,
Some Texas where real cowboys seem
Lost in a movie-cowboy's dream.
More even than in Europe, here
The choice of patterns is made clear
Which the machine imposes, what
Is possible and what is not,
To what conditions we must bow
In building the Just City now.

New Year Letter, part 3, 1940

ALL MEN ARE CREATED EQUAL

As a nation we began by declaring that 'all men are created equal.' We now practically read it 'all men are created equal, except the Negroes.' When the Know-Nothings get control, it will read 'all men are created equal, except Negroes and foreigners and Catholics.' When it comes to this, I shall prefer emigrating to some country where they make no pretense of loving liberty – to Russia, for instance, where despotism can be taken pure, and without the base alloy of hypocrisy.

Abraham Lincoln, letter to Joshua F. Speed, 24 August 1855

America

Centre of equal daughters, equal sons,
All, all alike endear'd, grown, ungrown, young or old,
Strong, ample, fair, enduring, capable, rich,
Perennial with the Earth, with Freedom, Law and Love,
A grand, sane, towering, seated Mother,
Chair'd in the adamant of Time.

Walt Whitman, *Leaves of Grass*, 1888

'An atrocious crime'

SYDNEY SMITH

If nations rank according to their wisdom and their virtue, what right has the American, a scourger and murderer of slaves, to compare himself with the least and lowest of the European nations? – much more with this great and humane country, where the greatest lord dare not lay a finger upon the meanest peasant? What is freedom, where all are not free? where the greatest of God's blessings is limited, with impious caprice, to the colour of the body? And these are the men who taunt the English with their corrupt Parliament, with their buying and selling votes. Let the world judge which is the most liable to censure – we who, in the midst of our rottenness, have torn off the manacles of slaves all over the world; – or they who, with their idle purity, and useless perfection, have remained mute and careless, while groans echoed and whips clank'd round the very walls of their spotless Congress. We wish well to America – we rejoice in her prosperity – and are delighted to resist the absurd impertinence with which the character of her people is often treated in this country: but the existence of slavery in America is an atrocious crime, with which no measures can be kept – for which her situation affords no sort of apology – which makes liberty itself distrusted, and the boast of it disgusting.

Edinburgh Review, December 1818

'A peep into a slave-mart'

JOSEPH INGRAHAM

'Will you ride with me into the country?' said a young planter. 'I am about purchasing a few negroes and a peep into a slave-mart may not be uninteresting to you.' I readily embraced the opportunity and in a few minutes our horses were at the door.

*

A mile from Natchez we came to a cluster of rough wooden buildings, in the angle of two roads, in front of which several saddle-horses, either tied or held by servants, indicated a place of popular resort.

'This is the slave market,' said my companion, pointing to a building in the rear; and alighting, we left our horses in charge of a neatly dressed yellow boy belonging to the establishment. Entering through a wide gate into a narrow court-yard, partially enclosed by low buildings, a scene of a novel character was at once presented. A line of negroes, commencing at the entrance with the tallest, who was not more than five feet eight or nine inches in height – for negroes are a low rather than a tall race of men – down to a little fellow about ten years of age, extended in a semicircle around the right side of the yard. There were in all about forty. Each was dressed in the usual uniform of slaves, when in market, consisting of a fashionably shaped, black fur hat, roundabout and trowsers of coarse corduroy velvet, precisely such as are worn by Irish labourers, when they first 'come over the water'; good vests, strong shoes, and white cotton shirts, completed their equipment. This dress they lay aside after they are sold, or wear out as soon as may be; for the negro dislikes to retain the indication of his having recently been in the market. With their hats in their hands, which hung down by their sides, they stood perfectly still, and in close order, while some gentlemen were passing from one to another examining for the purpose of buying. With the exception of displaying their teeth when addressed, and rolling their great white eyes about the court – they were so many statues of the most glossy ebony.

As we entered the mart, one of the slave merchants – for a 'lot' of slaves is usually accompanied, if not owned, by two or three individuals – approached us, saying 'Good morning, gentlemen! Would you like to examine my lot of boys? I have as fine a lot as ever came into market.' – We approached them, one of us as a curious spectator, the other as a purchaser; and as my friend passed along the line, with a scrutinizing eye – giving that singular look, peculiar to the buyer of slaves as he glances from head to foot over each individual – the passive subjects of his observations betrayed no other signs of curiosity than that evinced by an occasional glance. The entrance of a stranger into a mart is by no means an unimportant event to the slave, for every stranger may soon become his master and command his future destinies.

*

'For what service in particular did you want to buy?' inquired the trader of my friend, 'A coachman.' 'There is one I think may suit you, sir,' said he; George, step out here.' Forthwith a light-coloured negro, with a fine figure and good face, bating an enormous pair of lips, advanced a step from the line, and looked with some degree of intelligence, though with an air of indifference, upon his intended purchaser.

'How old are you, George?' he inquired. 'I don't recollect, sir 'zactly – b'lieve I'm somewhere 'bout twenty-dree.' 'Where were you raised?' 'On master R—'s farm in Wirginny.' 'Then you are a Virginia negro.' 'Yes, master, me full blood Wirginny.' 'Did you drive your master's carriage?' 'Yes, master, I drove ole missus' carage, more dan four year.' 'Have you a wife?' 'Yes, master, I lef' young wife in Richmond, but I got new wife here in de lot. I wishy you buy her, master, if you gwine to buy me.'

Then came a series of the usual questions from the intended purchaser. 'Let me see your teeth – your tongue – open your hands – roll up your sleeves – have you a good appetite? are you good tempered? 'Me get mad sometime,' replied George to the last query, 'but neber wid my horses.' 'What do you ask for this boy, sir?' inquired the planter, after putting a few more questions to the unusually loquacious slave. 'I have held him at one thousand dollars, but I will take nine hundred and seventy-five cash.' The bargain was in a few minutes concluded, and my companion took the negro at nine hundred and fifty, giving negotiable paper – the customary way of paying for slaves – at four months. It is, however, generally understood, that if servants prove unqualified for the particular service for which they are bought, the sale is dissolved. So there is general perfect safety in purchasing servants untried, and merely on the warrant of the seller.

George, in the meanwhile, stood by, with his hat in his hand, apparently unconcerned in the negotiations going on, and when the trader said to him, 'George, the gentleman has bought you; get ready to go with him,' he appeared gratified at the tidings, and smiled upon his companions apparently quite pleased, and then bounded off to the buildings for his little bundle. In a few minutes he returned and took leave of several of his companions, who, having been drawn up into line only to be shown to purchasers, were now once more at liberty, and moving about the court, all the visitors having left except my friend and myself. 'You mighty lucky, George,' said one, congratulating him, 'to get sol so quick,' 'Oh, you neber min', Charly,' replied the delighted George; 'your turn come soon too.'

The South-West, by a Yankee, 1835, chs. 38, 39

'A visit from two women'

FRANCES ANNE KEMBLE

This morning [28 February] I had a visit from two of the women, Charlotte and Judy, who came to me for help and advice for a complaint, which it really seems to me every other woman on the estate is cursed with, and which is a direct result of the conditions of their existence; the practice of sending women to labor in the fields in the third week after their confinement is a specific for causing this infirmity, and I know no specific for curing it under these circumstances. As soon as these poor things had departed with such comfort as I could give them, and the bandages they especially begged for, three other sable graces introduced themselves, Edie, Louisa, and Diana; the former told me she had had a family of seven children, but had lost them all through 'ill luck', as she denominated the ignorance and ill-treatment which were answerable for the loss of these, as of so many other poor little creatures their fellows. Having dismissed her and Diana with the sugar and rice they came to beg, I detained Louisa, whom I had never seen but in the presence of her old grandmother, whose version of the poor child's escape to, and hiding in the woods, I had a desire to compare with the heroine's own story.

She told it very simply, and it was most pathetic. She had not finished her task one day, when she said she felt ill, and unable to do so, and had been severely flogged by driver Bran, in whose 'gang' she then was. The next day, in spite of this encouragement to labor, she had again been unable to complete her appointed work; and Bran having told her that he'd tie her up and flog her if she did not get it done, she had left the field and run into the swamp.

'Tie you up, Louisa!' said I; 'what is that?'

She then described to me that they were fastened up by their wrists to a beam or a branch of a tree, their feet barely touching the ground, so as to allow them no purchase for resistance or evasion of the lash, their clothes turned over their heads, and their backs scored with a leather thong, either by the driver himself, or, if he pleases to inflict their punishment by deputy, any of the men he may choose to summon to the office; it might be father, brother, husband, or lover, if the overseer so ordered it. I turned sick, and my blood curdled listening to these details from the slender young slip of a lassie, with her poor piteous face and murmuring, pleading voice.

'Oh,' said I, 'Louisa; but the rattlesnakes – the dreadful rattlesnakes in the swamps; were you not afraid of those horrible creatures?'

'Oh, missis,' said the poor child, 'me no tink of dem; me forget all 'bout dem for de fretting.'

'Why did you come home at last?'

'Oh, missis, me starve with hunger, me most dead with hunger before me come back.'

'And were you flogged, Lousia?' said I, with a shudder at what the answer might be.

'No, missis, me go to hospital; me almost dead and sick so long, 'spec driver Bran him forgot 'bout de flogging.'

I am getting perfectly savage over all these doings, E[lizabeth], and really think I should consider my own throat and those of my children well cut if some night the people were to take it into their heads to clear off scores in that fashion.

Journal of a Residence on a Georgian Plantation in 1838–1839,
1863, ch. 19

Go Down, Moses

ANONYMOUS

When Israel was in Egypt's land,
    Let my people go;
Oppressed so hard they could not stand,
    Let my people go.

CHORUS
Go down, Moses, way down in Egypt's land;
Tell old Pharoah, to let my people go.

Thus saith the Lord, bold Moses said,
    Let my people go;
If not I'll smite your first born dead,
    Let my people go.

No more shall they in bondage toil,
    Let my people go;
Let them come out with Egypt's spoil,
    Let my people go.

O 'twas a dark and dismal night,
    Let my people go;
When Moses led the Israelites,
    Let my people go.

The Lord told Moses what to do,
    Let my people go;
To lead the children of Israel through,
    Let my people go.

O come along, Moses, you won't get lost,
    Let my people go;
Stretch out your rod and come across,
    Let my people go.

As Israel stood by the water side,
    Let my people go;
At the command of God it did divide,
    Let my people go.

And when they reached the other side,
    Let my people go;
They sang a song of triumph o'er,
    Let my people go.

You won't get lost in the wilderness,
    Let my people go;
With a lighted candle in your breast,
    Let my people go.

O let us all from bondage flee,
    Let my people go;
And let us all in Christ be free,
    Let my people go.

We need not always weep and moan,
    Let my people go;
And wear these slavery chains forlorn,
    Let my people go.

What a beautiful morning that will be,
    Let my people go;
When time breaks up in eternity,
Let my people go.

                                Early nineteenth century

Prejudice Against Color

FREDERICK DOUGLASS

Let no one imagine that we are about to give undue prominence to this subject. Regarding, as we do, the feeling named above to be the greatest of all
obstacles in the way of the anti-slavery cause, we think there is little danger
of making the subject of it too prominent. The heartless apathy which prevails in this community on the subject of slavery – the cold blooded indifference with which the wrongs of the perishing and heart-broken slave are
regarded – the contemptuous, slanderous, and malicious manner in which

the names and characters of Abolitionists are handled by the American pulpit and press generally, may be traced mainly to the *malign* feeling which passes under the name of prejudice against color. Every step in our experience in this country since we commenced our anti-slavery labors, has been marked by facts demonstrative of what we have just said. The day that we started on our first anti-slavery journey to Nantucket, now nine years ago, the steamer was detained at the wharf in New Bedford two hours later than the usual time of starting, in an attempt on the part of the captain to compel the colored passengers to separate from the white passengers, and to go on the forward deck of the steamer; and during this time, the most savage feelings were evinced towards every colored man who asserted his right to enjoy equal privileges with other passengers. – Aside from the twenty months which we spent in England, (where color is no crime, and where a man's fitness for respectable society is measured by his moral and intellectual worth,) we do not remember to have made a single anti-slavery tour in any direction in this country, when we have not been assailed by this mean spirit of caste. A feeling so universal and so powerful for evil, cannot well be too much commented upon. We have used the term prejudice against color to designate the feeling to which we allude, not because it expresses correctly what that feeling is, but simply because that *innocent* term is usually employed for that purpose.

Properly speaking, *prejudice against color* does not exist in this country. The feeling (or whatever it is) which we call *prejudice*, is no less than a *murderous, hell-born hatred* of every virtue which may adorn the character of a *black man*. It is not the black man's color which makes him the object of brutal treatment. When he is drunken, idle, ignorant and vicious, 'Black Bill' is a source of amusement: he is called a good-natured fellow; he is the first to [give] service in holding his horse, or blacking his boots. The white gentleman tells the landlord to give 'Bill' '*something to drink*', and actually drinks with 'Bill' himself! – While poor black 'Bill' will minister to the pride, vanity and laziness of white American gentlemen – while he consents to play the buffoon for their sport, he will share their regard. But let him cease to be what we have described him to be – let him shake off the filthy rags that cover him – let him abandon drunkenness for sobriety, industry for indolence, ignorance for intelligence, and give up his menial occupation for respectable employment – let him quit the hotel and go to the church, and assume there the rights and privileges of one for whom the Son of God died, and he will be pursued with the fiercest hatred. His name will be cast out as evil; and his life will be embittered with all the venom which hate and malice can generate. Thousands of colored men can bear witness to the truth of this representation. While we are servants, we are never offensive to the whites, or marks of popular displeasure. We have been often dragged or driven from the tables of hotels where colored men were officiating acceptably as waiters; and from steamboat cabins where twenty or thirty colored men in light jackets and white aprons were frisking about as servants among the whites in every direction. On the very day we were brutally assaulted in New York for riding down Broadway in company with ladies, we saw several white ladies riding with *black servants*. These servants were well-dressed, proud looking men, evidently living on the fat of the land – yet they were servants. They rode not for their own, but for the pleasure and convenience of white persons. They were not in those carriages as friends or equals. – They were there as appendages; they constituted a part of the magnificent equipages. – They were there as the fine black horses which they drove were there – to minister to the pride and splendor of their employers. As they passed down Broadway, they were observed with admiration by the multitude; and even the *poor* wretches who assaulted us might have said in their hearts, as they looked upon such splendor, 'We would do so too if we could.' We repeat, then, that color is not the cause of our persecution; that is, it *is not our color* which makes our proximity to white men disagreeable. The evil lies deeper than prejudice against color. It is, as we have said, an intense hatred of the colored man when he is distinguished for any ennobling qualities of head or heart. If the feeling which persecutes us were prejudice against color, the colored servant would be as obnoxious as the colored gentleman, for the color is the same in both cases; and being the same in both cases, it would produce the *same* result in both cases.

We are then a persecuted people; not because we are *colored*, but simply because that color has for a series of years been coupled in the public mind with the degradation of slavery and servitude. In these conditions, we are thought to be in our place; and to aspire to anything above them, is to contradict the established views of the community – to get out of our sphere, and commit the provoking sin of *impudence*. Just here is our sin: we have been a slave; we have passed through all the grades of servitude, and have, under God, secured our freedom; and if we have become the special object of attack, it is because we speak and act among our fellow-men without the slightest regard to their or our own complexion; – and further, because we claim and exercise the right to associate with just such persons as are willing to associate with us, and who are agreeable to our tastes, and suited to our moral and intellectual tendencies, without reference to the color of their skin, and without giving ourselves the slightest trouble to inquire whether the world are pleased or displeased by our conduct. We believe in human equality; that character, not color, should be the criterion by which to choose associates; and we pity the pride of the poor pale dust and ashes which would erect any other standard of social fellowship.

This doctrine of human equality is the bitterest yet taught by the abolitionists. It is swallowed with more difficulty than all the other points of the anti-slavery creed put together. 'What, make a Negro equal to a *white* man? No, we will never consent to that! No, that won't do!' But stop a moment; don't be in a passion; keep cool. What *is* a white man that you do so revolt at the idea of making a Negro equal with him? Who made . . . an angel of a man? 'A man.' Very well, he is a man, and nothing but a man – possessing the same weaknesses, liable to the same diseases, and under the same necessities to which a black man is subject. Wherein does the white man differ from the black? Why, one is white and the other is black. Well, what of that? Does the sun shine more brilliantly upon the one than it does upon the other? Is nature more lavish with her gifts toward the one than toward the other? Do earth, sea and air yield their united treasures to the one more readily than to the other? In a word, 'have we not all one Father?' Why then do you revolt at that equality which God and nature instituted?

The very apprehension which the American people betray on this point, is proof of the fitness of treating all men equally. The fact that they fear an acknowledgment of our equality, shows that they see a fitness in such an acknowledgment. Why are they not apprehensive lest the horse should be placed on an equality with man? Simply because the horse is not a man; and no amount of reasoning can convince the world, against its common sense, that the horse is anything else than a horse. So here all can repose without fear. But not so with the Negro. He stands erect. Upon his brow he bears the seal of manhood, from the hand of the living God. Adopt any mode of reasoning you please with respect to him, he is a man, possessing an immortal soul, illuminated by intellect, capable of heavenly aspirations, and in all things pertaining to manhood, he is at once self-evidently a man, and therefore entitled to all the rights and privileges which belong to human nature.

The North Star, June 1850

'The day of freedom came'

BOOKER T. WASHINGTON

Finally the war closed, and the day of freedom came. It was a momentous and eventful day to all upon our plantation. We had been expecting it. Freedom was in the air, and had been for months. Deserting soldiers returning to their homes were to be seen every day. Others who had been discharged, or whose regiments had been paroled, were constantly passing near our place. The 'grape-vine telegraph' was kept busy night and day. The news and mutterings of great events were swiftly carried from one plantation to

another. In the fear of 'Yankee' invasions, the silverware and other valu-
ables were taken from the 'big house', buried in the woods, and guarded by
trusted slaves. Woe be to anyone who would have attempted to disturb the
buried treasure. The slaves would give the Yankee soldiers food, drink,
clothing – anything but that which had been specifically entrusted to their
care and honour. As the great day drew nearer, there was more singing in
the slave quarters than usual. It was bolder, had more ring, and lasted later
into the night. Most of the verses of the plantation songs had some reference
to freedom. True, they had sung those same verses before, but they had
been careful to explain that the 'freedom' in these songs referred to the next
world, and had no connection with life in this world. Now they gradually
threw off the mask; and were not afraid to let it be known that the 'freedom'
in their songs meant freedom of the body in this world. The night before
the eventful day, word was sent to the slave quarters to the effect that something unusual was going to take place at the 'big house' the next morning.
There was little, if any, sleep that night. All was excitement and expectancy.
Early the next morning word was sent to all the slaves, old and young, to
gather at the house. In company with my mother, brother, and sister, and
a large number of other slaves, I went to the master's house. All of our
master's family were either standing or seated on the veranda of the house,
where they could see what was to take place and hear what was said. There
was a feeling of deep interest, or perhaps sadness, on their faces, but not
bitterness. As I now recall the impression they made upon me, they did not
at the moment seem to be sad because of the loss of property, but rather
because of parting with those whom they had reared and who were in many
ways very close to them. The most distinct thing that I now recall in connection with the scene was that some man who seemed to be a stranger (a
United States officer, I presume) made a little speech and then read a rather
long paper – the Emancipation Proclamation, I think. After the reading we
were told that we were all free, and could go when and where we pleased.
My mother, who was standing by my side, leaned over and kissed her children, while tears of joy ran down her cheeks. She explained to us what it
all meant, that this was the day for which she had been so long praying,
but fearing that she would never live to see.

For some minutes there was great rejoicing, and thanksgiving, and wild
scenes of ecstasy. But there was no feeling of bitterness. In fact, there was
pity among the slaves for our former owners. The wild rejoicing on the part
of the emancipated coloured people lasted but for a brief period, for I noticed that by the time they returned to their cabins there was a change in
their feelings. The great responsibility of being free, of having charge of
themselves, of having to think and plan for themselves and their children,
seemed to take possession of them. It was very much like suddenly turning

a youth of ten or twelve years out into the world to provide for himself. In a few hours the great question with which the Anglo-Saxon race had been grappling for centuries had been thrown upon these people to be solved. These were the questions of a home, a living, the rearing of children, education, citizenship, and the establishment and support of churches. Was it any wonder that within a few hours the wild rejoicing ceased and a feeling of deep gloom seemed to pervade the slave quarters? To some it seemed that, now that they were in actual possession of it, freedom was a more serious thing than they had expected to find it. Some of the slaves were seventy or eighty years old; their best days were gone. They had no strength with which to earn a living in a strange place and among strange people, even if they had been sure where to find a new place of abode. To this class the problem seemed especially hard. Besides, deep down in their hearts there was a strange and peculiar attachment to 'old Marster' and 'old Missus', and to their children, which they found it hard to think of breaking off. With these they had spent in some cases nearly a half-century, and it was no light thing to think of parting. Gradually, one by one, stealthily at first, the older slaves began to wander from the slave quarters back to the 'big house' to have whispered conversation with their former owners as to the future.

Up from Slavery, 1901, ch. 1

'This double-consciousness'

W. E. B. DU BOIS

Between me and the other world there is ever an unasked question: unasked by some through feelings of delicacy; by others through the difficulty of rightly framing it. All, nevertheless, flutter round it. They approach me in a half-hesitant sort of way, eye me curiously or compassionately, and then, instead of saying directly, How does it feel to be a problem? they say, I know an excellent colored man in my town; or, I fought at Mechanicsville; or, Do not these Southern outrages make your blood boil? At these I smile, or am interested, or reduce the boiling to a simmer, as the occasion may require. To the real question, How does it feel to be a problem? I answer seldom a word.

And yet, being a problem is a strange experience, – peculiar even for one who has never been anything else, save perhaps in babyhood and in Europe. It is in the early days of rollicking boyhood that the revelation first bursts upon one, all in a day, as it were. I remember well when the shadow swept across me. I was a little thing, away up in the hills of New England, where the dark Housatonic winds between Hoosac and Taghkanic to the sea. In a wee wooden schoolhouse, something put it into the boys' and girls' heads to buy gorgeous visiting-cards – ten cents a package – and exchange. The exchange was merry, till one girl, a tall newcomer, refused my card, – refused it peremptorily, with a glance. Then it dawned upon me with a certain suddenness that I was different from the others; or like, mayhap, in heart and life and longing, but shut out from their world by a vast veil. I had thereafter no desire to tear down that veil, to creep through; I held all beyond it in common contempt, and lived above it in a region of blue sky and great wandering shadows. That sky was bluest when I could beat my mates at examination-time, or beat them at a foot-race, or even beat their stringy heads. Alas, with the years all this fine contempt began to fade; for the words I longed for, and all their dazzling opportunities, were theirs, not mine. But they should not keep these prizes, I said; some, all, I would wrest from them. Just how I would do it I could never decide: by reading law, by healing the sick, by telling the wonderful tales that swam in my head – some way. With other black boys the strife was not so fiercely sunny: their youth shrunk into tasteless sycophancy, or into silent hatred of the pale world about them and mocking distrust of everything white; or wasted itself in a bitter cry, Why did God make me an outcast and a stranger in mine own house? The shades of the prison-house closed round about us all: walls strait and stubborn to the whitest, but relentlessly narrow, tall, and unscalable to sons of night who must plod darkly on in resignation, or beat unavailing palms against the stone, or steadily, half hopelessly, watch the streak of blue above.

After the Egyptian and Indian, the Greek and Roman, the Teuton and Mongolian, the Negro is a sort of seventh son, born with a veil, and gifted with second-sight in this American world, – a world which yields him no true self-consciousness, but only lets him see himself through the revelation of the other world. It is a peculiar sensation, this double-consciousness, this sense of always looking at one's self through the eyes of others, of measuring one's soul by the tape of a world that looks on in amused contempt and pity. One ever feels his twoness, – an American, a Negro; two souls, two thoughts, two unreconciled strivings; two warring ideals in one dark body, whose dogged strength alone keeps it from being torn asunder.

The history of the American Negro is the history of this strife, – this longing to attain self-conscious manhood, to merge his double self into a better and truer self. In this merging he wishes neither of the older selves to be lost. He would not Africanize America, for America has too much to teach the world and Africa. He would not bleach his Negro soul in a flood of white Americanism, for he knows that Negro blood has a message for the world. He simply wishes to make it possible for a man to be both a Negro and an American, without being cursed and spit upon by his fellows, without having the doors of Opportunity closed roughly in his face.

*

Work, culture, liberty, – all these we need, not singly but together, not successively but together, each growing and aiding each, and all striving toward that vaster ideal that swims before the Negro people, the ideal of human brotherhood, gained through the unifying ideal of Race; the ideal of fostering and developing the traits and talents of the Negro, not in opposition to or contempt for other races, but rather in large conformity to the greater ideals of the American Republic, in order that some day on American soil two world-races may give each to each those characteristics both so sadly lack. We the darker ones come even now not altogether empty-handed: there are to-day no truer exponents of the pure human spirit of the Declaration of Independence than the American Negroes; there is no true American music but the wild sweet melodies of the Negro slave; the American fairy tales and folklore are Indian and African; and, all in all, we black men seem the sole oasis of simple faith and reverence in a dusty desert of dollars and smartness. Will America be poorer if she replace her brutal dyspeptic blundering with light-hearted but determined Negro humility? or her coarse and cruel wit with loving jovial good-humor? or her vulgar music with the soul of the Sorrow Songs?

Merely a concrete test of the underlying principles of the great republic is the Negro Problem, and the spiritual striving of the freedmen's sons is the travail of souls whose burden is almost beyond the measure of their strength, but who bear it in the name of an historic race, in the name of this the land of their fathers' fathers, and in the name of human opportunity.

The Souls of Black Folk, 1903, ch. 1

Theme for English B

LANGSTON HUGHES

The instructor said,

> *Go home and write*
> *a page tonight.*
> *And let that page come out of you –*
> *Then, it will be true.*

I wonder if it's that simple?
I am twenty-two, colored, born in Winston-Salem.
I went to school there, then Durham, then here
to this college on the hill above Harlem.
I am the only colored student in my class.
The steps from the hill lead down into Harlem,
through a park, then I cross St Nicholas,
Eighth Avenue, Seventh, and I come to the Y,
the Harlem Branch Y, where I take the elevator
up to my room, sit down, and write this page:

It's not easy to know what is true for you or me
at twenty-two, my age. But I guess I'm what
I feel and see and hear, Harlem, I hear you:
hear you, hear me – we two – you, me, talk on this page.
(I hear New York, too.) Me – who?
Well, I like to eat, sleep, drink, and be in love.
I like to work, read, learn, and understand life.
I like a pipe for a Christmas present,
or records – Bessie, bop, or Bach.
I guess being colored doesn't make me *not* like
the same things other folks like who are other races.
So will my page be colored that I write?
Being me, it will not be white.
But it will be
a part of you, instructor.
You are white –
yet a part of me, as I am a part of you.
That's American.
Sometimes perhaps you don't want to be a part of me.
Nor do I often want to be a part of you.
But we are, that's true!
As I learn from you,
I guess you learn from me –
although you're older – and white –
and somewhat more free.

This is my page for English B.

(1949) *Selected Poems*, 1959

'Cheating on a large scale'

A. BARTLETT GIAMATTI

When those running a sport do not believe their own conventions, then the essential convention of a sport as a meritocracy in every sense will be undermined. When laxity on that scale occurs, then cheating on a large scale metastasizes. Then the social cheating of racism can occur. For instance, when baseball desegregated itself in 1947 on the field, the first American institution ever to do so voluntarily (before an executive order desegregated the US Army, and before the Supreme Court, the public schools, and Congress passed the Civil Rights Act of 1964), baseball changed America. Baseball changed how blacks and whites felt about themselves and about each other. Late, late as it was, the arrival in the Majors of Jack Roosevelt Robinson was an extraordinary moment in American history. For the first time, a black American was on America's most privileged version of a level field. He was there as an equal because of his skill, as those whites who preceded him had been and those blacks and whites who succeeded him would be. Merit will win, it was promised by baseball.

Take Time for Paradise, 1989, ch. 2

'Our Nation of Islam'

MALCOLM X

Before very long, radio and television people began asking me to defend our Nation of Islam in panel discussions and debates. I was to be confronted by handpicked scholars, both whites and some of those Ph.D. 'house' and 'yard' Negroes who had been attacking us. Every day, I was more incensed with the general misrepresentation and distortion of Mr Muhammad's teachings; I truly think that not once did it cross my mind that previously I never had been *inside* a radio or television station – let alone faced a microphone to audiences of millions of people. Prison debating had been my only experience speaking to anyone but Muslims.

*

The program hosts would start with some kind of dice-loading non-religious introduction for me. It would be something like " – and we have with us today the fiery, angry chief Malcolm X of the New York Muslims. . . . " I made up my own introduction. At home, or driving my car,

I practiced until I could interrupt a radio or television host and introduce myself.

"I represent Mr Elijah Muhammad, the spiritual head of the fastest-growing group of Muslims in the Western Hemisphere. We who follow him know that he has been divinely taught and sent to us by God Himself. We believe that the miserable plight of America's twenty million black people is the fulfillment of divine prophesy. We also believe the presence today in America of The Honorable Elijah Muhammad, his teachings among the so-called Negroes, and his naked warning to America concerning her treatment of these so-called Negroes, is all the fulfillment of divine prophecy. I am privileged to be the minister of our Temple Number Seven here in New York City which is a part of the Nation of Islam, under the divine leadership of The Honorable Elijah Muhammad – "

I would look around at those devils and their trained black parrots staring at me, while I was catching my breath – and I had set my tone.

They would outdo each other, leaping in on me, hammering at Mr Muhammad, at me, and at the Nation of Islam. Those 'integration'-mad Negroes – you know what they jumped on. *Why* couldn't Muslims *see* that 'integration' was the answer to American Negroes' problems? I'd try to rip that to pieces.

'No *sane* black man really wants integration! No *sane* white man really wants integration! No sane black man really believes that the white man ever will give the black man anything more than token integration. No! The Honorable Elijah Muhammad teaches that for the black man in America the only solution is complete *separation* from the white man!'

Anyone who has ever heard me on the radio or television programs knows that my technique is non-stop, until what I want to get said is said. I was developing the technique then.

'The Honorable Elijah Muhammad teaches us that since Western society is deteriorating, it has become overrun with immorality, and God is going to judge it, and destroy it. And the only way the black people caught up in this society can be saved is not to *integrate* into this corrupt society, but to *separate* from it, to a land of our *own*, where we can reform ourselves, lift up our moral standards, and try to be godly. The Western world's most learned diplomats have failed to solve this grave race problem. Her learned legal experts have failed. Her sociologists have failed. Her civil leaders have failed. Her fraternal leaders have failed. Since all of these have *failed* to solve this race problem, it is time for us to sit down and *reason*! I am certain that we will be forced to agree that it takes *God Himself* to solve this grave racial dilemma.'

Every time I mentioned 'separation', some of them would cry that we Muslims were standing for the same thing that white racists and demagogues stood for. I would explain the difference. 'No! We reject *segregation* even more militantly than you say you do! We want *separation*, which is not the same! The Honorable Elijah Muhammad teaches us that *segregation* is when your life and liberty are controlled, regulated, *by someone else*. To *segregate* means to control. Segregation is that which is forced upon inferiors by superiors. But *separation* is that which is done voluntarily, by two equals – for the good of both! The Honorable Elijah Muhammad teaches us that as long as our people here in America are dependent upon the white man, we will always be begging him for jobs, food, clothing, and housing. And he will always control our lives, regulate our lives, and have the power to segregate us. The Negro here in America has been treated like a child. A child stays within the mother until the time of birth! When the time of birth arrives, the child must be separated, or it will *destroy* its mother and itself. The mother can't carry that child after its time. The child cries for and needs its own world!'

Anyone who has listened to me will have to agree that I believed in Elijah Muhammad and represented him one hundred per cent. I never tried to take any credit for myself.

I was never in one of those panel discussions without some of them just waiting their chance to accuse me of 'inciting Negroes to violence'. I didn't even have to do any special studying to prepare for that one.

'The greatest miracle Christianity has achieved in America is that the black man in white Christian hands has not grown violent. It *is* a miracle that 22 million black people have not *risen up* against their oppressors – in which they would have been justified by all moral criteria, and even by the democratic tradition! It is a miracle that a nation of black people has so fervently continued to believe in a turn-the-other-cheek and heaven-for-you-after-you-die philosophy! It *is a miracle* that the American black people have remained a peaceful people, while catching all the centuries of hell that they have caught, here in white man's heaven! The *miracle* is that the white man's puppet Negro "leaders", his preachers and the educated Negroes laden with degrees, and others who have been allowed to wax fat off their black poor brothers, have been able to hold the black masses quiet until now.'

I guarantee you one thing – every time I was mixed up in those studios with those brainwashed, 'integration'-mad black puppets, and those tricky devils trying to rip and tear me down, as long as the little red light glowed 'on the air', I tried to represent Elijah Muhammad and the Nation of Islam to the utmost.

The Autobiography of Malcolm X, 1965, ch. 14

I Have a Dream

MARTIN LUTHER KING, JR

I am happy to join with you today in what will go down in history as the greatest demonstration for freedom in the history of our nation.

Fivescore years ago, a great American, in whose symbolic shadow we stand today, signed the Emancipation Proclamation. This momentous decree came as a great beacon light of hope to millions of Negro slaves who had been seared in the flame of withering injustice. It came as a joyous daybreak to end the long night of their captivity.

But one hundred years later, the Negro still is not free; one hundred years later, the life of the Negro is still sadly crippled by the manacles of segregation and the chains of discrimination; one hundred years later, the Negro lives on a lonely island of poverty in the midst of a vast ocean of material prosperity; one hundred years later, the Negro is still languished in the corners of American society and finds himself in exile in his own land.

So we've come here today to dramatize a shameful condition. In a sense we've come to our nation's capital to cash a check. When the architects of our republic wrote the magnificent words of the Constitution and the Declaration of Independence, they were signing a promissory note to which every American was to fall heir. This note was the promise that all men, yes, black men as well as white men, would be guaranteed the unalienable rights of life, liberty, and the pursuit of happiness.

It is obvious today that America has defaulted on this promissory note in so far as her citizens of color are concerned. Instead of honoring this sacred obligation, America has given the Negro people a bad check; a check which has come back marked 'insufficient funds'. We refuse to believe that there are insufficient funds in the great vaults of opportunity of this nation. And so we've come to cash this check, a check that will give us upon demand the riches of freedom and the security of justice.

We have also come to this hallowed spot to remind America of the fierce urgency of now. This is no time to engage in the luxury of cooling off or to take the tranquilizing drug of gradualism. Now is the time to make real the promises of democracy; now is the time to rise from the dark and desolate valley of segregation to the sunlit path of racial justice; now is the time to lift our nation from the quicksands of racial injustice to the solid rock of brotherhood; now is the time to make justice a reality for all God's children. It would be fatal for the nation to overlook the urgency of the moment. This sweltering summer of the Negro's legitimate discontent will not pass until there is an invigorating autumn of freedom and equality.

Nineteen sixty-three is not an end, but a beginning. And those who hope that the Negro needed to blow off stream and will now be content, will have a rude awakening if the nation returns to business as usual.

There will be neither rest nor tranquility in America until the Negro is granted his citizenship rights. The whirlwinds of revolt will continue to shake the foundations of our nation until the bright day of justice emerges.

But there is something that I must say to my people who stand on the warm threshold which leads into the palace of justice. In the process of gaining our rightful place we must not be guilty of wrongful deeds.

Let us not seek to satisfy our thirst for freedom by drinking from the cup of bitterness and hatred. We must forever conduct our struggle on the high plane of dignity and discipline. We must not allow our creative protest to degenerate into physical violence. Again and again we must rise to the majestic heights of meeting physical force with soul force.

The marvelous new militancy which has engulfed the Negro community must not lead us to a distrust of all white people, for many of our white brothers, as evidenced by their presence here today, have come to realize that their destiny is tied up with our destiny and they have come to realize that their freedom is inextricably bound to our freedom. This offense we share mounted to storm the battlements of injustice must be carried forth by a biracial army. We cannot walk alone.

And as we walk, we must make the pledge that we shall always march ahead. We cannot turn back. There are those who are asking the devotees of civil rights, 'When will you be satisfied?' We can never be satisfied as long as the Negro is the victim of the unspeakable horrors of police brutality.

We can never be satisfied as long as our bodies, heavy with fatigue of travel, cannot gain lodging in the motels of the highways and the hotels of the cities. We cannot be satisfied as long as the Negro's basic mobility is from a smaller ghetto to a larger one.

We can never be satisfied as long as our children are stripped of their selfhood and robbed of their dignity by signs stating 'for whites only'. We cannot be satisfied as long as a Negro in Mississippi cannot vote and a Negro in New York believes he has nothing for which to vote. No, we are not satisfied, and we will not be satisfied until justice rolls down like waters and righteousness like a mighty stream.

I am not unmindful that some of you have come here out of excessive trials and tribulation. Some of you have come fresh from narrow jail cells. Some of you have come from areas where your quest for freedom left you battered by the storms of persecution and staggered by the winds of police brutality. You have been the veterans of creative suffering. Continue to work with the faith that unearned suffering is redemptive.

Go back to Mississippi; go back to Alabama; go back to South Carolina; go back to Georgia; go back to Louisiana; go back to the slums and ghettos of the northern cities, knowing that somehow this situation can, and will be changed. Let us not wallow in the valley of despair.

So I say to you, my friends, that even though we must face the difficulties of today and tomorrow, I still have a dream. It is a dream deeply rooted in the American dream that one day this nation will rise up and live out the true meaning of its creed – we hold these truths to be self-evident, that all men are created equal.

I have a dream that one day on the red hills of Georgia, sons of former slaves and sons of former slave-owners will be able to sit down together at the table of brotherhood.

I have a dream that one day, even the state of Mississippi, a state sweltering with the heat of injustice, sweltering with the heat of oppression, will be transformed into an oasis of freedom and justice.

I have a dream my four little children will one day live in a nation where they will not be judged by the color of their skin but by the content of their character. I have a dream today!

I have a dream that one day, down in Alabama, with its vicious racists, with its governor having his lips dripping with the words of interposition and nullification, that one day, right there in Alabama, little black boys and black girls will be able to join hands with little white boys and white girls as sisters and brothers. I have a dream today!

I have a dream that one day every valley shall be exalted, every hill and mountain shall be made low, the rough places shall be made plain, and the crooked places shall be made straight and the glory of the Lord will be revealed and all flesh shall see it together.

This is our hope. This is the faith that I go back to the South with.

With this faith we will be able to tear out of the mountain of despair a stone of hope. With this faith we will be able to transform the jangling discords of our nation into a beautiful symphony of brotherhood.

With this faith we will be able to work together, to pray together, to struggle together, to go to jail together, to stand up for freedom together, knowing that we will be free one day. This will be the day when all of God's children will be able to sing with new meaning – 'my country 'tis of thee; sweet land of liberty; of thee I sing; land where my fathers died, land of the pilgrim's pride; from every mountain side, let freedom ring' – and if America is to be a great nation, this must become true.

So let freedom ring from the prodigious hilltops of New Hampshire.

Let freedom ring from the mighty mountains of New York.

Let freedom ring from the heightening Alleghenies of Pennsylvania.

Let freedom ring from the snow-capped Rockies of Colorado.

Let freedom ring from the curvaceous slopes of California.

But not only that.

Let freedom ring from Stone Mountain of Georgia.

Let freedom ring from Lookout Mountain of Tennessee.

Let freedom ring from every hill and molehill of Mississippi, from every mountainside, let freedom ring.

And when we allow freedom to ring, when we let it ring from every village and hamlet, from every state and city, we will be able to speed up that day when all of God's children – black men and white men, Jews and Gentiles, Catholics and Protestants – will be able to join hands and to sing in the words of the old Negro spiritual, 'Free at last, free at last; thank God Almighty, we are free at last.'

Speech, 28 August 1963

On Watts

ELDRIDGE CLEAVER

Folsom Prison
August 16, 1965

As we left the Mess Hall Sunday morning and milled around in the prison yard, after four days of abortive uprising in Watts, a group of low riders[1] from Watts assembled on the basketball court. They were wearing jubilant, triumphant smiles, animated by a vicarious spirit by which they, too, were in the thick of the uprising taking place hundreds of miles away to the south in the Watts ghetto.

'Man,' said one, 'what they doing out there? Break it down for me, Baby.'

They slapped each other's outstretched palms in a cool salute and burst out laughing with joy.

'Home boy, them Brothers is taking care of Business!' shrieked another ecstatically.

Then one low rider, stepping into the center of the circle formed by the others, rared back on his legs and swaggered, hunching his belt up with his forearms as he'd seen James Cagney and George Raft do in too many gangster movies. I joined the circle. Sensing a creative moment in the offing, we all got very quiet, very still, and others passing by joined the circle and did likewise.

'Baby,' he said, 'they walking in fours and kicking in doors; dropping Reds[2] and busting heads; drinking wine and committing crime, shooting and looting; high-siding[3] and low-riding, setting fires and slashing tires; turning over cars and burning down bars; making Parker mad and making me glad; putting an end to that "go slow" crap and putting sweet Watts on the map – my black ass is in Folsom this morning but my black heart is in Watts!' Tears of joy were rolling from his eyes.

It was a cleansing, revolutionary laugh we all shared, something we have not often had occasion for.

Watts was a place of shame. We used to use Watts as an epithet in much the same way as city boys used 'country' as a term of derision. To deride one as a 'lame', who did not know what was happening (a rustic bumpkin), the 'in-crowd' of the time from L.A. would bring a cat down by saying that he had just left Watts, that he ought to go back to Watts until he had learned what was happening, or that he had just stolen enough money to move out of Watts and was already trying to play a cool part. But now, blacks are seen in Folsom saying, 'I'm from Watts, Baby!' – whether true or no, but I think their meaning is clear. Confession: I, too, have participated in this game, saying, I'm from Watts. In fact, I did live there for a time, and I'm *proud* of it, the tired lamentations of Whitney Young, Roy Wilkins, and The Preacher [M. L. King] notwithstanding.

1 *Low rider*. A Los Angeles nickname for ghetto youth. Originally the term was coined to describe the youth who had lowered the bodies of their cars so that they rode low, close to the ground; also implied was the style of driving that these youngsters perfected. Sitting behind the steering wheel and slumped low down in the seat, all that could be seen of them was from their eyes up, which used to be the cool way of driving. When these youthful hipsters alighted from their vehicles, the term *low rider* stuck with them, evolving to the point where all black ghetto youth – but *never* the soft offspring of the black bourgeoisie – are referred to as low riders.
2 *Reds*. A barbiturate, called Red Devils; so called because of the color of the capsule and because they are reputed to possess a vicious kick.
3 *High-siding*. Cutting up. Having fun at the expense of another.

Soul on Ice, 1968

Nikki-Rosa

NIKKI GIOVANNI

childhood remembrances are always a drag
if you're Black
you always remember things like living in Woodlawn
with no inside toilet
and if you become famous or something
they never talk about how happy you were to have
your mother

all to yourself and
how good the water felt when you get your bath
from one of those
big tubs that folk in chicago barbecue in
and somehow when you talk about home
it never gets across how much you
understood their feelings
as the whole family attended meetings about Hollydale
and even though you remember
your biographers never understand
your father's pain as he sells his stock
and another dream goes
and though you're poor it isn't poverty that
concerns you
and though they fought a lot
it isn't your father's drinking that makes any difference
but only that everybody is together and you
and your sister have happy birthdays and very good
Christmases
and I really hope no white person ever has cause
to write about me
because they never understand
Black love is Black wealth and they'll
probably talk about my hard childhood
and never understand that
all the while I was quite happy.

Black Feeling, Black Talk, Black Judgment, 1968

'Remember the ladies'

ABIGAIL ADAMS

[Written to her husband, who was at the Second Continental Congress in Philadelphia]

I long to hear that you have declared an independency. And by the way, in the new Code of Laws which I suppose it will be necessary for you to make, I desire you would remember the ladies and be more generous and favorable to them than your ancestors. Do not put such unlimited power into the hands of the husbands. Remember all men would be tyrants if they could. If particular care and attention is not paid to the ladies, we are determined to foment a rebellion, and will not hold ourselves bound by any laws in which we have no voice or representation.

That your sex are naturally tyrannical is a truth so thoroughly established as to admit of no dispute, but such of you as wish to be happy willingly give up the harsh title of master for the more tender and endearing one of friend. Why then not put it out of the power of the vicious and the lawless to use us with cruelty and indignity with impunity? Men of sense in all ages abhor those customs which treat us only as the vassals of your sex. Regard us then as beings placed by providence under your protection, and in imitation of the Supreme Being make use of that power only for our happiness.

To John Adams, 31 March 1776

'Another tribe more numerous'

JOHN ADAMS

As to Declarations of Independency, be patient. Read our privateering laws and our commercial laws. What signifies a word?

As to your extraordinary Code of Laws, I cannot but laugh. We have been told that our struggle has loosened the bonds of government everywhere; that children and apprentices were disobedient, that schools and colleges were grown turbulent, that Indians slighted their guardians and Negroes grew insolent to their masters. But your letter was the first intimation that another tribe more numerous and powerful than all the rest were grown discontented. This is rather too coarse a compliment, but you are so saucy I won't blot it out.

Depend upon it, we know better than to repeal our masculine systems. Although they are in full force, you know they are little more than theory. We dare not exert our power in its full latitude. We are obliged to go fair and softly, and in practice you know we are the subjects. We have only the name of masters, and rather than give up this, which would completely subject us to the despotism of the petticoat, I hope General Washington and all our brave heroes would fight. I am sure every good politician would plot as long as he would against despotism, empire, monarchy, aristocracy, oligarchy, or ochlocracy. – A fine story indeed. I begin to think the ministry as deep as they are wicked. After stirring up Tories, landjobbers, trimmers, bigots, Canadians, Indians, Negroes, Hanoverians, Hessians, Russians, Irish Roman Catholics, Scotch renegadoes, at last they have stimulated the [—] to demand new privileges and threaten to rebel.

To Abigail Adams, 14 April 1776

'A little mite 'bout Woman's Rights'

SOJOURNER TRUTH

[Report of an address at a convention for women's rights held in New York City in 1853]

Sojourner Truth, a tall colored woman, well known in anti-slavery circles, and called the Lybian Sybil, made her appearance on the platform. This was the signal for a fresh outburst from the mob; for at every session every man of them was promptly in his place, at twenty-five cents a head. And this was the one redeeming feature of this mob – it paid all expenses, and left a surplus in the treasury. Sojourner combined in herself, as an individual, the two most hated elements of humanity. She was black, and she was a woman, and all the insults that could be cast upon color and sex were together hurled at her; but there she stood, calm and dignified, a grand, wise woman, who could neither read nor write, and yet with deep insight could penetrate the very soul of the universe about her. As soon as the terrible turmoil was in a measure quelled

She said: Is it not good for me to come and draw forth a spirit, to see what kind of spirit people are of? I see that some of you have got the spirit of a goose, and some have got the spirit of a snake. I feel at home here. I come to you, citizens of New York, as I suppose you ought to be. I am a citizen of the State of New York; I was born in it, and I was a slave in the State of New York; and now I am a good citizen of this State. I was born here, and I can tell you I feel at home here. I've been lookin' round and watchin' things, and I know a little mite 'bout Woman's Rights, too. I come forth to speak 'bout Woman's Rights, and want to throw in my little mite, to keep the scales a-movin'. I know that it feels a kind o' hissin' and ticklin' like to see a colored woman get up and tell you about things, and Woman's Rights. We have all been thrown down so low nobody thought we'd ever get up again; but we have been long enough trodden now; we will come up again, and now I am here.

I was a-thinkin', when I see women contendin' for their rights, I was a-thinkin' what a difference there is now, and what there was in old times. I have only a few minutes to speak; but in the old times the kings of the earth would hear a woman. There was a king in the Scriptures; and then it was the kings of the earth would kill a woman if she come into their presence; but Queen Esther come forth, for she was oppressed, and felt there was a great wrong, and she said I will die or I will bring my complaint before the king. Should the king of the United States be greater, or more crueler, or more harder? But the king, he raised up his sceptre and said:

'Thy request shall be granted unto thee – to the half of my kingdom will I grant it to thee!' Then he said he would hang Haman on the gallows he had made up high. But that is not what women come forward to contend. The women want their rights as Esther. She only wanted to explain her rights. And he was so liberal that he said, 'the half of my kingdom shall be granted to thee,' and he did not wait for her to ask, he was so liberal with her.

Now, women do not ask half of a kingdom, but their rights, and they don't get 'em. When she comes to demand 'em, don't you hear how sons hiss their mothers like snakes, because they ask for their rights; and can they ask for anything less? The king ordered Haman to be hung on the gallows which he prepared to hang others; but I do not want any man to be killed, but I am sorry to see them so short-minded. But we'll have our rights; see if we don't; and you can't stop us from them; see if you can. You may hiss as much as you like, but it is comin'. Women don't get half as much rights as they ought to; we want more, and we will have it. Jesus says: 'What I say to one, I say to all – watch!' I'm a-watchin'. God says: 'Honor your father and your mother.' Sons and daughters ought to behave themselves before their mothers, but they do not. I can see them a-laughin', and pointin' at their mothers up here on the stage. They hiss when an aged woman comes forth. If they'd been brought up proper they'd have known better than hissing like snakes and geese. I'm 'round watchin' these things, and I wanted to come up and say these few things to you, and I'm glad of the hearin' you give me. I wanted to tell you a mite about Woman's Rights, and so I came out and said so. I am sittin' among you to watch; and every once and awhile I will come out and tell you what time of night it is.

E. C. Stanton et al., *History of Woman Suffrage*, vol. 1, 1881

'The world is at their feet'

JAMES BRYCE

In no country are women, and especially young women, so much made of. The world is at their feet. Society seems organized for the purpose of providing enjoyment for them. Parents, uncles, aunts, elderly friends, even brothers, are ready to make their comfort and convenience bend to the girls' wishes. The wife has fewer opportunities for reigning over the world of amusements, because, except among the richest people, she has more to do in household management than in England, owing to the scarcity of servants. But she holds in her own house a more prominent, if not a more substantially powerful, position than in England or even in France. With the German *Hausfrau*, who is too often content to be a mere housewife, there is of course no comparison. The best proof of the superior place American ladies occupy is to be found in the notions they profess to entertain of the relations of an English married pair. They talk of the English wife as little better than a slave, declaring that when they stay with English friends, or receive an English couple in America, they see the wife always deferring to the husband and the husband always assuming that his pleasure and convenience are to prevail. The European wife, they admit, often gets her own way, but she gets it by tactful arts, by flattery or wheedling or playing on the man's weaknesses; whereas in America the husband's duty and desire is to gratify the wife and render to her those services which the English tyrant exacts from his consort.[1] One may often hear an American matron commiserate a friend who has married in Europe, while the daughters declare in chorus that they will never follow the example. Laughable as all this may seem to Englishwomen, it is perfectly true that the theory as well as the practice of conjugal life is not the same in America as in England. There are overbearing husbands in America, but they are more condemned by the opinion of the neighbourhood than in England. There are exacting wives in England, but their husbands are more pitied than would be the case in America. In neither country can one say that the principle of perfect equality reigns, for in America the balance inclines nearly though not quite as much in favour of the wife as it does in England in favour of the husband. No one man can have a sufficiently large acquaintance in both countries to entitle his individual opinion on the results to much weight. So far as I have been able to collect views from those observers who have lived in both countries, they are in favour of the American practice, perhaps because the theory it is based on departs less from pure equality than does that of England. These observers do not mean that the recognition of women as equals or superiors makes them any better or sweeter or wiser than Englishwomen; but rather that the principle of equality, by correcting the characteristic faults of men, and especially their selfishness and vanity, is more conducive to the concord and happiness of a home. They conceive that, to make the wife feel her independence and responsibility more strongly than she does in Europe, tends to brace and expand her character, while conjugal affection, usually stronger in her than in the husband, inasmuch as there are fewer competing interests, saves her from abusing the precedence yielded to her. This seems to be true, but I have heard others maintain that the American system, since it does not require the wife habitually to forego her own wishes, tends, if not to make her self-indulgent and capricious, yet slightly to impair the more delicate charms of character; as it is written, 'It is more blessed to give than to receive.'

A European cannot spend an evening in an American drawing-room without perceiving that the attitude of men to women is not that with which he is familiar at home. The average European man has usually a slight sense of condescension when he talks to a woman on serious subjects. Even if she is his superior in intellect, in character, in social rank, he thinks that as a man he is her superior, and consciously or unconsciously talks down to her. She is too much accustomed to this to resent it, unless it becomes tastelessly palpable. Such a notion does not cross an American's mind. He talks to a woman just as he would to a man, of course with more deference of manner, and with a proper regard to the topics likely to interest her, but giving her his intellectual best, addressing her as a person whose opinion is understood by both to be worth as much as his own. Similarly an American lady does not expect to have conversation made to her. It is just as much her duty or pleasure to lead it as the man's is, and more often than not she takes the burden from him, darting along with a gay vivacity which puts to shame his slower wits.

*

Some one may ask how far the differences between the position of women in America and their position in Europe are due to democracy? or if not to this, then to what other cause?

They are due to democratic feeling in so far as they spring from the notion that all men are free and equal, possessed of certain inalienable rights, and owing certain corresponding duties. This root idea of democracy cannot stop at defining men as male human beings, any more than it could ultimately stop at defining them as white human beings. For many years the Americans believed in equality with the pride of discoverers as well as with the fervour of apostles. Accustomed to apply it to all sorts and conditions of men, they were naturally the first to apply it to women also; not, indeed, as respects politics, but in all the social as well as legal relations of life. Democracy is in America more respectful of the individual, less disposed to infringe his freedom or subject him to any sort of legal or family control, than it has shown itself in Continental Europe, and this regard for the individual enured to the benefit of women. Of the other causes that have worked in the same direction two may be mentioned. One is the usage of the Congregationalist, Presbyterian, and Baptist churches, under which a woman who is a member of the congregation has the same rights in choosing a deacon, elder, or pastor, as a man has. Another is the fact that among the westward-moving settlers women were at first few in number, and were therefore treated with special respect. The habit then formed was retained as the communities grew, and propagated itself all over the country.

What have been the results on the character and usefulness of women themselves?

Favourable. They have opened to them a wider life and more variety of career. While the special graces of the feminine character do not appear to have suffered, there has been produced a sort of independence and a capacity for self-help which are increasingly valuable as the number of unmarried women increases. More resources are open to an American woman who has to lead a solitary life, not merely in the way of employment, but for the occupation of her mind and tastes, than to a European spinster or widow; while her education has not rendered the American wife less competent for the discharge of household duties.

How has the nation at large been affected by the development of this new type of womanhood, or rather perhaps of this variation on the English type?

If women have on the whole gained, it is clear that the nation gains through them. As mothers they mould the character of their children; while the function of forming the habits of society and determining its moral tone rests greatly in their hands. But there is reason to think that the influence of the American system tells directly for good upon men as well as upon the whole community. Men gain in being brought to treat women as equals rather than as graceful playthings or useful drudges. The respect for women which every American man either feels or is obliged by public sentiment to profess, has a wholesome effect on his conduct and character, and serves to check the cynicism which some other peculiarities of the country foster. The nation as a whole owes to the active benevolence of its women, and their zeal in promoting social reforms, benefits which the customs of Continental Europe would scarcely have permitted women to confer. Europeans have of late years begun to render a well-deserved admiration to the brightness and vivacity of American ladies. Those who know the work they have done and are doing in many a noble cause will admire still more their energy, their courage, their self-devotion. No country seems to owe more to its women than America does, nor to owe to them so much of what is best in social institutions and in the beliefs that govern conduct.

1 I have heard American ladies say, for instance, that they have observed that an Englishman who has forgotten his keys, sends his wife to the top of the house to fetch them; whereas an American would do the like errand for his wife, and never suffer her to do it for him.

The American Commonwealth, 1888, ch. 107

Frankie and Johnny

ANONYMOUS

1

Frankie and Johnny were lovers,
Lordy, how they could love,
Swore to be true to each other,
True as the stars above,
  He was her man, but he done her wrong.

2

Little Frankie was a good gal,
As everybody knows,
She did all the work around the house,
And pressed her Johnny's clothes,
  He was her man, but he done her wrong.

3

Johnny was a yeller man,
With coal black, curly hair,
Everyone up in St Louis
Thought he was a millionaire,
  He was her man, but he done her wrong.

4

Frankie went down to the bar-room,
Called for a bottle of beer,
Says, 'Looky here, Mister Bartender,
Has my lovin' Johnny been here?
  He is my man, and he's doin' me wrong.'

5

'I will not tell you no story,
I will not tell you no lie,
Johnny left here about an hour ago,
With a gal named Nelly Bly,
  He is your man and he's doin' you wrong.'

6

Little Frankie went down Broadway,
With a pistol in her hand,
Said, 'Stand aside you chorus gals,
I'm lookin' for my man,
  He is my man, and he's doin' me wrong.'

7

The first time she shot him, he staggered,
The next time she shot him, he fell,
The last time she shot, O Lawdy,
There was a new man's face in hell,
  She shot her man, for doin' her wrong.

8

'Turn me over doctor,
Turn me over slow,
I got a bullet in my left hand side,
Great God, it's hurtin' me so.
  I was her man, but I done her wrong.'

9

It was a rubber-tyred buggy,
Decorated hack,
Took poor Johnny to the graveyard,
Brought little Frankie back,
  He was her man, but he done her wrong.

10

It was not murder in the first degree,
It was not murder in the third.
A woman simply dropped her man
Like a hunter drops his bird,
  She shot her man, for doin' her wrong.

11

The last time I saw Frankie,
She was sittin' in the 'lectric chair,
Waitin' to go and meet her God
With the sweat runnin' out of her hair,
  She shot her man, for doin' her wrong.

12

Walked on down Broadway,
As far as I could see,
All I could hear was a two string bow
Playin' 'Nearer my God to thee',
  He was her man, and he done her wrong.

c. 1870–5

'The equality of rights in America'

JAMES FENIMORE COOPER

The equality of the United States is no more absolute than that of any other country. There may be less inequality in this nation than in most others, but inequality exists, and, in some respects, with stronger features than it is usual to meet with in the rest of Christendom.

The rights of property being an indispensable condition of civilization, and its quiet possession every where guarantied, equality of condition is rendered impossible. One man must labor, while another may live luxuriously on his means; one has leisure and opportunity to cultivate his tastes, to increase his information, and to refine his habits, while another is compelled to toil, that he may live. One is reduced to serve, while another commands, and, of course, there can be no equality in their social conditions.

*

By the inequality of civil and political rights that exists in certain parts of the Union, and the great equality that exists in others, we see the necessity of referring the true character of the institutions to those of the states, without a just understanding of which, it is impossible to obtain any general and accurate ideas of the real polity of the country.

The same general exceptions to civil and political equality, that are found in other free countries, exist in this, though under laws peculiar to ourselves. Women and minors are excluded from the suffrage, and from maintaining suits at law, under the usual provisions, here as well as elsewhere. None but natives of the country can fill many of the higher offices, and paupers, felons and all those who have not fixed residences, are also excluded from the suffrage. In a few of the states property is made the test of political rights, and, in nearly half of them, a large portion of the inhabitants, who are of a different race from the original European occupants of the soil, are entirely excluded from all political, and from many of the civil rights, that are enjoyed by those who are deemed citizens. A slave can neither choose, nor be chosen to office, nor, in most of the states, can even a free man, unless a white man. A slave can neither sue nor be sued; he can not hold property, real or personal, nor can he, in many of the states, be a witness in any suit, civil or criminal.

It follows from these facts, that absolute equality of condition, of political rights, or of civil rights, does not exist in the United States, though they all exist in a much greater degree in some states than in others, and in some of the states, perhaps, to as great a degree as is practicable. In what are usually called the free states of America, or those in which domestic slavery is abolished, there is to be found as much equality in every respect as comports with safety, civilization and the rights of property. This is also true, as respects the white population, in those states in which domestic slavery does exist; though the number of the bond is in a large proportion to that of the free.

As the tendency of the institutions of America is to the right, we learn in these truths, the power of facts, every question of politics being strictly a question of practice. They who fancy it possible to frame the institutions of a country, on the pure principles of abstract justice, as these principles exist in theories, know little of human nature, or of the restraints that are necessary to society. Abuses assail us in a thousand forms, and it is hopeless to aspire to any condition of humanity, approaching perfection. The very necessity of a government at all, arises from the impossibility of controlling the passions by any other means than that of force.

The celebrated proposition contained in the declaration of independence is not to be understood literally. All men are not 'created equal', in a physical, or even a moral sense, unless we limit the signification to one of political rights. This much is true, since human institutions are a human invention, with which nature has had no connection. Men are not born equals, physically, since one has a good constitution, another a bad; one is handsome, another ugly; one white, another black. Neither are men born equals morally, one possessing genius, or a natural aptitude, while his brother is an idiot. As regards all human institutions men are born equal, no sophistry being able to prove that nature intended one should inherit power and wealth, another slavery and want. Still artificial inequalities are the inevitable consequences of artificial ordinances, and in founding a new governing principle for the social compact, the American legislators instituted new modes of difference.

The very existence of government at all, infers inequality. The citizen who is preferred to office becomes the superior of those who are not, so long as he is the repository of power, and the child inherits the wealth of the parent as a controlling law of society. All that the great American proposition, therefore, can mean, is to set up new and juster notions of natural rights than those which existed previously, by asserting, in substance, that God has not instituted political inequalities, as was pretended by the advocates of the Jus Divinum, and that men possessed a full and natural authority to form such social institutions as best suited their necessities.

There are numerous instances in which the social inequality of America may do violence to our notions of abstract justice, but the compromise of interests under which all civilized society must exist, renders this unavoidable. Great principles seldom escape working injustice in particular things, and this so much the more, in establishing the relations of a community, for in them many great, and frequently conflicting principles enter, to maintain the more essential features of which sacrifices of parts become necessary. If we would have civilization and the exertion indispensable to its success, we must have property; if we have property, we must have its rights; if we have the rights of property, we must take those consequences of the rights of property which are inseparable from the rights themselves.

The equality of rights in America, therefore, after allowing for the striking exception of domestic slavery, is only a greater extension of the principle than common, while there is no such thing as an equality of condition. All that can be said of the first, is that it has been carried as far as a prudent discretion will at all allow, and of the last, that the inequality is the simple result of civilization, unaided by any of those factitious plans that have been elsewhere devised in order to augment the power of the strong, and to enfeeble the weak.

Equality is nowhere laid down as a governing principle of the institutions of the United States, neither the word, nor any inference that can be fairly deduced from its meaning, occurring in the constitution. As respect the states, themselves, the professions of an equality of rights are more clear, and slavery excepted, the intention in all their governments is to maintain it, as far as practicable, though equality of condition is nowhere mentioned, all political economists knowing that it is unattainable, if, indeed, it be desirable. Desirable in practice, it can hardly be, since the result would be to force all down to the level of the lowest.

All that a good government aims at, therefore, is to add no unnecessary and artificial aid to the force of its own unavoidable consequences, and to abstain from fortifying and accumulating social inequality as a means of increasing political inequalities.

'On American Equality' in *The American Democrat*, 1838

'Call me "Cobbett" '

WILLIAM COBBETT

343. Now, then, my dear sir, this people contains very few persons very much raised in men's estimation, above the general mass; for, though there are some men of immense *fortunes*, their wealth does very little indeed in the way of purchasing even the outward signs of respect; and, as to *adulation*, it is not to be purchased with love or money. Men, be they what they may, are generally called by their *two names*, without any thing prefixed

or added. I am one of the greatest men in this country at present; for people in general call me '*Cobbett*', though the Quakers provokingly persevere in putting the *William* before it, and my old friends in Pennsylvania, use even the word *Billy*, which, in the very sound of the letters, is an antidote to everything like thirst for distinction.

344. Fielding, in one of his romances, observes that there are but few cases, in which a husband can be justified in availing himself of the right which the law gives him to bestow manual chastisement upon his wife, and that one of these, he thinks is, when any pretensions to *superiority of blood* make their appearance in her language and conduct. They have a better cure for this malady here; namely; silent, but, *ineffable contempt*.

345. It is supposed, in England, that this equality of estimation must beget a general coarseness and rudeness of behaviour. Never was there a greater mistake. No man likes to be treated with disrespect; and, when he finds that he can obtain respect only by treating others with respect, he will use that only means. When he finds that neither haughtiness nor wealth will bring him a civil word, he becomes civil himself; and, I repeat it again and again, this is a country of *universal civility*.

346. The causes of *hypocrisy* are the fear of loss and the hope of gain. Men crawl to those, whom, in their hearts, they despise, because they fear the effects of their ill-will and hope to gain by their good-will. The circumstances of all ranks are so easy here, that there is no cause for hypocrisy; and the thing is not of so fascinating a nature, that men should love it for its own sake.

347. The boasting of wealth, and the endeavouring to disguise poverty, these two acts, so painful to contemplate, are almost total strangers in this country; for, no man can gain adulation or respect by his wealth, and no man dreads the effects of poverty, because no man sees any dreadful effects arising from poverty.

348. That *anxious eagerness to get on*, which is seldom unaccompanied with some degree of *envy* of more successful neighbours, and which has its foundation first in *a dread of future want*, and next in a *desire to obtain distinction by means of wealth*; this anxious eagerness, so unamiable in itself, and so unpleasant an inmate of the breast, so great a sourer of the temper, is a stranger to America, where accidents and losses, which would drive an Englishman half mad, produce but very little agitation.

349. From the absence of so many causes of uneasiness, of envy, of jealousy, of rivalship, and of mutual dislike, *society*, that is to say, the intercourse between man and man, and family and family, becomes easy and pleasant; while the universal plenty is the cause of universal hospitality. I know, and have ever known, but little of the people in the cities and towns

in America; but, the difference between them and the people in the country can only be such as is found in all other countries.

A Year's Residence in the United States of America, 1818, part 2, ch. 11

'With respect to Aristocracy'

THOMAS JEFFERSON

With respect to Aristocracy, we should further consider that, before the establishment of the American states, nothing was known to history but the Man of the old world, crowded within limits either small or overcharged, and steeped in the vices which that situation generates. A government adapted to such men would be one thing; but a very different one than that for the Man of these states. Here every one may have land to labor for himself if he chooses; or, preferring the exercise of any other industry, may exact for it such compensation as not only to afford a comfortable subsistence, but wherewith to provide for a cessation from labor in old age. Every one, by his property, or by his satisfactory situation, is interested in the support of law and order. And such men may safely and advantageously reserve to themselves a wholesome control over their public affairs, and a degree of freedom, which in the hands of the canaille of the cities of Europe, would be instantly perverted to the demolition and destruction of every thing public and private. The history of the last 25 years of France, and of the last 40 years in America, nay of its last 200 years, proves the truth of both parts of this observation.

To John Adams, 28 October 1813

'A nod from an American'

GEORGE GORDON, LORD BYRON

I would rather, however, have a nod from an American, than a snuff-box from an emperor.

To Thomas Moore, 8 June 1822

'Any man's son'

FRANCES TROLLOPE

There was one man whose progress in wealth I watched with much interest and pleasure. When I first became his neighbour, himself, his wife, and four children, were living in one room, with plenty of beef-steaks and onions for breakfast, dinner, and supper, but with very few other comforts. He was one of the finest men I ever saw, full of natural intelligence and activity of mind and body, but he could neither read nor write. He drank but little whiskey, and but rarely chewed tobacco, and was therefore more free from that plague spot of spitting which rendered male colloquy so difficult to endure. He worked for us frequently, and often used to walk into the drawing-room and seat himself on the sofa, and tell me all his plans. He made an engagement with the proprietor of the wooded hill before mentioned, by which half the wood he could fell was to be his own. His unwearied industry made this a profitable bargain, and from the proceeds he purchased the materials for building a comfortable frame (or wooden) house; he did the work almost entirely himself. He then got a job for cutting rails, and, as he could cut twice as many in a day as any other man in the neighbourhood, he made a good thing of it. He then let half his pretty house, which was admirably constructed, with an ample portico, that kept it always cool. His next step was contracting for the building of a wooden bridge, and when I left Mohawk he had fitted up his half of the building as an hotel and grocery store; and I have no doubt that every sun that sets sees him a richer man than when it rose. He hopes to make his son a lawyer, and I have little doubt that he will live to see him sit in Congress; when this time arrives, the woodcutter's son will rank with any other member of Congress, not of courtesy, but of right, and the idea that his origin is a disadvantage, will never occur to the imagination of the most exalted of his fellow-citizens.

This is the only feature in American society that I recognise as indicative of the equality they profess. Any man's son may become the equal of any other man's son, and the consciousness of this is certainly a spur to exertion; on the other hand, it is also a spur to that coarse familiarity, untempered by any shadow of respect, which is assumed by the grossest and the lowest in their intercourse with the highest and most refined. This is a positive evil, and, I think, more than balances its advantages.

And here again it may be observed, that the theory of equality may be very daintily discussed by English gentlemen in a London dining-room, when the servant, having placed a fresh bottle of cool wine on the table, respectfully shuts the door, and leaves them to their walnuts and their wisdom; but it will be found less palatable when it presents itself in the shape of a hard, greasy paw, and is claimed in accents that breathe less of freedom than of onions and whiskey. Strong, indeed, must be the love of equality in an English breast if it can survive a tour through the Union.

Domestic Manners of the Americans, 1832, ch. 12

'The kingly commons'

HERMAN MELVILLE

Men may seem detestable as joint stock-companies and nations; knaves, fools, and murderers there may be; men may have mean and meagre faces; but man, in the ideal, is so noble and so sparkling, such a grand and glowing creature, that over any ignominious blemish in him all his fellows should run to throw their costliest robes. That immaculate manliness we feel within ourselves, so far within us, that it remains intact though all the outer character seem gone; bleeds with keenest anguish at the undraped spectacle of a valor-ruined man. Nor can piety itself, at such a shameful sight, completely stifle her upbraidings against the permitting stars. But this august dignity I treat of, is not the dignity of kings and robes, but that abounding dignity which has no robed investiture. Thou shalt see it shining in the arm that wields a pick or drives a spike; that democratic dignity which, on all hands, radiates without end from God, Himself! The great God absolute! The centre and circumference of all democracy! His omnipresence, our divine equality!

If, then, to meanest mariners, and renegades and castaways, I shall hereafter ascribe high qualities, though dark; weave round them tragic graces; if even the most mournful, perchance the most abased, among them all, shall at times lift himself to the exalted mounts; if I shall touch that workman's arm with some ethereal light; if I shall spread a rainbow over his disastrous set of sun; then against all mortal critics bear me out in it, thou just Spirit of Equality, which has spread one royal mantle of humanity over all my kind! Bear me out in it, thou great democratic God! who didst not refuse to the swart convict, Bunyan, the pale, poetic pearl; Thou who didst clothe with double hammered leaves of finest gold, the stumped and paupered arm of old Cervantes; Thou who didst pick up Andrew Jackson from the pebbles; who didst hurl him upon a warhorse; who didst thunder him higher than a throne! Thou who, in all Thy mighty, earthly marchings, ever cullest Thy selectest champions from the kingly commons; bear me out in it, O God!

Moby-Dick, 1851, ch. 26

'The pitifulest thing out is a mob'

MARK TWAIN

[Episode based upon an actual murder in Hannibal, Missouri, in 1845]

'Here comes old Boggs! – in from the country for his little old monthly drunk – here he comes, boys!'

All the loafers looked glad – I reckoned they was used to having fun out of Boggs. One of them says –

'Wonder who he's a gwyne to chaw up this time. If he'd a chawed up all the men he's been a gwyne to chaw up in the last twenty year, he'd have considerble ruputation, now.'

Another one says, 'I wisht old Boggs'd threaten me, 'cuz then I'd know I warn't gwyne to die for a thousan' year.'

Boggs comes a-tearing along on his horse, whooping and yelling like an Injun, and singing out –

'Cler the track, thar. I'm on the waw-path, and the price uv coffins is a gwyne to raise.'

He was drunk, and weaving about in his saddle; he was over fifty year old, and had a very red face. Everybody yelled at him, and laughed at him, and sassed him, and he sassed back, and said he'd attend to them and lay them out in their regular turns, but he couldn't wait now, because he'd come to town to kill old Colonel Sherburn, and his motto was, 'meat first, and spoon vittles to top off on'.

He see me, and rode up and says –

'Whar'd you come f'm, boy? You prepared to die?'

Then he rode on. I was scared; but a man says –

'He don't mean nothing; he's always a carryin' on like that, when he's drunk. He's the best-naturedest old fool in Arkansas – never hurt nobody, drunk nor sober.'

Boggs rode up before the biggest store in town and bent his head down so he could see under the curtain of the awning, and yells –

'Come out here, Sherburn! Come out and meet the man you've swindled. You're the houn' I'm after, and I'm a gwyne to have you, too!'

And so he went on, calling Sherburn everything he could lay his tongue to, and the whole street packed with people listening and laughing and go-ing on. By-and-by a proud-looking man about fifty-five – and he was a heap the best dressed man in that town, too – steps out of the store, and the crowd drops back on each side to let him come. He says to Boggs, mighty ca'm and slow – he says:

'I'm tired of this; but I'll endure it till one o'clock. Till one o'clock, mind – no longer. If you open your mouth against me only once, after that time, you can't travel so far but I will find you.'

Then he turns and goes in. The crowd looked mighty sober; nobody stirred, and there warn't no more laughing. Boggs rode off blackguarding Sherburn as loud as he could yell, all down the street; and pretty soon back he comes and stops before the store, still keeping it up. Some men crowded around him and tried to get him to shut up, but he wouldn't; they told him it would be one o'clock in about fifteen minutes, and so he *must* go home – he must go right away. But it didn't do no good. He cussed away, with all his might, and throwed his hat down in the mud and rode over it, and pretty soon away he went a-raging down the street again, with his gray hair a-flying. Everybody that could get a chance at him tried their best to coax him off of his horse so they could lock him up and get him sober; but it warn't no use – up the street he would tear again, and give Sherburn another cussing. By-and-by somebody says –

'Go for his daughter – quick, go for his daughter; sometimes he'll listen to her. If anybody can persuade him, she can.'

So somebody started on a run. I walked down street a ways, and stopped. In about five or ten minutes, here comes Boggs again – but not on his horse. He was a-reeling across the street towards me, bareheaded, with a friend on both sides of him aholt of his arms and hurrying him along. He was quiet, and looked uneasy; and he warn't hanging back any, but was doing some of the hurrying himself. Somebody sings out –

'Boggs!'

I looked over there to see who said it, and it was that Colonel Sherburn. He was standing perfectly still, in the street, and had a pistol raised in his right hand – not aiming it, but holding it out with the barrel tilted up towards the sky. The same second I see a young girl coming on the run, and two men with her. Boggs and the men turned round, to see who called him, and when they see the pistol the men jumped to one side, and the pistol barrel come down slow and steady to a level – both barrels cocked. Boggs throws up both of his hands, and says, 'O Lord, don't shoot!' Bang! goes the first shot, and he staggers back clawing at the air – bang! goes the second one, and he tumbles backwards onto the ground, heavy and solid, with his arms spread out. That young girl screamed out, and comes rushing, and down she throws herself on her father, crying, and saying, 'Oh, he's killed him, he's killed him!' The crowd closed up around them, and shouldered and jammed one another, with their necks stretched, trying to see, and people on the inside trying to shove them back, and shouting, 'Back, back! give him air, give him air!'

Colonel Sherburn he tossed his pistol onto the ground, and turned around on his heels and walked off.

They took Boggs to a little drug store, the crowd pressing around, just the same, and the whole town following, and I rushed and got a good place at the window, where I was close to him and could see in. They laid him on the floor, and put one large Bible under his head, and opened another one and spread it on his breast – but they tore open his shirt first, and I seen where one of the bullets went in. He made about a dozen long gasps, his breast lifting the Bible up when he drawed in his breath, and letting it down again when he breathed it out – and after that he laid still; he was dead. Then they pulled his daughter away from him, screaming and crying, and took her off. She was about sixteen, and very sweet and gentle-looking, but awful pale and scared.

Well, pretty soon the whole town was there, squirming and scrouging and pushing and shoving to get at the window and have a look, but people that had the places wouldn't give them up, and folks behind them was saying all the time, 'Say, now, you've looked enough, you fellows; 'taint right and 'taint fair, for you to stay thar all the time, and never give nobody a chance; other folks has their rights as well as you.'

There was considerable jawing back, so I slid out, thinking maybe there was going to be trouble. The streets was full, and everybody was excited. Everybody that seen the shooting was telling how it happened, and there was a big crowd packed around each one of these fellows, stretching their necks and listening. One long lanky man, with long hair and a big white fur stove-pipe hat on the back of his head, and a crooked-handled cane, marked out the places on the ground where Boggs stood, and where Sherburn stood, and the people following him around from one place to t'other and watching everything he done, and bobbing their heads to show they understood, and stooping a little and resting their hands on their thighs to watch him mark the places on the ground with his cane; and then he stood up straight and stiff where Sherburn had stood, frowning and having his hat-brim down over his eyes, and sung out, 'Boggs!' and then fetched his cane down slow to a level, and says 'Bang!' staggered backwards, says 'Bang!' again, and fell down flat on his back. The people that had seen the thing said he done it perfect; said it was just exactly the way it all happened. Then as much as a dozen people got out their bottles and treated him.

Well, by-and-by somebody said Sherburn ought to be lynched. In about a minute everybody was saying it; so away they went, mad and yelling, and snatching down every clothes-line they come to, to do the hanging with.

They swarmed up the street towards Sherburn's house, a-whooping and yelling and raging like Injuns, and everything had to clear the way or get run over and tromped to mush, and it was awful to see. Children was heeling it ahead of the mob, screaming and trying to get out of the way; and

every window along the road was full of women's heads, and there was nigger boys in every tree, and bucks and wenches looking over every fence; and
as soon as the mob would get nearly to them they would break and skaddle
back out of reach. Lots of the women and girls was crying and taking on,
scared most to death.

They swarmed up in front of Sherburn's palings as thick as they could jam
together, and you couldn't hear yourself think for the noise. It was a little
twenty-foot yard. Some sung out 'Tear down the fence! tear down the
fence!' Then there was a racket of ripping and tearing and smashing, and
down she goes, and the front wall of the crowd begins to roll in like a wave.

Just then Sherburn steps out onto the roof of his little front porch, with
a double-barrel gun in his hand, and takes his stand, perfectly ca'm and
deliberate, not saying a word. The racket stopped, and the wave sucked
back.

Sherburn never said a word – just stood there, looking down. The stillness was awful creepy and uncomfortable. Sherburn run his eye slow along
the crowd; and wherever it struck, the people tried a little to outgaze him,
but they couldn't; they dropped their eyes and looked sneaky. Then pretty
soon Sherburn sort of laughed; not the pleasant kind, but the kind that
makes you feel like when you are eating bread that's got sand in it.

Then he says, slow and scornful:

'The idea of *you* lynching anybody! It's amusing. The idea of you thinking you had pluck enough to lynch a *man*! Because you're brave enough to
tar and feather poor friendless cast-out women that come along here, did
that make you think you had grit enough to lay your hands on a *man*? Why,
a *man's* safe in the hands of ten thousand of your kind – as long as it's daytime and you're not behind him.

'Do I know you? I know you clear through. I was born and raised in the
South, and I've lived in the North; so I know the average all around. The
average man's a coward. In the North he lets anybody walk over him that
wants to, and goes home and prays for a humble spirit to bear it. In the
South one man, all by himself, has stopped a stage full of men, in the daytime, and robbed the lot. Your newspapers call you a brave people so much
that you think you *are* braver than any other people – whereas you're just
as brave, and no braver. Why don't your juries hang murderers? Because
they're afraid the man's friends will shoot them in the back, in the dark –
and it's just what they *would* do.

'So they always acquit; and then a *man* goes in the night, with a hundred
masked cowards at his back, and lynches the rascal. Your mistake is, that
you didn't bring a man with you; that's one mistake, and the other is that
you didn't come in the dark, and fetch your masks. You brought *part* of a

man – Buck Harkness, there – and if you hadn't had him to start you, you'd a taken it out in blowing.

'You didn't want to come. The average man don't like trouble and danger. *You* don't like trouble and danger. But if only *half* a man – like Buck Harkness, there – shouts "Lynch him, lynch him!" you're afraid to back down – afraid you'll be found out to be what you are – *cowards* – and so you raise a yell, and hang yourselves onto that half-a-man's coat tail, and come raging up here, swearing what big things you're going to do. The pitifulest thing out is a mob; that's what an army is – a mob; they don't fight with courage that's born in them, but with courage that's borrowed from their mass, and from their officers. But a mob without any *man* at the head of it, is *beneath* pitifulness. Now the thing for you to do, is to droop your tails and go home and crawl in a hole. If any real lynching's going to be done, it will be done in the dark, Southern fashion; and when they come they'll bring their masks, and fetch a *man* along. Now *leave* – and take your half-a-man with you' – tossing his gun up across his left arm and cocking it, when he says this.

The crowd washed back sudden, and then broke all apart and went tearing off every which way, and Buck Harkness he heeled it after them, looking tolerable cheap. I could a staid, if I'd a wanted to, but I didn't want to.

The Adventures of Huckleberry Finn, 1884, chs. 21–22

'All due to democracy'

JOHN BUTLER YEATS

Charles is a good talker – because he is so frank, never concealing his thought – and then he has the open ingenuous and *wide* mind of the American which nothing startles and nothing frightens. Elsewhere people are so anxious and timid, and from deadly fear, so distrustful of each other. Here the idea still exists, handed down from Early Settler days, of mutual helpfulness. They have a weak sense of law and of property, and are not enthusiastic over their civic duties but they easily become your friend – a real friend with an open hand. And *there is no class*. You have to come to America to find out the blessedness of those words.

To Ruth Hart, 15 December 1910

The ethical doctrine most popular in America is expressed by the word *service*. Every man, woman and child is brought up with the idea of service and it is fatal to sincerity. In America there is no such thing as sincerity. The effect of democracy is that each citizen regards himself as holding, by virtue of his citizenship and his vote, a kind of *public position*.

To W. B. Yeats, 10 February 1916

I see in the papers that important people engaged in teaching are making a tremendous 'to do' about the immorality in the schools. I fancy they are right. The cause of this thing is to me quite apparent. It is that the American boy and girl have lost the feeling for *personal pride and honour* and it is all due to democracy. It is undemocratic in America for anyone to have pride. That is why Quinn when he chooses is quite ready to treat me as an office boy, and he treats his clerks in the same way, and that is why George was asked such extraordinary questions about things quite intimate . . . There are no proud girls in America. Feminine beauty has not that *touch-me-not quality* which is half the charm of the well-bred girl (of other countries). It is the pride of the democracies and the Americans to have no pride, and it does make life pleasant and easy, but it leaves the American girl naked and defenceless against all these false ideas that are so abundant among socialists.

To Lily Yeats, 26 February 1921

Impromptu: The Suckers

WILLIAM CARLOS WILLIAMS

[At their trial in Dedham, Massachusetts, in 1921, Nicola Sacco and Bartolomeo Vanzetti were convicted of murdering two men during a robbery. After prolonged public protest and gubernatorial review, they were executed in 1927.]

Take it out in vile whisky, take it out
in lifting your skirts to show your silken
crotches; it is this that is intended.
You are it. Your pleas will always be denied.
You too will always go up with the two guys,
scapegoats to save the Republic and

especially the State of Massachusetts. The
Governor says so and you ain't supposed
to ask for details –

Your case has been reviewed by high-minded
and unprejudiced observers (like hell
they were!) the president of a great
university, the president of a noteworthy
technical school and a judge too old to sit
on the bench, men already rewarded for
their services to pedagogy and the enforcement
of arbitrary statutes. In other words
pimps to tradition –

Why in hell didn't they choose some other
kind of 'unprejudiced adviser' for their
death council? instead of sticking to that
autocratic strain of Boston backwash, except
that the council was far from unprejudiced
but the product of a rejected, discredited
class long since outgrown except for use in
courts and school, and that they
wanted it so –

Why didn't they choose at least one decent
Jew or some fair-minded Negro or anybody
but such a triumvirate of inversion, the
New England aristocracy, bent on working off
a grudge against you, Americans, you
are the suckers, you are the ones who will
be going up on the eleventh to get the current
shot into you, for the glory of the state
and the perpetuation of abstract justice –

And all this in the face of the facts: that
the man who swore, and deceived the jury
wilfully by so doing, that the bullets found
in the bodies of the deceased could be
identified as having been fired from the pistol
of one of the accused – later
acknowledged that he could not so identify
them; that the jurors now seven years after
the crime do not remember the details and
have wanted to forget them; that the

prosecution has never succeeded in
apprehending the accomplices nor in connecting
the prisoners with any of the loot stolen –

The case is perfect against you, all the
documents say so – in spite of the fact that
it is reasonably certain that you were not
at the scene of the crime, shown, quite as
convincingly as the accusing facts in the
court evidence, by better reasoning to have
been committed by someone else with whom
the loot can be connected and among whom the
accomplices can be found –

It's no use, you are Americans, just the dregs.
It's all you deserve. You've got the cash,
what the hell do you care? You've got
nothing to lose. You are inheritors of a great
tradition. My country right or wrong!
You do what you're told to do. You don't
answer back the way Tommy Jeff did or Ben
Frank or Georgie Washing. I'll say you
don't. You're civilized. You let your
betters tell you where you get off. Go
ahead –

But after all, the thing that swung heaviest
against you was that you were scared when
they copped you. Explain that you
nature's nobleman! For you know that every
American is innocent and at peace in his
own heart. He hasn't a damned thing to be
afraid of. He knows the government is for
him. Why, when a cop steps up and grabs
you at night you just laugh and think it's
a hell of a good joke –

That is what was intended from the first.
So take it out in your rotten whisky and
silk underwear. That's what you get out of
it. But put it down in your memory that this
is the kind of stuff that they can't get away
with. It is there and it's loaded. No one
can understand what makes the present age

what it is. They are mystified by certain insistences.

(1938) *Collected Earlier Poems*, 1951

'All right we are two nations'

JOHN DOS PASSOS

they have clubbed us off the streets they are stronger they are rich they hire and fire the politicians the newspapereditors the old judges the small men with reputations the collegepresidents the wardheelers (listen businessmen collegepresidents judges America will not forget her betrayers) they hire the men with guns the uniforms the policecars the patrolwagons

all right you have won you will kill the brave men our friends tonight

there is nothing left to do we are beaten we the beaten crowd together in these old dingy schoolrooms on Salem Street   shuffle up and down the gritty creaking stairs sit hunched with bowed heads on benches and hear the old words of the haters of oppression made new in sweat and agony tonight

our work is over the scribbled phrases the nights typing releases the smell of the printshop the sharp reek of newprinted leaflets the rush for Western Union stringing words into wires the search for stinging words to make you feel who are your oppressors America

America our nation has been beaten by strangers who have turned our language inside out who have taken the clean words our fathers spoke and made them slimy and foul

their hired men sit on the judge's bench they sit back with their feet on the tables under the dome of the State House they are ignorant of our beliefs they have the dollars the guns the armed forces the powerplants

they have built the electricchair and hired the executioner to throw the switch

all right we are two nations

American our nation has been beaten by strangers who have bought the laws and fenced off the meadows and cut down the woods for pulp and turned our pleasant cities into slums and sweated the wealth out of our people and when they want to they hire the executioner to throw the switch

but do they know that the old words of the immigrants are being renewed in blood and agony tonight do they know that the old American speech of the haters of oppression is new tonight in the mouth of an old woman from

Pittsburgh of a husky boilermaker from Frisco who hopped freights clear from the Coast to come here in the mouth of a Back Bay socialworker in the mouth of an Italian printer of a hobo from Arkansas   the language of the beaten nation is not forgotten in our ears tonight

the men in the deathhouse made the old words new before they died

If it had not been for these things, I might have lived out my life talking at streetcorners to scorning men. I might have died unknown, unmarked, a failure. This is our career and our triumph. Never in our full life can we hope to do such work for tolerance, for justice, for man's understanding of man as now we do by an accident.

now their work is over   the immigrants haters of oppression lie quiet in black suits in the little undertaking parlor in the North End   the city is quiet   the men of the conquering nation are not to be seen on the streets

they have won why are they scared to be seen on the streets? on the streets you see only the downcast faces of the beaten   the streets belong to the beaten nation   all the way to the cemetery where the bodies of the immigrants are to be burned   we line the curbs in the drizzling rain we crowd the wet sidewalks elbow to elbow silent pale looking with scared eyes at the coffins

we stand defeated America

'The Camera Eye (50)' in *The Big Money*, 1936

'An unworldly assumption'

MARY MCCARTHY

This republic was founded on an unworldly assumption, a denial of 'the facts of life'. It is manifestly untrue that all men are created equal; interpreted in worldly terms, this doctrine has resulted in a pseudo-equality, that is, in standardization, in an equality of things rather than of persons. The inalienable rights to life, liberty, and the pursuit of happiness appear, in practice, to have become the inalienable right to a bathtub, a flush toilet, and a can of Spam. Left-wing critics of America attribute this result to the intrusion of capitalism; right-wing critics see it as the logical dead end of democracy. Capitalism, certainly, now depends on mass production, which depends on large-scale distribution of uniform goods, till the consumer to-day is the victim of the manufacturer who launches on him a regiment of products for which he must make house-room in his soul. The buying impulse, in its original force and purity, was not nearly so crass, however, or so meanly acquisitive as many radical critics suppose. The purchase of a bathtub was the exercise of a spiritual right. The immigrant or the poor native American bought a bathtub, not because he wanted to take a bath, but because he wanted to be in a *position* to do so. This remains true in many fields today; possessions, when they are desired, are not wanted for their own sakes but as tokens of an ideal state of freedom, fraternity, and franchise. 'Keeping up with the Joneses' is a vulgarization of Jefferson's concept, but it too is a declaration of the rights of man, and decidedly unfeasible and visionary. Where for a European, a fact is a fact, for us Americans, the real, if it is relevant at all, is simply symbolic appearance. We are a nation of twenty million bathrooms, with a humanist in every tub. One such humanist I used to hear of on Cape Cod had, on growing rich, installed two toilets side by side in his marble bathroom, on the model of the two-seater of his youth. He was a clear case of Americanism, hospitable, gregarious, and impractical, a theorist of perfection. Was his dream of the conquest of poverty a vulgar dream or a noble one, a material demand or a spiritual insistence? It is hard to think of him as a happy man, and in this too he is characteristically American, for the parity of the radio, the movies, and the washing machine has made Americans sad, reminding them of another parity of which these things were to be but emblems.

'America the Beautiful: The Humanist in the Bathtub' (1947) in
On the Contrary, 1962

CHARACTER

Americans – like omelettes:
there is no such thing
as a pretty good one.

W. H. Auden, 'Marginalia', 1965–8

What is an American?

J. HECTOR ST JOHN DE CRÈVECŒUR

In this great American asylum, the poor of Europe have by some means met together, and in consequence of various causes; to what purpose should they ask one another what countrymen they are? Alas, two thirds of them had no country. Can a wretch who wanders about, who works and starves, whose life is a continual scene of sore affliction or pinching penury; can that man call England or any other kingdom his country? A country that had no bread for him, whose fields procured him no harvest, who met with nothing but the frowns of the rich, the severity of the laws, with jails and punishments; who owned not a single foot of the extensive surface of this planet? No! urged by a variety of motives, here they came. Every thing has tended to regenerate them; new laws, a new mode of living, a new social system; here they are become men: in Europe they were as so many useless plants, wanting vegetative mould, and refreshing showers; they withered, and were mowed down by want, hunger, and war; but now by the power of transplantation, like all other plants they have taken root and flourished! Formerly they were not numbered in any civil lists of their country, except in those of the poor; here they rank as citizens. By what invisible power has this surprising metamorphosis been performed? By that of the laws and that of their industry. The laws, the indulgent laws, protect them as they arrive, stamping on them the symbol of adoption; they receive ample rewards for their labours; these accumulated rewards procure them lands; those lands confer on them the title of freemen, and to that title every benefit is affixed which men can possibly require. This is the great operation daily performed by our laws. From whence proceed these laws? From our government. Whence the government? It is derived from the original genius and strong desire of the people ratified and confirmed by the crown. This is the great chain which links us all, this is the picture which every province exhibits, Nova Scotia excepted. There the crown has done all; either there were no people who had genius, or it was not much attended to: the consequence is, that the province is very thinly inhabited indeed; the power of the crown in conjunction with the musketos has prevented men from settling there. Yet some parts of it flourished once, and it contained a mild harmless set of people. But for the fault of a few leaders, the whole were banished. The greatest political error the crown ever committed in America, was to cut off men from a country which wanted nothing but men!

What attachment can a poor European emigrant have for a country where he had nothing? The knowledge of the language, the love of a few kindred as poor as himself, were the only cords that tied him: his country is now that which gives him land, bread, protection, and consequence: *Ubi panis ibi patria*, is the motto of all emigrants. What then is the American, this new man? He is either an European, or the descendant of an European, hence that strange mixture of blood, which you will find in no other country. I could point out to you a family whose grandfather was an Englishman, whose wife was Dutch, whose son married a French woman, and whose present four sons have now four wives of different nations. *He* is an American, who leaving behind him all his ancient prejudices and manners, receives new ones from the new mode of life he has embraced, the new government he obeys, and the new rank he holds. He becomes an American by being received in the broad lap of our great *Alma Mater*. Here individuals of all nations are melted into a new race of men, whose labours and posterity will one day cause great changes in the world. Americans are the western pilgrims, who are carrying along with them that great mass of arts, sciences, vigour, and industry which began long since in the east; they will finish the great circle. The Americans were once scattered all over Europe; here they are incorporated into one of the finest systems of population which has ever appeared, and which will hereafter become distinct by the power of the different climates they inhabit. The American ought therefore to love this country much better than that wherein either he or his forefathers were born. Here the rewards of his industry follow with equal steps the progress of his labour; his labour is founded on the basis of nature, *self-interest*; can it want a stronger allurement? Wives and children, who before in vain demanded of him a morsel of bread, now, fat and frolicsome, gladly help their father to clear those fields whence exuberant crops are to arise to feed and to clothe them all; without any part being claimed, either by a despotic prince, a rich abbot, or a mighty lord. Here religion demands but little of him; a small voluntary salary to the minister, and gratitude to God; can he refuse these? The American is a new man, who acts upon new principles; he must therefore entertain new ideas, and form new opinions. From involuntary idleness, servile dependence, penury, and useless labour, he has passed to toils of a very different nature, rewarded by ample subsistence. – This is an American.

Letters from an American Farmer, 1782, letter 3

'My countrymen'

THOMAS JEFFERSON

With respect to my countrymen there is surely nothing which can render them uneasy, in the observations made on them. They know that they are not perfect, and will be sensible that you have viewed them with a philanthropic eye. You say much good of them, and less ill than they are conscious may be said with truth. I have studied their character with attention. I have thought them, as you found them, aristocratical, pompous, clannish, indolent, hospitable, and I should have added, disinterested, but you say attached to their interest. This is the only trait in their character wherein our observations differ. I have always thought them so careless of their interests, so thoughtless in their expenses and in all their transactions of business that I had placed it among the vices of their character, as indeed most virtues when carried beyond certain bounds degenerate into vices. I had even ascribed this to its cause, to that warmth of their climate which unnerves and unmans both body and mind. While on this subject I will give you my idea of the characters of the several states.

In the North they are	In the South they are
cool	fiery
sober	voluptuary
laborious	indolent
persevering	unsteady
independent	independent
jealous of their own liberties, and just to those of others	zealous for their own liberties, but trampling on those of others
interested	generous
chicaning	candid
superstitious and hypocritical in their religion	without attachment or pretensions to any religion but that of the heart

These characteristics grow weaker and weaker by gradation from North to South and South to North, insomuch that an observing traveller, without the aid of the quadrant, may always know his latitude by the character of the people among whom he finds himself. It is in Pennsylvania that the two characters seem to meet and blend, and form a people free from the extremes both of vice and virtue. Peculiar circumstances have given to New York the character which climate would have given had she been placed on the South instead of the north side of Pennsylvania. Perhaps too other circumstances may have occasioned in Virginia a transplantation of a particular vice foreign to its climate. You could judge of this with more impartiality than I could, and the probability is that your estimate of them is the most just. I think it for their good that the vices of their character should be pointed out to them that they may amend them; for a malady of either body or mind once known is half cured.

To the Marquis of Chastellux, 2 September 1785

General Washington

S. T. COLERIDGE

We would fain believe that the whole of General Washington's Will has been perused by no man without some portion of that calm and pleasurable elevation which uniformly leaves us better and wiser beings. It would have been deeply interesting, considered only as the last deliberate act of a life so beneficial to the human race; but independently of this sublime association, it is in itself an affecting and most instructive composition. Like all the former manifestations of his character, it gives proof that a true and solid greatness may exist, and make itself felt, without any admixture of wildness, without any obtrusive appeals to the imagination: it gives proof, consolatory and inspiriting proof, how many virtues, too often deemed incompatible with each other, a thinking and upright mind may unite in itself. It were scarcely too much to affirm of this Will, that all the main elements of public and private morals, of civil and domestic wisdom, are conveyed in it either directly or by implication. It is, indeed, no less than an abstract of his opinions and feelings, as a Patriot, Friend, and Relation; and all arising naturally and unostentatiously out of the final disposal of a fortune not more honourably earned than beneficently employed. Appertaining to his character, as the American Patriot, more exclusively than the other pages of his Will, is the plan and endowment of a central University. The motives which impelled the General to this bequest, he has stated with such beauty and precision, as scarcely leave any thing for the philosopher or the eulogist to add. We can only subjoin to the advantages so ably enumerated, that such an institution must be eminently serviceable to America, as having a direct tendency to soften and liberalise the too great commercial spirit of that country, in as far as it will connect the pleasures and ambition of its wealthier citizens, in the most impressible period of life, with objects abstract and unworldly; and that while by friendships and literary emulations it may remove local jealousies, it will tend to decorate the American character with an ornament hitherto wanting in it, viz. genuine local attachments, unconnected with pecuniary interests.

Of a mixed nature, partly belonging to the patriot, and partly to the master of a family, is the humane, earnest, and solemn wish concerning the emancipation of the slaves on his estate. It explains, with infinite delicacy and manly sensibility, the true cause of his not having emancipated them in his life time; and should operate as a caution against those petty libellers, who interpret the whole of a character by a part, instead of interpreting a part by the whole. We feel ourselves at a loss which most to admire in this interesting paragraph, the deep and weighty feeling of the general principle of universal liberty; or the wise veneration of those fixed laws in society, without which that universal liberty must for ever remain impossible, and which, therefore, must be obeyed even in those cases, where they *suspend* the action of that general principle; or, lastly, the affectionate attention to the particular feelings of the slaves themselves, with the ample provision for the aged and infirm. Washington was no 'architect of ruin'!

In the bequests to his friends, the composition evidences the peculiar delicacy and correctness of his mind. The high value which he attached to his old friend Dr Franklin's legacy of the gold-headed cane, by bequeathing it, and it alone, to his brother, Charles Washington; the spy-glasses, left, with the modest parenthesis, 'because they will be useful to them where they live'; yet not without stamping the value on those precious relicts, as having been useful to himself in the deliverance of his country; the wisdom of remitting the box to Lord Buchan, with the gentle implication of the impracticability and impropriety of performing the conditions, with which the box had been originally accompanied; that reverence for the primary designation of a gift, implied in the words 'agreeably to the original design of the Goldsmiths' Company of Edinburgh', and which words were besides necessary, in order to prevent the interpretation, that he had remitted it from inability to find any man in his own country equally deserving of it with the Earl; the bequest of the bible, and of the swords, the first without annotation, the last with the solemnity of a Christian hero; all and each of these we have dwelt upon, as evidences of a mind strong and healthful, yet with a fineness and rapidity of the associating power, seldom found even in those who derive sensibility from nervous disease. The gratitude, the deep and immortal gratitude, displayed in the declaration of the motives of his bequest to his nephew, Bushrod Washington, is of a still higher class of excellence; and the virtue is individualized, and has a new interest given it, by his attention to the very letter of an old promise, no longer in force. The accuracy with which the estates are marked out will aid the distant posterity of the present Americans, in their reverential pilgrimages to the seat of their great PATER PATRIAE. The attachment which he has shewn to all his relations; the provisions he has made for them all; and the attention to honourable causes of local preferment in these provisions; are circumstances highly noticeable. Highly noticeable too is the disjunction of this family attachment from that desire of the aggrandisement of some one branch of the family, so commonly adherent to it. He has weakened by evidence the best and almost the only argument for primogeniture, *in new countries*. One fact strikes us particularly in the perusal of this Will. – Of all Washington's numerous relations, not one appears as a placeman or beneficiary of the government – not one appears to have received any thing from their kinsman as President and Influencer of the United States, yet all have evidences of the zeal and affection of the President, as their kinsman. *It is not so every where.*

There is something in the arrangement of the Will, beyond any example, which we recollect, instructive and judicious. He commences with a positive or perfect duty, the payment of duties; then goes immediately to the most respectful and affectionate attention to his wife, which becomes more intellectual, more moral, from the circumstances, which he after notices, of his having remained without issue: he proceeds to his concerns as master of his family, and provides for the emancipation of his slaves; and having finished his most immediate and *most* sacred offices, viz. the domestic duties, he rises, *then*, and *not till then*, into the Patriot; and founds a central University.

After his own family comes his country, and then his relations by consanguinity not of his own family – after these his friends; and all those whom fellowship in arms, or old acquaintance had endeared to him; and last of all, he proceeds to the circumstantial disposal of his estate. Throughout the whole, there reigns a *humanness* of feeling, a complete union of himself with the mass of his fellow-citizens, so as even to avoid references to any public characters in that country; and above all, an ardent wish for improvement, combined with reverential observance, and affectionate awe for present and existing customs and feelings. But Washington was too great a man to court singularity. The dwarf, that steps aside from the crowd, and walks by himself, may gain the whole crowd to turn and stare at him – Washington could attract their admiration, while he moved on with them, and in the midst of them.

Morning Post, 25 March 1800

'Spanish character'

WALT WHITMAN

Camden, New Jersey, July 20, 1883
To Messrs Griffin, Martinez, Prince, and other Gentlemen at Santa Fé:

Dear Sirs: – Your kind invitation to visit you and deliver a poem for the 333d Anniversary of founding Santa Fé has reach'd me so late that I have to decline, with sincere regret. But I will say a few words off hand.

We Americans have yet to really learn our own antecedents, and sort them, to unify them. They will be found ampler than has been supposed, and in widely different sources. Thus far, impress'd by New England writers and schoolmasters, we tacitly abandon ourselves to the notion that our United States have been fashion'd from the British Islands only, and essentially form a second England only – which is a very great mistake. Many leading traits for our future national personality, and some of the best ones, will certainly prove to have originated from other than British stock. As it is, the British and German, valuable as they are in the concrete, already threaten excess. Or rather, I should say, they have certainly reach'd that excess. To-day, something outside of them, and to counterbalance them, is seriously needed.

The seething materialistic and business vortices of the United States, in their present devouring relations, controlling and belittling everything else, are, in my opinion, but a vast and indispensable stage in the new world's development, and are certainly to be follow'd by something entirely different – at least by immense modifications. Character, literature, a society worthy of the name, are yet to be establish'd, through a nationality of noblest spiritual, heroic and democratic attributes – not one of which at present definitely exists – entirely different from the past, though unerringly founded on it, and to justify it.

To that composite American identity of the future, Spanish character will supply some of the most needed parts. No stock shows a grander historic retrospect – grander in religiousness and loyalty, or for patriotism, courage, decorum, gravity and honor. It is time to dismiss utterly the illusion-compound, half raw-head-and-bloody-bones and half Mysteries-of-Udolpho, inherited from the English writers of the past 200 years. It is time to realize – for it is certainly true – that there will not be found any more cruelty, tyranny, superstition, &c., in the *résumé* of past Spanish history than in the corresponding *résumé* of Anglo-Norman history. Nay, I think there will not be found so much.

Then another point, relating to American ethnology, past and to come,

I will here touch upon at a venture. As to our aboriginal or Indian population – the Aztec in the South, and many a tribe in the North and West – I
know it seems to be agreed that they must gradually dwindle as time rolls
on, and in a few generations more leave only a reminiscence, a blank. But
I am not at all clear about that. As America, from its many far-back sources
and current supplies, develops, adapts, entwines, faithfully identifies its
own – are we to see it cheerfully accepting and using all the contributions
of foreign lands from the whole outside globe – and then rejecting the only
ones distinctively its own – the autochthonic ones?

As to the Spanish stock of our Southwest, it is certain to me that we do
not begin to appreciate the splendor and sterling value of its race element.
Who knows but that element, like the course of some subterranean river,
dipping invisibly for a hundred or two years, is now to emerge in broadest
flow and permanent action?

Philadelphia Press, 5 August 1883

'Their chief businesss'

ALEXIS DE TOCQUEVILLE

I readily admit that public tranquillity is a great good; but at the same time,
I cannot forget that all nations have been enslaved by being kept in good
order. Certainly, it is not to be inferred that nations ought to despise public
tranquillity; but that state ought not to content them. A nation which asks
nothing of its government but the maintenance of order is already a slave
at heart, – the slave of its own well-being, awaiting but the hand that will
bind it.

By such a nation, the despotism of faction is not less to be dreaded than
the despotism of an individual. When the bulk of the community are engrossed by private concerns, the smallest parties need not despair of getting
the upper hand in public affairs. At such times, it is not rare to see upon
the great stage of the world, as we see at our theatres, a multitude represented by a few players, who alone speak in the name of an absent or inat-
tentive crowd: they alone are in action, whilst all others are stationary; they
regulate everything by their own caprice; they change the laws, and tyran-
nize at will over the manners of the country; and then men wonder to see
into how small a number of weak and worthless hands a great people may
fall.

Hitherto, the Americans have fortunately escaped all the perils which I
have just pointed out; and in this respect they are really deserving of admira-

tion. Perhaps there is no country in the world where fewer idle men are to be met with than in America, or where all who work are more eager to promote their own welfare. But if the passion of the Americans for physical gratifications is vehement, at least it is not indiscriminate; and reason, though unable to restrain it, still directs its course.

An American attends to his private concerns as if he were alone in the world, and the next minute he gives himself up to the common weal as if he had forgotten them. At one time, he seems animated by the most selfish cupidity; at another, by the most lively patriotism. The human heart cannot be thus divided. The inhabitants of the United States alternately display so strong and so similar a passion for their own welfare and for their freedom, that it may be supposed that these passions are united and mingled in some part of their character. And indeed, the Americans believe their freedom to be the best instrument and surest safeguard of their welfare: they are attached to the one by the other. They by no means think that they are not called upon to take a part in public affairs; they believe, on the contrary, that their chief business is to secure for themselves a government which will allow them to acquire the things they covet, and which will not debar them from the peaceful enjoyment of those possessions which they have already acquired.

Democracy in America, vol. 2, book 2, ch. 14, 1840, trans. Henry Reeve;
rev. Francis Bowen, 1862

'Idealistic'

WOODROW WILSON

Sometimes people call me an idealist. Well, that is the way I know I am an American. America, my fellow citizens – I do not say it in disparagement of any other great people – America is the only idealistic Nation in the world.

Speech, 8 September 1919

'Self-glorification'

MATTHEW ARNOLD

But now the Americans seem, in certain matters, to have agreed, as a people, to deceive themselves, to persuade themselves that they have what they have not, to cover the defects in their civilisation by boasting, to fancy that they well and truly solve, not only the political and social problem, but the human problem too. One would say that they do really hope to find in tall talk and inflated sentiment a substitute for that real sense of elevation which human nature, as I have said, instinctively craves – and a substitute which may do as well as the genuine article. The thrill of awe, which Goethe pronounces to be the best thing humanity has, they would fain create by proclaiming themselves at the top of their voices to be 'the greatest nation upon earth', by assuring one another, in the language of their national historian [George Bancroft], that American democracy proceeds in its ascent 'as uniformly and majestically as the laws of being, and is as certain as the decrees of eternity'.

Or, again, far from admitting that their newspapers are a scandal, they assure one another that their newspaper press is one of their most signal distinctions. Far from admitting that in literature they have as yet produced little that is important, they play at treating American literature as if it were a great independent power; they reform the spelling of the English language by the insight of their average man. For every English writer they have an American writer to match. And him good Americans read; the Western States are at this moment being nourished and formed, we hear, on the novels of a native author called Roe, instead of those of Scott and Dickens. Far from admitting that their average man is a danger, and that his predominance has brought about a plentiful lack of refinement, distinction, and beauty, they declare in the words of my friend Colonel Higginson, a prominent critic at Boston, that 'Nature said, some years since: "Thus far the English is my best race, but we have had Englishmen enough; put in one drop more of nervous fluid and make the American." And with that drop a new range of promise opened on the human race, and a lighter, finer, more highly organised type of mankind was born.' Far from admitting that the American accent, as the pressure of their climate and of their average man has made it, is a thing to be striven against, they assure one another that it is the right accent, the standard English speech of the future.

*

The new West promises to beat in the game of brag even the stout champions I have been quoting. Those belong to the old Eastern States; and the other day there was sent to me a Californian newspaper which calls all the Easterners 'the unhappy denizens of a forbidding clime', and adds: 'The time will surely come when all roads will lead to California. Here will be the home of art, science, literature, and profound knowledge.'

Common-sense criticism, I repeat, of all this hollow stuff there is in America next to none. There are plenty of cultivated, judicious, delightful individuals there. They are our hope and America's hope; it is through their means that improvement must come. They know perfectly well how false and hollow the boastful stuff talked is; but they let the storm of self-laudation rage, and say nothing. For political opponents and their doings there are in America hard words to be heard in abundance; for the real faults in American civilisation, and for the foolish boasting which prolongs them, there is hardly a word of regret or blame, at least in public. Even in private, many of the most cultivated Americans shrink from the subject, are irritable and thin-skinned when it is canvassed. Public treatment of it, in a cool and sane spirit of criticism, there is none. In vain I might plead that I had set a good example of frankness, in confessing over here, that, so far from solving our problems successfully, we in England find ourselves with an upper class materialised, a middle class vulgarised, and a lower class brutalised. But it seems that nothing will embolden an American critic to say firmly and aloud to his countrymen and to his newspapers, that in America they do not solve the human problem successfully, and that with their present methods they never can. Consequently the masses of the American people do really come to believe all they hear about their finer nervous organisation, and the rightness of the American accent, and the importance of American literature; that is to say, they see things not as they are, but as they would like them to be; they deceive themselves totally. And by such self-deception they shut against themselves the door to improvement, and do their best to make the reign of *das Gemeine* eternal. In what concerns the solving of the political and social problem they see clear and think straight; in what concerns the higher civilisation they live in a fool's paradise. This it is which makes a famous French critic [Michelet] speak of 'the hard unintelligence of the people of the United States' – *la dure inintelligence des Américains du Nord* – of the very people who in general pass for being specially intelligent – and so, within certain limits, they are. But they have been so plied with nonsense and boasting that outside those limits, and where it is a question of things in which their civilisation is weak, they seem, very many of them, as if in such things they had no power of perception whatever, no idea of a proper scale, no sense of the difference between good and bad. And at this rate they can never, after solving the political and social problem with success, go on to solve happily the human problem too, and thus at last to make their civilisation full and interesting.

'Civilisation in the United States', 1888

'Purely as an American'

HENRY JAMES

Mr Theodore Roosevelt appears to propose – in 'American Ideals and Other Essays Social and Political' – to tighten the screws of the national consciousness as they have never been tightened before. The national consciousness for Mr Theodore Roosevelt is, moreover, at the best a very fierce affair. He may be said neither to wear it easily nor to enjoy any such wearing on any one else. Particularly interesting is the spirit of his plea at a time when the infatuated peoples in general, under the pressure of nearer and nearer neighbourhood, show a tendency to relinquish the mere theory of patriotism in favour of – as on the whole more convenient – the mere practice. It is not the practice, but the theory that is violent, or that, at any rate, may easily carry that air in an age when so much of the ingenuity of the world goes to multiplying contact and communication, to reducing separation and distance, to promoting, in short, an inter-penetration that would have been the wonder of our fathers, as the comparative inefficiency of our devices will probably be the wonder of our sons. We may have been great fools to develop the post office, to invent the newspaper and the railway; but the harm is done – it will be our children who will see it; we have created a Frankenstein monster at whom our simplicity can only gape. Mr Roosevelt leaves us gaping – deserts us as an adviser when we most need him. The best he can do for us is to turn us out, for our course, with a pair of smart, patent blinders.

It is 'purely as an American', he constantly reminds us, that each of us must live and breathe. Breathing, indeed, is a trifle; it is purely as Americans that we must think, and all that is wanting to the author's demonstration is that he shall give us a receipt for the process. He labours, however, on the whole question, under the drollest confusion of mind. To say that a man thinks as an American is to say that he expresses his thought, in whatever field, as one. That may be vividly – it may be superbly – to describe him after the fact; but to describe the way an American thought *shall* be expressed is surely a formidable feat, one that at any rate requires resources not brought by Mr Roosevelt to the question. His American subject has only to happen to be encumbered with a mind to put him out altogether. Mr Roosevelt, I surmise, deprecates the recognition of the encumbrance – would at least have the danger kept well under. He seems, that is, but just barely to allow for it, as when, for instance, mentioning that he would not deny, in the public sphere, the utility of criticism. 'The politician who cheats or swindles, or the newspaper man who lies in any form, should be made to feel that he is an object of scorn for all honest men.' That is luminous; but, none the less, 'an educated man must not go into politics as such; he must go in simply as an American, . . . or he will be upset by some other American with no education at all. . . . ' A better way perhaps than to barbarize the upset – already, surely, sufficiently unfortunate – would be to civilize the upsetter.

Mr Roosevelt makes very free with the 'American' name, but it is after all not a symbol revealed once for all in some book of Mormon dug up under a tree. Just as it is not criticism that makes critics, but critics who make criticism, so the national type is the result, not of what we take from it, but of what we give to it, not of our impoverishment, but of our enrichment of it. We are all making it, in truth, as hard as we can, and few of us will subscribe to any invitation to forgo the privilege – in the exercise of which stupidity is really the great danger to avoid. The author has a happier touch when he ceases to deal with doctrine. Excellent are those chapters in his volume – the papers on 'machine' politics in New York, on the work of the Civil Service Reform Commission, on the reorganization of the New York police force – that are in each case a record of experience and participation. These pages give an impression of high competence – of Mr Roosevelt's being a very useful force for example. But his value is impaired for intelligible percept by the puerility of his simplifications.

Literature, 23 April 1898

'The American gentleman'

JOHN BUTLER YEATS

The more I see of the Americans, the more I admire them – what you hear in Ireland and in England is all lies. I believe myself they are far ahead of all nations, and will in time produce the greatest poetry and the greatest art. At present, young and old, they have all the naïveté and attractiveness of young University students, that is, when those students are swept by some great wave of enthusiasm – loyalty or patriotism – or better still for some idea.

The American gentleman to my mind, is far ahead of the English or Irish gentleman, a truer dignity and unselfishness, and such an alert mind and will. I heard yesterday of a German schoolmarm who said the American man lacked dignity. Of course the poor slave missed the heavy foot of her German taskmaster placed upon her neck. A servile race like a strong master. It is always easier to obey *if you dare not disobey*. German women are to their lords like so many black beetles.

To Miss Grierson, 2 June 1909

Joe Louis

ALISTAIR COOKE

The day Joe Louis retired must have brought a moment's pause and a sigh from many people who don't care for sport, the sense of a promised date that would never be kept such as non-musical people felt when Caruso or Paderewski died. On the 1st of March 1949, it came home to some of us that we should very likely never again see him shuffle with great grace up to some wheezing hulk of a man, bait him with a long left before he brought up the shattering, awful thunderbolt of his right, and then toddle considerately away and wait for the referee to call the roll on yet another ruined reputation.

There are some idols you acquire too early, who later turn into walking parodies of themselves, like a favorite uncle who gets to be a vaudeville bore. There are others – the artists of popularity – who stay just far enough away from the hungry crowd and never glut the appetite they tease. Joe Louis was one of these. I doubt I should ever have seen him, or cared to, if he had not at one time connected with a private occasion. I went down to Baltimore the first day of summer in 1937 to stay with an old friend, a doctor at the Johns Hopkins Hospital, who promised himself next day an afternoon off from his messy labors with stomach-aches and corpses. We drove out into the blossoming Worthington and Green Spring valleys. The purple twilight fell. It had been a perfect day, of the kind that makes you grateful for your friendships and stirs the memory of how they first started. I had met this man years before on such an evening when he stopped by my room in college to admire a battered record I had carried across the Atlantic. It was Fats Waller singing the 'Dallas Blues'. Driving back into Baltimore he remembered that Fats was on tap in person just them. 'How about', he said, 'we go down to darktown and catch him?' There was a little vaudeville house deep in the colored section of town, and that's where we went. We packed ourselves in with several hundred Negroes too many. They clapped and stomped in time and sweated like the plebs at a Roman circus. It was possibly ninety-five degrees outdoors and a hundred and ten inside. Nobody seemed to care. In the middle of one number, though, something happened outside that rode above the rhythm of the band and the hallelujahs of the audience. Far off from somewhere came a high roar like a tidal wave. The band looked uneasy but played on. It came on nearer, a great sighing and cheering. Suddenly there was a noise of doors splintering and cops barking and women screaming and men going down grabbing their toes and snarling obscenities. The band stopped and the lights went up. The black faces all around us bobbed and flashed. Women threw their heads back and shrieked at the roof. Some people embraced each other and a little girl in pigtails cried. Other people cuffed and swung at each other. We managed to get out whole. Outside, in the villainously lit streets – they still have gaslight in darktown Baltimore – it was like Christmas Eve in darkest Africa. This, it turned out, was the night that Joe Louis won the heavyweight championship, and for one night, in all the lurid darktowns of America, the black man was king.

The memory of that night has terrified and exhilarated me ever since. The phrase, 'Arise, you have nothing to lose but your chains,' must have a terrible appeal to the Negro. Most Southerners know it, and it is why in some places they watch fearfully for every Negro flexing his muscles and wonder if he is somehow connected with the Communists. That immediate fear was not besetting America then as it is now. But the lesson was plain: one Negro had outboxed all the living contenders, no matter how white (and Braddock was whiter when he came out of the ring than when he went in), and he was a racial god.

It took several years and a run of inevitable victories, and wide familiarity with Joe in the ring and on the newsreels, for Americans to learn a special respect for this quiet, beautiful, mannerly youth, who never thought of himself as anybody's god, who never played his color up or down, who never questioned a ruling, never flirted with the crowd, kept his mind on his work, stepped scrupulously aside when an opponent stumbled; and who, when it was all over, said such embarrassing things over the radio that they had to whisk the mike away from him to the loser, who would usually say the clichés that were expected of him. They pushed the microphone up to Joe in December 1947, when he had been fought into a dazed parody of his younger self by another old Joe – Jersey Joe Walcott. A sharp little announcer chattered, 'Did he ever have you worried, Joe – at any time?' This is a question expecting the answer, 'No, I felt fine all the time, never better.' Joe said, 'I was worried all the way through. Yes, sir, I ain't twenty-three any more.'

I know it is hard, perhaps impossible, for any white man to appraise the character of any Negro. If you have lived all your life around Negroes, you inherit certain attitudes towards them. If you are a stranger to them, there is the danger of making them out to be quite the nicest people in America. In a way, nice Negroes have to be; for though Negroes are as good and as bad as anybody else, they have one thing in common: they have had, most of them, a worse deal than the white man. A variation of this condescension is to think so poorly of the Negro in general that when he does anything as well as a white man, you have to make him out to be unique. You hear a colored band and shout that nobody can play a trumpet like a black man (it depends, of course, which black man is being compared with which white). Then you run into Louis Armstrong, who tells you of the first time he heard a white boy – a very pasty-faced boy from Davenport, Iowa – play the cornet. And Armstrong broke into tears. 'Man!' he said, 'might as well lay you down and die, nigger.'

When you come to look at the life and career of Joe Louis, there is the special dilemma that he is a black man, and that even when you have done your best to judge him as other men, there's no way of denying that if he is not the best boxer that ever lived, he is as near to it as we are ever likely to know. He was born in 1914 on a sharecropper's cotton patch in Alabama and was as country-poor as it is possible to be. In theory the farm was – it had been rented as – a cotton and vegetable farm. But the vegetables did not feed the family, not by the time Joe, the seventh child, came along. His father broke, as sharecroppers do, from the daily strain of not making enough in crops either to feed his children or to put shoes on them. They had no money to send him to a hospital. So he was carried off to a state institution where he died. A widower came to help out and soon married Joe's mother. And his five children moved in with the eight Louises. Joe got a little more food and went to a one-room school. Then the family moved to Detroit, where the stepfather worked in an automobile factory. Joe went on to trade-school and worked in the evenings doing the rounds with an ice-wagon. Then came the depression, and the family went on relief. This, said Joe, made his mother feel very bad. Years later Joe wrote out a careful check, for two hundred and sixty-nine dollars, which was the amount of the relief checks they had had from the Government. That, said Joe, made Mrs Brooks, as she now was, feel better.

Whatever a big city means to the poor, Detroit meant to Joe. But it means something else to a hefty Negro lad short of cash. It means gymnasiums and the prospect of a quick take of two or three dollars in improvised fights. When Joe was eighteen he came home very late one night and found his stepfather blocking the door. 'Where you been, Joe?' he asked.

'Over to the gym,' said Joe, 'working out.'

'I thought so,' said Mr Brooks, and lectured him about the fate of no-goods getting punch-drunk in gymnasiums. 'You go on foolin' around with boxing, you're never gonna to amount to nothin'.'

He says this had him really worried. He asked his mother about it. She said it was all right to be a boxer if that's what you wanted to do most. And that was, in a way, the end of Joe's wayward life. The rest was practice, and workouts, and learning, learning, being knocked to pulp, and learning some more and coming again with a new trick or two.

There is a biography of Joe Louis, there may be several, that makes him talk the way sentimental writers always think simple men talk. It is a fairly nauseating work. But just before Joe retired, two first-rate newspapermen, Meyer Berger and Barney Negler, got hold of him for many long sessions and, presumably with one hand in their pockets, transcribed exactly how he talked and what he said, without paying any more attention than Joe Louis does to grammar, simplicity, or morals. From a few sentences of this report, I think you can get closer to the sort of man Louis is than from reams of official biographies. Take the bit about his being born with a catlike tread. 'When I got up in fighting,' he says, 'newspaper writers put a lot of words in my mouth. They wrote I was born with movements like a panther, and how I was a born killer. I never said it was wrong before, but the real truth is I was born kind of clumsy-footed. My mother says I liked to stumble a lot when I was a baby. . . . That footwork the writers say was cat-sense was something Chappie Blackburn drilled into me. That was learned, it wasn't a born thing. He saw I couldn't follow my left hook with a right cross without gettin' my right foot off the floor. It takes a lot of learnin' before you can do it without thinkin'.' Or his explanation of why he never says much. 'When I got to be champion, the writers made a lot of noise about how hard it was to get me to talk. My mother said I was no different when I was a kid. When I went to school the teacher made me say words over and over and by-and-by I got stubborn, I guess, and wouldn't say them at all.'

After he lost a fight in early 1934, before his professional career was technically on the books, his manager told him to stop staying out late with the gang. 'He treated me real good,' says Joe. 'I got to wear some of his clothes made over.' The night he became champion, the night it seemed the whole population of darktown Baltimore poured into that vaudeville theater, Joe summed up his feelings in an immortal sentence or two:

'He fell in a face-down dive. That made me heavyweight champion. People figure that was my biggest thrill. But I don't remember no special feelin', I just felt good . . . maybe it was because I figured I wouldn't feel a real champ until I got that Schmeling. That's what I fixed on.' (Schmeling it was who rang the only jarring note on Joe's professional record. At the end, it read – '61 bouts, 51 knockouts, 9 decisions, knocked out once. That was in 1936. And exactly one year to the night after he became champion, Joe had his revenge. He did what he 'fixed on'.)

Maybe you will get from this the idea that Joe Louis is a simple soul with quiet manners, a good boy who never had a crafty thought. Of course, he doesn't talk about his respect for his opponents, or his decency and casualness with the crowd, because these are fundamental, the characteristics that a man hardly knows about, or, if he does, keeps quiet about. But there is one remark he makes about his pride in money that should round out the picture. 'People ask me,' he says, "Joe, what will you do when the big money from fightin' stops coming' in? Won't you have to cut down?" I tell 'em, I'm gonna live good, retired or not retired. I got investments and I got ideas. I'll keep on livin' good. It's them who lived off me who won't be livin' so good.'

We ought to be able to stop there. And in a more artistic world, that is where Joe would have stopped too. But the Bureau of Internal Revenue is not noted for its artistic restraint or its sense of the dying close. Joe might announce his retirement, and the newspapers salute him with splendid tears. But there was a little matter of two hundred and twenty thousand unpaid dollars between Joe and the tax officials. He had 'lived good' when the money was rolling in like a Kansas harvest. And, true, he had 'got investments'. But many of them were grubstakes handed out in the flush days to acquaintances more remarkable for their enthusiasm than their financial foresight or prospecting genius. Some of these investments could charitably be written off as bad debts, but not on the merciless forms of the income-tax boys. So Joe was thrown back on those 'ideas' he had dared to boast about. In the end, there was only one idea that – in desperation and in decency – he could fall back on: it was the pitiful idea of going on fighting.

He won a fight and lost a fight, and then in the fall of 1950 he was battered like a sick old bull by a little dancing man called Ezzard Charles. With every beating, his price would go down. I suppose the Internal Revenue theory was that it was still Joe Louis fighting up there, with the terrible right hand that once earned about fifty thousand dollars per thrust. They allow working depreciation on a five-year-old car but not apparently on a worn-out thunderbolt. So the means to pay off the big debt grew limper every month.

There is no point in going on. Better far accept the word he gave in the spring of 1949, when he retired unbeaten in full view of a thousand fighters who dare not match him. Better recall only the memory of incredible speed, a slow shuffle, a solemn face, a gentleness, a shy acceptance of his greatness. All things considered – even the prospect of a fumbling end – a credit to his race; so long as you add Jimmy Cannon's good and necessary afterthought – the human race, that is.

One Man's America, 1952

'Violence'

H. RAP BROWN

I say violence is necessary. It is as American as cherry pie.

Speech, 27 July 1967

The Gangster as Tragic Hero

ROBERT WARSHOW

America, as a social and political organization, is committed to a cheerful view of life. It could not be otherwise. The sense of tragedy is a luxury of aristocratic societies, where the fate of the individual is not conceived of as having a direct and legitimate political importance, being determined by a fixed and supra-political – that is, non-controversial – moral order or fate. Modern equalitarian societies, however, whether democratic or authoritarian in their political forms, always base themselves on the claim that they are making life happier; the avowed function of the modern state, at least in its ultimate terms, is not only to regulate social relations, but also to determine the quality and the possibilities of human life in general. Happiness thus becomes the chief political issue – in a sense, the only political issue – and for that reason it can never be treated as an issue at all. If an American or a Russian is unhappy, it implies a certain reprobation of his society, and therefore, by a logic of which we can all recognize the necessity, it becomes an obligation of citizenship to be cheerful; if the authorities find it necessary, the citizen may even be compelled to make a public display of his cheerfulness on important occasions, just as he may be conscripted into the army in time of war.

Naturally, this civic responsibility rests most strongly upon the organs of mass culture. The individual citizen may still be permitted his private unhappiness so long as it does not take on political significance, the extent of this tolerance being determined by how large an area of private life the society can accommodate. But every production of mass culture is a public act and must conform with accepted notions of the public good. Nobody seriously questions the principle that it is the function of mass culture to maintain public morale, and certainly nobody in the mass audience objects to having his morale maintained.[1] At a time when the normal condition of the citizen is a state of anxiety, euphoria spreads over our culture like the broad smile of an idiot. In terms of attitudes towards life, there is very little difference between a 'happy' movie like *Good News*, which ignores death and suffering, and a 'sad' movie like *A Tree Grows in Brooklyn*, which uses death and suffering as incidents in the service of a higher optimism.

But, whatever its effectiveness as a course of consolation and a means of pressure for maintaining 'positive' social attitudes, this optimism is fundamentally satisfying to no one, not even to those who would be most disoriented without its support. Even within the area of mass culture, there always exists a current of opposition, seeking to express by whatever means are available to it that sense of desperation and inevitable failure which optimism itself helps to create. Most often, this opposition is confined to rudimentary or semi-literate forms: in mob politics and journalism, for example, or in certain kinds of religious enthusiasm. When it does enter the field of art, it is likely to be disguised or attenuated: in an unspecific form of expression like jazz, in the basically harmless nihilism of the Marx Brothers, in the continually reasserted strain of hopelessness that often seems to be the real meaning of the soap opera. The gangster film is remarkable in that it fills the need for disguise (though not sufficiently to avoid arousing uneasiness) without requiring any serious distortion. From its beginnings, it has been a consistent and astonishingly complete presentation of the modern sense of tragedy.[2]

In its initial character, the gangster film is simply one example of the movies' constant tendency to create fixed dramatic patterns that can be repeated indefinitely with a reasonable expectation of profit. One gangster film follows another as one musical or one Western follows another. But this rigidity is not necessarily opposed to the requirements of art. There have been very successful types of art in the past which developed such specific and detailed conventions as almost to make individual examples of the type interchangeable. This is true, for example, of Elizabethan revenge tragedy and Restoration comedy.

For such a type to be successful means that its conventions have imposed themselves upon the general consciousness and become the accepted vehicles of a particular set of attitudes and a particular aesthetic effect. One goes to any individual example of the type with very definite expectations, and originality is to be welcomed only in the degree that it intensifies the expected experience without fundamentally altering it. Moreover, the relationship between the conventions which go to make up such a type and the real experience of its audience or the real facts of whatever situation it pretends to describe is of only secondary importance and does not determine its aesthetic force. It is only in an ultimate sense that the type appeals to its audience's experience of reality; much more immediately, it appeals to previous experience of the type itself: it creates its own field of reference.

Thus the importance of the gangster film, and the nature and intensity of its emotional and aesthetic impact, cannot be measured in terms of the place of the gangster himself or the importance of the problem of crime in American life. Those European movie-goers who think there is a gangster on every corner in New York are certainly deceived, but defenders of the 'positive' side of American culture are equally deceived if they think it relevant to point out that most Americans have never seen a gangster. What matters is that the experience of the gangster *as an experience of art* is universal to Americans. There is almost nothing we understand better or react to more readily or with quicker intelligence. The Western film, though it seems never to diminish in popularity, is for most of us no more than the folklore of the past, familiar and understandable only because it has been repeated so often. The gangster film comes much closer. In ways that we do not easily or willingly define, the gangster speaks for us, expressing that part of the American psyche which rejects the qualities and the demands of modern life, which rejects 'Americanism' itself.

1 In her testimony before the House Committee on Un-American Activities, Mrs Leila Rogers said that the movie *None But the Lonely Heart* was un-American because it was gloomy. Like so much else that was said during the unhappy investigation of Hollywood, this statement was at once stupid and illuminating. One knew immediately what Mrs Rogers was talking about; she had simply been insensitive enough to carry her philistinism to its conclusion.

2 Efforts have been made from time to time to bring the gangster film into line with the prevailing optimism and social constructiveness of our culture; *Kiss of Death* is a recent example. These efforts are usually unsuccessful; the reasons for their lack of success are interesting in themselves, but I shall not be able to discuss them here.

Excerpt, *Partisan Review*, February 1948

'This kindness'

JOHN BUTLER YEATS

Remember I am as much in love with the country as ever. They don't understand art and have no manners, but there runs through all ranks a goodness and kindness, and their humour is all based on this kindness. It is as if the stern countenances of the Pilgrim Fathers had [word indecipherable] into a grim mother, full of pity . . . pity but yet no indulgence. When there is indulgence you get sentimentality which is just the opposite to humour – especially American humour. English humour is based in cruelty, in order that they may enjoy the consciousness of their strength and superiority. They strike bare your weakness and inadequacy, exposing you in shivering nakedness to their laughter and wits. The Americans are the kindest people

I ever met, but they are the grimmest. They keep their countenances sour. The little children do it . . . I look round the various tables and can at once 'spot' an English person by his smiling countenance and talkativeness for which he would not be distinguished anywhere else.

(Ellipses are Yeats's or his editor's.) To Harriet Jameson, 1908

'Mammy' Man

DAMON RUNYON

At the fights at Madison Square Garden one night and again in Moore's restaurant the following night, I saw Joley, otherwise Al Jolson. He was making his old rounds.

I thought he looked well despite a recent illness that called for the removal of a couple of ribs. It is thought he picked up the makings of the illness on one of his jaunts to the Caribbean or Alaska entertaining the service men. He was one of the first to go on those missions.

But he looked stouter than usual, it seemed to me, even allowing for the middle-aged spread inevitable to the 57 years to which Joley admits. (How is that, Neighbor? Yes, that is what he says: 57.)

He wore horn-rimmed spectacles. His apparel was the mixed-ale Hollywood type, pants different from the jacket. He was in good spirits. He recently acquired a new wife, a very pretty and intelligent young lady. I believe it is the third time around for Al, maybe the fourth. I never keep track of those things. (What is that, sir? Yes, I tell you he says: 57.)

'You going back to the coast?' Joley asked me.

'No,' I said. 'You?'

'Uh-huh,' he said. 'Gottuh.'

Jolson was never a great singer but he was always a super-stylist, and the closest any of the zillion imitators of him could come to his technique was to get down on one knee and yell, 'Mammy!'

In fact, I was thinking as I watched Joley the other night that there sat one old champion they have yet to equal.

Jolson may be the richest actor alive. He is reputed several times a millionaire. He made his money long before big taxes when he could keep most of his income, which the top money earners of the profession today like Bob Hope, Bing Crosby, Jack Benny and others cannot do. Besides Jolson was a highly successful investor for years.

He used to be a heavy plunger on the races and still makes a right neat bet if he likes the spot, but nothing compared to his less conservative days in the mid '20's. He can get pretty sore when he loses a bet, too, which I trust you will observe is a slight switch from the usual formula of putting away a subject as a good loser.

But it was not of his minor idiosyncrasies that I reflected the other night. It was of his career over at least forty years of American theatre history, most of those years a succession of triumphs. Joley reigned a long time as king of the boards. There is now no one on the stage that you can compare with him from the standpoint of an individual drawing card or on his unbroken line of successes.

He was one of the few performers I ever saw who could hold the stage as long as he pleased without tiring his audience. An hour is a pretty long stretch but that was duck soup for Joley. I would like to see one of the stage performers of today try that period of time on their customers some night.

Harry Lauder, the Scotchman, could do it. In fact, with an unsophisticated audience, Lauder might have been able to hold the stage even longer than Jolson, but not with an assemblage of the Broadway type. John McCormack, the great Irish singer, was another who could stay out there as long as he pleased.

You have to talk to veteran actors to get a true measure of Joley's stage stature in his prime. He was not the most popular man among them that ever lived but I never heard one deny that he was the greatest of all the entertainers they had ever known. A couple of years ago for some obscure reason, possibly to satisfy his own vanity, Joley made a comeback in a show in New York and was a sensation.

He played in it until he tired, which did not take long, though it is only fair to say that he was commencing to ail even then. A man cannot stand up forever against that grind. But when Joley folded he was still the old champ.

Short Takes, 1946

'Parents'

THE DUKE OF WINDSOR [FORMERLY KING EDWARD VIII]

The thing that impresses me most about America is the way parents obey their children.

Look, 5 March 1957

'American women'

ANTHONY TROLLOPE

All native American women are intelligent. It seems to be their birthright. In the eastern cities they have, in their upper classes, superadded womanly grace to this intelligence, and consequently they are charming as companions. They are beautiful also, and, as I believe, lack nothing that a lover can desire in his love. But I cannot fancy myself much in love with a western lady, or rather with a lady in the West. They are as sharp as nails, but then they are also as hard. They know, doubtless, all that they ought to know, but then they know so much more than they ought to know. They are tyrants to their parents, and never practise the virtue of obedience till they have half-grown-up daughters of their own. They have faith in the destiny of their country, if in nothing else; but they believe that that destiny is to be worked out by the spirit and talent of the young women. I confess that for me Eve would have had no charms had she not recognized Adam as her lord. I can forgive her in that she tempted him to eat the apple. Had she come from the West country she would have ordered him to make his meal, and then I could not have forgiven her.

North America, 1862, ch. 25

'This woman is an idol'

PAUL BOURGET

A great artist, foremost of this epoch by the ardor of his efforts, the conscientiousness of his study, and the sincerity of his vision, John Sargent, has shown what I have tried to express, in a portrait which I saw in an exhibition, – that of a woman whose name I do not know [Isabella Stewart Gardner]. It is a portrait such as the fifteenth-century masters painted, who, back of the individual found the real, and back of the model a whole social order. The canvas might be called 'The American Idol', so representative is it.

The woman is standing, her feet side by side, her knees close together, in an almost hieratic pose. Her body, rendered supple by exercise, is sheathed – you might say moulded – in a tight-fitting black dress. Rubies, like drops of blood, sparkle on her shoes. Her slender waist is encircled by a girdle of enormous pearls, and from this dress, which makes an intensely dark background for the stony brilliance of the jewels, the arms and shoulders shine out with another brilliance, that of a flower-like flesh, – fine, white flesh, through which flows blood perpetually invigorated by the air of the country and the ocean. The head, intellectual and daring, with a countenance as of one who has understood everything, has, for a sort of aureole, the vaguely gilded design of one of those Renascence stuffs which the Venetians call *sopra-risso*. The rounded arms, in which the muscles can hardly be seen, are joined by the clasped hands, – firm hands, the thumb almost too long, which might guide four horses with the precision of an English coachman. It is the picture of an energy at once delicate and invincible, momentarily in repose, and all the Byzantine Madonna is in that face, with its wide-open eyes.

Yes, this woman is an idol, for whose service man labors, which he has decked with the jewels of a queen, behind each one of whose whims lie days and days spent in the ardent battle of Wall Street. Frenzy of speculations in land, cities undertaken and built by sheer force of millions, trains launched at full speed over bridges built on a Babel-like sweep of arch, the creaking of cable cars, the quivering of electric cars, sliding along their wires with a crackle and a spark, the dizzy ascent of elevators, in buildings twenty stories high, immense wheat-fields of the West, its ranches, mines, colossal slaughter-houses, – all the formidable traffic of this country of effort and struggle, all its labor, – these are what have made possible this woman, this living orchid, unexpected masterpiece of this civilization.

Did not the very painter consecrate to her his intense toil? To be capable of such a picture, he must have absorbed some of the ardor of the Spanish masters, caught the subtlety of the great Italians, understood and practised the curiosities of impressionism, dreamed before the pictures in basilicas like Ravenna, and read and thought. Ah, how much of culture, of reflection, before one could fathom the secret depths of one's own race. He has expressed one of the most essential characteristics of the race, – the deification of woman, considered not as a Beatrice as in Florence, nor as a courtesan as at Milan, but as a supreme glory of the national spirit. This woman can do without being loved. She has no need of being loved. What she symbolizes is neither sensuality nor tenderness. She is like a living object of art, the last fine work of human skill, attesting that the Yankee, but yesterday despairing, vanquished by the Old World, has been able to draw from this savage world upon which fate has cast him a wholly new civilization, incarnated in this woman, her luxury, and her pride. Everything is illuminated by this civilization, at the gaze of these fathomless eyes, in the expression of which the painter has succeeded in putting all the idealism of this country which has no ideal; all that which, perhaps, will one day be its destruction, but up to the present time is still its greatness, – a faith in the human Will, absolute, unique, systematic, and indomitable.

Outre-Mer, 1895, ch. 4

'Bottled lightning'

WILLIAM JAMES

In a weekly paper not very long ago I remember reading a story in which, after describing the beauty and interest of the heroine's personality, the author summed up her charms by saying that to all who looked upon her an impression of 'bottled lightning' was irresistibly conveyed.

Bottled lightning, in truth, is one of our American ideals, even of a young girl's character! Now it is most ungracious, and it may seem to some persons unpatriotic, to criticize in public the physical peculiarities of one's own people, of one's own family, so to speak. Besides, it may be said, and said with justice, that there are plenty of bottled-lightning temperaments in other countries, and plenty of phlegmatic temperaments here; and that, when all is said and done, the more or less of tension about which I making such a fuss is a very small item in the sum total of a nation's life, and not worth solemn treatment at a time when agreeable rather than disagreeable things should be talked about. Well, in one sense the more or less of tension in our faces and in our unused muscles *is* a small thing: not much mechanical work is done by these contractions. But it is not always the material size of a thing that measures its importance: often it is its place and function. One of the most philosophical remarks I ever heard made was by an unlettered workman who was doing some repairs at my house many years ago. 'There is very little difference between one man and another,' he said, 'when you go to the bottom of it. But what little there is, is very important.' And the remark certainly applies to this case. The general over-contraction may be small when estimated in foot-pounds, but its importance is immense on account of its *effects on the over-contracted person's spiritual life*. This follows as a necessary consequence from the theory of our emotions to which I made reference at the beginning of this article. For by the sensations that so incessantly pour in from the over-tense excited body the over-tense and excited habit of mind is kept up; and the sultry, threatening, exhausting, thunderous inner atmosphere never quite clears away. If you never wholly give yourself up to the chair you sit in, but always keep your leg- and body-muscles half contracted for a rise; if you breathe eighteen or nineteen instead of sixteen times a minute, and never quite breathe out at that – what mental mood *can* you be in but one of inner panting and expectancy, and how can the future and its worries possibly forsake your mind? On the other hand, how can they gain admission to your mind if your brow be unruffled, your respiration calm and complete, and your muscles all relaxed?

Now what is the cause of this absence of repose, this bottled-lightning quality in us Americans? The explanation of it that is usually given is that it comes from the extreme dryness of our climate and the acrobatic performances of our thermometer, coupled with the extraordinary progressiveness of our life, the hard work, the railroad speed, the rapid success, and all the other things we know so well by heart. Well, our climate is certainly exciting, but hardly more so than that of many parts of Europe, where nevertheless no bottled-lightning girls are found. And the work done and the pace of life are as extreme in every great capital of Europe as they are here. To me both of these pretended causes are utterly insufficient to explain the facts.

To explain them, we must go not to physical geography, but to psychology and sociology. The latest chapter both in sociology and in psychology to be developed in a manner that approaches adequacy is the chapter on the imitative impulse. First Bagehot, then Tarde, then Royce and Baldwin here, have shown that invention and imitation, taken together, form, one may say, the entire warp and woof of human life, in so far as it is social. The American over-tension and jerkiness and breathlessness and intensity and agony of expression are primarily social, and only secondarily physiological, phenomena. They are *bad habits*, nothing more or less, bred of custom and example, born of the imitation of bad models and the cultivation of false personal ideals. How are idioms acquired, how do local peculiarities of phrase and accent come about? Through an accidental example set by someone, which struck the ears of others, and was quoted and copied till at last every one in the locality chimed in. Just so it is with national tricks of vocalization or intonation, with national manners, fashions of movement and gesture, and habitual expressions of face. We, here in America, through following a succession of pattern-setters whom it is now impossible to trace, and through influencing each other in a bad direction, have at last settled down collectively into what, for better or worse, is our own characteristic national type – a type with the production of which, so far as these habits go, the climate and conditions have had practically nothing at all to do.

This type, which we have thus reached by our imitativeness, we now have fixed upon us, for better or worse. Now no type can be *wholly* disadvantageous; but, so far as our type follows the bottled-lightning fashion, it cannot be wholly good. Dr Clouston was certainly right in thinking that eagerness, breathlessness, and anxiety are not signs of strength: they are signs of weakness and of bad coördination. The even forehead, the slab-like cheek, the codfish eye, may be less interesting for the moment; but they are more promising signs than intense expression is of what we may expect of their possessor in the long run. Your dull, unhurried worker gets over a great deal of ground, because he never goes backward or breaks down. Your intense, convulsive worker breaks down and has bad moods so often that you never know where he may be when you most need his help – he may be having one of his 'bad days'. We say that so many of our fellow-countrymen collapse, and have to be sent abroad to rest their nerves, because they work so hard. I suspect that this is an immense mistake. I suspect that neither the nature nor the amount of our work is accountable for the frequency and severity of our breakdowns, but that their cause lies rather in those absurd feelings of hurry and having no time, in that breathlessness and tension, that anxiety of feature and that solicitude for results, that lack of inner harmony and ease, in short, by which with us the work is so apt to be accompanied, and from which a European who should do the same work would nine times out of ten be free. These perfectly wanton and unnecessary tricks of inner attitude and outer manner in us, caught from the social atmosphere, kept up by tradition, and idealized by many as the admirable way of life, are the last straws that break the American camel's back, the final overflowers of our measure of wear and tear and fatigue.

The voice, for example, in a surprisingly large number of us has a tired and plaintive sound. Some of us are really tired (for I do not mean absolutely to deny that our climate has a tiring quality); but far more of us are not tired at all, or would not be tired at all unless we had got into a wretched trick of feeling tired, by following the prevalent habits of vocalization and expression. And if talking high and tired, and living excitedly and hurriedly, would only enable us to *do* more by the way, even while breaking us down in the end, it would be different. There would be some compensation, some excuse, for going on so. But the exact reverse is the case. It is your relaxed and easy worker, who is in no hurry, and quite thoughtless most of the while of consequences, who is your efficient worker; and tension and anxiety, and present and future, all mixed up together in our mind at once, are the surest drags upon steady progress and hindrances to our success.

'The Gospel of Relaxation' in *Talks to Teachers on Psychology*, 1899

Why the Americans Are So Restless in the Midst of Their Prosperity

ALEXIS DE TOCQUEVILLE

In certain remote corners of the Old World, you may still sometimes stumble upon a small district which seems to have been forgotten amidst the general tumult, and to have remained stationary whilst everything around it was in motion. The inhabitants are, for the most part, extremely ignorant and poor; they take no part in the business of the country, and are frequently oppressed by the government; yet their countenances are generally placid, and their spirits light.

In America, I saw the freest and most enlightened men placed in the happiest circumstances which the world affords: it seemed to me as if a cloud habitually hung upon their brow, and I thought them serious, and almost sad, even in their pleasures.

The chief reason of this contrast is, that the former do not think of the ills they endure, while the latter are forever brooding over advantages they do not possess. It is strange to see with what feverish ardor the Americans pursue their own welfare; and to watch the vague dread that constantly torments them, lest they should not have chosen the shortest path which may lead to it.

A native of the United States clings to this world's goods as if he were certain never to die; and he is so hasty in grasping at all within his reach, that one would suppose he was constantly afraid of not living long enough to enjoy them. He clutches everything, he holds nothing fast, but soon loosens his grasp to pursue fresh gratifications.

In the United States, a man builds a house in which to spend his old age, and he sells it before the roof is on; he plants a garden, and lets it just as the trees are coming into bearing; he brings a field into tillage, and leaves other men to gather the crops; he embraces a profession, and gives it up; he settles in a place, which he soon afterwards leaves, to carry his changeable longings elsewhere. If his private affairs leave him any leisure, he instantly plunges into the vortex of politics; and if, at the end of a year of unremitting labor, he finds he has a few days' vacation, his eager curiosity whirls him over the vast extent of the United States, and he will travel fifteen hundred miles in a few days, to shake off his happiness. Death at length overtakes him, but it is before he is weary of his bootless chase of that complete felicity which forever escapes him.

At first sight, there is something surprising in this strange unrest of so many happy men, restless in the midst of abundance. The spectacle itself is, however, as old as the world; the novelty is, to see a whole people furnish an exemplification of it.

Their taste for physical gratifications must be regarded as the original source of that secret inquietude which the actions of the Americans betray, and of that inconstancy of which they daily afford fresh examples. He who has set his heart exclusively upon the pursuit of worldly welfare is always in a hurry, for he has but a limited time at his disposal to reach, to grasp, and to enjoy it. The recollection of the shortness of life is a constant spur to him. Besides the good things which he possesses, he every instant fancies a thousand others, which death will prevent him from trying if he does not try them soon. This thought fills him with anxiety, fear, and regret, and keeps his mind in ceaseless trepidation, which leads him perpetually to change his plans and his abode.

If, in addition to the taste for physical well-being, a social condition be superadded, in which neither laws nor customs retain any person in his place, there is a great additional stimulant to this restlessness of temper. Men will then be seen continually to change their track, for fear of missing the shortest cut to happiness.

It may readily be conceived, that, if men, passionately bent upon physical gratifications, desire eagerly, they are also easily discouraged: as their ultimate object is to enjoy, the means to reach that object must be prompt and easy, or the trouble of acquiring the gratification would be greater than the gratification itself. Their prevailing frame of mind, then, is at once ardent and relaxed, violent and enervated. Death is often less dreaded by them than perseverance in continuous efforts to one end.

The equality of conditions leads by a still straighter road to several of the effects which I have here described. When all the privileges of birth and fortune are abolished, when all professions are accessible to all, and a man's own energies may place him at the top of any one of them, an easy and unbounded career seems open to his ambition, and he will readily persuade himself that he is born to no vulgar destinies. But this is an erroneous notion, which is corrected by daily experience. The same equality which allows every citizen to conceive these lofty hopes, renders all the citizens less able to realize them: it circumscribes their powers on every side, whilst it gives freer scope to their desires. Not only are they themselves powerless, but they are met at every step by immense obstacles, which they did not at first perceive. They have swept away the privileges of some of their fellow-creatures which stood in their way, but they have opened the door to universal competition; the barrier has changed its shape rather than its position. When men are nearly alike, and all follow the same track, it is very difficult for any one individual to walk quick and cleave a way through the dense throng which surrounds and presses him. This constant strife between the inclinations springing from the equality of condition and the means it supplies to satisfy them, harasses and wearies the mind.

It is possible to conceive men arrived at a degree of freedom which should completely content them; they would then enjoy their independence without anxiety and without impatience. But men will never establish any equality with which they can be contented. Whatever efforts a people may make, they will never succeed in reducing all the conditions of society to a perfect level; and even if they unhappily attained that absolute and complete equality of position, the inequality of minds would still remain, which, coming directly from the hand of God, will forever escape the laws of man. However democratic, then, the social state and the political constitution of a people may be, it is certain that every member of the community will always find out several points about him which overlook his own position; and we may foresee that his looks will be doggedly fixed in that direction. When inequality of conditions is the common law of society, the most marked inequalities do not strike the eye: when everything is nearly on the same level, the slightest are marked enough to hurt it. Hence, the desire of equality always becomes more insatiable in proportion as equality is more complete.

Amongst democratic nations, men easily attain a certain equality of condition; but they can never attain as much as they desire. It perpetually retires from before them, yet without hiding itself from their sight, and in retiring draws them on. At every moment they think they are about to grasp it; it escapes at every moment from their hold. They are near enough to see its charms, but too far off to enjoy them; and before they have fully tasted its delights, they die.

To these causes must be attributed that strange melancholy which oftentimes haunts the inhabitants of democratic countries in the midst of their abundance, and that disgust at life which sometimes seizes upon them in the midst of calm and easy circumstances. Complaints are made in France that the number of suicides increases; in America suicide is rare, but insanity is said to be more common there than anywhere else. These are all different symptoms of the same disease. The Americans do not put an end to their lives, however disquieted they may be, because their religion forbids it; and amongst them materialism may be said hardly to exist, notwithstanding the general passion for physical gratification. The will resists, but reason frequently gives way.

In democratic times, enjoyments are more intense than in the ages of aristocracy, and the number of those who partake in them is vastly larger: but, on the other hand, it must be admitted that man's hopes and desires are oftener blasted, the soul is more stricken and perturbed, and care itself more keen.

Democracy in America, vol. 2, book 2, ch. 13, 1840, trans. Henry Reeve;
rev. Francis Bowen, 1862

'Irreverent of themselves'

JOHN RUSKIN

My American friends, of whom one, Charles Eliot Norton, of Cambridge, is the dearest I have in the world, tell me I know nothing about America. It may be so, and they must do me the justice to observe that I, therefore, usually *say* nothing about America. But this much I have said, because the Americans, as a nation, set their trust in liberty and in equality, of which I detest the one, and deny the possibility of the other; and because, also, as a nation, they are wholly undesirous of Rest, and incapable of it; irreverent of themselves, both in the present and in the future; discontented with what they are, yet having no ideal of anything which they desire to become.

Fors Clavigera, vol. 1, letter 12, 1871

'Conformity'

FRANCES ANNE KEMBLE

Charleston has an air of eccentricity, too, and peculiarity, which formerly were not deemed unbecoming the well-born and well-bred gentlewoman, which her gentility itself sanctioned and warranted – none of the vulgar dread of vulgar opinion, forcing those who are possessed by it to conform to a general standard of manners, unable to conceive one peculiar to itself, – this 'what'll-Mrs-Grundy-say' devotion to conformity in small things and great, which pervades the American body-social from the matter of church-going to the trimming of women's petticoats, – this dread of singularity, which has eaten up all individuality amongst them, and makes their population like so many moral and mental lithographs, and their houses like so many thousand hideous brick-twins.

I believe I am getting excited; but the fact is, that being politically the most free people on earth, the Americans are socially the least so; and it seems as though, ever since that little affair of establishing their independence among nations, which they managed so successfully, every American mother's son of them has been doing his best to divest himself of his own private share of that great public blessing, liberty.

(1838) *Records of Later Life*, 1882

'This American character'

JOHN BUTLER YEATS

What would I give for a talk with your mother, at the chimney corner in your drawing room – in America people talk either to say or to listen to *memorable* things – but there is no atmosphere.

*

– and yet, you must not think I do not admire and really adore this American character, which is now growing up, even while it is so easy to laugh at and even sometimes hate. A sort of European old-maidishness gets between me and them. Depend upon it it is a mistake sometimes to have been too well brought up, it prevents you realising that in America everything hitherto respected including your politeness and reticence is *quite out of date*. Every day of my life, I meet with some fresh surprise. People will do and say anything, and except a few things like the multiplication table, nothing is sacred.

To Ruth Hart, 3 July 1912

'Benjamin Franklin'

D. H. LAWRENCE

Benjamin, in his sagacity, knew that the breaking of the old world was a long process. In the depths of his own under-consciousness he hated England, he hated Europe, he hated the whole corpus of the European being. He wanted to be American. But you can't change your nature and mode of consciousness like changing your shoes. It is a gradual shedding. Years must go by, and centuries must elapse before you have finished. Like a son escaping from the domination of his parents. The escape is not just one rupture. It is a long and half-secret process.

So with the American. He was a European when he first went over the Atlantic. He is in the main a recreant European still. From Benjamin Franklin to Woodrow Wilson may be a long stride, but it is a stride along the same road. There is no new road. The same old road, become dreary and futile. Theoretic and materialistic.

Why then did Benjamin set up this dummy of a perfect citizen as a pattern to America? Of course he did it in perfect good faith, as far as he knew. He thought it simply was the true ideal. But what we *think* we do is not very important. We never really know what we are doing. Either we are materialistic instruments, like Benjamin, or we move in the gesture of creation, from our deepest self, usually unconscious. We are only the actors, we are never wholly the authors of our own deeds or works. IT is the author, the unknown inside us or outside us. The best we can do is to try to hold ourselves in unison with the deeps which are inside us. And the worst we can do is to try to have things our own way, when we run counter to IT, and in the long run get our knuckles rapped for presumption.

So Benjamin contriving money out of the Court of France. He was contriving the first steps of the overthrow of all Europe, France included. You can never have a new thing without breaking an old. Europe happens to be the old thing. America, unless the people in America assert themselves too much in opposition to the inner gods, should be the new thing. The new thing is the death of the old. But you can't cut the throat of an epoch. You've got to steal the life from it through several centuries.

And Benjamin worked for this both directly and indirectly. Directly, at the Court of France, making a small but very dangerous hole in the side of England, through which hole Europe has by now almost bled to death. And indirectly in Philadelphia, setting up this unlovely, snuff-coloured little ideal, or automaton, of a pattern American. The pattern American, this dry, moral, utilitarian little democrat, has done more to ruin the old Europe than any Russian nihilist. He has done it by slow attrition, like a son who has stayed at home and obeyed his parents, all the while silently hating their authority, and silently, in his soul, destroying not only their authority but their whole existence. For the American spiritually stayed at home in Europe. The spiritual home of America was and still is Europe. This is the galling bondage, in spite of several billions of heaped-up gold. Your heaps of gold are only so many muck-heaps, America, and will remain so till you become a reality to yourselves.

All this Americanizing and mechanizing has been for the purpose of overthrowing the past. And now look at America, tangled in her own barbed wire, and mastered by her own machines. Absolutely got down by her own barbed wire of shalt-nots, and shut up fast in her own 'productive' machines like millions of squirrels running in millions of cages. It is just a farce.

Now is your chance, Europe. Now let Hell loose and get your own back, and paddle your own canoe on a new sea, while clever America lies on her muck-heaps of gold, strangled in her own barbed-wire of shalt-not ideals and shalt-not moralisms. While she goes out to work like millions of squir-rels in millions of cages. Production!

Let Hell loose, and get your own back, Europe!

Studies in Classic American Literature, 1922

'Not sublime man'

JOHN KEATS

Dilke, whom you know to be a Godwin perfectability man, pleases himself with the idea that America will be the country to take up the human intellect where England leaves off – I differ there with him greatly – A country like the United States whose greatest men are Franklins and Washingtons will never do that – They are great men doubtless but how are they to be com-pared to those our countrymen Milton and the two Sidneys – The one is a philosophical Quaker full of mean and thrifty maxims, the other sold the very charger who had taken him through all his battles – Those Americans are great but they are not sublime man – The humanity of the United States can never reach the sublime – Birkbeck's mind is too much in the American style – You must endeavour to infuse a little spirit of another sort into the settlement, always with great caution, for thereby you may do your descen-dants more good than you may imagine. If I had a prayer to make for any great good, next to Tom's [their brother's] recovery, it should be that one of your children should be the first American poet.

To George and Georgiana Keats in the USA, 14 October 1818

The American Sublime

WALLACE STEVENS

How does one stand
To behold the sublime,
To confront the mockers,
The mickey mockers
And plated pairs?

When General Jackson
Posed for his statue
He knew how one feels.

Shall a man go barefoot
Blinking and blank?

But how does one feel?
One grows used to the weather,
The landscape and that;
And the sublime comes down
To the spirit itself,

The spirit and space,
The empty spirit
In vacant space.
What wine does one drink?
What bread does one eat?

Ideas of Order, 1935

'The national chemical'

EZRA POUND

I might go on objecting to details of the American order, and that would be perhaps easier than convincing a foreign audience that I am right to believe in our future.

I detest an education which tends to separate a man from his fellows. For the humanities rightly taught can but give more points of contact with other men. I should like to see the universities and the arts and the system of publication linked together for some sort of mutual benefit and stimulus.

I detest what seems to me the pedantry of the 'germanic system', although I am not insensible to the arguments in favour of this method and mechanism. I want all the accuracy of this system, but I want a more able synthesis of the results.

I want the duty on foreign books removed.

'Si étais dieu le printemps soit eternel.'

Yet the question seems not so much what I should like to see altered in the affairs of the United States as what force I rely on; why I believe that these changes and others will follow in due course.

I trust in the national chemical, or, if the reader be of Victorian sensibility, let us say the 'spirit' or the 'temper' of the nation.

I have found in 'The Seafarer' and in 'The Wanderer' trace of what I should call the English national chemical. In those early Anglo-Saxon poems I find expression of that quality which seems to me to have transformed the successive arts of poetry that have been brought to England from the South. For the art has come mostly from the south, and it has found on the island something in the temper of the race which has strengthened it and given it fibre. And this is hardly more than a race conviction that words scarcely become a man.

> Nor may the weary-in-mind withstand his fate,
> Nor is high heart his helping.
> For the doom-eager oft bindeth fast his thought in
>   blood-bedabbled breast.

The word I have translated 'doom-eager' is 'domgeorne'. And 'dom' is both 'fate' and 'glory'. The 'Dom georne' man is the man ready for his deed, eager for it, eager for the glory of it, ready to pay the price.

If a man has this quality and be meagre of speech one asks little beyond this.

I find the same sort of thing in Whitman. I mean I find in him what I should be as ready to call our American keynote as I am to call this the English keynote.

It is, as nearly as I can define it, a certain generosity; a certain carelessness, or looseness, if you will; a hatred of the sordid, an ability to forget the part for the sake of the whole, a desire for largeness, a willingness to stand exposed.

> Camerado, this is no book;
> Who touches this touches a man.

The artist is ready to endure personally a strain which his craftsmanship would scarcely endure.

Here is a spirit, one might say, as hostile to the arts as was the Anglo-Saxon objection to speaking at all.

Yet the strength of both peoples is just here; that one undertakes to keep quiet until there is something worth saying, and the other will undertake nothing in its art for which it will not be in person responsible.

This is, of course, the high ideal, not the standard or the average of practice.

And my other hope is in this: that when an American in any art or *métier* has learned what is the best, he will never after be content with the second-rate. It is by this trait that we are a young nation and a strong one. An old nation weighs the cost of the best, and asks if the best is worth while.

Because we do not do this we shall move as fast as we learn, though knowledge and instinct are not to be over-quickly acquired; not in one generation.

Yet where we have now culture and a shell we shall have some day the humanities and a centre.

'Poems and materials of poems shall come from their lives, they shall be makers and finders.'

One reason why Whitman's reception in America has been so tardy is that he says so many things which we are accustomed, almost unconsciously, to take for granted. He was so near the national colour that the nation hardly perceived him against that background. He came at a time when America was proud of a few deeds and of a few principles. He came before the nation was self-conscious or introspective or subjective; before the nation was interested in being itself.

The nation had no interest in seeing its face in the glass. It wanted a tradition like other nations, and it got Longfellow's 'Tales of a Wayside Inn' and 'Hiawatha' and 'Evangeline'.

Whitman established the national *timbre*. One may not need him at home. It is in the air, this tonic of his. But if one is abroad; if one is ever likely to forget one's birth-right, to lose faith, being surrounded by disparagers, one can find, in Whitman, the reassurance. Whitman goes bail for the nation.

Whistler was our martinet and left his message, almost, it would seem, by accident. It was in substance, that being born of an American is no excuse for being content with a parochial standard. It is all very well to say that Whistler was European, but it does not affect my argument.

If a man's work require him to live in exile, let him suffer, or enjoy, his exile gladly. But it would be about as easy for an American to become a Chinaman or a Hindoo as for him to acquire an Englishness, or a Frenchness, or a European-ness that is more than half a skin deep.

Patria Mia (wr. 1911–13), 1950, part 1

Song of Myself [15]

WALT WHITMAN

The pure contralto sings in the organloft,
The carpenter dresses his plank . . . . the tongue of his foreplane
   whistles its wild ascending lisp,
The married and unmarried children ride home to their thanksgiving
   dinner,

The pilot seizes the king-pin, he heaves down with a strong arm,
The mate stands braced in the whaleboat, lance and harpoon are ready,
The duck-shooter walks by silent and cautious stretches,
The deacons are ordained with crossed hands at the altar,
The spinning-girl retreats and advances to the hum of the big wheel,
The farmer stops by the bars of a Sunday and looks at the oats and rye,
The lunatic is carried at last to the asylum a confirmed case,
He will never sleep any more as he did in the cot in his mother's
  bedroom;
The jour printer with gray head and gaunt jaws works at his case,
He turns his quid of tobacco, his eyes get blurred with the manuscript;
The malformed limbs are tied to the anatomist's table,
What is removed drops horribly in a pail;
The quadroon girl is sold at the stand . . . . the drunkard nods by the
  barroom stove,
The machinist rolls up his sleeves . . . . the policeman travels his
  beat . . . . the gate-keeper marks who pass,
The young fellow drives the express-wagon . . . . I love him though I do
  not know him;
The half-breed straps on his light boots to compete in the race,
The western turkey-shooting draws old and young . . . . some lean on
  their rifles, some sit on logs,
Out from the crowd steps the marksman and takes his position and
  levels his piece;
The groups of newly-come immigrants cover the wharf or levee,
The woollypates hoe in the sugarfield, the overseer views them from his
  saddle;
The bugle calls in the ballroom, the gentlemen run for their partners,
  the dancers bow to each other;
The youth lies awake in the cedar-roofed garret and harks to the
  musical rain,
The Wolverine sets traps on the creek that helps fill the Huron,
The reformer ascends the platform, he spouts with his mouth and nose,
The company returns from its excursion, the darkey brings up the rear
  and bears the well-riddled target,
The squaw wrapt in her yellow-hemmed cloth is offering moccasins and
  beadbags for sale.
The connoisseur peers along the exhibition-gallery with halfshut eyes
  bent sideways,
The deckhands make fast the steamboat, the plank is thrown for the
  shoregoing passengers,

The young sister holds out the skein, the elder sister winds it off in a ball and stops now and then for the knots,

The one-year wife is recovering and happy, a week ago she bore her first child,

The cleanhaired Yankee girl works with her sewing-machine or in the factory or mill,

The nine months' gone is in the parturition chamber, her faintness and pains are advancing;

The pavingman leans on his twohanded rammer – the reporter's lead flies swiftly over the notebook – the signpainter is lettering with red and gold,

The canal-boy trots on the towpath – the bookkeeper counts at his desk – the shoemaker waxes his thread,

The conductor beats time for the band and all the performers follow him,

The child is baptised – the convert is making the first professions,

The regatta is spread on the bay . . . . how the white sails sparkle!

The drover watches his drove, he sings out to them that would stray,

The pedlar sweats with his pack on his back – the purchaser higgles about the odd cent,

The camera and plate are prepared, the lady must sit for her daguerreotype,

The bride unrumples her white dress, the minutehand of the clock moves slowly,

The opium eater reclines with rigid head and just-opened lips,

The prostitute draggles her shawl, her bonnet bobs on her tipsy and pimpled neck,

The crowd laugh at her blackguard oaths, the men jeer and wink to each other,

(Miserable! I do not laugh at your oaths nor jeer you,)

The President holds a cabinet council, he is surrounded by the great secretaries,

On the piazza walk five friendly matrons with twined arms;

The crew of the fish-smack pack repeated layers of halibut in the hold,

The Missourian crosses the plains toting his wares and his cattle,

The fare-collector goes through the train – he gives notice by the jingling of loose change,

The floormen are laying the floor – the tinners are tinning the roof – the masons are calling for mortar,

In single file each shouldering his hod pass onward the laborers;

Seasons pursuing each other the indescribable crowd is gathered . . . . it is the Fourth of July . . . . what salutes of cannon and small arms!

Seasons pursuing each other the plougher ploughs and the mower mows
    and the wintergrain falls in the ground;
Off on the lakes the pikefisher watches and waits by the hole in the
    frozen surface,
The stumps stand thick round the clearing, the squatter strikes deep
    with his axe,
The flatboatmen make fast toward dusk near the cottonwood or
    pekantrees,
The coon-seekers go now through the regions of the Red river, or
    through those drained by the Tennessee, or through those of the
    Arkansas,
The torches shine in the dark that hangs on the Chattahoochee or
    Altamahaw;
Patriarchs sit at supper with sons and grandsons and great grandsons
    around them,
In walls of adobe, in canvass tents, rest hunters and trappers after their
    day's sport.
The city sleeps and the country sleeps,
The living sleep for their time. . . . the dead sleep for their time,
The old husband sleeps by his wife and the young husband sleeps by his
    wife;
And these one and all tend inward to me, and I tend outward to them,
And such as it is to be of these more or less I am.

Leaves of Grass, 1855

A Supermarket in California

ALLEN GINSBERG

What thoughts I have of you tonight, Walt Whitman, for I walked
down the sidestreets under the trees with a headache self-conscious
looking at the full moon.

In my hungry fatigue, and shopping for images, I went into the
neon fruit supermarket, dreaming of your enumerations!

What peaches and what penumbras! Whole families shopping at
night! Aisles full of husbands! Wives in the avocados, babies in the
tomatoes! – and you, García Lorca, what were you doing down by the
watermelons?

I saw you, Walt Whitman, childless, lonely old grubber, poking
among the meats in the refrigerator and eyeing the grocery boys.

I heard you asking questions of each: Who killed the pork chops?
What price bananas? Are you my Angel?

I wandered in and out of the brilliant stacks of cans following you,
and followed in my imagination by the store detective.

We strode down the open corridors together in our solitary fancy
tasting artichokes, possessing every frozen delicacy, and never passing
the cashier.

Where are we going, Walt Whitman? The doors close in an hour.
Which way does your beard point tonight?

(I touch your book and dream of our odyssey in the supermarket
and feel absurd.)

Will we walk all night through solitary streets? The trees add shade
to shade, lights out in the houses, we'll both be lonely.

Will we stroll dreaming of the lost America of love past blue
automobiles in driveways, home to our silent cottage?

Ah, dear father, graybeard, lonely old courage-teacher, what
America did you have when Charon quit poling his ferry and you got
out on a smoking bank and stood watching the boat disappear on the
black waters of Lethe?

Howl, 1956

'Their burial-places'

HARRIET MARTINEAU

As might have been predicted, one of the first directions in which the Americans have indulged their taste and indicated their refinement is in the preparation and care of their burial-places. This might have been predicted by
any one who meditates upon the influences under which the mind of
America is growing. The pilgrim origin of the New-England population,
whose fathers seemed to think that they lived only in order to die, is in
favour of all thoughts connected with death filling a large space in the people's minds. Then, in addition to the moving power of common human
affections, the Americans are subject to being more incessantly reminded
than others how small a section of the creation is occupied by the living in
comparison with that engrossed by the dead. In the busy, crowded empires
of the Old World, the invisible are liable to be forgotten in the stirring presence of visible beings, who inhabit every corner, and throng the whole surface on which men walk. In the New World it is not so. Living men are
comparatively scarce, and the general mind dwells more on the past and the

future (of both which worlds death is the atmosphere) than on the present. By various influences, death is made to constitute a larger element in their estimate of collective human experience, a more conspicuous object in their contemplation of the plan of Providence, than it is to, perhaps, any other people. As a natural consequence, all arrangements connected with death occupy much of their attention, and engage a large share of popular sentiment.

I have mentioned that family graveyards are conspicuous objects in country abodes in America. In the valley of the Mohawk, on the heights of the Alleghanies, in the centre of the northwestern prairie, wherever there is a solitary dwelling there is a domestic burying-place, generally fenced with neat white palings, and delicately kept, however full the settler's hands may be, and whatever may be the aspect of the abode of the living. The new burial-places which are laid out near the towns may already be known from a distance by the air of finish and taste about their plantations; and I believe it is allowed that Mount Auburn is the most beautiful cemetery in the world.

Retrospect of Western Travel, 1838

'A space of time'

GERTRUDE STEIN

Then at the same time is the question of time. The assembling of a thing to make a whole thing and each one of these whole things is one of a series, but beside this there is the important thing and the very American thing that everybody knows who is an American just how many seconds minutes or hours it is going to take to do a whole thing. It is singularly a sense for combination within a conception of the existence of a given space of time that makes the American thing the American thing, and the sense of this space of time must be within the whole thing as well as in the completed whole thing.

I felt this thing, I am an American and I felt this thing, and I made a continuous effort to create this thing in every paragraph that I made in *The Making of Americans*. And that is why after all this book is an American book an essentially American book, because this thing is an essentially American thing this sense of space of time and what is to be done within this space of time not in any way excepting in the way that it is inevitable that there is this space of time and anybody who is an American feels what is inside this space of time and so well they do what they do within this space of time, and so ultimately it is a thing contained within. I wonder if I at all convey to you what I mean by this thing. I will try to tell it in every

way I can as I have in all the writing that I have ever done. I am always trying to tell this thing that a space of time is a natural thing for an American
to always have inside them as something in which they are continuously
moving. Think of anything, of cowboys, of movies, of detective stories, of
anybody who goes anywhere or stays at home and is an American and you
will realize that it is something strictly American to conceive a space that
is filled with moving, a space of time that is filled always filled with moving
and my first real effort to express this thing which is an American thing began in writing *The Making of Americans*.

'The Gradual Making of *The Making of Americans*' in
Lectures in America, 1935

An American

RUDYARD KIPLING

The American Spirit speaks:

'If the Led Striker call it a strike,
    Or the papers call it a war,
They know not much what I am like,
    Nor what he is, my Avatar.'

Through many roads, by me possessed,
    He shambles forth in cosmic guise;
He is the Jester and the Jest,
    And he the Text himself applies.

The Celt is in his heart and hand,
    The Gaul is in his brain and nerve;
Where, cosmopolitanly planned,
    He guards the Redskin's dry reserve.

His easy unswept hearth he lends
    From Labrador to Guadeloupe;
Till, elbowed out by sloven friends,
    He camps, at sufferance, on the stoop.

Calm-eyed he scoffs at sword and crown,
    Or panic-blinded stabs and slays:
Blatant he bids the world bow down,
    Or cringing begs a crust of praise;

Or, sombre-drunk, at mine and mart,
    He dubs his dreary brethren Kings.
His hands are black with blood – his heart
    Leaps, as a babe's, at little things.

But, through the shift of mood and mood,
    Mine ancient humour saves him whole –
The cynic devil in his blood
    That bids him mock his hurrying soul;

That bids him flout the Law he makes,
    That bids him make the Law he flouts,
Till, dazed by many doubts, he wakes
    The drumming guns that – have no doubts;

That checks him foolish-hot and fond,
    That chuckles through his deepest ire,
That gilds the slough of his despond
    But dims the goal of his desire;

Inopportune, shrill-accented,
    The acrid Asiatic mirth
That leaves him, careless 'mid his dead,
    The scandal of the elder earth.

How shall he clear himself, how reach
    Your bar or weighed defence prefer?
A brother hedged with alien speech
    And lacking all interpreter.

Which knowledge vexes him a space;
    But while Reproof around him rings,
He turns a keen untroubled face
    Home, to the instant need of things.

Enslaved, illogical, elate,
    He greets th' embarrassed Gods, nor fears
To shake the iron hand of Fate,
    Or match with Destiny for beers.

Lo, imperturbable he rules,
    Unkempt, disreputable, vast –
And, in the teeth of all the schools,
    I – I shall save him at the last!

1894

CULTURE

Young man, there is America – which at this day serves for little more than to amuse you with stories of savage men, and uncouth manners; yet shall, before you taste of death, show itself equal to the whole of that commerce which now attracts the envy of the world.

Edmund Burke, *Speech on Conciliation with America*, 1775

This word Culture, or what it has come to represent, involves, by contrast, our whole theme, and has been, indeed, the spur, urging us to engagement [. . .] I do not so much object to the name, or word, but I should certainly insist, for the purposes of these States, on a radical change of category, in the distribution of precedence. I should demand a programme of culture, drawn out, not for a single class alone, or for the parlors or lecture-rooms, but with an eye to practical life, the west, the working-men, the facts of farms and jack-planes and engineers, and of the broad range of the women also of the middle and working strata, and with reference to the perfect equality of women, and of a grand and powerful motherhood.

Walt Whitman, *Democratic Vistas*, 1871

'Who reads an American book?'

SYDNEY SMITH

The Americans are a brave, industrious, and acute people; but they have hitherto given no indications of genius, and made no approaches to the heroic, either in their morality or character. They are but a recent offset indeed from England; and should make it their chief boast, for many generations to come, that they are sprung from the same race with Bacon and Shakespeare and Newton. Considering their numbers, indeed, and the favorable circumstances in which they have been placed, they have yet done marvellously little to assert the honour of such a descent, or to show that their English blood has been exalted or refined by their republican training and institutions. Their Franklins and Washingtons, and all the other sages and heroes of their revolution, were born and bred subjects of the King of England, – and not among the freest or most valued of his subjects. And, since the period of their separation, a far greater proportion of their statesmen and artists and political writers have been foreigners, than ever occurred before in the history of any civilised and educated people. During the thirty or forty years of their independence, they have done absolutely nothing for the Sciences, for the Arts, for Literature, or even for the statesman-like studies of Politics or Political Economy. Confining ourselves to our own country, and to the period that has elapsed since *they* had an independent existence, we would ask, Where are their Foxes, their Burkes, their Sheridans, their Windhams, their Horners, their Wilberforces? – where their Arkwrights, their Watts, their Davys? – their Robertsons, Blairs, Smiths, Stewarts, Paleys, and Malthuses? – their Porsons, Parrs, Burneys, or Blomfields? – their Scotts, Rogers's, Campbells, Byrons, Moores, or Crabbes? – their Siddons's, Kembles, Keans, or O'Neils? – their Wilkies, Laurences, Chantrys? – or their parallels to the hundred other names that have spread themselves over the world from our little island in the course of the last thirty years, and blest or delighted mankind by their works, inventions, or examples? In so far as we know, there is no such parallel to be produced from the whole annals of this self-adulating race. In the four quarters of the globe, who reads an American book? or goes to an American play? or looks at an American picture or statue? What does the world yet owe to American physicians or surgeons? What new substances have their chemists discovered? or what old ones have they analysed? What new constellations have been discovered by the telescopes of Americans? What have they done in the mathematics? Who drinks out of American glasses? or eats from American plates? or wears American coats or gowns? or sleeps in American blankets?

Finally, under which of the old tyrannical governments of Europe is every sixth man a slave, whom his fellow-creatures may buy and sell and torture?

When these questions are fairly and favourably answered, their laudatory epithets may be allowed: but, till that can be done, we would seriously advise them to keep clear of superlatives.

Edinburgh Review, January, 1820

'A national literature'

HERMAN MELVILLE

Let America then prize and cherish her writers; yea, let her glorify them. They are not so many in number as to exhaust her good will. And while she has good kith and kin of her own, to take to her bosom, let her not lavish her embraces upon the household of an alien. For believe it or not, England, after all, is, in many things, an alien to us. China has more bowels of real love for us than she. But even were there no strong literary individualities among us, as there are some dozen at least, nevertheless, let America first praise mediocrity even, in her own children, before she praises (for everywhere, merit demands acknowledgement from every one) the best excellence in the children of any other land. Let her own authors, I say, have the priority of appreciation. I was much pleased with a hot-headed Carolina cousin of mine, who once said, 'If there were no other American to stand by, in Literature – why, then, I would stand by Pop Emmons and his *Fredoniad*, and till a better epic came along, swear it was not very far behind the *Iliad*.' Take away the words, and in spirit he was sound.

Not that American genius needs patronage in order to expand. For that explosive sort of stuff will expand though screwed up in a vise, and burst it, though it were triple steel. It is for the nation's sake, and not for her authors' sake, that I would have America be heedful of the increasing greatness among her writers. For how great the shame, if other nations should be before her, in crowning her heroes of the pen! But this is almost the case now. American authors have received more just and discriminating praise (however loftily and ridiculously given, in certain cases) even from some Englishmen, than from their own countrymen. There are hardly five critics in America; and several of them are asleep. As for patronage, it is the American author who now patronizes his country, and not his country him. And if at times some among them appeal to the people for more recognition, it is not always with selfish motives, but patriotic ones.

It is true that but few of them as yet have evinced that decided originality which merits great praise.

*

But it is not meant that all American writers should studiously cleave to nationality in their writings; only this, no American writer should write like an Englishman, or a Frenchman; let him write like a man, for then he will be sure to write like an American. Let us away with this leaven of literary flunkyism towards England. If either must play the flunky in this thing, let England do it, not us. While we are rapidly preparing for that political supremacy among the nations, which prophetically awaits us at the close of the present century, in a literary point of view we are deplorably unprepared for it, and we seem studious to remain so. Hitherto, reasons might have existed why this should be; but no good reason exists now. And all that is requisite to amendment in this matter is simply this: that, while freely acknowledging all excellence, everywhere, we should refrain from unduly lauding foreign writers and, at the same time, duly recognize the meritorious writers that are our own; those writers who breathe that unshackled, democratic spirit of Christianity in all things, which now takes the practical lead in this world, though at the same time led by ourselves – us Americans. Let us boldly condemn all imitation, though it comes to us graceful and fragrant as the morning, and foster all originality, though, at first, it be crabbed and ugly as our own pine knots. And if any of our authors fail, or seem to fail, then, in the words of my enthusiastic Carolina cousin, let us clap him on the shoulder, and back him against all Europe for his second round. The truth is that, in our point of view, this matter of a national literature has come to such a pass with us that in some sense we must turn bullies, else the day is lost, or superiority so far beyond us, that we can hardly say it will ever be ours.

'Hawthorne and His Mosses', 1850

'The renovated English speech'

WALT WHITMAN

In a little while, in the United States, the English language, enriched with contributions from all languages, old and new, will be spoken by a hundred millions of people: – perhaps a hundred thousand words ('seventy or eighty thousand words' – Noah Webster, of the English language).

The Americans are going to be the most fluent and melodious voiced people in the world – and the most perfect users of words. – Words follow character – nativity, independence, individuality.

I see that the time is nigh when the etiquette of saloons is to be discharged from that great thing, the renovated English speech in America. – The occasions of the English speech in America are immense, profound – stretch over ten thousand vast cities, over millions of miles of meadows, farms, mountains, men, through thousands of years – the occasions of saloons are for a coterie, a bon soir or two, – involve waiters standing behind chairs, silent, obedient, with backs that can bend and must often bend.

*

The appetite of the people of These States, in popular speeches and writings, is for unhemmed latitude, coarseness, directness, live epithets, expletives, words of opprobrium, resistance. – This I understand because I have the taste myself as large as largely as any one. – I have pleasure in the use, on fit occasions, of traitor, coward, liar, shyster, skulk, doughface, trickster, mean curse, backslider, thief, impotent, lickspittle.

The great writers are often select of their audiences. – The greatest writers only are well-pleased and at their ease among the unlearned – are received by common men and women familiarly, do not hold out obscure, but come welcome to table, bed, leisure, by day and night.

A perfect writer would make words sing, dance, kiss, do the male and female act, bear children, weep, bleed, rage, stab, steal, fire cannon, steer ships, sack cities, charge with cavalry or infantry, or do any thing, that man or woman or the natural powers can do.

*

What name a city has – What name a State, river, sea, mountain, wood, prairie, has – is no indifferent matter. – All aboriginal names sound good. I was asking for something savage and luxuriant, and behold here are the aboriginal names. I see how they are being preserved. They are honest words – they give the true length, breadth, depth. They all fit. Mississippi! – the word winds with chutes – it rolls a stream three thousand miles long. Ohio, Connecticut, Ottawa, Monongahela, all fit.

*

The nigger dialect furnishes hundreds of outré words, many of them adopted into the common speech of the mass of the people. – Curiously, these words show the old English instinct for wide open pronunciations, as *yallah* for yellow – *massah* for master – and for rounding off all the corners of words. The nigger dialect has hints of the future theory of the modification of all the words of the English language, for musical purposes, for a native grand opera in America, leaving the words just as they are for writing and speaking, but the same words so modified as to answer perfectly for musical purposes, on grand and simple principles. – Then we should have two sets of words, male and female as they should be, in these states, both equally understood by the people, giving a fit much-needed medium to that passion for music, which is deeper and purer in America than in any other land in the world. – The music of America is to adopt the Italian method, and expand it to vaster, simpler, far superber effects. – It is not to be satisfied till it comprehends the people and is comprehended by them.

*

California is sown thick with the names of all the little and big saints. Chase them away and substitute aboriginal names. What is the fitness – What the strange charm of aboriginal names? – Monongahela – it rolls with venison richness upon the palate. Among names to be revolutionized: that of the city of 'Baltimore'.

Never will I allude to the English Language or tongue without exultation. This is the tongue that spurns laws, as the greatest tongue must. It is the most capacious vital tongue of all – full of ease, definiteness and power – full of sustenance. – An enormous treasure-house, or range of treasure-houses, arsenals, granary, chock full with so many contributions from the north and from the south, from Scandinavia, from Greece and Rome – from Spaniards, Italians and the French – that its own sturdy home-dated Angles-bred words have long been outnumbered by the foreigners whom they lead – which is all good enough, and indeed must be. – America owes immeasurable respect and love to the past, and to many ancestries, for many inheritances – but of all that America has received from the past, from the mothers and fathers of laws, arts, letters, &c., by far the greatest inheritance is the English Language – so long in growing – so fitted.

An American Primer (wr. 1855–60), 1904

'The negative side of the spectacle'

HENRY JAMES

There is a phrase in the preface to his [Hawthorne's] novel of *Transformation*, which must have lingered in the minds of many Americans who have tried to write novels and to lay the scene of them in the western world. 'No author, without a trial, can conceive of the difficulty of writing a romance about a country where there is no shadow, no antiquity, no mystery, no picturesque and gloomy wrong, nor anything but a commonplace prosperity, in broad and simple daylight, as is happily the case with my dear native land.' The perusal of Hawthorne's American Note-Books operates as a practical commentary upon this somewhat ominous text. It does so at least to my own mind; it would be too much perhaps to say that the effect would be the same for the usual English reader. An American reads between the lines – he completes the suggestions – he constructs a picture. I think I am not guilty of any gross injustice in saying that the picture he constructs from Hawthorne's American diaries, though by no means without charms of its own, is not, on the whole, an interesting one. It is characterised by an extraordinary blankness – a curious paleness of colour and paucity of detail. Hawthorne, as I have said, has a large and healthy appetite for detail, and one is therefore the more struck with the lightness of the diet to which his observation was condemned. For myself, as I turn the pages of his journals, I seem to see the image of the crude and simple society in which he lived. I use these epithets, of course, not invidiously, but descriptively; if one desires to enter as closely as possible into Hawthorne's situation, one must endeavour to reproduce his circumstances. We are struck with the large number of elements that were absent from them, and the coldness, the thinness, the blankness, to repeat my epithet, present themselves so vividly that our foremost feeling is that of compassion for a romancer looking for subjects in such a field. It takes so many things, as Hawthorne must have felt later in life, when he made the acquaintance of the denser, richer, warmer European spectacle – it takes such an accumulation of history and custom, such a complexity of manners and types, to form a fund of suggestion for a novelist. If Hawthorne had been a young Englishman, or a young Frenchman of the same degree of genius, the same cast of mind, the same habits, his consciousness of the world around him would have been a very different affair; however obscure, however reserved, his own personal life, his sense of the life of his fellow-mortals would have been almost infinitely more various. The negative side of the spectacle on which Hawthorne looked out, in his contemplative saunterings and reveries, might, indeed, with a little ingenuity, be made almost ludicrous; one might enumerate the items of high civilization, as it exists in other countries, which are absent from the texture of American life, until it should become a wonder to know what was left. No State, in the European sense of the word, and indeed barely a specific national name. No sovereign, no court, no personal loyalty, no aristocracy, no church, no clergy, no army, no diplomatic service, no country gentlemen, no palaces, no castles, nor manors, nor old country-houses, nor parsonages, nor thatched cottages nor ivied ruins, no cathedrals, nor abbeys, nor little Norman churches; no great Universities nor public schools – no Oxford, nor Eton, nor Harrow; no literature, no novels, no museums, no pictures, no political society, no sporting class – no Epsom nor Ascot!

Some such list as that might be drawn up of the absent things in American life – especially in the American life of forty years ago, the effect of which, upon an English or a French imagination, would probably as a general thing be appalling. The natural remark, in the almost lurid light of such an indict-ment, would be that if these things are left out, everything is left out. The American knows that a good deal remains; what it is that remains – that is his secret, his joke, as one may say. It would be cruel, in this terrible denu-dation, to deny him the consolation of his national gift, that 'American hu-mour' of which of late years we have heard so much.

Hawthorne, 1879, ch. 2

'Distinctively American'

T. S. ELIOT

Like many other terms, the term 'American literature' has altered and devel oped its meaning in the course of time. It means something different for us today from what it could have meant a hundred years ago. It has much fuller meaning now than it could have had then. By this I do not mean that American literature of the nineteenth century is less deserving of the name than American literature of the twentieth. I mean that the phrase could not mean quite the same thing to the writers of a century ago that it means to us; that it is only in retrospect that their Americanness is fully visible. At the beginning, to speak of 'American literature' would have been only to es-tablish a geographical distinction: Jonathan Edwards could hardly have un-derstood what the term means today. Early American literature, without the achievements of later writers, would merely be literature written in Eng-lish by men born or living in America. Washington Irving is less distinctively American than Fenimore Cooper. I suspect that the Leather-stocking novels, to a contemporary English reader, must have appeared to depict, not a new and different society, but the adventures of English pioneers in new and undeveloped country; just as I suppose they still have, for English boys, much the same fascination as good tales of adventure of early life in British dominions and colonies anywhere. (Cooper has suffered, like Walter Scott, from being read in early youth, and by many people never read again: it remained for D. H. Lawrence, who discovered Cooper later in life, to write probably the most brilliant of critical essays on him.) The English reader of the day, certainly, would hardly have recognized in Natty Bumppo a new kind of man: it is only in retrospect that such differences are visible.

The literature of nineteenth century New England, however, is patently marked by something more than the several personalities of its authors: it has its own particular *civilized* landscape and the ethos of a local society of English origin with its own distinct traits. It remains representative of New England, rather than of America: and Longfellow, Whittier, Bryant, Emerson, Thoreau – and even the last of the pure New Englanders, Robert Frost – yield more of themselves, I believe, to people of New England origin than to others; they have, in addition to their qualities of wider appeal, a peculiar nostalgic charm for New Englanders settled elsewhere. And as for the writer who to me is the greatest among them, Nathaniel Hawthorne, it seems to me that there is something in Hawthorne that can best be appreciated by the reader with Calvinism in his bones and witch-hanging (*not* witch-hunting) on his conscience.

*

I think it is just to say that the pioneers of twentieth-century poetry were more conspicuously the Americans than the English, both in number and in quality. Why this should have been must remain a matter for conjecture. I do not believe that it is attributable to the fact that so many more Britons were killed in the first war: the most remarkable of the British poets killed in that war whose work has been published is, in my opinion, Isaac Rosenberg, who was outside the movement. Perhaps the young Americans of that age were less oppressed by the weight of the Victorian tradition, more open to new influences and more ready for experiment. (So far as my observation goes, I should say in general, of contemporary verse, that the most dangerous tendency of American versifiers is towards eccentricity and formlessness, whereas that of English versifiers is rather towards conventionality and reversion to the Victorian type.) But, looking at my own generation, the names that come immediately to mind are those of Ezra Pound, W. C. Williams, Wallace Stevens – and you may take pride in one who is a St Louisan by birth: Miss Marianne Moore. Even of a somewhat younger generation, the names of Americans come to my mind most readily: Cummings, Hart Crane, Ransom, Tate. And I am choosing names only from among those whose work places them among the more radical experimenters: among poets of an intermediate type of technique the names of distinction are as numerous here as in England. And this is a new thing. In the nineteenth century, Poe and Whitman stand out as solitary international figures: in the last forty years, for the first time, there has been assembled a *body* of American poetry which has made its total impression in England and in Europe.

I am merely stating what seem to me cold facts. During the thirties the tide seemed to be turning the other way: the representative figure of that decade is W. H. Auden, though there are other British poets of the same generation whose best work will I believe prove equally permanent. Now, I do not know whether Auden is to be considered as an English or as an American poet: his career has been useful to me in providing me with an answer to the same question when asked about myself, for I can say: 'whichever Auden is, I suppose I must be the other'. Today there are several interesting younger poets in both countries, and England has acquired some valuable recruits from Wales. But my point in making this hurried review is simply this. In my time, there have been influences in both directions, and I think, to the mutual profit of literature on both sides of the Atlantic. But English and American poetry do not in consequence tend to become merged into one common international type, even though the poetry of today on one side of the ocean may show a closer kinship with poetry on the other side, than either does with that of an earlier generation. I do not think that a satisfactory statement of what constitutes the difference between an English and an American 'tradition' in poetry could be arrived at: because the moment you produce your definition, and the neater the definition is, the more surely some poet will turn up who doesn't fit into it at all, but who is nevertheless definitely either English or American. And the tradition itself, as I have said long ago, is altered by every new writer of genius. The difference will remain undefined, but it will remain; and this is I think as it should be: for it is because they are different that English poetry and American poetry can help each other, and contribute towards the endless renovation of both.

'American Literature and the American Language' (1953)
in *To Criticize the Critic*, 1965

'British and American poetry'

W. H. AUDEN

Normally, in comparing the poetry of two cultures, the obvious and easiest point at which to start is with a comparison of the peculiar characteristics, grammatical, rhetorical, rhythmical, of their respective languages, for even the most formal and elevated styles of poetry are more conditioned by the spoken tongue, the language really used by the men of that country, than by anything else. In the case of British and American poetry, however, this is the most subtle difference of all and the hardest to define. Any Englishman, with a little effort, can learn to pronounce 'the letter *a* in psalm and calm . . . with the sound of *a* in candle', to say *thumb-tacks* instead of *drawing-pins* or twenty-minutes-*of*-one instead of twenty-minutes-*to*-one, and discover that, in the Middle West, *bought* rhymes with *hot*, but he will still be as far from speaking American English as his Yankee cousin who comes to England will be from speaking the Queen's. No dramatist in either country who has introduced a character from the other side has, to my knowledge, been able to make his speech convincing. What the secret of the difference is, I cannot put my finger on; William Carlos Williams, who has thought more than most about this problem, says that 'Pace is one of its most important manifestations' and to this one might add another. Pitch. If undefinable, the difference is, however, immediately recognizable by the ear, even in verse where the formal conventions are the same.

> He must have had a father and a mother –
> In fact I've heard him say so – and a dog,
> As a boy should, I venture; and the dog,
> Most likely, was the only man who knew him.
> A dog, for all I know, is what he needs
> As much as anything right here today,
> To counsel him about his disillusions,
> Old aches, and parturitions of what's coming –
> A dog of orders, an emeritus,
> To wag his tail at him when he comes home,
> And then to put his paws up on his knees
> And say, 'For God's sake, what's it all about?'

(E. A. Robinson, 'Ben Jonson Entertains a Man from Stratford')

Whatever this may owe to Browning, the fingering is quite different and un-British. Again, how American in rhythm as well as in sensibility is this stanza by Robert Frost:

> But no, I was out for stars:
> I would not come in.
> I meant not even if asked,
> And I hadn't been.

('Come In')

Until quite recently an English writer, like one of any European country, could presuppose two conditions, a nature which was mythologized, humanized, on the whole friendly, and a human society which had become in time, whatever succession of invasions it may have suffered in the past, in race and religion more or less homogeneous and in which most people lived and died in the locality where they were born.

Christianity might have deprived Aphrodite, Apollo, the local genius, of their divinity but as figures for the forces of nature, as a mode of thinking about the creation, they remained valid for poets and their readers alike. Descartes might reduce the non-human universe to a mechanism but the feelings of Europeans about the sun and moon, the cycle of the seasons, the local landscape remained unchanged. Wordsworth might discard the mythological terminology but the kind of relation between nature and man which he described was the same personal one. Even when nineteenth-century biology began to trouble men's minds with the thought that the universe might be without moral values, their immediate experience was still of a friendly and lovable nature. Whatever their doubts and convictions about the purpose and significance of the universe as a whole, Tennyson's Lincolnshire or Hardy's Dorset were places where they felt completely at home, landscapes with faces of their own which a human being could recognize and trust.

But in America, neither the size nor the condition nor the climate of the continent encourages such intimacy. It is an unforgettable experience for anyone born on the other side of the Atlantic to take a plane journey by night across the United States. Looking down he will see the lights of some town like a last outpost in a darkness stretching for hours ahead, and realize that, even if there is no longer an actual frontier, this is still a continent only partially settled and developed, where human activity seems a tiny thing in comparison to the magnitude of the earth, and the equality of men not some dogma of politics or jurisprudence but a self-evident fact. He will behold a wild nature, compared with which the landscapes of Salvator Rosa are as cosy as Arcadia and which cannot possibly be thought of in human or personal terms. If Henry Adams could write:

> When Adams was a boy in Boston, the best chemist in the place had probably never heard of Venus except by way of scandal, or of the Virgin except as idolatry. . . . The force of the Virgin was still felt at Lourdes, and seemed to be as potent as X-rays; but in America neither Venus nor Virgin ever had value as force – at most as sentiment. No American had ever been truly afraid of either

the reason for this was not simply that the *Mayflower* carried iconophobic dissenters but also that the nature which Americans, even in New England, had every reason to fear could not possibly be imagined as a mother. A white whale whom man can neither understand nor be understood by, whom only a madman like Gabriel can worship, the only relationship with whom is a combat to the death by which a man's courage and skill are tested and judged, or the great buck who answers the poet's prayer for 'someone else additional to him' in 'The Most of It' are more apt symbols. Thoreau, who certainly tried his best to become intimate with nature, had to confess

> I walk in nature still alone
> And know no one,
> Discern no lineament nor feature
> Of any creature.
> Though all the firmament
> Is o'er me bent,
> Yet still I miss the grace
> Of an intelligent and kindred face.
> I still must seek the friend
> Who does with nature blend,
> Who is the person in her mask,
> He is the man I ask. . . .

Many poets in the Old World have become disgusted with human civilization but what the earth would be like if the race became extinct they cannot imagine; an American like Robinson Jeffers can quite easily, for he has seen with his own eyes country as yet untouched by history.

In a land which is fully settled, most men must accept their local environment or try to change it by political means; only the exceptionally gifted or adventurous can leave to seek his fortune elsewhere. In America, on the other hand, to move on and make a fresh start somewhere else is still the normal reaction to dissatisfaction or failure. Such social fluidity has important psychological effects. Since movement involves breaking social and personal ties, the habit creates an attitude towards personal relationships in which impermanence is taken for granted.

(Ellipses are Auden's.) 'American Poetry' (1956)
in *The Dyer's Hand*, 1963

Responses to *Twentieth Century Verse* Questionnaire

WALLACE STEVENS

ENQUIRY

1. *Do you think a representative 'American poetry' exists now [1938], distinct from English poetry, that an 'American tradition' is in process of creation? To put the question another way, do you think the American Renaissance of 1912 and the following years had permanent value?*
2. *Do you regard yourself as part of the 'American tradition', as an American poet, regional or national; or as a poet simply, dissociated from nationality?*
3. *Do you think the poetry written by Americans during the last ten years shows any line of development (progression)?*

QUESTION 1 –

The relationship between Americans is at least approximately racial, and does not pretend to be anything else. We have the country in common, even if we do not always have each other. This does not make for tradition. In the case of any poem professing to be an American poem, most Englishmen would be competent to determine for themselves, by now, whether it was genuinely American. In short, there exists a clear sense of what is American. Conceding that we are racially a bit tentative, does not the sense of what we are answer your question? The less said about permanent values now-a-days, the better.

QUESTION 2 –

I should not say that I was flagrantly American, but I hope that I am American.

QUESTION 3 –

The older poets have to be considered as individuals; the younger poets, whom it is easier to see as a group, lack a leader. After all, the fury of poetry always comes from the presence of a madman or two and, at the moment, all the madmen are politicians.

(1938) *Opus Posthumous*, rev. ed. 1989

American Poetry

LOUIS SIMPSON

Whatever it is, it must have
A stomach that can digest
Rubber, coal, uranium, moons, poems.

Like the shark, it contains a shoe.
It must swim for miles through the desert
Uttering cries that are almost human.

At the End of the Open Road, 1963

On the Ball

ROGER ANGELL

It weighs just over five ounces and measures between 2.86 and 2.94 inches in diameter. It is made of a composition-cork nucleus encased in two thin layers of rubber, one black and one red, surrounded by 121 yards of tightly wrapped blue-gray wool yarn, 45 yards of white wool yarn, 53 more yards of blue-gray wool yarn, 150 yards of fine cotton yarn, a coat of rubber cement, and a cowhide (formerly horsehide) exterior, which is held together with 216 slightly raised red cotton stitches. Printed certifications, endorsements, and outdoor advertising spherically attest to its authenticity. Like most institutions, it is considered inferior in its present form to its ancient archetypes, and in this case the complaint is probably justified; on occasion in recent years it has actually been known to come apart under the demands of its brief but rigorous active career. Baseballs are assembled and hand-stitched in Taiwan (before this year the work was done in Haiti, and before 1973 in Chicopee, Massachusetts), and contemporary pitchers claim that there is a tangible variation in the size and feel of the balls that now come into play in a single game; a true peewee is treasured by hurlers, and its departure from the premises, by fair means or foul, is secretly mourned. But never mind: any baseball is beautiful. No other small package comes as close to the ideal in design and utility. It is a perfect object for a man's hand. Pick it up and it instantly suggests its purpose; it is meant to be thrown a considerable distance – thrown hard and with precision. Its feel and heft are the beginning of the sport's critical dimensions; if it were a fraction of an inch larger or smaller, a few centigrams heavier or lighter, the game of baseball would be utterly different. Hold a baseball in your hand. As it happens, this one is not brand-new. Here, just to one side of the curved surgical welt of stitches, there is a pale-green grass smudge, darkening on one edge almost to black – the mark of an old infield play, a tough grounder now lost in memory. Feel the ball, turn it over in your hand; hold it across the seam or the other way, with the seam just to the side of your middle finger. Speculation stirs. You want to get outdoors and throw this spare and sensual object to somebody or, at the very least, watch somebody else throw it. The game has begun.

Thinking about the ball and its attributes seems to refresh our appreciation of this game. A couple of years ago, I began to wonder why it was that pitchers, taken as a group, seemed to be so much livelier and more garrulous than hitters. I considered the possibility of some obscure physiological linkage (the discobologlottal syndrome) and the more obvious occupational discrepancies (pitchers have a lot more spare time than other players), but then it came to me that a pitcher is the only man in baseball who can properly look on the ball as being his instrument, his accomplice. He is the only player who is granted the privilege of making offensive plans, and once the game begins he is (in concert with his catcher) the only man on the field who knows what is meant to happen next. Everything in baseball begins with the pitch, and every other part of the game – hitting, fielding, and throwing – is reflexive and defensive. (The hitters on a ball team are referred to as the 'offense', but almost three quarters of the time this is an absolute misnomer.) The batter tapping the dirt off his spikes and now stepping into the box looks sour and glum, and who can blame him, for the ball has somehow been granted in perpetuity to the wrong people. It is already an object of suspicion and hatred, and the reflex that allows him occasionally to deflect that tiny onrushing dot with his bat, and sometimes even to relaunch it violently in the opposite direction, is such a miraculous response of eye and body as to remain virtually inexplicable, even to him. There are a few dugout flannelmouths (Ted Williams, Harry Walker, Pete Rose) who can talk convincingly about the art of hitting, but, like most arts, it does not in the end seem communicable. Pitching is different. It is a craft ('the crafty portsider . . . ') and is thus within reach.

The smiling pitcher begins not only with the advantage of holding his fate in his own hands, or hand, but with the knowledge that every advantage of physics and psychology seems to be on his side. A great number of surprising and unpleasant things can be done to the ball as it is delivered from the grasp of a two-hundred-pound optimist, and the first of these is simply to transform it into a projectile. Most pitchers seem hesitant to say so, but if you press them a little they will admit that the prime ingredient in their intense personal struggle with the batter is probably fear. A few pitchers in the majors have thrived without a real fastball – junk men like Eddie Lopat and Mike Cuellar, superior control artists like Bobby Shantz and Randy Jones, knuckleballers like Hoyt Wilhelm and Charlie Hough – but almost everyone else has had to hump up and throw at least an occasional no-nonsense hard one, which crosses the plate at eighty-five miles per hour, or better, and thus causes the hitter to – well, to *think* a little. The fastball sets up all the other pitches in the hurler's repertoire – the curve, the slider, the sinker, and so on – but its other purpose is to intimidate. Great fastballers like Bob Gibson, Jim Bunning, Sandy Koufax, and Nolan Ryan have always run up high strikeout figures because their money pitch was almost untouchable, but their deeper measures of success – twenty-victory seasons and low earned-run averages – were due to the fact that none of the hitters they faced, not even the best of them, was immune to the thought of what a 90-mph missile could do to a man if it struck him. They had been ever so slightly distracted, and distraction is bad for hitting. The intention of the pitcher has almost nothing to do with this; very few pitches are delivered with intent to maim. The bad dream, however, will not go away. Walter Johnson, the greatest fireballer of them all, had almost absolute control, but he is said to have worried constantly about what might happen if one of his pitches got away from him. Good hitters know all this and resolutely don't think about it (a good hitter is a man who can keep his back foot firmly planted in the box even while the rest of him is pulling back or bailing out on an inside fastball), but even these icy customers are less settled in their minds than they would like to be, just because the man out there on the mound is hiding that cannon behind his hip. Hitters, of course, do not call this fear. The word is 'respect'.

Excerpt, *Five Seasons*, 1977

Baseball and Writing

MARIANNE MOORE

Suggested by post-game broadcasts.

Fanaticism? No. Writing is exciting
and baseball is like writing.
　　You can never tell with either
　　　　how it will go
　　　　or what you will do;
　　generating excitement –
　　a fever in the victim –

pitcher, catcher, fielder, batter.
      Victim in what category?
*Owl*man watching from the press box?
      To whom does it apply?
      Who is excited? Might it be I?

It's a pitcher's battle all the way – a duel –
a catcher's, as, with cruel
    puma paw, Elston Howard lumbers lightly
      back to plate. (His spring
      de-winged a bat swing.)
They have that killer instinct;
yet Elston – whose catching
arm has hurt them all with the bat –
    when questioned, says, unenviously,
'I'm very satisfied. We won.'
      Shorn of the batting crown, says, 'We';
      robbed by a technicality.

When three players on a side play three positions
and modify conditions,
    the massive run need not be everything.
    'Going, going . . . ' Is
    it? Roger Maris
has it, running fast. You will
never see a finer catch. Well . . .
'Mickey, leaping like the devil' – why
      gild it, although deer sounds better –
snares what was speeding towards its treetop nest,
      one-handing the souvenir-to-be
      meant to be caught by you or me.

Assign Yogi Berra to Cape Canaveral;
he could handle any missile.
    He is no feather. 'Strike! . . . Strike *two*!'
    Fouled back. A blur.
    It's gone. You would infer
that the bat had eyes.
He put the wood to that one.
Praised, Skowron says, 'Thanks, Mel.
I think I helped a *little* bit.'
      All business, each, and modesty.
    Blanchard, Richardson, Kubek, Boyer.

In that galaxy of nine, say which
won the pennant? *Each*. It was he.

Those two magnificent saves from the knee – throws
by Boyer, finesses in twos –
  like Whitey's three kinds of pitch and pre-
    diagnosis
    with pick-off psychosis.
  Pitching is a large subject.
  Your arm, too true at first, can learn to
  catch the corners – even trouble
      Mickey Mantle ('Grazed a Yankee!
My baby pitcher, Montejo!'
      With some pedagogy,
      you'll be tough, premature prodigy.)

They crowd him and curve him and aim for the knees. Trying
indeed! The secret implying:
  'I can stand here, bat held steady.'
    One may suit him;
    none has hit him.
  Imponderables smite him.
  Muscle kinks, infections, spike wounds
  require food, rest, respite from ruffians. (Drat it!
      Celebrity costs privacy!)
Cow's milk, 'tiger's milk', soy milk, carrot juice,
      brewer's yeast (high-potency) –
      concentrates presage victory

sped by Luis Arroyo, Hector Lopez –
deadly in a pinch. And 'Yes,
  it's work; I want you to bear down,
    but enjoy it
    while you're doing it.'
  Mr Houk and Mr Sain,
  if you have a rummage sale,
  don't sell Roland Sheldon or Tom Tresh.
      Studded with stars in belt and crown,
the Stadium is an adastrium.
      O flashing Orion,
      your stars are muscled like the lion.

Tell Me, Tell Me, 1966

Casey at the Bat

E. L. THAYER

The outlook wasn't brilliant for the Mudville nine that day;
The score stood four to two with but one inning more to play.
And then when Cooney died at first, and Barrows did the same,
A sickly silence fell upon the patrons of the game.

A straggling few got up to go in deep despair. The rest
Clung to that hope which springs eternal in the human breast;
They thought if only Casey could but get a whack at that –
We'd put up even money now with Casey at the bat.

But Flynn preceded Casey, as did also Johnnie Blake,
And the former was a lulu and the latter was a cake;
So upon that stricken multitude grim melancholy sat,
For there seemed but little chance of Casey's getting to the bat.

But Flynn let drive a single, to the wonderment of all,
And Blake, the much despised, tore the cover off the ball;
And when the dust had lifted, and the men saw what had occurred,
There was Johnnie safe at second and Flynn a-hugging third.

Then from 5,000 throats and more there rose a lusty yell;
It rumbled through the valley; it rattled in the dell;
It knocked upon the mountain and recoiled upon the flat,
For Casey, mighty Casey, was advancing to the bat.

There was ease in Casey's manner as he stepped into his place;
There was pride in Casey's bearing and a smile on Casey's face.
And when, responding to the cheers, he lightly doffed his hat,
No stranger in the crowd could doubt 'twas Casey at the bat.

Ten thousand eyes were on him as he rubbed his hands with dirt;
Five thousand tongues applauded when he wiped them on his shirt.
Then while the writhing pitcher ground the ball into his hip,
Defiance gleamed in Casey's eye, a sneer curled Casey's lip.

And now the leather-covered sphere came hurtling through the air,
And Casey stood a-watching it in haughty grandeur there.
Close by the sturdy batsman the ball unheeded sped –
'That ain't my style,' said Casey. 'Strike one,' the umpire said.

From the benches, black with people, there went up a muffled roar,
Like the beating of the storm-waves on a stern and distant shore.
'Kill him! Kill the umpire!' shouted some one on the stand;
And it's likely they'd have killed him had not Casey raised his hand.

With a smile of Christian charity great Casey's visage shone;
He stilled the rising tumult; he bade the game go on;
He signaled to the pitcher, and once more the spheroid flew;
But Casey still ignored it, and the umpire said, 'Strike two.'

'Fraud!' cried the maddened thousands, and echo answered fraud;
But one scornful look from Casey and the audience was awed.
They saw his face grow stern and cold, they saw his muscles strain,
And they knew that Casey wouldn't let that ball go by again.

The sneer is gone from Casey's lip, his teeth are clenched in hate;
He pounds with cruel violence his bat upon the plate.
And now the pitcher holds the ball, and now he lets it go,
And now the air is shattered by the force of Casey's blow.

Oh, somewhere in this favored land the sun is shining bright;
The band is playing somewhere, and somewhere hearts are light,
And somewhere men are laughing, and somewhere children shout;
But there is no joy in Mudville – mighty Casey has struck out.

San Francisco Examiner, 3 June 1888

'Two things about football'

GERTRUDE STEIN

The players were longer and thinner than I remembered them, both sides
were, they did not seem to have such bulky clothing on them, they seem to
move more. But there are two things about football that anybody can like.
They live by numbers, numbers are everything to them and their preparation is like any savage dancing, they do what red Indians do when they are
dancing and their movement is angular like the red Indians move. When
they lean over and when they are on their hands and feet and when they
are squatting they are like an Indian dance. The Russians squat and jump
too but it looks different, art is inevitable everybody is as their air and land
is everybody is as their food and weather is and the Americans and the red
Indians had the same so how could they not be the same how could they
not, the country is large but somehow it is the same if it were not somehow

the same it would not remain our country and that would be a shame. I like it as it is.

Everybody's Autobiography, 1937, ch. 4

'Among the hunters'

JOHN STEINBECK

There are customs, attitudes, myths and directions and changes that seem to be part of the structure of America. And I propose to discuss them as they were first thrust on my attention. While these discussions go on you are to imagine me bowling along on some little road or pulled up behind a bridge, or cooking a big pot of lima beans and salt pork. And the first of these has to do with hunting. I could not have escaped hunting if I had wanted to, for open seasons spangle the autumn. We have inherited many attitudes from our recent ancestors who wrestled this continent as Jacob wrestled the angel, and the pioneers won. From them we take a belief that every American is a natural-born hunter. And every fall a great number of men set out to prove that without talent, training, knowledge, or practice they are dead shots with rifle or shotgun. The results are horrid. From the moment I left Sag Harbor the guns were booming at the migrating ducks, and as I drove in Maine the rifle shots in the forest would have frightened off any number of redcoats so long as they didn't know what was happening. This is bound to get me a bad name as a sportsman, but let me say at once that I have nothing against the killing of animals. Something has to kill them, I suppose. In my youth I often crawled miles on my belly through freezing wind for the pure glory of blasting a mudhen which even soaked in salt water made poor eating. I don't greatly care for venison or bear or moose or elk except for the livers. The recipes, the herbs, the wine, the preparation that goes into a good venison dish would make an old shoe a gourmet's delight. If I were hungry, I would happily hunt anything that runs or crawls or flies, even relatives, and tear them down with my teeth. But it isn't hunger that drives millions of armed American males to forests and hills every autumn, as the high incidence of heart failure among the hunters will prove. Somehow the hunting process has to do with masculinity, but I don't quite know how. I know there are any number of good and efficient hunters who know what they are doing; but many more are overweight gentlemen, primed with whiskey and armed with high-powered rifles. They shoot at anything that moves or looks as though it might, and their success in killing one another may well prevent a population explosion. If the casualties were limited to their own kind there would be no problem, but the slaughter of cows, pigs, farmers, dogs, and highway signs makes autumn a dangerous season in which to travel. A farmer in upper New York State painted the word cow in big black letters on both sides of his white bossy, but the hunters shot it anyway. In Wisconsin, as I was driving through, a hunter shot his own guide between the shoulder blades. The coroner questioning this nimrod asked, 'Did you think he was a deer?'

'Yes, sir, I did.'

'But you weren't sure he was a deer.'

'Well, no sir. I guess not.'

Travels with Charley, 1962

'Arrowheads'

HENRY DAVID THOREAU

I have not decided whether I had better publish my experience in searching for arrowheads in three volumes, with plates and an index, or try to compress it into one. These durable implements seem to have been suggested to the Indian mechanic with a view to my entertainment in a succeeding period. After all the labor expended on it, the bolt may have been shot but once perchance, and the shaft which was devoted to it decayed, and there lay the arrowhead, sinking into the ground, awaiting me. They lie all over the hills with like expectations, and in due time the husbandman is sent, and, tempted by the promise of corn or rye, he plows the land and turns them up to my view. Many as I have found, methinks the last one gives me about the same delight that the first did. Some time or other, you would say, it had rained arrowheads, for they lie all over the surface of America. You may have your peculiar tastes. Certain localities in your town may seem from association unattractive and uninhabitable to you. You may wonder that the land bears any money value there, and pity some poor fellow who is said to survive in that neighborhood. But plow up a new field there, and you will find the omnipresent arrow-points strewn over it, and it will appear that the red man, with other tastes and associations, lived there too. No matter how far from the modern road or meeting-house, no matter how near. They lie in the meeting-house cellar, and they lie in the distant cow-pasture. And some collections which were made a century ago by the curious like myself have been dispersed again, and they are still as good as new. You cannot tell the third-hand ones (for they are all second-hand) from the others, such is their persistent out-of-door durability; for they were chiefly made to be lost. They are sown, like a grain that is slow to germinate, broadcast over the earth. Like the dragon's teeth which bore a crop of soldiers, these bear crops of philosophers and poets, and the same seed is just as good to plant again. It is a stone fruit. Each one yields me a thought. I come nearer to the maker of it than if I found his bones. His bones would not prove any wit that wielded them, such as this work of his bones does. It is humanity inscribed on the face of the earth, patent to my eyes as soon as the snow goes off, not hidden away in some crypt or grave or under a pyramid. No disgusting mummy, but a clean stone, the best symbol or letter that could have been transmitted to me.

The Red Man, his mark

At every step I see it, and I can easily supply the 'Tahatawan' or 'Mantatuket' that might have been written if he had had a clerk. It is no single inscription on a particular rock, but a footprint – rather a mindprint – left everywhere, and altogether illegible. No vandals, however vandalic in their disposition, can be so industrious as to destroy them.

Journal, 28 March 1859

'The simple feast'

GEORGE CATLIN

I spoke in a former Letter of Mah-to-toh-pa (the four bears), the second chief of the nation, and the most popular man of the Mandans – a high-minded and gallant warrior.

*

About a week since, this noble fellow stepped into my painting-room about twelve o'clock in the day, in full and splendid dress, and passing his arm through mine, pointed the way, and led me in the most gentlemanly manner, through the village and into his own lodge, where a feast was prepared in a careful manner and waiting our arrival. The lodge in which he dwelt was a room of immense size, some forty or fifty feet in diameter, in a circular form, and about twenty feet high – with a sunken curb of stone in the centre, of five or six feet in diameter and one foot deep, which contained the fire over which the pot was boiling. I was led near the edge of this curb, and seated on a very handsome robe, most ingeniously garnished and painted with hieroglyphics; and he seated himself gracefully on another one at a little distance from me; with the feast prepared in several dishes, resting on a beautiful rush mat, which was placed between us.

The simple feast which was spread before us consisted of three dishes only, two of which were served in wooden bowls, and the third in an earthen vessel of their own manufacture, somewhat in shape of a bread-tray in our own country. This last contained a quantity of *pem-i-can* and *marrow-fat*; and one of the former held a fine brace of buffalo ribs, delight-fully roasted; and the other was filled with a kind of paste or pudding, made of the flour of the '*pomme blanche*', as the French call it, a delicious turnip of the prairie, finely flavoured with the buffalo berries, which are collected in great quantities in this country, and used with divers dishes in cooking, as we in civilized countries use dried currants, which they very much resemble.

A handsome pipe and a tobacco-pouch made of the otter skin, filled with k'nick-k'neck (Indian tobacco), laid by the side of the feast; and when we were seated, mine host took up his pipe, and deliberately filled it; and in-stead of lighting it by the fire, which he could easily have done, he drew from his pouch his flint and steel, and raised a spark with which he kindled it. He drew a few strong whiffs through it, and presented the stem of it to my mouth, through which I drew a whiff or two while he held the stem in his hands. This done, he laid down the pipe, and drawing his knife from his belt, cut off a very small piece of the meat from the ribs, and pronounc-ing the word 'Ho-pe-ne-chee wa-pa-shee' (meaning a *medicine* sacrifice), threw it into the fire.

He then (by signals) requested me to eat, and I commenced, after drawing out from my belt my knife (which it is supposed that every man in this coun-try carries about him, for at an Indian feast a knife is never offered to a guest). Reader, be not astonished that I sat and ate my dinner *alone*, for such is the custom of this strange land. In all tribes in these western regions it is an invariable rule that a chief never eats with his guests invited to a feast; but while they eat, he sits by, at their service, and ready to wait upon them; deliberately charging and lighting the pipe which is to be passed around after the feast is over. Such was the case in the present instance, and while I was eating, Mah-to-toh-pa sat cross-legged before me, cleaning his pipe and preparing it for a cheerful smoke when I had finished my meal. For this ceremony I observed he was making unusual preparation, and I ob-served as I ate, that after he had taken enough of the k'nick-k'neck or bark of the red willow, from his pouch, he rolled out of it also a piece of the '*cas-tor*', which it is customary amongst these folks to carry in their tobacco-sack to give it a flavour; and, shaving off a small quantity of it, mixed it with the bark, with which he charged his pipe. This done, he drew also from his sack a small parcel containing a fine powder, which was made of dried buffalo dung, a little of which he spread over the top, (according also to custom), which was like tinder, having no other effect than that of lighting the pipe with ease and satisfaction. My appetite satiated, I straightened up, and with a whiff the pipe was lit, and we enjoyed together for a quarter of an hour the most delightful exchange of good feelings, amid clouds of smoke and pantomimic signs and gesticulations.

The dish of 'pemican and marrow-fat', of which I spoke, was thus: – The first, an article of food used throughout this country, as familiarly as we use bread in the civilized world. It is made of buffalo meat dried very hard, and afterwards pounded in a large wooden mortar until it is made nearly as fine as sawdust, then packed in this dry state in bladders or sacks of skin, and is easily carried to any part of the world in good order. 'Marrow-fat' is collected by the Indians from the buffalo bones which they break to pieces, yielding a prodigious quantity of marrow, which is boiled out and put into buffalo bladders which have been distended; and after it cools, becomes quite hard like tallow, and has the appearance, and very nearly the flavour, of the richest yellow butter. At a feast, chunks of this marrow-fat are cut off and placed in a tray or bowl, with the pemican, and eaten together.

*

In this dish laid a spoon made of the buffalo's horn, which was black as jet, and beautifully polished; in one of the others there was another of still more ingenious and beautiful workmanship, made of the horn of the mountain-sheep, or 'Gros corn', as the French trappers call them; it was large enough to hold of itself two or three pints, and was almost entirely transparent.

I spoke also of the earthen dishes or bowls in which these viands were served out; they are a familiar part of the culinary furniture of every Mandan lodge, and are manufactured by the women of this tribe in great quantities, and modelled into a thousand forms and tastes. They are made by the hands of the women, from a tough black clay, and baked in kilns which are made for the purpose, and are nearly equal in hardness to our own manufacture of pottery; though they have not yet got the art of glazing, which would be to them a most valuable secret. They make them so strong and serviceable, however, that they hang them over the fire as we do our iron pots, and boil their meat in them with perfect success. I have seen some few specimens of such manufacture, which have been dug up in Indian mounds and tombs in the southern and middle states, placed in our Eastern Museums and looked upon as a great wonder, when here this novelty is at once done away with, and the whole mystery; where women can be seen handling and using them by hundreds, and they can be seen every day in the summer also, moulding them into many fanciful forms, and passing them through the kiln where they are hardened.

Whilst sitting at this feast the wigwam was as silent as death, although we were not alone in it. This chief, like most others, had a plurality of wives, and all of them (some six or seven) were seated around the sides of the lodge, upon robes or mats placed upon the ground, and not allowed to speak, though they were in readiness to obey his orders or commands, which were uniformly given by signs-manual, and executed in the neatest and most silent manner.

When I arose to return, the pipe through which we had smoked was presented to me; and the robe on which I had sat, he gracefully raised by the corners and tendered it to me, explaining by signs that the paintings which were on it were the representations of the battles of his life, where he had fought and killed with his own hand fourteen of his enemies; that he had been two weeks engaged in painting it for me, and that he had invited me here on this occasion to present it to me.

Letters and Notes on the Manners, Customs, and Condition
of the North American Indians, 1841, letter 16

'Stuffing their children'

FRANCES ANNE KEMBLE

My only trial here [on the train to Baltimore] was one which I have to encounter in whatever direction I travel in America, and which, though apparently a trivial matter in itself, has caused me infinite trouble, and no little compassion for the rising generation of the United States – I allude to the ignorant and fatal practice of the women of stuffing their children from morning till night with every species of trash which comes to hand.

(1838) *Records of Later Life*, 1882

'Good cooking'

EDITH WHARTON

My father had inherited from his family a serious tradition of good cooking, with a cellar of vintage clarets, and of Madeira which had rounded the Cape. The 'Jones' Madeira (my father's) and the 'Newbold' (my uncle's) enjoyed a particular celebrity even in that day of noted cellars. The following generation, interested only in champagne and claret, foolishly dispersed these precious stores. My brothers sold my father's cellar soon after his death; and after my marriage, dining in a *nouveau riche* house of which the master was unfamiliar with old New York cousinships, I had pressed on me, as a treat not likely to have come the way of one of my modest condition, a glass of 'the famous Newbold Madeira'.

My mother, if left to herself, would probably not have been much interested in the pleasures of the table. My father's Dutch blood accounted for his gastronomic enthusiasm; his mother, who was a Schermerhorn, was reputed to have the best cook in New York. But to know about good cooking was a part of every young wife's equipment, and my mother's favourite cookery books (Francatelli's and Mrs Leslie's) are thickly interleaved with sheets of yellowing note paper, on which, in a script of ethereal elegance, she records the making of 'Mrs Joshua Jones's scalloped oysters with cream', 'Aunt Fanny Gallatin's fried chicken', 'William Edgar's punch', and the special recipes of our two famous negro cooks, Mary Johnson and Susan Minneman. These great artists stand out, brilliantly turbaned and earringed, from a Snyders-like background of game, fish and vegetables transformed into a succession of succulent repasts by their indefatigable blue-nailed hands: Mary Johnson, a gaunt towering woman of a rich bronzy black, with huge golden hoops in her ears, and crisp African crinkles under vividly patterned kerchiefs; Susan Minneman, a small smiling mulatto, more quietly attired, but as great a cook as her predecessor.

Ah, what artists they were! How simple yet sure were their methods – the mere perfection of broiling, roasting and basting – and what an unexampled wealth of material, vegetable and animal, their genius had to draw upon! Who will ever again taste anything in the whole range of gastronomy to equal their corned beef, their boiled turkeys with stewed celery and oyster sauce, their fried chickens, broiled red-heads, corn fritters, stewed tomatoes, rice griddle cakes, strawberry short-cake and vanilla ices? I am now enumerating only our daily fare, that from which even my tender years did not exclude me; but when my parents 'gave a dinner', and terrapin and canvas-back ducks, or (in their season) broiled Spanish mackerel, soft-shelled crabs with a mayonnaise of celery, and peach-fed Virginia hams cooked in champagne (I am no doubt confusing all the seasons in this allegoric evocation of their riches), lima-beans in a cream, corn soufflés and salads of oyster-crabs, poured in varied succulence from Mary Johnson's lifted cornucopia – ah, then, the *gourmet* of that long-lost day, when cream was cream and butter butter and coffee coffee, and meat fresh every day, and game hung just for the proper number of hours, might lean back in his chair and murmur 'Fate cannot harm me' over his cup of Moka and his glass of authentic Chartreuse.

I have lingered over these details because they formed a part – a most important and honourable part – of that ancient curriculum of house-keeping which, at least in Anglo-Saxon countries, was so soon to be swept aside by the 'monstrous regiment' of the emancipated: young women taught by their elders to despise the kitchen and the linen room, and to substitute the acquiring of University degrees for the more complex art of civilized living. The movement began when I was young, and now that I am old, and have watched it and noted its results, I mourn more than ever the extinction of the household arts. Cold storage, deplorable as it is, has done far less harm to the home than the Higher Education.

A Backward Glance, 1934, ch. 3

Soul Food

ELDRIDGE CLEAVER

Folsom Prison
November 3, 1965

You hear a lot of jazz about Soul Food. Take chitterlings: the ghetto blacks eat them from necessity while the black bourgeoisie has turned it into a mocking slogan. Eating chitterlings is like going slumming to them. Now that they have the price of a steak, here they come prattling about Soul Food. The people in the ghetto want steaks. *Beef Steaks*. I wish I had the power to see to it that the bourgeoisie really *did* have to make it on Soul Food.

The emphasis on Soul Food is counter-revolutionary black bourgeois ideology. The main reason Elijah Muhammad outlawed pork for Negroes had nothing to do with dietary laws. The point is that when you get all those blacks cooped up in the ghetto with beef steaks on their minds – with the weight of religious fervor behind the desire to chuck – then something's got to give. The system has made allowances for the ghettoites to obtain a little pig, *but there are no provisions for the elite to give up any beef*. The walls come tumbling down.

Soul on Ice, 1968

'The most beautiful city'

EZRA POUND

America is the only place where contemporary architecture may be held to be of any great interest. That art at least is alive.

And New York is the most beautiful city in the world?

It is not far from it. No urban nights are like the nights there. I have looked down across the city from high windows. It is then that the great buildings lose reality and take on their magical powers. They are immaterial; that is to say one sees but the lighted windows.

Squares after squares of flame, set and cut into the ether. Here is our poetry, for we have pulled down the stars to our will.

As for the harbour, and the city from the harbour. A huge Irishman stood beside me the last time I went back there and he tried vainly to express himself by repeating: –

'It uccedes Lundun.'

'It uccedes Lundun.'

I have seen Cadiz from the water. The thin, white lotus beyond a dazzle of blue. I know somewhat of cities. The Irishman thought of size alone. I thought of the beauty, and beside it Venice seems like a tawdry scene in a play-house. New York is out of doors.

Patria Mia (wr. 1911–13), 1950, part 1

'The architectural art'

LOUIS H. SULLIVAN

The work completed, the gates [of the World's Fair, Chicago] thrown open 1 May, 1893, the crowds flowed in from every quarter, continued to flow throughout a fair-weather summer and a serenely beautiful October. Then came the end. The gates were closed.

These crowds were astonished. They beheld what was for them an amazing revelation of the architectural art, of which previously they in comparison had known nothing. To them it was a veritable Apocalypse, a message inspired from on high. Upon it their imagination shaped new ideals. They went away, spreading again over the land, returning to their homes, each one of them carrying in the soul the shadow of the white cloud, each of them permeated by the most subtle and slow-acting of poisons; an imperceptible miasm within the white shadow of a higher culture. A vast multitude, exposed, unprepared, they had not had time nor occasion to become immune to forms of sophistication not their own, to a higher and more dexterously insidious plausibility. Thus they departed joyously, carriers of contagion, unaware that what they had beheld and believed to be truth was to prove, in historic fact, an appalling calamity. For what they saw was not at all what they believed they saw, but an imposition of the spurious upon their eyesight, a naked exhibitionism of charlatanry in the higher feudal and domineering culture, conjoined with expert salesmanship of the materials of decay. Adventitiously, to make the stage setting complete, it happened by way of apparent but unreal contrast that the structure representing the United States Government was of an incredible vulgarity, while the building at the peak of the north axis, stationed there as a symbol of 'The Great State of Illinois' matched it as a lewd exhibit of drooling imbecility and political debauchery. The distribution at the northern end of the grounds of many state and foreign headquarters relieved the sense of stark immensity. South of them, and placed on the border of a small lake, stood the Palace of the Arts, the most vitriolic of them all – the most impudently thievish. The landscape work, in its genial distribution of lagoons, wooded islands, lawns, shrubbery and plantings, did much to soften an otherwise mechanical display; while far in the southeast corner, floating in a small lagoon or harbor, were replicas of the three caravels of Columbus, and on an adjacent artificial mound a representation of the Convent of La Rabida. Otherwhere there was no evidence of Columbus and his daring deed, his sufferings, and his melancholy end. No keynote, no dramatic setting forth of that deed which, recently, has aroused some discussion as to whether the discovery of America had proven to be a blessing or a curse to the world of mankind.

*

From the height of its Columbian Ecstasy, Chicago drooped and subsided with the rest, in a common sickness, the nausea of overstimulation. This in turn passed, toward the end of the decade, and the old game began again with intensified fury, to come to a sudden halt in 1907. There are those who say this panic was artificial and deliberate, that the battle of the saber-toothed tigers and the mastodons was on.

Meanwhile the virus of the World's Fair, after a period of incubation in the architectural profession and in the population at large, especially the influential, began to show unmistakable signs of the nature of the contagion. There came a violent outbreak of the Classic and the Renaissance in the East, which slowly spread westward, contaminating all that it touched, both at its source and outward. The selling campaign of the bogus antique was remarkably well managed through skillful publicity and propaganda, by those who were first to see its commercial possibilities. The market was

ripe, made so through the hebetude of the populace, big business men, and
eminent educators alike. By the time the market had been saturated, all
sense of reality was gone. In its place had come deep-seated illusions, hallu-
cinations, absence of pupillary reaction to light, absence of knee-reac-
tion – symptoms all of progressive cerebral meningitis: The blanketing of
the brain. Thus Architecture died in the land of the free and the home of
the brave, – in a land declaring its fervid democracy, its inventiveness, its
resourcefulness, its unique daring, enterprise and progress. Thus did the virus of a culture, snobbish and alien to the land, perform its work of disintegration; and thus ever works the pallid academic mind, denying the real,
exalting the fictitious and the false, incapable of adjusting itself to the flow
of living things, to the reality and the pathos of man's follies, to the valiant
hope that ever causes him to aspire, and again to aspire; that never lifts a
hand in aid because it cannot; that turns its back upon man because that
is its tradition; a culture lost in ghostly *mésalliance* with abstractions, when
what the world needs is courage, common sense and human sympathy, and
a moral standard that is plain, valid and livable.

The damage wrought by the World's Fair will last for half a century from
its date, if not longer. It has penetrated deep into the constitution of the
American mind, effecting there lesions significant of dementia.

'Retrospect' in *Autobiography of an Idea*, 1924

The Master's Work

FRANK LLOYD WRIGHT

The new in the old and old in the new is ever principle.

Principle is all and single the reality the beloved master, Louis Sullivan,
ever loved. It gave to the man stature and to his work true significance.

His loyalty to principle was the more remarkable as *vision* when all
around him poisonous cultural mists hung low to obscure or blight any
bright hope of finer beauty in the matter of this world.

The buildings he has left with us for a brief time are the least of him. In
the heart of him he was of infinite value to the countrymen who wasted him
not because they would; but because *they could not know him.*

Any work, great as human expression, must be studied in relation to the
time in which it insisted upon its own virtues and got itself into human view.

So it is with the work he has left to us.

Remember, you who can, the contemporaries of the Chicago Auditorium, his first great building.

They were the hectic Pullman Building, W. W. Boyington's chamfered 'Board of Trade', the hideous Union Station and many other survivors in the idiom of that harsh, insensate period.

Outside the initial impetus of John Edelman in his early days, H. H. Richardson (great emotionalist of the Romanesque revival) was the one whose influence the master most felt. And John Root, another fertile rival of that time who knew less than the master but felt almost as much. The master admitted he sometimes shot very straight indeed. They were his only peers. And they were only feeling their way. But he was thinking *and* feeling – far in advance of either – to the new.

The Auditorium Building is largely what it is, physically, owing to Dankmar Adler's good judgment and restraining influence. It was Louis Sullivan who made it sing; made it music for Music.

The Getty Tomb in Graceland Cemetery was entirely his own; fine sculpture. A statue. A great poem addressed to human sensibilities as such. Outside the realm of music what finer requiem?

But – when he brought the drawing board with the motive for the Wainwright outlined in profile and elevation upon it and threw the board down on my table I was perfectly aware of what had happened.

This was a great Louis H. Sullivan moment. The tall building was born tall. His greatest effort? No. But here was the 'skyscraper': a new thing beneath the sun, entity imperfect, but with virtue, individuality, beauty all its own. Until Louis Sullivan showed the way, high buildings lacked unity. They were built-up in layers. All were fighting height instead of gracefully and honestly accepting it. What unity those false masonry masses have that now pile up toward big-city skies is due to the master mind that first perceived the high building as a harmonious unit – its height triumphant.

The Wainwright Building was *tall*. It prophesied the way for these tall office-building effects we now point to with pride. And so to this day the Wainwright remains the master key to the 'skyscraper' so far as 'skyscraper' is a matter of architecture.

Only the golden interior of the Chicago Auditorium, the golden doorway of the purely pictorial Transportation Building (for what it is worth), the Getty Tomb, and the Wainwright Building are necessary to show the great reach of creative activity that was Louis Sullivan's. Other buildings the firm did, but all were more or less on these stems. Some were grafted upon these, some where grown from alongside them. But all were relatively inferior in point of the quality which we finally associate with the primitive strength of the thing that got itself born regardless, *true* to the idea.

Excerpt (1949) *Genius and the Mobocracy*, 1971, book 3, ch. 5

'High of necessity'

GERTRUDE STEIN

We settled down to ten days in Chicago, we did not know then that we were coming back again.

The central part is a beautiful city. They told us that the modern high buildings had been invented in Chicago and not in New York. That is interesting. It is interesting that it should have been done where there was plenty of land to build on and not in New York where it is narrow and so must be high of necessity. Choice is always more pleasing than anything necessary.

I had no idea that they would throw such a beautiful dark gray light on the city at night but they do. I mean the lights do. The lighting of the buildings in Chicago is very interesting and then I liked the advertisement for dancing that they had at the end of the beginning of everything they had a room and figures dancing solemnly dancing and in the daytime it was the daytime and at night it was nightime and I never tired of seeing them, the sombre gray light on the buildings and the simple solemn mechanical figures dancing, there were other things I liked but I liked that the most.

Chicago may have thought of it first but New York has made it higher much higher. It was the Rockefeller Center building that pleased me the most and they were building the third piece of it when we left New York so quietly so thinly and so rapidly, and when we came back it was already so much higher that it did not take a minute to end it quickly.

It is not delicate it is not slender it is not thin but it is something that does make existence a non-existent real thing. Alice Toklas said it is not the way they go into the air but the way they come out of the ground that is the thing. European buildings sit on the ground but American ones come out of the ground. And then of course there is the air. And that air is everywhere, everywhere in America, there is no sky, there is air and that makes religion and wandering and architecture.

When I used to try to explain America to Frenchmen of course before I had gone over this time, I used to tell them you see there is no sky over there there is only air, when you look up at the tall buildings at that time I left America the Flatiron was the tallest one and now it is not one at all it is just a house like any house but at that time it was the tallest one and I said you see you look up and you see the cornice way on top clear in the air, but now in the new ones there is no cornice up there and that is right because why end anything, well anyway I always explained everything in America by this thing, the lack of passion that they call repression and gangsters, and savagery, and everybody being nice, and everybody not thinking because they had to drink and keep moving, in Europe when they drink they sit still but not in America no not in America and that is because there is no sky, there is no lid on top of them and so they move around or stand still and do not say anything. That makes that American language that says everything in two words and mostly in words of one syllable two words of one syllable and that makes all the conversation. That is the reason they like long books novels and things of a thousand pages it is to calm themselves from the need of two words and those words of one syllable that say everything.

Everybody's Autobiography, 1937, ch. 4

Arizona Nature Myth

JAMES MICHIE

Up in the heavenly saloon
Sheriff sun and rustler moon
Gamble, stuck in the sheriff's mouth
The fag end of an afternoon.

There in the bad town of the sky
Sheriff, nervy, wonders why
He's let himself wander so far West
On his own; he looks with a smoky eye

At the rustler opposite turning white,
Lays down a king for Law, sits tight
Bluffing. On it that crooked moon
Plays an ace and shoots for the light.

Spurs, badge and uniform red,
(It looks like blood, but he's shamming dead),
Down drops the marshal, and under cover
Crawls out dogwise, ducking his head.

But Law that don't get its man ain't Law.____
Next day, faster on the draw,
Sheriff creeping up from the other side
Blazes his way in through the back door.

But moon's not there. He'd ridden out on
A galloping phenomenon,

A wonder horse, quick as light.
Moon's left town. Moon's clean gone.

Possible Laughter, 1959

'Disneyland'

UMBERTO ECO

In an excellent essay on Disneyland as 'degenerate utopia' ('a degenerate utopia is an ideology realized in the form of myth'), Louis Marin analyzed the structure of that nineteenth-century frontier city street that receives entering visitors and distributes them through the various sectors of the magic city. Disneyland's Main Street seems the first scene of the fiction whereas it is an extremely shrewd commercial reality. Main Street – like the whole city, for that matter – is presented as at once absolutely realistic and absolutely fantastic, and this is the advantage (in terms of artistic conception) of Disneyland over the other toy cities. The houses of Disneyland are full-size on the ground floor, and on a two-thirds scale on the floor above, so they give the impression of being inhabitable (and they are) but also of belonging to a fantastic past that we can grasp with our imagination. The Main Street façades are presented to us as toy houses and invite us to enter them, but their interior is always a disguised supermarket, where you buy obsessively, believing that you are still playing.

In this sense Disneyland is more hyperrealistic than the wax museum, precisely because the latter still tries to make us believe that what we are seeing reproduces reality absolutely, whereas Disneyland makes it clear that within its magic enclosure it is fantasy that is absolutely reproduced. The Palace of Living Arts presents its Venus de Milo as almost real, whereas Disneyland can permit itself to present its reconstructions as masterpieces of falsification, for what it sells is, indeed, goods, but genuine merchandise, not reproductions. What is falsified is our will to buy, which we take as real, and in this sense Disneyland is really the quintessence of consumer ideology.

But once the 'total fake' is admitted, in order to be enjoyed it must seem totally real. So the Polynesian restaurant will have, in addition to a fairly authentic menu, Tahitian waitresses in costume, appropriate vegetation, rock walls with little cascades, and once you are inside nothing must lead you to suspect that outside there is anything but Polynesia. If, between two trees, there appears a stretch of river that belongs to another sector, Adventureland, then that section of stream is so designed that it would not be unrealistic to see in Tahiti, beyond the garden hedge, a river like this. And if in the wax museums wax is not flesh, in Disneyland, when rocks are involved, they are rock, and water is water, and a baobab a baobab. When there is a fake – hippopotamus, dinosaur, sea serpent – it is not so much because it wouldn't be possible to have the real equivalent but because the public is meant to admire the perfection of the fake and its obedience to the program. In this sense Disneyland not only produces illusion, but – in confessing it – stimulates the desire for it: A real crocodile can be found in the zoo, and as a rule it is dozing or hiding, but Disneyland tells us that faked nature corresponds much more to our daydream demands. When, in the space of twenty-four hours, you go (as I did deliberately) from the fake New Orleans of Disneyland to the real one, and from the wild river of Adventureland to a trip on the Mississippi, where the captain of the paddle-wheel steamer says it is possible to see alligators on the banks of the river, and then you don't see any, you risk feeling homesick for Disneyland, where the wild animals don't have to be coaxed. Disneyland tells us that technology can give us more reality than nature can.

In this sense I believe the most typical phenomenon of this universe is not the more famous Fantasyland – an amusing carousel of fantastic journeys that take the visitor into the world of Peter Pan or Snow White, a wondrous machine whose fascination and lucid legitimacy it would be foolish to deny – but the Caribbean Pirates and the Haunted Mansion. The pirate show lasts a quarter of an hour (but you lose any sense of time, it could be ten minutes or thirty); you enter a series of caves, carried in boats over the surface of the water, you see first abandoned treasures, a captain's skeleton in a sumptuous bed of moldy brocade, pendent cobwebs, bodies of executed men devoured by ravens, while the skeleton addresses menacing admonitions to you. Then you navigate an inlet, passing through the crossfire of a galleon and the cannon of a fort, while the chief corsair shouts taunting challenges at the beleaguered garrison; then, as if along a river, you go by an invaded city which is being sacked, with the rape of the women, theft of jewels, torture of the mayor; the city burns like a match, drunken pirates sprawled on piles of kegs sing obscene songs; some, completely out of their heads, shoot at the visitors; the scene degenerates, everything collapses in flames, slowly the last songs die away, you emerge into the sunlight. Everything you have seen was on human scale, the vault of the caves became confused with that of the sky, the boundary of this underground world was that of the universe and it was impossible to glimpse its limits. The pirates moved, danced, slept, popped their eyes, sniggered, drank – really. You realize that they are robots, but you remain dumbfounded by their verisimilitude. And, in fact, the 'Audio-Animatronic' technique represented a great source of pride for Walt Disney, who had finally managed to achieve his own dream and reconstruct a fantasy world more real than reality, breaking down the wall of the second dimension, creating not a movie, which is illusion, but total theater, and not with anthropomorphized animals, but with human beings. In fact, Disney's robots are masterpieces of electronics; each was devised by observing the expressions of a real actor, then building models, then developing skeletons of absolute precision, authentic computers in human form, to be dressed in 'flesh' and 'skin' made by craftsmen, whose command of realism is incredible. Each robot obeys a program, can synchronize the movements of mouth and eyes with the words and sounds of the audio, repeating ad infinitum all day long his established part (a sentence, one or two gestures) and the visitor, caught off guard by the succession of events, obliged to see several things at once, to left and right and straight ahead, has no time to look back and observe that the robot he has just seen is already repeating his eternal scenario.

'City of Robots' in *Travels in Hyper-Reality*, 1986; trans. William Weaver

To the Film Industry in Crisis

FRANK O'HARA

Not you, lean quarterlies and swarthy periodicals
with your studious incursions toward the pomposity of ants,
nor you, experimental theatre in which Emotive Fruition
is wedding Poetic Insight perpetually, nor you,
promenading Grand Opera, obvious as an ear (though you
are close to my heart), but you, Motion Picture Industry,
it's you I love!

In times of crisis, we must all decide again and again whom we love.
And give credit where it's due: not to my starched nurse, who taught
    me
how to be bad and not bad rather than good (and has lately availed
herself of this information), not to the Catholic Church
which is at best an oversolemn introduction to cosmic entertainment,
not to the American Legion, which hates everybody, but to you,
glorious Silver Screen, tragic Technicolor, amorous Cinemascope,
stretching Vistavision and startling Stereophonic Sound, with all
your heavenly dimensions and reverberations and iconoclasms! To
Richard Barthelmess as the 'tol'able' boy barefoot and in pants,
Jeanette MacDonald of the flaming hair and lips and long, long neck,
Sue Carroll as she sits for eternity on the damaged fender of a car

and smiles, Ginger Rogers with her pageboy bob like a sausage
on her shuffling shoulders, peach-melba-voiced Fred Astaire of the feet,
Eric von Stroheim, the seducer of mountain-climbers' gasping spouses,
the Tarzans, each and every one of you (I cannot bring myself to prefer
Johnny Weissmuller to Lex Barker, I cannot!), Mae West in a furry sled,
her bordello radiance and bland remarks, Rudolph Valentino of the moon,
its crushing passions, and moonlike, too, the gentle Norma Shearer,
Miriam Hopkins dropping her champagne glass off Joel McCrea's yacht
and crying into the dappled sea, Clark Gable rescuing Gene Tierney
from Russia and Allan Jones rescuing Kitty Carlisle from Harpo Marx,
Cornel Wilde coughing blood on the piano keys while Merle Oberon
    berates,
Marilyn Monroe in her little spike heels reeling through Niagara Falls,
Joseph Cotten puzzling and Orson Welles puzzled and Dolores del Rio
eating orchids for lunch and breaking mirrors, Gloria Swanson reclining,
and Jean Harlow reclining and wiggling, and Alice Faye reclining
and wiggling and singing, Myrna Loy being calm and wise, William Powell
in his stunning urbanity, Elizabeth Taylor blossoming, yes, to you

and to all you others, the great, the near-great, the featured, the extras
who pass quickly and return in dreams saying your one or two lines,
my love!
Long may you illumine space with your marvellous appearances, delays
and enunciations, and may the money of the world glitteringly cover you
as you rest after a long day under the kleig lights with your faces
in packs for our edification, the way the clouds come often at night
but the heavens operate on the star system. It is a divine precedent
you perpetuate! Roll on, reels of celluloid, as the great earth rolls on!

Meditations in an Emergency, 1957

'A woman like Marilyn Monroe'

WENDY LESSER

To give an actress in a movie or play the profession of actress or performer
is to create a hollow circularity. What is she when she's not being an actress?
What is she *besides* an actress? Nothing; zero; the empty hole.

It seems amazing, in this light, that Marilyn Monroe never worked with
Hitchcock, who was so repeatedly and obsessively interested in questions
about deception, authenticity, and the female empty-vessel actress whom
the male director fills with meaning. Marilyn may not have been empty

enough for Hitchcock: she had the blondeness and the potential for victimization, but she lacked the utter vacuousness, the blank-slate quality, of actresses like Eva Marie Saint, Kim Novak, and Tippi Hedren. She didn't, at any rate, make any movies with Hitchcock. But she made a very Hitchcock-like movie with Henry Hathaway – the best film of his career, and one of the best of hers.

Niagara is a thriller set at an enormously symbolic and symbolically enormous American monument; it was filmed in 1953, six years before Hitchcock used the gigantic presidents' faces of Mount Rushmore in *North by Northwest*. It has the *Suspicion, Notorious*, and *Dial M For Murder* plot of attempted murder of a spouse, the *Spellbound* plot of possibly murderous insanity, and a squeaky-clean American couple – complete with dominant-but-dense husband and smart, endangered wife – who might have stepped straight out of the remade *Man Who Knew Too Much*. It also has Joseph Cotten, whom Hitchcock had used ten years earlier in his own favorite movie, *Shadow of a Doubt*. As Marilyn Monroe's husband in *Niagara*, Cotten is both her victim and her murderer – a classic role for the men in her life, as her real husband was eventually to show in *After the Fall*. In many ways, though it comes relatively early in her career and uses her uncharacteristically, *Niagara* portrays Marilyn more astutely than any other film she made.

The movie opens, for instance, with Joseph Cotten looking out over the falls, muttering neurotically to himself about his obsession with the torrent of water, and then turning away to walk back to his tourist cabin. The falls themselves are shimmering with rainbows; as he walks back along the lawn-lined streets, the sprinklers he passes have rainbows in them too; and the place he is staying turns out to be called Rainbow Cabins. Capturing a rainbow on film must be a rather hard thing to do. It's a visual object – anyone can see it – but on the other hand it's not really there. It's a mere thing of beauty that has no solid reality, and yet it's one of the strongest positive images in mythical thinking: fairy tales place their pot of gold at the end of it. It's a perfect emblem for Marilyn Monroe.

Cotten goes inside the cabin and we get a glimpse of Marilyn, who is pretending to be asleep in the other twin bed. The bed is a classic Monroe location in her films: it stands for both her sexuality and her innocence (as a child is innocent when it sleeps). Our first glimpse of her in *The Asphalt Jungle* – her earliest noteworthy film, released in 1950 – shows her asleep on a couch; and we again see her asleep (with an older, worn-faced man standing over her, as Cotten does here in *Niagara*) at the end of her career, in *The Misfits*. Sleep is the daily habit that Marilyn, in life, was to find far from habitual: she had to force herself into it with pills and alcohol. It is also the oblivion into which she sank toward her barbiturate-induced death.

Meanwhile, the Cutlers arrive at Rainbow Cabins – the fresh-faced, obnoxiously conventional pair so reminiscent of Hitchcock's Jimmy Stewart and Doris Day. As the plot suggests (the Cutlers can't get into their reserved cabin because the Loomises, played by Marilyn Monroe and Joseph Cotten, are still there), these two are a foil, an opposite, to the mysterious, murderous Loomises. As opposed to Cotten's shell-shocked veteran, Mr Cutler is boringly, conventionally sane; he makes up prize-winning slogans like a character in a Preston Sturges movie and doesn't see anything humorous about it. His wife is far more interesting, and interested (it is she who collects all the clues in the Loomis plot), but she too is presented as an opposite to Marilyn, a good girl as opposed to a bad one. 'That dress is cut down to the kneecaps,' Loomis complains to Mrs Cutler about one of his wife's slinkier outfits. 'Would *you* wear that dress?' 'I'm not the kneecap type,' she calmly and self-effacingly replies. Yet her husband wants her to be a litle more that type – to be less straightforward and pal-like, more self-displayingly sexy. He tries to get her to take a cheesecake pose for a tourist photo he's taking, and she complies, though it irks her almost invisibly. The photo session is interrupted by Marilyn (who is laying the groundwork for her role of grieving widow), and when she leaves the husband says, 'Get back into that pose again.' Like the Tom Ewell character in *The Seven Year Itch*, Mr Cutler is the kind of wimpy guy who fantasizes about being with a woman like Marilyn Monroe and therefore undervalues his pretty, courageous wife. And, again as in *The Seven Year Itch*, he's a toady to a more powerful boss; he's a man who likes or needs to play up to a stronger man, and therefore wants to play down to women.

Niagara is, in subtle ways, a movie that comments on sexual roles. When the tourists go out onto the falls, for instance, the men all wear dark blue slickers and the women all wear yellow. (This may be how it actually worked at Niagara Falls in the real-life 1950s, but in a color film it's more than a fact: it's a statement.) The Cutlers are supposed to represent this simple variety of gender division – he, the strong male, brings in the money and faces reality; she, the flightier woman, 'imagines' seeing the supposedly dead Joseph Cotten – but in fact the indeterminacy of the Loomis marriage, where power shifts back and forth from moment to moment, invades the Cutlers as well, and in the end Mr Cutler stands helplessly aside while his wife hurtles toward the falls on a boat with Joseph Cotten. 'Scuttle it! Scuttle it!' is all he can pray; it's an acknowledgment that some situations (like conventional marriage, perhaps?) can be corrected only by shipwreck and destruction.

His Other Half, 1991

Of the Sorrow Songs

W. E. B. DU BOIS

I walk through the churchyard
 To lay this body down;
I know moon-rise, I know star-rise;
I walk in the moonlight, I walk in the starlight;
I'll lie in the grave and stretch out my arms,
I'll go to judgment in the evening of the day,
And my soul and thy soul shall meet that day,
 When I lay this body down.

NEGRO SONG

*

Little of beauty has America given the world save the rude grandeur God himself stamped on her bosom; the human spirit in this new world has expressed itself in vigor and ingenuity rather than in beauty. And so by fateful chance the Negro folk-song – the rhythmic cry of the slave – stands to-day not simply as the sole American music, but as the most beautiful expression of human experience born this side the seas. It has been neglected, it has been, and is, half despised, and above all it has been persistently mistaken and misunderstood; but notwithstanding, it still remains as the singular spiritual heritage of the nation and the greatest gift of the Negro people.

Away back in the thirties the melody of these slave songs stirred the nation, but the songs were soon half forgotten. Some, like 'Near the lake where drooped the willow', passed into current airs and their source was forgotten; others were caricatured on the 'minstrel' stage and their memory died away. Then in war-time came the singular Port Royal experiment after the capture of Hilton Head, and perhaps for the first time the North met the Southern slave face to face and heart to heart with no third witness. The Sea Islands of the Carolinas, where they met, were filled with a black folk of primitive type, touched and moulded less by the world about them than any other outside the Black Belt. Their appearance was uncouth, their language funny, but their hearts were human and their singing stirred men with a mighty power. Thomas Wentworth Higginson hastened to tell of these songs, and Miss McKim and others urged upon the world their rare beauty. But the world listened only half credulously until the Fisk Jubilee Singers sang the slave songs so deeply into the world's heart that it can never wholly forget them again.

There was once a blacksmith's son born at Cadiz, New York, who in the changes of time taught school in Ohio and helped defend Cincinnati from

Kirby Smith. Then he fought at Chancellorsville and Gettysburg and finally served in the Freedman's Bureau at Nashville. Here he formed a Sunday-school class of black children in 1866, and sang with them and taught them to sing. And then they taught him to sing, and when once the glory of the Jubilee songs passed into the soul of George L. White, he knew his life-work was to let those Negroes sing to the world as they had sung to him. So in 1871 the pilgrimage of the Fisk Jubilee Singers began. North to Cincinnati they rode, – four half-clothed black boys and five girl-women, – led by a man with a cause and a purpose. They stopped at Wilberforce, the oldest of Negro schools, where a black bishop blessed them. Then they went, fighting cold and starvation, shut out of hotels, and cheerfully sneered at, ever northward; and ever the magic of their song kept thrilling hearts, until a burst of applause in the Congregational Council at Oberlin revealed them to the world. They came to New York and Henry Ward Beecher dared to welcome them, even though the metropolitan dailies sneered at his 'Nigger Minstrels'. So their songs conquered till they sang across the land and across the sea, before Queen and Kaiser, in Scotland and Ireland, Holland and Switzerland. Seven years they sang, and brought back a hundred and fifty thousand dollars to found Fisk University.

Since their day they have been imitated – sometimes well, by the singers of Hampton and Atlanta, sometimes ill, by straggling quartettes. Caricature has sought again to spoil the quaint beauty of the music, and has filled the air with many debased melodies which vulgar ears scarce know from the real. But the true Negro folk-song still lives in the hearts of those who have heard them truly sung and in the hearts of the Negro people.

What are these songs, and what do they mean? I know little of music and can say nothing in technical phrase, but I know something of men, and knowing them, I know that these songs are the articulate message of the slave to the world. They tell us in these eager days that life was joyous to the black slave, careless and happy. I can easily believe this of some, of many. But not all the past South, though it rose from the dead, can gainsay the heart-touching witness of these songs. They are the music of an unhappy people, of the children of disappointment; they tell of death and suffering and unvoiced longing toward a truer world, of misty wanderings and hidden ways.

Excerpt, *The Souls of Black Folk*, 1903

On Being American

VIRGIL THOMSON

What is an American composer? The Music Critics' Circle of New York City says it is any musical author of American citizenship. This group, however, and also the Pulitzer Prize Committee, finds itself troubled about people like Stravinsky, Schönberg, and Hindemith. Can these composers be called American, whose styles were formed in Europe and whose most recent work, if it shows any influence of American ways, shows this certainly in no direction that could possibly be called nationalistic? Any award committee would think a second time before handing these men a certificate, as Americans, for musical excellence. The American section of the International Society for Contemporary Music has more than once been reproached in Europe for allowing the United States to be represented at international festivals of the society by composers of wholly European style and formation, such as Ernest Bloch and Ernst Krenek. And yet a transfer of citizenship cannot with justice be held to exclude any artist from the intellectual privileges of the country that has, both parties consenting, adopted him, no matter what kind of music he writes.

Neither can obvious localisms of style be demanded of any composer, native-born or naturalized. If Schönberg, who writes in an ultrachromatic and even atonal syntax and who practically never uses folk material, even that of his native Austria, is to be excluded by that fact from the ranks of American composers, then we must exclude along with him that stalwart Vermonter, Carl Ruggles, who speaks a not dissimilar musical language. And among the native-born young, Harold Shapero and Arthur Berger are no more American for writing in the international neoclassic manner (fountainhead Stravinsky) than Lou Harrison and Merton Brown are, who employ the international chromatic techniques (fountainhead Schönberg). All these gifted young writers of music are American composers, though none employs a nationalistic trademark.

The fact is, of course, that citizens of the United States write music in every known style. From the post-Romantic eclecticism of Howard Hanson and the post-Romantic expressionism of Bernard Rogers through the neoclassicized impressionism of Edward Burlingame Hill and John Alden Carpenter, the strictly Parisian neoclassicism of Walter Piston, the romanticized neoclassicism of Roy Harris and William Schuman, the elegant neo-Romanticism of Samuel Barber, the sentimental neo-Romanticism of David Diamond, the folksy neo-Romanticism of Douglas Moore, Randall Thompson, and Henry Cowell, the Germano-eclectic modernism of Roger Sessions, the neoprimitive polytonalism of Charles Ives, and the ecstatic chromaticism of Carl Ruggles, to the percussive and rhythmic research fellows Edgard Varèse and John Cage, we have everything. We have also the world-famous European atonalists Schönberg and Krenek, the neoclassic masters Stravinsky and Hindemith. We have, moreover, a national glory in the form of Aaron Copland, who so skillfully combines, in the Bartók manner, folk feeling with neoclassic techniques that foreigners often fail to recognize his music as American at all.

All this music is American, nevertheless, because it is made by Americans. If it has characteristic traits that can be identified as belonging to this continent only, our composers are largely unconscious of them. These are shared, moreover, by composers of all the schools and probably by our South American neighbors. Two devices typical of American practice (I have written about these before) are the nonaccelerating crescendo and a steady ground rhythm of equalized eighth notes (expressed or not). Neither of these devices is known to Europeans, though practically all Americans take them for granted. Further study of American music may reveal other characteristics. But there can never be any justice in demanding their presence as a proof of musical Americanism. Any American has the right to write music in any way he wishes or is able to do. If the American school is beginning to be visible to Europeans as something not entirely provincial with regard to Vienna and Paris, something new, fresh, real, and a little strange, none of this novel quality is a monopoly, or even a specialty, of any group among us. It is not limited to the native born or to the German trained or to the French influenced or to the self-taught or to the New York–resident or to the California bred. It is in the air and belongs to us all. It is a set of basic assumptions so common that everybody takes them for granted. This is why, though there is no dominant style in American music, there is, viewed from afar (say from Europe), an American school.

National feelings and local patriotisms are as sound sources of inspiration as any other. They are not, however, any nobler than any other. At best they are merely the stated or obvious subject of a piece. Music that has life in it always goes deeper than its stated subject or than what its author thought about while writing it. Nobody becomes an American composer by thinking about America while composing. If that were true George Auric's charming fox-trot *Adieu New York* would be American music and not French music, and *The Road to Mandalay* would be Burmese. The way to write American music is simple. All you have to do is to be an American and then write any kind of music you wish. There is precedent and model here for all the kinds. And any Americanism worth bothering about is everybody's property anyway. Leave it in the unconscious; let nature speak.

Nevertheless, the award-giving committees do have a problem on their hands. I suggest they just hedge and compromise for a while. That, after all, is a way of being American, too.

(1948) *A Virgil Thomson Reader*, 1981

The Weary Blues

LANGSTON HUGHES

Droning a drowsy syncopated tune,
Rocking back and forth to a mellow croon,
 I heard a Negro play.
Down on Lenox Avenue the other night
By the pale dull pallor of an old gas light
 He did a lazy sway . . .
 He did a lazy sway . . .
To the tune o' those Weary Blues.
With his ebony hands on each ivory key
He made that poor piano moan with melody.
 O Blues!
Swaying to and fro on his rickety stool
He played that sad raggy tune like a musical fool.
 Sweet Blues!
Coming from a black man's soul.
 O Blues!
In a deep song voice with a melancholy tone
I heard that Negro sing, that old piano moan –
 'Ain't got nobody in all this world,
 Ain't got nobody but ma self.
 I's gwine to quit ma frownin'
 And put ma troubles on the shelf.'
Thump, thump, thump, went his foot on the floor.
He played a few chords then he sang some more –
 'I got the Weary Blues
 And I can't be satisfied.
 Got the Weary Blues
 And can't be satisfied –
 I ain't happy no mo'
 And I wish that I had died.'
And far into the night he crooned that tune.
The stars went out and so did the moon.

The singer stopped playing and went to bed
While the Weary Blues echoed through his head.
He slept like a rock or a man that's dead.

The Weary Blues, 1926

'Jazzmen'

RALPH ELLISON

It has been a long time now, and not many remember how it was in the old days; not really. Not even those who were there to see and hear as it happened, who were pressed in the crowds beneath the dim rosy lights of the bar in the smoke-veiled room, and who shared, night after night, the mysterious spell created by the talk, the laughter, grease paint, powder, perfume, sweat, alcohol and food – all blended and simmering, like a stew on the restaurant range, and brought to a sustained moment of elusive meaning by the timbres and accents of musical instruments locked in passionate recitative. It has been too long now, some seventeen years.

Above the bandstand there later appeared a mural depicting a group of jazzmen holding a jam session in a narrow Harlem bedroom. While an exhausted girl with shapely legs sleeps on her stomach in a big brass bed, they bend to their music in a quiet concatenation of unheard sound; a trumpeter, a guitarist, a clarinetist, a drummer; their only audience a small, cock-eared dog. The clarinetist is white. The guitarist strums with an enigmatic smile. The trumpet is muted. The barefooted drummer, beating a folded newspaper with whisk-brooms in lieu of a drum, stirs the eye's ear like a blast of brasses in a midnight street. A bottle of port rests on a dresser, but it, like the girl, is ignored. The artist, Charles Graham, adds mystery to, as well as illumination within, the scene by having them play by the light of a kerosene lamp. The painting, executed in a harsh documentary style reminiscent of WPA art, conveys a feeling of musical effort caught in timeless and unrhetorical suspension, the sad remoteness of a scene observed through a wall of crystal.

Except for the lamp, the room might well have been one in the Hotel Cecil, the building on 118th Street in which Minton's Playhouse is located, and although painted in 1946, some time after the revolutionary doings there had begun, the mural should help recall the old days vividly. But the décor of the place has been changed and now it is covered, most of the time, by draperies. These require a tricky skill of those who would draw them aside. And even then there will still only be the girl who must sleep forever unhearing, and the men who must forever gesture the same soundless tune. Besides, the time it celebrates is dead and gone and perhaps not even those who came when it was still fresh and new remember those days as they were.

Neither do those remember who knew Henry Minton, who gave the place his name. Nor those who shared the noisy lostness of New York the rediscovered community of the feasts, evocative of home, of South, of good times, the best and most unself-conscious of times, created by the generous portions of Negro American cuisine – the hash, grits, fried chicken, the ham-seasoned vegetables, the hot biscuits and rolls and the free whiskey – with which, each Monday night, Teddy Hill honored the entire cast of current Apollo Theatre shows. They were gathered here from all parts of America and they broke bread together and there was a sense of good feeling and promise, but what shape the fulfilled promise would take they did not know, and few except the more restless of the younger musicians even questioned. Yet it was an exceptional moment and the world was swinging with change.

Most of them, black and white alike, were hardly aware of where they were or what time it was; nor did they wish to be. They thought of Minton's as a sanctuary, where in an atmosphere blended of nostalgia and a music-and-drink-lulled suspension of time they could retreat from the wartime tensions of the town. The meaning of time-present was not their concern; thus when they try to tell it now the meaning escapes them.

For they were caught up in events which made that time exceptionally and uniquely *then*, and which brought, among the other changes which have reshaped the world, a momentous modulation into a new key of musical sensibility; in brief, a revolution in culture.

So how *can* they remember? Even in swiftly changing America there are few such moments, and at best Americans give but a limited attention to history. Too much happens too rapidly, and before we can evaluate it, or exhaust its meaning or pleasure, there is something new to concern us. Ours is the tempo of the motion picture, not that of the still camera, and we waste experience as we wasted the forest. During the time it was happening the sociologists were concerned with the riots, unemployment and industrial tensions of the time, the historians with the onsweep of the war; and the critics and most serious students of culture found this area of our national life of little interest. So it was left to those who came to Minton's out of the needs of feeling, and when the moment was past no one retained more than a fragment of its happening. Afterward the very effort to put the fragments together transformed them – so that in place of true memory they now summon to mind pieces of legend. They retell the stories as they have been told and written, glamorized, inflated, made neat and smooth, with all incomprehensible details vanished along with most of the wonder – not how it was as they themselves knew it.

When asked how it was back then, back in the forties, they will smile, then, frowning with the puzzlement of one attempting to recall the details of a pleasant but elusive dream, they'll say: 'Oh, man, it was a hell of a time! A wailing time! Things were jumping, you couldn't get in here for the people. The place was packed with celebrities. Park Avenue, man! Big people in show business, college professors along with the pimps and their women. And college boys and girls. Everybody came. You know how the old words to the "Basin Street Blues" used to go before Sinatra got hold of it? *Basin Street is the street where the dark and the light folks meet* – that's what I'm talking about. That was Minton's, man. It was a place where everybody could come to be entertained because it was a place that was jumping with good times.'

Or some will tell you that it was here that Dizzy Gillespie found his own trumpet voice; that here Kenny Clarke worked out the patterns of his drumming style; where Charlie Christian played out the last creative and truly satisfying moments of his brief life, his New York home; where Charlie Parker built the monument of his art; where Thelonius Monk formulated his contribution to the chordal progressions and the hide-and-seek melodic methods of modern jazz. And they'll call such famous names as Lester Young and Ben Webster, Coleman Hawkins; or Fats Waller, who came here in the after-hour stillness of the early morning to compose. They'll tell you that Benny Goodman, Art Tatum, Count Basie and Lena Horne would drop in to join in the fun; that it was here that George Shearing played on his first night in the United States; or of Tony Scott's great love of the place; and they'll repeat all the stories of how, when and by whom the word 'bebop' was coined here – but, withal, few actually remember, and these leave much unresolved.

Usually music gives resonance to memory (and Minton's was a hotbed of jazz), but not the music then in the making here. It was itself a texture of fragments, repetitive, nervous, not fully formed; its melodic lines underground, secret and taunting; its riffs jeering – 'Salt peanuts! Salt peanuts!' Its timbres flat or shrill, with a minimum of thrilling vibrato. Its rhythms were out of stride and seemingly arbitrary, its drummers frozen-faced introverts dedicated to chaos. And in it the steady flow of memory, desire and defined experience summed up by the traditional jazz beat and blues mood seemed swept like a great river from its old, deep bed. We know better now, and recognize the old moods in the new sounds, but what we know is that which was then becoming. For most of those who gathered here, the enduring meaning of the great moment at Minton's took place off to the side, beyond the range of attention, like a death blow glimpsed from the corner of the eye, the revolutionary rumpus sounding like a series of flubbed notes blasting the talk with discord. So that the events which made Minton's *Min-*

ton's arrived in conflict and ran their course – then the heat was gone and all that is left to mark its passage is the controlled fury of the music itself, sealed pure and irrevocable, banalities and excellencies alike, in the early recordings; or swept along by our restless quest for the new, to be diluted in more recent styles, the best of it absorbed like drops of fully distilled technique, mood and emotions into the great stream of jazz.

'The Golden Age, Time Past' (1958) in *Shadow and Act*, 1964

To Whistler, American

EZRA POUND

On the loan exhibit of his paintings at the Tate Gallery.

You also, our first great,
Had tried all ways;
Tested and pried and worked in many fashions,
And this much gives me heart to play the game.

Here is part that's slight, and part gone wrong,
And much of little moment, and some few
Perfect as Dürer!
'In the Studio' and these two portraits,[1] if I had my choice!
And then these sketches in the mood of Greece?

You had your searches, your uncertainties.
And this is good to know – for us, I mean,
Who bear the brunt of our America
And try to wrench her impulse into art.

You were not always sure, not always set
To hiding night or tuning 'symphonies';
Had not one style from birth, but tried and pried
And stretched and tampered with the media.

You and Abe Lincoln from that mass of dolts
Show us there's chance at least of winning through.

[1] 'Brown and Gold – de Race.' 'Grenat et Or – Le Petit Cardinal.'

(1912) *Collected Shorter Poems*, 1952

Photographs from a Book: Six Poems

DAVID FERRY

I

A poem again, of several parts, each having to do
With a photograph. The first, by Eakins, is of his student,
Samuel C. Murray, about twenty-five years old.
Naked, a life study, in the cold light and hungry
Shadow of Eakins's studio in Philadelphia.
The picture was taken in eighteen ninety-two.
The young man's face is unsmiling, shy, or appears to be so
Because of the shadow. One knows from other
Images in the book that Murray's unshadowed gaze
Can look out clear, untroubled, without mystery or guile.
His body is easy in its selfhood, in its self and strength;
The virtue of its perfection is only of its moment
In the light and shadow. In the stillness of the photograph
I cannot see the light and shadow moving
As light and shadow move in the moving of a river.

II

He stands against what looks like the other side
Of a free-standing bookcase, with a black cloth
Draped over it, and a shelf as the top of it,
And on the shelf, sad, some bits and pieces
Of old 'fine' culture and bric-a-brac;
An urn; a child's head; a carved animal
Of some sort, a dog or a wolf, it's hard to tell;
A bust of a goddess staring out at nothing;
Something floral in wood or plaster. 'The Arcadians
Are said to have inhabited the earth
Before the birth of Jupiter; their tribe
Was older than the moon. Not as yet enhanced
By discipline or manners, their life
Resembled that of beasts; they were an uncouth
People, who were still ignorant of art.'

III

There is a strange, solemn, silent, graceless
Gayety in their dancing, the dancing of the young
Ladies of Philadelphia in the anxious
Saffron light of Eakins's photograph;

There in the nineteenth century, dressed in their 'Grecian'
Long white dresses, so many years ago,
They are dancing or standing still before the camera.
Selfhood altered to an alien poetry,
The flowers in their hair already fading;
Persephone, Dryope, Lotis, or maybe only
Some general Philadelphia notion of Grecian
Nymph or maiden, posing, there by the river.
'If those who suffer are to be believed,
I swear by the gods my fate is undeserved.'
The light in Eakins's photograph is ancient.

IV

Plate 134. By Eakins. 'A cowboy in the West.
An unidentified man at the Badger Company Ranch.'
His hat, his gun, his gloves, his chair, his place
In the sun. He sits with his feet in a dried-up pool
Of sunlight. His face is the face of a hero
Who has read nothing at all about heroes.
He is without splendor, utterly without
The amazement of self that glorifies Achilles
The sunlike, the killer. He is without mercy
As he is without the imagination that he is
Without mercy. There is nothing to the East of him
Except the camera, which is almost entirely without
Understanding of what it sees in him,
His hat, his gun, his gloves, his homely and
Heartbreaking canteen, empty on the ground.

V

The Anasazi drink from underground rivers.
The petroglyph cries out in the silence of the rock
The tourist looks at. The past is beautiful.
How few the implements and how carefully made
The dwelling place, against the wind and heat.
Looking at a photograph, as at a petroglyph,
How little there is to go on. 'The darkest objects
Reflect almost no light, or none at all.
Causing no changes in the salts in the emulsion.'
In the brilliant light and heart-stifling heat,
The scratchings on the surface of the rock,
Utterings, scriptions, bafflings of the spirit,
The bewildered eye reads nonsense in the dazzle;

In the black depth of the rock the river says nothing,
Reflectionless, swift, intent, purposeless, flowing.

VI

A picture of Eakins and a couple of other people,
One of them Murray, bathing in a river,
The Cohansey, near Fairton, New Jersey; Eakins
An old man, Murray no longer young; the other man,
Elderly, smiling, 'probably Charlie Boyers.'
They are patiently waiting for the picture to be taken.
It is a summer evening. The photograph
Is overexposed, so the light and the water are almost
Impossible to distinguish one from the other,
In their mutual weakness; an oarless rowboat waits
In the water, just clear of the rivergrass and weeds;
The opposite bank of the river is hard to see
In the washy blankness of the light; the sallow
Flat South Jersey landscape, treeless almost,
Almost featureless, stretches vaguely beyond.

Strangers, 1983

Georgia O'Keeffe

JOAN DIDION

'Where I was born and where and how I have lived is unimportant,' Georgia
O'Keeffe told us in the book of paintings and words published in her nine-
tieth year on earth. She seemed to be advising us to forget the beautiful face
in the Stieglitz photographs. She appeared to be dismissing the rather condescending romance that had attached to her by then, the romance of extreme good looks and advanced age and deliberate isolation. 'It is what I
have done with where I have been that should be of interest.' I recall an August afternoon in Chicago in 1973 when I took my daughter, then seven, to
see what Georgia O'Keeffe had done with where she had been. One of the
vast O'Keeffe 'Sky Above Clouds' canvases floated over the back stairs in
the Chicago Art Institute that day, dominating what seemed to be several
stories of empty light, and my daughter looked at it once, ran to the landing, and kept on looking. 'Who drew it,' she whispered after a while. I told
her. 'I need to talk to her,' she said finally.

My daughter was making, that day in Chicago, an entirely unconscious
but quite basic assumption about people and the work they do. She was as-

suming that the glory she saw in the work reflected a glory in its maker, that the painting was the painter as the poem is the poet, that every choice one made alone – every word chosen or rejected, every brush stroke laid or not laid down – betrayed one's character. *Style is character.* It seemed to me that afternoon that I had rarely seen so instinctive an application of this familiar principle, and I recall being pleased not only that my daughter responded to style as character but that it was Georgia O'Keeffe's particular style to which she responded: this was a hard woman who had imposed her 192 square feet of clouds on Chicago.

'Hardness' has not been in our century a quality much admired in women, nor in the past twenty years has it even been in official favor for men. When hardness surfaces in the very old we tend to transform it into 'crustiness' or eccentricity, some tonic pepperiness to be indulged at a distance. On the evidence of her work and what she has said about it, Georgia O'Keeffe is neither 'crusty' nor eccentric. She is simply hard, a straight shooter, a woman clean of received wisdom and open to what she sees. This is a woman who could early on dismiss most of her contemporaries as 'dreamy', and would later single out one she liked as 'a very poor painter'. (And then add, apparently by way of softening the judgment: 'I guess he wasn't a painter at all. He had no courage and I believe that to create one's own world in any of the arts takes courage.') This is a woman who in 1939 could advise her admirers that they were missing her point, that their appreciation of her famous flowers was merely sentimental. 'When I paint a red hill,' she observed coolly in the catalogue for an exhibition that year, 'you say it is too bad that I don't always paint flowers. A flower touches almost everyone's heart. A red hill doesn't touch everyone's heart.' This is a woman who could describe the genesis of one of her most well-known paintings – the 'Cow's Skull: Red, White and Blue' owned by the Metropolitan – as an act of quite deliberate and derisive orneriness. 'I thought of the city men I had been seeing in the East,' she wrote. 'They talked so often of writing the Great American Novel – the Great American Play – the Great American Poetry . . . So as I was painting my cow's head on blue I thought to myself, "I'll make it an American painting. They will not think it great with the red stripes down the sides – Red, White and Blue – but they will notice it." '

The city men. The men. They. The words crop up again and again as this astonishingly aggressive woman tells us what was on her mind when she was making her astonishingly aggressive paintings. It was those city men who stood accused of sentimentalizing her flowers: 'I made you take time to look at what I saw and when you took time to really notice my flower you hung all your associations with flowers on my flower and you write about my flower as if I think and see what you think and see – and I don't.'

And I don't. Imagine those words spoken, and the sound you hear is *don't tread on me.* 'The men' believed it impossible to paint New York, so Georgia O'Keeffe painted New York. 'The men' didn't think much of her bright color, so she made it brighter. The men yearned toward Europe so she went to Texas, and then New Mexico. The men talked about Cézanne, 'long involved remarks about the "plastic quality" of his form and color', and took one another's long involved remarks, in the view of this angelic rattlesnake in their midst, altogether too seriously. 'I can paint one of those dismal-colored paintings like the men,' the woman who regarded herself always as an outsider remembers thinking one day in 1922, and she did; a painting of a shed 'all low-toned and dreary with the tree beside the door'. She called this act of rancor 'The Shanty' and hung it in her next show. 'The men seemed to approve of it,' she reported fifty-four years later, her contempt undimmed. 'They seemed to think that maybe I was beginning to paint. That was my only low-toned dismal-colored painting.'

Some women fight and others do not. Like so many successful guerrillas in the war between the sexes, Georgia O'Keeffe seems to have been equipped early with an immutable sense of who she was and a fairly clear understanding that she would be required to prove it. On the surface her upbringing was conventional. She was a child on the Wisconsin prairie who played with china dolls and painted watercolors with cloudy skies because sunlight was too hard to paint and, with her brother and sisters, listened every night to her mother read stories of the Wild West, of Texas, of Kit Carson and Billy the Kid. She told adults that she wanted to be an artist and was embarrassed when they asked what kind of artist she wanted to be: she had no idea 'what kind'. She had no idea what artists did. She had never seen a picture that interested her, other than a pen-and-ink Maid of Athens in one of her mother's books, some Mother Goose illustrations printed on cloth, a tablet cover that showed a little girl with pink roses, and the painting of Arabs on horseback that hung in her grandmother's parlor. At thirteen, in a Dominican convent, she was mortified when the sister corrected her drawing. At Chatham Episcopal Institute in Virginia she painted lilacs and sneaked time alone to walk out to where she could see the line of the Blue Ridge Mountains on the horizon. At the Art Institute in Chicago she was shocked by the presence of live models and wanted to abandon anatomy lessons. At the Art Students League in New York one of her fellow students advised her that, since he would be a great painter and she would end up teaching painting in a girls' school, any work of hers was less important than modeling for him. Another painted over her work to show her how the Impressionists did trees. She had not before heard how the Impressionists did trees and she did not much care.

At twenty-four she left all those opinions behind and went for the first time to live in Texas, where there were no trees to paint and no one to tell her how not to paint them. In Texas there was only the horizon she craved. In Texas she had her sister Claudia with her for a while, and in the late afternoons they would walk away from town and toward the horizon and watch the evening star come out. 'That evening star fascinated me,' she wrote, 'It was in some way very exciting to me. My sister had a gun, and as we walked she would throw bottles into the air and shoot as many as she could before they hit the ground. I had nothing but to walk into nowhere and the wide sunset space with the star. Ten watercolors were made from that star.' In a way one's interest is compelled as much by the sister Claudia with the gun as by the painter Georgia with the star, but only the painter left us this shining record. Ten watercolors were made from that star.

(1976) *The White Album*, 1979

'The greatest revolution in modern art'

FRANK O'HARA

A symbolic tale of our times, comparable to the legend of Apelles' leaving his sign on the wall, is that of the modern artist who, given the wrappings from issues of a foreign review by a friend, transforms them into two collage masterpieces; and who, given a stack of Japan paper, makes six drawings and on seeing them the next day is so excited by the black ink having bled into orange at its edges that he decides to make six hundred more drawings. The collages are *N.R.F. Numbers One and Two*, the drawings are the group called 'Lyric Suite', and the artist is Robert Motherwell. Does art choose the artist, or does the man choose art?

Motherwell's choice is one of the most fascinating in modern art. As a young man of twenty-five, a university student who majored in philosophy, he decided to devote himself completely to painting, a decision which at the time held promise of little but hard work and probable discouragement. Yet, a few short years later, he was to find himself one of the leading figures in the greatest revolution in modern art since cubism, abstract expressionism.

Recently, in a television interview, Robert Motherwell remembered the aims of the early period of abstract expressionism as being 'really quite simple in a way, almost too simple, considering what has happened in the last twenty years. But really I suppose most of us felt that our passionate allegiance was not to American art or in that sense to any national art, but that there was such a thing as modern art: that it was essentially international in character, that it was the greatest painting adventure of our time, that we wished to participate in it, that we wished to plant it here, that it would blossom in its own way here as it had elsewhere, because beyond national differences there are human similarities that are more consequential . . . '

The measure of the success of the abstract expressionist artists may be gauged by our response to the movement's ethical stand – today it seems an inevitable development, it is surrounded by an atmosphere of 'of course'. But in the late '30s and early '40s there was violent resistance to this 'passionate allegiance'. We forget, in the complexity of our present worldwide artistic and political engagements, that period's artistic and political isolationism (how controversial then were Gertrude Stein and Wendell Willkie!), the mania for the impressionist masters, the conviction, where there was any interest at all, that avant-garde was not only a French word but an Ecole de Paris monopoly. But the greatest resistance of all came from other American painters – the regionalists, the social realists and the traditionalists.

No account of the period can ignore Motherwell's role as an internationalist. In a sense a turn toward both revolution and internationalism were in the air, for the various national financial depressions had united most of the Western countries in crisis, if not in political agreement. And the artists, like the philosophers and the religious, had been the least economically valued members of distressed societies.

Without transition the struggle against Depression conditions became the struggle against War. War on such a scale that 'conditions' became an obsolete word, faced down by the appalling actual and philosophical monolith of historical event. But the artists were not faced down by the war vocabulary. With the advent of war a heterogeneous number of American artists whose only common passion was the necessity of contemporary art's being Modern began to emerge as a movement which, in Boris Pasternak's famous description of a far different emergency, as he relates in his autobiography *Safe Conduct*, ' . . . turned with the same side towards the times, stepping forward with its first declaration about its learning, its philosophy and its art'.

Underlying, and indeed burgeoning within, every great work of the abstract expressionists, whether subjectively lyrical as in Gorky, publicly explosive as in de Kooning, or hieratical as in Newman, exists the traumatic consciousness of emergency and crisis experienced as personal event, the artist assuming responsibility for being, however accidentally, alive here and now. Their gift was for a somber and joyful art; somber because it does not merely reflect but sees what is about it, and joyful because it is able to exist. It is just as possible for art to look out at the world as it is for the world to look at art. But the abstract expressionists were frequently the first violators of their own gifts; to this we often owe the marvelously demonic, sullen or mysterious quality of their work, as they moved from the pictorial image to the hidden subject.

Motherwell's special contribution to the American struggle for modernity was a strong aversion to provincialism, both political and aesthetic, a profound immersion in modern French culture (especially School of Paris art and the poetry and theories of the Symbolist and Surrealist poets – conquest by absorption, like the Chinese), and a particular affinity for what he has sometimes called 'Mediterranean light', which in his paintings seems to mean a mingling of the light of the California of his childhood with that of Mexico and the South of France. This affinity may explain somewhat the ambiguity between the relatively soft painted edges of many of his forms and the hard, clear contour they convey, especially in the series of 'Elegies to the Spanish Republic'. He can employ a rough, spontaneous stroke while evoking from the picture plane with great economy a precise personal light. There is no atmospheric light in his paintings; if he uses grey it is never twilight or dawn. One of his important early paintings is called *Western Air* and the light in it persists in many later works.

*

It is no wonder then that when Meyer Schapiro introduced him to the European refugee artists who had fled here from the Fall of France, he was strongly drawn to them, both as emblems of art and also as emblems of experience – an experience which no American artist save Gertrude Stein suffered as the French themselves did. Their insouciant survival in the face of disaster, partly through character, partly through belief in art, is one of the great legends, and it did not escape him. To recall the presence of these artists is indeed staggering. Motherwell's affinity for French Symbolist and Surrealist aesthetics made him a quick liaison between the refugees and certain New York artists whom he scarcely knew at the time. The capitulation of France had brought about an intense Francophilism among all liberal intellectuals, especially those who felt strongly about the tragedy of the Spanish Civil War; and the fate of Great Britain was still in question. It was not too difficult to feel a strong identification, and of course these artists were already heroes of the modern artistic revolution; if some of them hadn't invented it, they had certainly aided, abetted and extended it. In the artistic imagination these refugees represented everything valuable in modern civilization that was being threatened by physical extermination. It had never been more clear that a modern artist stands for civilization.

Modern artists ideologically, as the Jews racially, were the chosen enemies of the authoritarian states because their values were the most in opposition, so that one had a heightened sense, beyond the artistic, of seeing a Lipchitz or a Chagall walk free on the streets of New York. It is impossible for a society to be at war without each responsible element joining the endeavor, whether military, philosophical or artistic, and whether consciously or not. The perspectives may be different, but the temper of the time is inexorable and demanding for all concerned. I think that it was the pressure of this temper and this time that forced from abstract expressionism its statement of values, which is, and probably shall remain, unique in the history of culture. While the other protesting artistic voices of the time were bound by figuration and overt symbolism, the abstract expressionists chose the open road of personal responsibility, naked nerve-ends and possible hubris, and this separated them from the surrealists, the Mexican School and the American social realists. Belief in their personal and ethical responses saved them from aestheticism on the one hand and programmatic contortion on the other. Abstract expressionism for the first time in American painting insisted upon an artistic identity. This, of course, is what made abstract expressionism so threatening to other contemporaneous tendencies then, and even now. The abstract expressionists decided, instead of imitating the style of the European moderns, to do instead what they had done, to venture into the unknown, to give up looking at reproductions in *Verve* and *Cahiers d'Art* and to replace them with first-hand experimentation. This was the great anguish of the American artists. They had a sound theoretical, but no practical, knowledge of the suffering involved in being extreme; but they would learn. They shot off in every direction, risking everything. They were never afraid of having a serious idea, and the serious idea was never self-referential. Theirs was a struggle as ultimate as their painting. A struggle which, in the poet Edwin Denby's description in his reminiscence of the '30s, was against ' . . . the cliché about downtown painting in the depression – the accepted idea that everybody had doubts and imitated Picasso and talked politics. None of these features seemed to me remarkable at the time, and they don't now. Downtown everybody loved Picasso then, and why not. But what they painted made no sense as an imitation of him. For myself, something in his steady wide light reminded me then of the light in the streets and lofts we lived in. At that time Tchelitchew was the uptown master, and he had a flickering light.'

Robert Motherwell, 1965

'America leads the world'

JOHN BUTLER YEATS

You and Great Britain and Ireland must resign yourselves to it – America leads the world. She has been doing it for a long time in several devious ways, unknown even to herself. From now on she will do it openly, and I am glad of it. She has the right ideas and the right methods, in which she is miles ahead of any other nation – more than France. She has the collective mind; – *man himself* in the mass, as a unit in a vast crowd, is destined to be her pupil for years upon years. Hope, the great divinity, is domiciled in America, as the Pope lives in Rome. This all sounds a little eloquent, not to say grandiloquent. America will pay for it a great price. She loses literature and art and poetry – I mean of the great kind, the kind that matters. There the leadership remains with England, if she keeps her presence of mind, her equanimity, her equilibrium, and is not seduced into attempting that for which she has a most blessed incapacity. For England through all the centuries has been the home of the individualistic mind, which is the soul of the *great* poetry and the *great* art. Under English civilization a poet like Willie [W. B. Yeats] comes to a natural birth; he is impossible in America.

To Oliver Elton, 17 September 1918

MONEY AND THINGS

———

THE ALMIGHTY DOLLAR. The Romans worshipped their standards; and the Roman standard happened to be an eagle. Our standard is only one-tenth of an Eagle – a Dollar – but we make all even by adoring it with tenfold devotion.

Edgar Allan Poe, Southern Literary Messenger, June 1849

The chief business of the American people is business.

Calvin Coolidge, Speech, 1925

I think lots of men die of their wives and *thousands* of women die of their husbands. But not an American. Here, if there is a little trouble over a hand glass or a tooth brush, they shake hands and part, unless of course, there is a lot of money, when the lawyers take a hand.

John Butler Yeats to Lily Yeats, 21 March 1921

'The recent rush to California'

HENRY DAVID THOREAU

The recent rush to California and the attitude of the world, even of its philosophers and prophets, in relation to it appears to me to reflect the greatest disgrace on mankind. That so many are ready to get their living by the lottery of gold-digging without contributing any value to society, and that the great majority who stay at home justify them in this both by precept and example! It matches the infatuation of the Hindoos who have cast themselves under the car of Juggernaut. I know of no more startling development of the morality of trade and all the modes of getting a living than the rush to California affords. Of what significance the philosophy, or poetry, or religion of a world that will rush to the lottery of California gold-digging on the receipt of the first news, to live by luck, to get the means of commanding the labor of others less lucky, *i. e.* of slaveholding, without contributing any value to society? And that is called enterprise, and the devil is only a little more enterprising! The philosophy and poetry and religion of such a mankind are not worth the dust of a puffball. The hog that *roots* his own living, and so makes manure, would be ashamed of such company. If I could command the wealth of all the worlds by lifting my finger, I would not pay such a price for it. It makes God to be a moneyed gentleman who scatters a handful of pennies in order to see mankind scramble for them. Going to California. It is only three thousand miles nearer to hell. I will resign my life sooner than live by luck. The world's raffle. A subsistence in the domains of nature a thing to be raffled for! No wonder that they gamble there. I never heard that they did anything else there. What a comment, what a satire, on our institutions! The conclusion will be that mankind will hang itself upon a tree. And who would interfere to cut it down. And have all the precepts in all the bibles taught men only this? and is the last and most admirable invention of the Yankee race only an improved muck-rake? – patented too! If one came hither to sell lottery tickets, bringing satisfactory credentials, and the prizes were seats in heaven, this world would buy them with a rush.

Did God direct us so to get our living, digging where we never planted, – and He would perchance reward us with lumps of gold? It is a text, oh! for the Jonahs of this generation, and yet the pulpits are as silent as immortal Greece, silent, some of them, because the preacher is gone to California himself. The gold of California is a touchstone which has betrayed the rottenness, the baseness, of mankind. Satan, from one of his elevations, showed mankind the kingdom of California, and they entered into a compact with him at once.

Journal, 1 February 1852

'A share in the speculation'

MARK TWAIN

[Young Washington Hawkins visits Colonel Beriah Sellars in Hawkeye, Missouri.]

Washington slept in a cold bed in a carpetless room and woke up in a palace in the morning; at least the palace lingered during the moment that he was rubbing his eyes and getting his bearings – and then it disappeared and he recognized that the Colonel's inspiring talk had been influencing his dreams. Fatigue had made him sleep late; when he entered the sitting-room he noticed that the old haircloth sofa was absent; when he sat down to breakfast the Colonel tossed six or seven dollars in bills on the table, counted them over, said he was a little short and must call upon his banker; then returned the bills to his wallet with the indifferent air of a man who is used to money. The breakfast was not an improvement upon the supper, but the Colonel talked it up and transformed it into an oriental feast. By and by, he said:

'I intend to look out for you, Washington, my boy. I hunted up a place for you yesterday, but I am not referring to that, now – that is a mere livelihood – mere bread and butter; but when I say I mean to look out for you I mean something very different. I mean to put things in your way that will make a mere livelihood a trifling thing. I'll put you in a way to make more money than you'll ever know what to do with. You'll be right here where I can put my hand on you when anything turns up. I've got some prodigious operations on foot; but I'm keeping quiet; mum's the word; your old hand don't go around pow-wowing and letting everybody see his k'yards and find out his little game. But all in good time, Washington, all in good time. You'll see. Now, there's an operation in corn that looks well. Some New York men are trying to get me to go into it – buy up all the growing crops and just boss the market when they mature – ah, I tell you it's a great thing. And it only costs a trifle; two millions or two and a half will do it. I haven't exactly promised yet – there's no hurry – the more indifferent I seem, you know, the more anxious those fellows will get. And then there is the hog speculation – that's bigger still. We've got quiet men at work,' (he was very impressive here,) 'mousing around, to get propositions out of all the farmers in the whole West and Northwest for the hog crop, and other agents quietly getting propositions and terms out of all the manufactories – and don't you see, if we can get all the hogs and all the slaughter-houses into our hands on the dead quiet – whew! it would take three ships to carry the money. I've looked into the thing – calculated all the chances for and all the chances against, and though I shake my head and hesitate and keep on thinking, apparently, I've got my mind made up that if the thing can be done on a capital of six millions, that's the horse to put up money on! Why, Washington – but what's the use of talking about it – any man can see that there's whole Atlantic oceans of cash in it, gulfs and bays thrown in. But there's a bigger thing than that, yet – a bigger – '

'Why, Colonel, you can't want anything bigger!' said Washington, his eyes blazing. 'Oh, I wish I could go into either of those speculations – I only wish I had money – I wish I wasn't cramped and kept down and fettered with poverty, and such prodigious chances lying right here in sight! Oh, it is a fearful thing to be poor. But don't throw away those things – they are so splendid and I can see how sure they are. Don't throw them away for something still better and maybe fail in it! I wouldn't, Colonel. I would stick to these. I wish father were here and were his old self again. Oh, he never in his life had such chances as these are. Colonel, you *can't* improve on these – no man can improve on them!'

A sweet, compassionate smile played about the Colonel's features, and he leaned over the table with the air of a man who is 'going to show you' and do it without the least trouble:

'Why Washington, my boy, these things are nothing. They *look* large – of course they look large to a novice, but to a man who has been all his life accustomed to large operations – shaw! They're well enough to while away an idle hour with, or furnish a bit of employment that will give a trifle of idle capital a chance to earn its bread while it is waiting for something to *do*, but – now just listen a moment – just let me give you an idea of what we old veterans of commerce call "business". Here's the Rothschilds' proposition – this is between you and me, you understand – '

Washington nodded three or four times impatiently, and his glowing eyes said, 'Yes, yes – hurry – I understand – '

' – for I wouldn't have it get out for a fortune. They want me to go in with them on the sly – agent was here two weeks ago about it – go in on the sly' (voice down to an impressive whisper, now) 'and buy up a hundred and thirteen wildcat banks in Ohio, Indiana, Kentucky, Illinois, and Missouri – notes of these banks are at all sorts of discount now – average discount of the hundred and thirteen is forty-four percent – buy them all up, you see, and then all of a sudden let the cat out of the bag! Whiz! the stock of every one of those wildcats would spin up to a tremendous premium before you could turn a handspring – profit on the speculation not a dollar less than forty millions!' (An eloquent pause, while the marvelous vision settled into W's focus.) 'Where's your hogs now! Why, my dear innocent boy, we would just sit down on the front doorsteps and peddle banks like lucifer matches!'

Washington finally got his breath and said:

'Oh, it is perfectly wonderful! Why couldn't these things have happened in father's day? And I – it's of no use – they simply lie before my face and mock me. There is nothing for me but to stand helpless and see other people reap the astonishing harvest.'

'Never mind, Washington, don't you worry. I'll fix you. There's plenty of chances. How much money have you got?'

In the presence of so many millions, Washington could not keep from blushing when he had to confess that he had but eighteen dollars in the world.

'Well, all right – don't despair. Other people have been obliged to begin with less. I have a small idea that may develop into something for us both, all in good time. Keep your money close and add to it. I'll make it breed. I've been experimenting (to pass away the time) on a little preparation for curing sore eyes – a kind of decoction nine-tenths water and the other tenth drugs that don't cost more than a dollar a barrel; I'm still experimenting; there's one ingredient wanted yet to perfect the thing, and somehow I can't just manage to hit upon the thing that's necessary, and I don't dare talk with a chemist, of course. But I'm progressing, and before many weeks I wager the country will ring with the fame of Beriah Sellers' Infallible Imperial Oriental Optic Liniment and Salvation for Sore Eyes – the Medical Wonder of the Age! Small bottles fifty cents, large ones a dollar. Average cost, five and seven cents for the two sizes. The first year sell, say, ten thousand bottles in Missouri, seven thousand in Iowa, three thousand in Arkansas, four thousand in Kentucky, six thousand in Illinois, and say twenty-five thousand in the rest of the country. Total, fifty-five thousand bottles; profit clear of all expenses, twenty thousand dollars at the very lowest calculation. All the capital needed is to manufacture the first two thousand bottles – say a hundred and fifty dollars – then the money would begin to flow in. The second year, sales would reach 200,000 bottles – clear profit, say, $75,000 – and in the meantime the great factory would be building in St Louis, to cost, say, $100,000. The third year we could easily sell 1,000,000 bottles in the United States and – '

'O, splendid!' said Washington. 'Let's commence right away – let's – '

' – 1,000,000 bottles in the United States – profit at least $350,000 – and *then* it would begin to be time to turn our attention toward the *real* idea of the business.'

'The *real* idea of it! Ain't $350,000 year a pretty real' –

'Stuff! Why, what an infant you are, Washington – what a guileless, short-sighted, easily-contented innocent you are, my poor little country-bred know-nothing! Would I go to all that trouble and bother for the poor crumbs a body might pick up in *this* country? Now do I look like a man who – does my history suggest that I am a man who deals in trifles, contents

himself with the narrow horizon that hems in the common herd, sees no further than the end of his nose? Now, *you* know that that is not me – couldn't
be me. *You* ought to know that if I throw my time and abilities into a patent
medicine, it's a patent medicine whose field of operations is the solid earth!
its clients the swarming nations that inhabit it! Why what is the republic of
America for an eye-water country? Lord bless you, it is nothing but a barren
highway that you've got to cross to get *to* the true eye-water market! Why,
Washington, in the Oriental countries people swarm like the sands of the
desert; every square mile of ground upholds its thousands upon thousands
of struggling human creatures – and every separate and individual devil of
them's got the ophthalmia! It's as natural to them as noses are – and sin.
It's born with them, it stays with them, it's all that some of them have left
when they die. Three years of introductory trade in the Orient and what will
be the result? Why, our headquarters would be in Constantinople and our
hindquarters in Further India! Factories and warehouses in Cairo, Ispahan,
Bagdad, Damascus, Jerusalem, Yedo, Peking, Bangkok, Delhi, Bombay,
and Calcutta! Annual income – well, God only knows how many millions
and millions apiece!'

Washington was so dazed, so bewildered – his heart and his eyes had
wandered so far away among the strange lands beyond the seas, and such
avalanches of coin and currency had fluttered and jingled confusedly down
before him, that he was now as one who has been whirling round and round
for a time, and, stopping all at once, finds his surroundings still whirling
and all objects a dancing chaos. However, little by little the Sellers family
cooled down and crystallized into shape, and the poor room lost its glitter
and resumed its poverty. Then the youth found his voice and begged Sellers
to drop everything and hurry up the eye-water; and he got his eighteen dollars and tried to force it upon the Colonel – pleaded with him to take
it – implored him to do it. But the Colonel would not; said he would not
need the capital (in his native magnificent way he called that eighteen dollars
capital) till the eye-water was an accomplished fact. He made Washington
easy in his mind, though, by promising that he would call for it just as soon
as the invention was finished, and he added the glad tidings that nobody but
just they two should be admitted to a share in the speculation.

The Gilded Age, 1873 (with Charles Dudley Warner), ch. 8

'The habit of speculation'

JAMES BRYCE

This eager interest centres itself in New York, for finance, more perhaps than any other kind of business, draws to few points, and New York, which has as little claim to be the social or intellectual as to be the political capital of the country, is emphatically its financial capital. And as the centre of America is New York, so the centre of New York is Wall Street. This famous thoroughfare is hardly a quarter of a mile long, a little longer than Lombard Street in London. It contains the Sub-Treasury of the United States and the Stock Exchange. In it and the three or four streets that open into it are situated the Produce Exchange, the offices of the great railways, and the places of business of the financiers and stockbrokers, together representing an accumulation of capital and intellect comparable to the capital and intellect of London, and destined before many years to surpass every similar spot in either hemisphere. Wall Street is the great nerve centre of all American business; for finance and transportation, the two determining powers in business, have here their headquarters. It is also the financial barometer of the country, which every man engaged in large affairs must constantly consult, and whose only fault is that it is too sensitive to slight and transient variations of pressure.

The share market of New York, or rather of the whole Union in 'the Street', as it is fondly named, is the most remarkable sight in the country after Niagara and the Yellowstone Geysers. It is not unlike those geysers in the violence of its explosions, and in the rapid rise and equally rapid subsidence of its active paroxysms. And as the sparkling column of the geyser is girt about and often half concealed by volumes of steam, so are the rise and fall of stocks mostly surrounded by mists and clouds of rumour, some purposely created, some self-generated in the atmosphere of excitement, curiosity, credulity, and suspicion which the denizens of Wall Street breathe. Opinions change from moment to moment; hope and fear are equally vehement and equally irrational; men are constant only in inconstancy, superstitious because they are sceptical, distrustful of patent probabilities, and therefore ready to trust their own fancies or some unfathered tale. As the eagerness and passion of New York leave European stock markets far behind, for what the Paris and London exchanges are at rare moments Wall Street is for weeks, or perhaps, with a few intermissions, for months together, so the operations of Wall Street are vaster, more boldly conceived, executed with a steadier precision, than those of European speculators. It is not only their bearing on the prosperity of railroads or other great undertakings that is eagerly watched all over the country, but also their personal and dramatic aspects. The various careers and characters of the leading operators are familiar to every one who reads a newspaper; his schemes and exploits are followed as Europe followed the fortunes of Prince Alexander of Battenberg or General Boulanger. A great 'corner', for instance, is one of the exciting events of the year, not merely to those concerned with the stock or species of produce in which it is attempted, but to the public at large.

*

The more serious question remains: How does Wall Street tell on the character of the people? They are naturally inclined to be speculative. The pursuit of wealth is nowhere so eager as in America, the opportunities for acquiring it are nowhere so numerous. Nowhere is one equally impressed by the progress which the science and arts of gain – I do not mean the arts that add to the world's wealth, but those by which individuals appropriate an exceptionally large share of it – make from year to year. The materials with which the investor or the speculator has to work may receive no sensible addition; but the constant application of thousands of keen intellects, spurred by sharp desire, evolves new combinations out of these old materials, devises new methods and contrivances apt for a bold and skilful hand, just as electricians go on perfecting the machinery of the telegraph, just as the accumulated labours of scholars present us with always more trustworthy texts of the classical writers and more precise rules of Greek and Latin syntax. Under these new methods of business, speculation, though it seems to become more of a science, does not become less speculative. People seem to buy and sell on even slighter indications than in Paris or London. The processes of 'bulling' and 'bearing' are more constant and more skilfully applied. The whole theory and practice of 'margins' has been more completely worked out. However, it is of less consequence for our present purpose to dwell on the proficiency of the professional operator than to note the prevalence of the habit of speculation; it is not intensity so much as extension that affects an estimate of the people at large.

Except in New York, and perhaps in Chicago, which is more and more coming to reproduce and surpass the characteristics of New York, Americans bet less upon horse-races than the English do. Horse-races are, indeed, far less common, though there is a good deal of fuss made about trotting-matches. However, much money changes hands, especially in Eastern cities, over yacht-races, and plenty everywhere over elections. The purchase and sale of 'produce futures', *i.e.* of cotton, wheat, maize, bacon, lard, and other staples not yet in existence but to be delivered at some distant day, has reached an enormous development. There is, even in the Eastern cities, where the value of land might be thought to have become stable, a real estate market in which land and houses are dealt in as matter for pure speculation, with no intention of holding except for a rise within the next few hours or days; while in the new West the price of lands, especially near cities, undergoes fluctuations greater than those of the most unstable stocks in the London market. It can hardly be doubted that the pre-existing tendency to encounter risks and 'back one's opinion', inborn in the Americans, and fostered by the circumstances of their country, is further stimulated by the existence of so vast a number of joint-stock enterprises, and by the facilities they offer to the smallest capitalists. Similar facilities exist in the Old World; but few of the inhabitants of the Old World have yet learned how to use and abuse them. The Americans, quick at everything, have learned long ago. The habit of speculation is now a part of their character, and it increases that constitutional excitability and high nervous tension of which they are proud.

Some may think that when the country fills up and settles down, and finds itself altogether under conditions more nearly resembling those of the Old World, these peculiarities will fade away. I doubt it. They seem to have already passed into the national fibre.

The American Commonwealth, 1888, ch. 104

'The American scale of gain'

HENRY JAMES

These reflections connect themselves moreover with that most general of his restless hauntings in the United States – not only with the lapse of all wonderment at the immense number of absentees unrestored and making their lives as they may in other countries, but with the preliminary American postulate or basis for any successful accommodation of life. This basis is that of active pecuniary gain and of active pecuniary gain only – that of one's making the conditions so triumphantly pay that the prices, the manners, the other inconveniences, take their place as a friction it is comparatively easy to salve, wounds directly treatable with the wash of gold. What prevails, what sets the tune, is the American scale of gain, more magnificent than any other, and the fact that the whole assumption, the whole theory of life, is that of the individual's participation in it, that of his being more or less punctually and more or less effectually 'squared'. To make so much money that you won't, that you don't 'mind', don't mind anything – that is absolutely, I think, the main American formula. Thus your making no money – or so little that it passes there for none – and being thereby distinctly reduced to minding, amounts to your being reduced to the knowledge that America is no place for you. To mind as one minds, for instance, in Europe, under provocation or occasion offered, and yet to have to live under the effect of American pressure, is speedily to perceive that the knot can be untied but by a definite pull of one or the other string. The immense majority of people pull, luckily for the existing order, the string that consecrates their connection with it; the minority (small, however, only in comparison) pull the string that loosens that connection. The existing order is meanwhile safe, inasmuch as the faculty of making money is in America the commonest of all and fairly runs the streets; so simple a matter does it appear there, among vast populations, to make betimes enough *not* to mind. Yet the withdrawal of the considerable group of the pecuniarily disqualified seems no less, for the present, an assured movement; there will always be scattered individuals condemned to mind on a scale beyond any scale of making. The relation of this modest body to the country of their birth, which asks so much, on the whole – so many surrenders and compromises, and the possession above all of such a prodigious head for figures – before it begins, in its wonderful way, to give or to 'pay', would appear to us supremely touching, I think, as a case of communion baffled and blighted, if we had time to work it out. It would bathe in something of a tragic light the vivid truth that the 'great countries' are all, more and more, happy lands (so far as any can be called such) for any, for every sort of person rather than the middle sort. The upper sort – in the scale of wealth, the only scale now – can to their hearts' content build their own castles and move by their own motors; the lower sort, masters of gain in *their* degree, can profit, also to their hearts' content, by the enormous extension of those material facilities which may be gregariously enjoyed; they are able to rush about, as never under the sun before, in promiscuous packs and hustled herds, while to the act of so rushing about all felicity and prosperity appear for them to have been comfortably reduced. The frustrated American, as I have hinted at him, scraping for *his* poor practical solution in the depleted silver-mine of history, is the American who 'makes' too little for the castle and yet 'minds' too much for the hustled herd, who can neither achieve such detachment nor surrender to such society, and who most of all accordingly, in the native order, fails of a working basis. The salve, the pecuniary salve, in Europe, is sensibly less, but less on the other hand also the excoriation that makes it necessary, whether from above or below.

The American Scene, 1907, ch. 7

'This pressure of self-interest'

JOHN JAY CHAPMAN

We have seen that our more recent misgovernment has not been due to democracy, and we now see that the most striking weakness of our social life is not and never has been due to democracy.

Let us take an example: A party of men meet in a club, and the subject of free trade is launched. Each of these men has been occupied all day in an avocation where silence is golden. Shall he be the one to speak first? Who knows but what some phase of the discussion may touch his pocket? But the matter is deeper. Free speech is a habit. It cannot be expected from such men, because a particular subject is free from danger. Let the subject be dress reform, and the traders will be equally politic.

This pressure of self-interest which prevents a man from speaking his mind comes on top of that familiar moral terrorism of any majority, even a majority of two persons against one, which is one of the ultimate phenomena of human intercourse.

It is difficult to speak out a sentiment that your table companions disapprove of. Even Don Quixote was afraid to confess that it was he who had set the convicts at liberty, because he heard the barber and curate denounce the thing as an outrage. Now the weight of this normal social pressure in any particular case will depend on how closely the individuals composing the majority resemble each other. But men, lighted by the same passion, pursuing one object under the similar conditions, of necessity grow alike. By a process of natural selection, the self-seekers of Europe have for sixty years been poured into the hopper of our great mill. The Suabian and the Pole each drops his costume, his language, and his traditions as he goes in. They come out American business men; and in the second generation they resemble each other more closely in ideals, in aims, and in modes of thought than two brothers who had been bred to different trades in Europe.

The uniformity of occupation, the uniformity of law, the absence of institutions, like the church, the army, family pride, in fact, the uniformity of the present and the sudden evaporation of all the past, have ground the men to a standard.

America turns out only one kind of man. Listen to the conversation of any two men in a street car. They are talking about the price of something – building material, advertising, bonds, cigars.

We have, then, two distinct kinds of pressure, each at its maximum, both due to commerce: the pressure of fear that any unpopular sentiment a man utters will show in his bank account; the pressure of a unified majority who are alike in their opinions, have no private opinions, nor patience with the private opinions of others. Of these two pressures, the latter is by far the more important.

It cannot be denied that the catchwords of democracy have been used to intensify this tyranny. If the individual must submit when outvoted in politics, he ought to submit when outvoted in ethics, in opinion, or in sentiment. Private opinion is a thing to be stamped out, like private law. A prejudice is aroused by the very fact that a man thinks for himself; he is dangerous; he is anarchistic.

But this misapplication of a dogma is not the cause but the cloak of oppression. It is like the theory of the divine right of Kings – a thing invoked by conservatism to keep itself in control, a shibboleth muttered by men whose cause will not bear argument.

We must never expect to find in a dogma the explanation of the system which it props up. That explanation must be sought for in history. The dogma records but does not explain a supremacy. Therefore, when we hear some one appeal to democratic principle for a justification in suppressing the individual, we have to reflect how firmly must this custom be established, upon what a strong basis of interest must it rest, that it has power so to pervert the ideas of democracy. A distrust of the individual running into something like hatred may be seen reflected in the press of the United States. The main point is that Americans have by business training been growing more alike every day, and have seized upon any and every authority to aid them in disciplining a recusant.

We have then a social life in which caution and formalism prevail, and can see why it is that the gathering at the club was a dull affair.

'Society' (1898) in *Causes and Consequences*, 1909

'The love of *business*'

GEORGE SANTAYANA

[Addressed to the graduating students of Oberlin College, Ohio]

You are eager to be done with tradition: it is practice you feel that will free your souls. Such a premonition cannot well be deceptive. It may be frustrated by chance in one or another of you, for in the most brilliant victories many fall by the way; but it can hardly be frustrated on the whole for a race and a generation that feels it distinctly. Much less can it be frustrated in America, where an altogether unprecedented career is open to human effort. This country has had the privilege of beginning with all the advantages of tradition and with none of its trammels. The advantages were a seasoned moral character, a religion free from gross superstition, possessed of the various practical arts and crafts current in Europe, and an almost empty continent in the temperate zone. Under such conditions practice ought to yield fruit quickly, and not to be much misinterpreted by the traditions to which it gives rise. Such traditions have in fact arisen – first in politics, and industry. New and appropriate moulds have been given to political and industrial life which not only secure efficiency but which engross intellect and inspire emotion. American life, every one has heard, has extraordinary intensity; it goes at a great rate. This is not due, I should say, to any particular urgency in the object pursued. Other nations have more pressing motives to bestir themselves than America has: and it is observable that not all the new nations, in either hemisphere, are energetic. This energy can hardly spring either from unusually intolerable conditions which people wish to overcome, nor from unusually important objects which they wish to attain. It springs, I should venture to say, from the harmony which subsists between the task and the spirit, between the mind's vitality and the forms which, in America, political and industrial tradition has taken on. It is sometimes said that the ruling passion in America is the love of money. That seems to me a complete mistake. The ruling passion is the love of *business*, which is something quite different. The lover of money would be jealous of it; he would spend it carefully; he would study to get out of it the most he could. But the lover of business, when he is successful, does not much change his way of living; he does not think out what further advantages he can get out of his success. His joy is in that business itself and in its further operation, in making it greater and better organized and a mightier engine in the general life. The adventitious personal profit in it is the last thing he thinks of, the last thing he is skillful in bringing about; and the same zeal and intensity is applied in managing a college, or a public office, or a naval establishment, as is lavished on private business, for it is not a motive of personal gain that stimulates to such exertions. It is the absorbing, satisfying character of the activities themselves: it is the art, the happiness, the greatness of them. So that in beginning life in such a society, which has developed a native and vital tradition out of its practice, you have good reason to feel that your spirit will be freed, that you will begin to realize a part of what you are living for.

Speech, 'Tradition and Practice', 1904

'I think better of business'

H. G. WELLS

I spent a curious day amidst the memories of that strangely interesting social experiment, the Oneida community, and met a most significant contempory, a 'live American' of the newer school, in the son of the founder and the present head of 'Oneida Limited'.

There are moments when that visit I paid to Oneida seems to me to stand for all America. The place, you know, was once the seat of a perfectionist community; the large red community buildings stand now among green lawns and ripening trees, and I dined in the communal dining-room and visited the library, and saw the chain and trap factory, and the silk-spinning factory, and something of all its industries. I talked to old and middle-aged people, who told me all sorts of interesting things of 'community days', looked through curious old-fashioned albums of photographs showing the women in their bloomers and cropped hair, and the men in the ill-fitting frock-coats of the respectable mediocre person in early Victorian times. I think that some of the reminiscences I awakened had been voiceless for some time. At moments it was like hearing the story of a flattened, dry, and colourless flower between the pages of a book, of a verse written in faded ink, or some daguerreotype spotted and faint beyond recognition. It was extraordinarily New England in its quality as I looked back at it all. They claimed a quiet perfection of soul, they searched each other marvellously for spiritual chastening, they defied custom and opinion, they followed their reasoning and their theology to the most amazing abnegations, and they kept themselves solvent by the manufacture of steel traps that catch the legs of beasts in their strong and pitiless jaws . . .

But this book is not about the things that concerned Oneida in community days, and I mention them here only because of the curious developments of the present time. Years ago, when the founder, John Humphrey Noyes, grew old and unable to control the new dissensions that arose out of the sceptical attitude of the younger generation towards his ingenious theology, and such-like stresses, communism was abandoned, the religious life and services discontinued, the concern turned into a joint-stock company, and the members made shareholders on strictly commercial lines. For some years its prosperity declined. Many of the members went away; but a nucleus remained as residents in the old buildings, and after a time there were returns. I was told that in the early days of the new period there was a violent reaction against communistic methods, a jealous, inexperienced insistence upon property. 'It was difficult to borrow a hammer,' said one of my informants.

Then, as the new generation began to feel its feet, came a fresh development of vitality. The Oneida company began to set up new machinery, to seek wider markets, to advertise, and fight competitors.

This Mr P.B. Noyes was the leader into the new paths. He possesses all the force of character, the constructive passion, the imaginative power of his progenitor, and it has all gone into business competition. I have heard much talk of the romance of business, chiefly from people I heartily despised, but in Mr Noyes I found business indeed romantic. It had got hold of him, it possessed him like a passion. He has inspired all his half-brothers and cousins and younger fellow-members of the community with his own imaginative motive. They, too, are enthusiasts for business. Before the old perfectionists of the former generation realized what had happened, the Oneida corporation had started out upon the road of commercial adventure, to fight and capture, to form and control 'combines', to be in traps and chains what Standard Oil is in petroleum, to lead the market in plated knives and forks throughout the world. Some of the poor dears, I perceive, are growing rich in the profoundest dismay of soul; and there are no weekly criticisms, no prayers, no fires upon the deserted altars of Oneida any more for ever . . .

Mr Noyes is a tall man, who looks down when he talks to one. He showed me over the associated factories, told me how the trap trade of all North America is in Oneida's hands, told me of how they fight and win against the British traps in South America and Burmah. He showed me photographs of panthers in traps, tigers in traps, bears snarling at the approaching death, unfortunate deer, foxes caught by the paws . . .

I did my best to forget those photographs at once in the interest of his admirable machinery, which busied itself with chain-making as though it had eyes and hands. I went beside him, full of that respect that a literary man must needs feel when a creative business controller displays his quality.

'But the old religion of Oneida?' I would interpolate.

'Each one of us is free to follow his own religion. Here is a new sort of chain we are making for hanging lamps. Hitherto – .'

Presently I would try again. 'Are the workers here in any way members of the community?'

'Oh no! Many of them are Italian immigrants. We think of building a school for them . . . No, we get no labour troubles. We pay always above the trade-union rates, and so we get the pick of the workmen. Our class of work can't be sweated . . .'

Yes, he was an astonishing personality, so immensely concentrated in these efficient manufacturing and trading developments, so evidently careless of theology, philosophy, social speculation, beauty.

'Your father was a philosopher,' I said.

'I think in ten years' time I may give up control here,' he threw out, 'and write something.'

'I've thought of the publishing trade myself,' I had to retort, 'when my wits are old and stiff . . . '

I never met a man before so firmly gripped by the romantic, constructive, and adventurous element of business, so little concerned about personal riches or the accumulation of wealth. He illuminated much that had been dark to me in the American character. I think better of business by reason of him. And time after time I tried him upon politics. It came to nothing. Making a new world was, he thought, a rhetorical flourish about futile and troublesome activities, and politicians merely a disreputable sort of parasite upon honourable people who made chains and plated spoons. All his constructive instincts, all his devotion, were for Oneida and its enterprises. America was just the impartial space, the large liberty, in which Oneida grew, the stars and stripes a wide sanction akin to the impartial, irresponsible harbouring sky overhead. Sense of the state had never grown in him; can now, I feel convinced, never grow . . .

But some day, I like to imagine, it will be the World State, and not Oneida corporations, and a nobler trade than traps, that will command such services as his.

(Ellipses are Wells's.) 'State-Blindness' in *The Future in America*, 1906

'A College President *must* be worldly'

JOHN JAY CHAPMAN

James Croswell is my candidate for President of Harvard. But he is not worldly enough to suit. He'd get fifty blackballs out of fifty-one votes. A College President *must* be worldly. You said so yourself – though not in those words. Well, it's not true. I used to care somewhat about Harvard College; but since those circulars about Eliot's seventieth birthday and the three million fund, and all that bombast and vulgarity, I cannot go it. I cannot bear to be called 'a loyal son of Harvard'. This chest-thumping, back-slapping, vociferous and cheap emotionalism, done to get money and land money, is too much like everything else. I felt so clearly that the whole age's decay of scholarship and decent feeling could be shown from the Eliot circular, that if I hadn't been sick (and sworn off anyway) I should have come to Boston and given a lecture on the *English* of the document – the mere tone of it. Everything seems to be a base-ball team – jollying, rough good-feeling, and a thoroughgoing belief in money and *us* – and it's bad form to be accurate about anything except cash. Harvard is a base-ball team, and they'll bid high to get the best man they can, even if they have to outbid the Sioux City Nine. The truth is, I don't know much about Harvard, and don't doubt there's much else in it – only I always happen to meet the boom-side of it. Eliot has boomed and boomed – till we think it's the proper way to go on. He *must*, or lose foothold. Well, why not a man who does not boom? Is boom the best thing in life? Is it all boom? Is there now and to be nothing ever but boom, boom, boom? Is there not something that operates without money – not anywhere?

Why, my dear fellow, Eliot and the crew of howlers have wasted and destroyed more by their buildings and their gates – they are submerged in their improvements. It will take hairshirts to get the sky clear. It is no one's fault. They done the best they knew; and the next generation can pick up the pieces and painfully recover and reconstruct the idea that a university is a place of thought, truth, religion.

Pierpont Morgan is the actual apex as well as the type, of the commercial perversions of the era. The political corruption, etc., the power behind all . . . Now then, at the dedication of the New Medical School, Eliot goes about in a cab with Pierpont, hangs laurel wreaths on his nose, and gives him his papal kiss. Now what I want to know is this – what has Eliot got to say to the young man entering business or politics who is about to be corrupted by Morgan and his class? How eloquently can Eliot present the case for honesty? Can he say anything that will reverberate through the chambers of that young man's brain more loudly than that kiss?

If Eliot is a great man, I want a small man.

All this sounds to you remote – because you never, perhaps, were in an office – but in the offices of men entering the field, comes one form of the struggle between light and darkness, and it comes very quick, within a month or a few days – and it always comes; and it is always elementally the same – lawyers, architects, engineers, doctors are up against the commercial forces just now – very distinctly. Well, they are daily doing better, seeing more clearly, understanding the thing more clearly, but they need light, not fog, from the headlights of humanity and progress.

Of course you will say, 'Yes, but they never have got it from them in the history of the world.' That's all I mean.

To William James, 13 February 1907

The House of Morgan

JOHN DOS PASSOS

I commit my soul into the hands of my savior, wrote John Pierpont Morgan in his will, *in full confidence that having redeemed it and washed it in His most precious blood, He will present it faultless before my heavenly father, and I entreat my children to maintain and defend at all hazard and at any cost of personal sacrifice the blessed doctrine of complete atonement for sin through the blood of Jesus Christ once offered and through that alone,*

and into the hands of the House of Morgan represented by his son,

he committed,

when he died in Rome in 1913,

the control of the Morgan interests in New York, Paris, and London, four national banks, three trust companies, three life insurance companies, ten railroad systems, three streetrailway companies, an express company, the International Mercantile Marine,

power,

on the cantilever principle, through interlocking directorates,

over eighteen other railroads, US Steel, General Electric, American Tel. and Tel., five major industries;

the interwoven cables of the Morgan-Stillman-Baker combination held credit up like a suspension bridge, thirteen per cent of the banking resources of the world.

The first Morgan to make a pool was Joseph Morgan, a hotelkeeper in Hartford, Connecticut, who organized stagecoach lines and bought up Aetna Life Insurance stock in a time of panic caused by one of the big New York fires in the 1830's;

his son Junius followed in his footsteps, first in the drygoods business, and then as partner to George Peabody, a Massachusetts banker who built up an enormous underwriting and mercantile business in London and became a friend of Queen Victoria;

Junius married the daughter of John Pierpont, a Boston preacher, poet, eccentric, and abolitionist; and their eldest son,

John Pierpont Morgan,

arrived in New York to make his fortune

after being trained in England, going to school at Vevey, proving himself a crack mathematician at the University of Göttingen,

a lanky morose young man of twenty,

just in time for the panic of '57

(war and panics on the stock exchange, bankruptcies, war-loans, good growing weather for the House of Morgan).

When the guns started booming at Fort Sumter, young Morgan turned some money over reselling condemned muskets to the US Army and began to make himself felt in the Gold Room in downtown New York; there was more in trading in gold than in trading in muskets; so much for the Civil War.

During the Franco-Prussian War Junius Morgan floated a huge bond issue for the French government at Tours.

At the same time young Morgan was fighting Jay Cooke and the German-Jew bankers in Frankfort over the funding of the American war debt (he never did like the Germans or the Jews).

The panic of '73 ruined Jay Cooke and made J. Pierpont Morgan the boss croupier of Wall Street; he united with the Philadelphia Drexels and built the Drexel Building where for thirty years he sat in his glassedin office, red-faced and insolent, writing at his desk, smoking great black cigars, or, if important issues were involved, playing solitaire in his inner office; he was famous for his few words, Yes or No, and for his way of suddenly blowing up in a visitor's face and for that special gesture of the arm that meant, *What do I get out of it?*

In '77 Junius Morgan retired; J. Pierpont got himself made a member of the board of directors of the New York Central Railroad and launched the first *Corsair*. He liked yachting and to have pretty actresses call him Commodore.

He founded the Lying-in Hospital on Stuyvesant Square, and was fond of going into Saint George's church and singing a hymn all alone in the afternoon quiet.

In the panic of '93
at no inconsiderable profit to himself
Morgan saved the US Treasury; gold was draining out, the country was ruined, the farmers were howling for a silver standard, Grover Cleveland and his cabinet were walking up and down in the Blue Room at the White House without being able to come to a decision, in Congress they were making speeches while the gold reserves melted in the Subtreasuries; poor people were starving; Coxey's army was marching to Washington; for a long time Grover Cleveland couldn't bring himself to call in the representative of the Wall Street moneymasters; Morgan sat in his suite at the Arlington smoking cigars and quietly playing solitaire until at last the President sent for him;

he had a plan all ready for stopping the gold hemorrhage.

After that what Morgan said went; when Carnegie sold out he built the Steel Trust.

J. Pierpont Morgan was a bullnecked irascible man with small black magpie's eyes and a growth on his nose; he let his partners work themselves to death over the detailed routine of banking, and sat in his back office smoking black cigars; when there was something to be decided he said Yes or No or just turned his back and went back to his solitaire.

Every Christmas his librarian read him Dickens's *A Christmas Carol* from the original manuscript.

He was fond of canarybirds and pekinese dogs and liked to take pretty actresses yachting. Each *Corsair* was a finer vessel than the last.

When he dined with King Edward he sat at His Majesty's right; he ate with the Kaiser tête-à-tête; he liked talking to cardinals or the Pope, and never missed a conference of Episcopal bishops;

Rome was his favorite city.

He liked choice cookery and old wines and pretty women and yachting, and going over his collections, now and then picking up a jeweled snuffbox and staring at it with his magpie's eyes.

He made a collection of the autographs of the rulers of France, owned glass cases full of Babylonian tables, seals, signets, statuettes, busts,

Gallo-Roman bronzes,

Merovingian jewels, miniatures, watches, tapestries, porcelains, cuneiform inscriptions, paintings by all the old masters, Dutch, Italian, Flemish, Spanish,

manuscripts of the Gospels and the Apocalypse,

a collection of the works of Jean-Jacques Rousseau,

and the letters of Pliny the Younger.

His collectors bought anything that was expensive or rare or had the glint of empire on it, and he had it brought to him and stared hard at it with his magpie's eyes. Then it was put in a glass case.

The last year of his life he went up the Nile on a dahabeeyah and spent a long time staring at the great columns of the Temple of Karnak.

The panic of 1907 and the death of Harriman, his great opponent in railroad financing, in 1909, had left him the undisputed ruler of Wall Street, most powerful private citizen in the world;

an old man tired of the purple, suffering from gout, he had deigned to go to Washington to answer the questions of the Pujo Committee during the Money Trust Investigation: Yes, I did what seemed to me to be for the best interests of the country.

So admirably was his empire built that his death in 1913 hardly caused

a ripple in the exchanges of the world: the purple descended to his son,
J. P. Morgan,

who had been trained at Groton and Harvard and by associating with the
British ruling class

to be a more constitutional monarch: *J. P. Morgan suggests . . .*

By 1917 the Allies had borrowed one billion, ninehundred million dollars
through the House of Morgan: we went overseas for democracy and the
flag;

and by the end of the Peace Conference the phrase *J. P. Morgan suggests*
had compulsion over a power of seventyfour billion dollars.

J. P. Morgan is a silent man, not given to public utterances, but during
the great steel strike he wrote Gary: *Heartfelt congratulations on your stand
for the open shop, with which I am, as you know, absolutely in accord. I
believe American principles of liberty are deeply involved, and must win if
we stand firm.*

(Wars and panics on the stock exchange,
machinegunfire and arson,
bankruptcies, warloans,
starvation, lice, cholera and typhus:
good growing weather for the House of Morgan.)

1919,   32

'The towers of Zenith'

SINCLAIR LEWIS

I

The towers of Zenith aspired above the morning mist; austere towers of
steel and cement and limestone, sturdy as cliffs and delicate as silver rods.
They were neither citadels nor churches, but frankly and beautifully office-
buildings.

The mist took pity on the fretted structures of earlier generations: the
Post Office with its shingle-tortured mansard, the red brick minarets of
hulking old houses, factories with stingy and sooted windows, wooden
tenements colored like mud. The city was full of such grotesqueries, but the
clean towers were thrusting them from the business center, and on the farther hills were shining new houses, homes – they seemed – for laughter and
tranquility.

Over a concrete bridge fled a limousine of long sleek hood and noiseless
engine. These people in evening clothes were returning from an all-night re-

hearsal of a Little Theater play, an artistic adventure considerably illumi-nated by champagne. Below the bridge curved a railroad, a maze of green and crimson lights. The New York Flyer boomed past, and twenty lines of polished steel leaped into the glare.

In one of the skyscrapers the wires of the Associated Press were closing down. The telegraph operators wearily raised their celluloid eye-shades af-ter a night of talking with Paris and Peking. Through the building crawled the scrubwomen, yawning, their old shoes slapping. The dawn mist spun away. Cues of men with lunch-boxes clumped toward the immensity of new factories, sheets of glass and hollow tile, glittering shops where five thou-sand men worked beneath one roof, pouring out the honest wares that would be sold up the Euphrates and across the veldt. The whistles rolled out in greeting a chorus cheerful as the April dawn; the song of labor in a city built – it seemed – for giants.

II

There was nothing of the giant in the aspect of the man who was beginning to awaken on the sleeping-porch of a Dutch Colonial house in that residen-tial district of Zenith known as Floral Heights.

His name was George F. Babbitt. He was forty-six years old now, in April, 1920, and he made nothing in particular, neither butter nor shoes nor poetry, but he was nimble in the calling of selling houses for more than peo-ple could afford to pay.

His large head was pink, his brown hair thin and dry. His face was baby-ish in slumber, despite his wrinkles and the red spectacle-dents on the slopes of his nose. He was not fat but he was exceedingly well fed; his cheeks were pads, and the unroughened hand which lay helpless upon the khaki-colored blanket was slightly puffy. He seemed prosperous, extremely married and unromantic; and altogether unromantic appeared this sleeping-porch, which looked on one sizable elm, two respectable grassplots, a cement driveway, and a corrugated iron garage. Yet Babbitt was again dreaming of the fairy child, a dream more romantic than scarlet pagodas by a silver sea.

For years the fairy child had come to him. Where others saw but Georgie Babbitt, she discerned gallant youth. She waited for him, in the darkness beyond mysterious groves. When at last he could slip away from the crowded house he darted to her. His wife, his clamoring friends, sought to follow, but he escaped, the girl fleet beside him, and they crouched together on a shadowy hillside. She was so slim, so white, so eager! She cried that he was gay and valiant, that she would wait for him, that they would sail –

Rumble and bang of the milk-truck.

Babbitt moaned, turned over, struggled back toward his dream. He could see only her face now, beyond misty waters. The furnace-man slammed the basement door. A dog barked in the next yard. As Babbitt sank blissfully into a dim warm tide, the paper-carrier went by whistling, and the rolled-up *Advocate* thumped the front door. Babbitt roused, his stomach constricted with alarm. As he relaxed, he was pierced by the familiar and irritating rattle of some one cranking a Ford: snap-ah-ah, snap-ah-ah, snap-ah-ah. Himself a pious motorist, Babbitt cranked with the unseen driver, with him waited through taut hours for the roar of the starting engine, with him agonized as the roar ceased and again began the infernal patient snap-ah-ah – a round, flat sound, a shivering cold-morning sound, a sound infuriating and inescapable. Not till the rising voice of the motor told him that the Ford was moving was he released from the panting tension. He glanced once at his favorite tree, elm twigs against the gold patina of sky, and fumbled for sleep as for a drug. He who had been a boy very credulous of life was no longer greatly interested in the possible and improbable adventures of each new day.

He escaped from reality till the alarm-clock rang, at seven-twenty.

III

It was the best of nationally advertised and quantitatively produced alarm-clocks, with all modern attachments, including cathedral chime, intermittent alarm, and a phosphorescent dial. Babbitt was proud of being awakened by such a rich device. Socially it was almost as creditable as buying expensive cord tires.

He sulkily admitted now that there was no more escape, but he lay and detested the grind of the real-estate business, and disliked his family, and disliked himself for disliking them. The evening before, he had played poker at Vergil Gunch's till midnight, and after such holidays he was irritable before breakfast. It may have been the tremendous home-brewed beer of the prohibition-era and the cigars to which that beer enticed him; it may have been resentment of return from this fine, bold man-world to a restricted region of wives and stenographers, and of suggestions not to smoke so much.

From the bedroom beside the sleeping-porch, his wife's detestably cheerful 'Time to get up, Georgie boy,' and the itchy sound, the brisk and scratchy sound, of combing hairs out of a stiff brush.

He grunted; he dragged his thick legs, in faded baby-blue pajamas, from under the khaki blanket; he sat on the edge of the cot, running his fingers through his wild hair, while his plump feet mechanically felt for his slippers. He looked regretfully at the blanket – forever a suggestion to him of freedom and heroism. He had bought it for a camping trip which had never come off. It symbolized gorgeous loafing, gorgeous cursing, virile flannel shirts.

He creaked to his feet, groaning at the waves of pain which passed behind his eyeballs. Though he waited for their scorching recurrence, he looked blurrily out at the yard. It delighted him, as always; it was the neat yard of a successful business man of Zenith, that is, it was perfection, and made him also perfect. He regarded the corrugated iron garage. For the three-hundred-and-sixty-fifth time in a year he reflected, 'No class to that tin shack. Have to build me a frame garage. But by golly it's the only thing on the place that isn't up-to-date!' While he stared he thought of a community garage for his acreage development, Glen Oriole. He stopped puffing and jiggling. His arms were akimbo. His petulant, sleep-swollen face was set in harder lines. He suddenly seemed capable, an official, a man to contrive, to direct, to get things done.

On the vigor of his idea he was carried down the hard, clean, unused-looking hall into the bathroom.

Though the house was not large it had, like all houses on Floral Heights, an altogether royal bathroom of porcelain and glazed tile and metal sleek as silver. The towel-rack was a rod of clear glass set in nickel. The tub was long enough for a Prussian Guard, and above the set bowl was a sensational exhibit of tooth-brush holder, shaving-brush-holder, soap-dish, sponge-dish, and medicine-cabinet, so glittering and so ingenious that they resembled an electrical instrument-board. But the Babbitt whose god was Modern Appliances was not pleased. The air of the bathroom was thick with the smell of a heathen toothpaste. 'Verona been at it again! 'Stead of sticking to Lilidol, like I've re-peat-ed-ly asked her, she's gone and gotten some confounded stinkum stuff that makes you sick!'

The bath-mat was wrinkled and the floor was wet. (His daughter Verona eccentrically took baths in the morning, now and then.) He slipped on the mat, and slid against the tub. He said 'Damn!' Furiously he snatched up his tube of shaving-cream, furiously he lathered, with a belligerent slapping of the unctuous brush, furiously he raked his plump cheeks with a safety-razor. It pulled. The blade was dull. He said, 'Damn – oh – oh – damn it!'

He hunted through the medicine-cabinet for a packet of new razor-blades (reflecting, as invariably, 'Be cheaper to buy one of these dinguses and strop your own blades,') and when he discovered the packet, behind the round box of bicarbonate of soda, he thought ill of his wife for putting it there and very well of himself for not saying 'Damn.' But he did say it, immediately afterward, when with wet and soap-slippery fingers he tried to remove the horrible little envelope and crisp clinging oiled paper from the new blade.

Then there was the problem, oft-pondered, never solved, of what to do with the old blade, which might imperil the fingers of his young. As usual, he tossed it on top of the medicine-cabinet, with a mental note that some day he must remove the fifty or sixty other blades that were also temporarily, piled up there. He finished his shaving in a growing testiness increased by his spinning headache and by the emptiness in his stomach. When he was done, his round face smooth and streamy and his eyes stinging from soapy water, he reached for a towel. The family towels were wet, wet and clammy and vile, all of them wet, he found, as he blindly snatched them – his own face-towel, his wife's, Verona's, Ted's, Tinka's, and the lone bath-towel with the huge welt of initial. Then George F. Babbitt did a dismaying thing. He wiped his face on the guest-towel! It was a pansy-embroidered trifle which always hung there to indicate that the Babbitts were in the best Floral Heights society. No one had ever used it. No guest had ever dared to. Guests secretively took a corner of the nearest regular towel.

He was raging, 'By golly, here they go and use up all the towels, every doggone one of 'em, and they use 'em and get 'em all wet and sopping, and never put out a dry one for me – of course, I'm the goat! – and then I want one and – I'm the only person in the doggone house that's got the slightest doggone bit of consideration for other people and thoughtfulness and consider there may be others that may want to use the doggone bathroom after me and consider – '

He was pitching the chill abominations into the bath-tub, pleased by the vindictiveness of that desolate flapping sound; and in the midst his wife serenely trotted in, observed serenely, 'Why Georgie dear, what are you doing? Are you going to wash out the towels? Why, you needn't wash out the towels. Oh, Georgie, you didn't go and use the guest-towel, did you?'

It is not recorded that he was able to answer.

For the first time in weeks he was sufficiently roused by his wife to look at her.

*

v

Before he followed his wife, Babbitt stood at the westernmost window of their room. This residential settlement, Floral Heights, was on a rise; and though the center of the city was three miles away – Zenith had between three and four hundred thousand inhabitants now – he could see the top of the Second National Tower, an Indiana limestone building of thirty-five stories.

Its shining walls rose against April sky to a simple cornice like a streak of white fire. Integrity was in the tower, and decision. It bore its strength lightly as a tall soldier. As Babbitt stared, the nervousness was soothed from his face, his slack chin lifted in reverence. All he articulated was 'That's one lovely sight!' but he was inspired by the rhythm of the city; his love of it renewed. He beheld the tower as a temple-spire of the religion of business,

a faith passionate, exalted, surpassing common men; and as he clumped
down to breakfast he whistled the ballad 'Oh, by gee, by gosh, by jingo' as
though it were a hymn melancholy and noble.

Babbitt, 1922, ch. I

Chicago

CARL SANDBURG

Hog Butcher for the World,
Tool Maker, Stacker of Wheat,
Player with Railroads and the Nation's Freight Handler;
Stormy, husky, brawling,
City of the Big Shoulders:

They tell me you are wicked and I believe them, for I have seen your
painted women under the gas lamps luring the farm boys.
And they tell me you are crooked and I answer: Yes, it is true I have
seen the gunman kill and go free to kill again.
And they tell me you are brutal and my reply is: On the faces of
women and children I have seen the marks of wanton hunger.
And having answered so I turn once more to those who sneer at this my
city, and I give them back the sneer and say to them:
Come and show me another city with lifted head singing so proud to be
alive and coarse and strong and cunning.
Flinging magnetic curses amid the toil of piling job on job, here is a tall
bold slugger set vivid against the little soft cities;
Fierce as a dog with tongue lapping for action, cunning as a savage
pitted against the wilderness,
Bareheaded,
Shoveling,
Wrecking,
Planning,
Building, breaking, rebuilding,
Under the smoke, dust all over his mouth, laughing with white teeth,
Under the terrible burden of destiny laughing as a young man laughs,
Laughing even as an ignorant fighter laughs who has never lost a battle,
Bragging and laughing that under his wrist is the pulse, and under his
ribs the heart of the people,
Laughing!

Laughing the stormy, husky, brawling laughter of Youth, half-naked, sweating, proud to be Hog Butcher, Tool Maker, Stacker of Wheat, Player with Railroads and Freight Handler to the Nation.

(1914) *Chicago Poems*, 1916

'Rackets on strictly American lines'

CLAUD COCKBURN

In Chicago the director of the Illinois Central Bank, to whom I had been putting solemn questions on the subject of car loadings, commodity prices and the like, said moodily, 'Hell, boy, the capitalist system's on the skids anyway, let's go and get a drink.' I was glad of this attitude on his part because I had not really come to Chicago to discuss commodity prices in the Middle West, but to report the background to a murder. A couple of days before, we in New York had read the news of the killing in broad daylight of Jake Lingle, then crime reporter of the *Chicago Tribune* and – as emerged later – an important liaison officer between the Capone gang and the police department. It was one of the most spectacular and, for many reasons, looked like being one of the most revealing Chicago killings of the period when Al Capone was at approximately the height of his power. From a friend in New York who knew Chicago I learned enough of the background of the crime to make me very eager to go to Chicago myself. Hinrichs, who thought it would be a splendid story, was nevertheless hesitant. He explained to me that whenever *The Times* published a crime story from the United States somebody from the American Embassy or the English-Speaking Union or some other agency for promoting Anglo-American relations would ring up or would attack the editor at dinner, saying how much he had always previously admired *The Times*'s treatment of American affairs, and could there not be at least one British newspaper which did not represent the United States as a land dominated by gunmen and hoodlums? Hinrichs thought we had better cable London asking whether they wished me to go to Chicago.

As an assignment to report a murder the reply from *The Times* was probably a classic. 'By all means', it said, 'Cockburn Chicagowards. Welcome stories ex-Chicago not unduly emphasising crime.'

By the time I was in the air over Cleveland the difficulty of carrying out this directive successfully had notably increased. Ex-Ambassador Charlie Gates Dawes had impetuously been 'drafted' or had drafted himself to act as 'strong man' of the situation, to put himself, it was stated, at the head of 'the better element' and to 'clean up' Chicago. Before I touched down at Chicago Airport he had arrested nearly six hundred people and a number of others had been wounded in indiscriminate gunplay. I drove to the Criminal Courts Building and sought the advice of the dean of Chicago crime reporters, the original, I believe, of one of the central characters in Ben Hecht's play *The Front Page*. I showed him my cable. His deep laughter shook the desk. What, he asked, did I want to do? I said I supposed the first thing to do was to interview Mr Capone. He suggested that I listen in on an extension while he telephoned Mr Capone at the Lexington Hotel where he then had his offices. Presently I heard Capone's voice on the wire asking what went on. The crime reporter explained that there was a Limey from the London *Times* who wanted to talk with him. They fixed up an appointment for the following afternoon and just before he rang off the crime reporter said, 'Listen, Al, there's just one thing. You know this bird's assignment says he's to cover all this "not unduly emphasising crime".' Bewilderment exploded at the other end of the line. 'Not what?' Capone said. 'You heard me,' said the crime reporter. 'Not unduly emphasising crime.'

The Lexington Hotel had once, I think, been a rather grand family hotel, but now its large and gloomy lobby was deserted except for a couple of bulging Sicilians and a reception clerk who looked at once across the counter with the expression of a speakeasy proprietor looking through the grille at a potential detective. He checked on my appointment with some superior upstairs, and as I stepped into the elevator I felt my hips and sides being gently frisked by the tapping hands of one of the lounging civilians. There were a couple of ante-rooms to be passed before you got to Capone's office and in the first of them I had to wait for a quarter of an hour or so, drinking whisky poured by a man who used his left hand for the bottle and kept the other in his pocket.

Except that there was a sub-machine gun, operated by a man called Mac-Gurn – whom I later got to know and somewhat esteem – poking through the transom of a door behind the big desk, Capone's own room was nearly indistinguishable from that of – say a 'newly arrived' Texan oil millionaire. Apart from the jowly young murderer on the far side of the desk, what took the eye were a number of large, flattish, solid silver bowls upon the desk, each filled with roses. They were nice to look at, and they had another purpose too, for Capone, when agitated stood up and dipped the tips of his fingers in the water in which floated the roses.

I had been a little embarrassed as to how the interview was to be launched. Naturally the nub of all such interviews is somehow to get around to the question 'What makes you tick?' but in the case of this millionaire killer the approach to this central question seemed mined with dangerous impediments. However, on the way down to the Lexington Hotel I had had the good fortune to see, in I think the *Chicago Daily News*, some statistics offered by an insurance company which dealt with the average expectation of life of gangsters in Chicago. I forgot exactly what the average expectation was, and also what was the exact age of Capone at that time – I think he was in his very early thirties. The point was, however, that in any case he was four years older than the upper limit considered by the insurance company to be the proper average expectation of life for a Chicago gangster. This seemed to offer a more or less neutral and academic line of approach, and after the ordinary greetings I asked Capone whether he had read this piece of statistics in the paper. He said that he had. I asked him whether he considered the estimate reasonably accurate. He said that he thought that the insurance companies and the newspaper boys probably knew their stuff. 'In that case,' I asked him, 'how does it feel to be, say, four years over the age?'

He took the question quite seriously and spoke of the matter with neither more nor less excitement or agitation than a man would who, let us say, had been asked whether he, as the rear machine-gunner of a bomber, was aware of the average incidence of casualties in that occupation. He apparently assumed that sooner or later he would be shot despite the elaborate precautions which he regularly took. The idea that – as afterwards turned out to be the case – he would be arrested by the Federal authorities for income-tax evasion had not, I think, at that time so much as crossed his mind. And, after all, he said with a little bit of corn-and-ham somewhere at the back of his throat, supposing he had not gone into this racket? What would he have been doing? He would, he said, 'have been selling newspapers barefoot on the street in Brooklyn.'

He stood up as he spoke, cooling his finger-tips in the rose bowl in front of him. He sat down again, brooding and sighing. Despite the ham-and-corn, what he said was quite probably true and I said so, sympathetically. A little bit too sympathetically, as immediately emerged, for as I spoke I saw him looking at me suspiciously, not to say censoriously. My remarks about the harsh way the world treats barefoot boys in Brooklyn were interrupted by an urgent angry waggle of his podgy hand.

'Listen,' he said, 'don't you get the idea I'm one of these goddam radicals. Don't get the idea I'm knocking the American system. The American system . . . ' As though an invisible chairman had called upon him for a few words, he broke into an oration upon the theme. He praised freedom, enterprise and the pioneers. He spoke of 'our heritage'. He referred with contemptuous disgust to Socialism and Anarchism. 'My rackets,' he repeated several times, 'are run on strictly American lines and they're going to stay that way.' This turned out to be a reference to the fact that he had recently been elected the President of the Unione Siciliano, a slightly mysterious, partially criminal society which certainly had its roots in the Mafia. Its power and importance varied sharply from year to year. Sometimes there did seem to be evidence that it was a secret society of real power, and at other times it seemed more in the nature of a mutual benefit association not essentially much more menacing than, say, the Elks. Capone's complaint just now was that the Unione was what he called 'lousy with black-hand stuff'. 'Can you imagine,' he said, 'people going in for what they call these blood feuds – some guy's grandfather was killed by some other guy's grandfather, and this guy thinks that's good enough reason to kill the other.' It was, he said, entirely unbusinesslike. His vision of the American system began to excite him profoundly and now he was on his feet again, leaning across the desk like chairman of a board meeting, his fingers plunged in the rose bowls.

'This American system of ours,' he shouted, 'call it Americanism, call it Capitalism, call it what you like, gives to each and every one of us a great opportunity if we only seize it with both hands and make the most of it.' He held out his hands towards me, the fingers dripping a little, and stared at me sternly for a few seconds before reseating himself.

A month later in New York I was telling this story to Mr John Walter, minority owner of *The Times*. He asked me why I had not written the Capone interview for the paper. I explained that when I had come to put my notes together I saw that most of what Capone had said was in essence identical with what was being said in the leading articles of *The Times* itself, and I doubted whether the paper would be best pleased to find itself seeing eye to eye with the most notorious gangster in Chicago. Mr Walter, after a moment's wry reflection, admitted that probably my idea had been correct.

Even so, when I did start writing my thesis from Chicago – not unduly emphasising crime – I became aware, really for the first time, that about fifty per cent of what seemed to me to be the truth about the situation in Chicago would certainly be unpalatable and perhaps in parts unintelligible to *The Times*. I struggled with the article, produced a couple of readable pieces, and *The Times* wired me quite a large and much-needed bonus on the strength of it.

(1929) *In Time of Trouble*, 1956

Late Lamented Fame of the Giant City of New York

BERTOLT BRECHT

I

Who is there still remembers
The fame of the giant city of New York
In the decade after the Great War?

*

II

What people they were! Their boxers the strongest!
Their inventors the most practical! Their trains the fastest!
And also the most crowded!
And it all looked like lasting a thousand years
For the people of the city of New York put it about themselves:
That their city was built on the rock and hence
Indestructible.

12

Truly their whole system of communal life was beyond compare.
What fame! What a century!

13

Admittedly that century lasted
A bare eight years.

14

For one day there ran through the world the rumour of strange
    collapses
On a famous continent, and its banknotes, hoarded only yesterday
Were rejected in disgust like rotten stinking fish.

15

Today, when the word has gone round
That these people are bankrupt
We on the other continents (which are indeed bankrupt as well)
See many things differently and, so we think, more clearly.

16

What of the skyscrapers?
We observe them more coolly.

What contemptible hovels skyscrapers are when they no longer yield rents!
Rising so high, full of poverty? Touching the clouds, full of debt?
What of the railroad trains?
In the railroad trains, which resemble hotels on wheels, they say
Often nobody lives.
He travels nowhere
With incomparable rapidity.
What of the bridges? The longest in the world, they now link
Scrapheap with scrapheap.
And what of the people?

17
They still make up, we hear, but now
It's to grab a job. Twenty-two year old girls
Sniff cocaine now before setting out
To capture a place at a typewriter.
Desperate parents inject poison into their daughters' thighs
To make them look red hot.

18
Gramophone records are still sold, not many of course
But what do they tell us, these cows who have not learned
To sing? What
Is the sense of these songs? What have they really
Been singing to us all these years long?
Why do we now dislike these once celebrated voices?
Why
Do these photos of cities no longer make the slightest impression on us?
Because word has gone round
That these people are bankrupt.

19
For their machines, it is said, lie in huge heaps (the biggest in the world)
And rust
Like the machines of the Old World (in smaller heaps).

*

23
What a bankruptcy! How
Great a fame has departed! What a discovery:
That their system of communal life displays
The same miserable flaw as that of
More modest people.

(c. 1930) Poems 1913–1956, 1976; trans. Frank Jellinek

Americans in 1933–4–5–6–7–8–, Etc.

MERRILL MOORE

We filled our ears with so much noise that
There was no room for anything but that.

We stuffed our bellies full of so much bread
That we forgot what else we might be fed.

We smelt so much smoke, and so much perfume,
We could not sense an odor in the room
Other than what we might have thought was there
Whether it were decent or unfair.

We saw so many sights, we could not tell
Whether we liked them not at all or well.

We felt so much sensation, we could not
Tell what we were bringing from what was brought
Us on the laden platters of the years

Now so empty and so full of tears.

M, 1938

At the Dam

JOAN DIDION

Since the afternoon in 1967 when I first saw Hoover Dam, its image has never been entirely absent from my inner eye. I will be talking to someone in Los Angeles, say, or New York, and suddenly the dam will materialize, its pristine concave face gleaming white against the harsh rusts and taupes and mauves of that rock canyon hundreds or thousands of miles from where I am. I will be driving down Sunset Boulevard, or about to enter a freeway, and abruptly those power transmission towers will appear before me, canted vertiginously over the tailrace. Sometimes I am confronted by the in-takes and sometimes by the shadow of the heavy cable that spans the can-yon and sometimes by the ominous outlets to unused spillways, black in the lunar clarity of the desert light. Quite often I hear the turbines. Frequently I wonder what is happening at the dam this instant, at this precise intersec-tion of time and space, how much water is being released to fill downstream orders and what lights are flashing and which generators are in full use and which just spinning free.

I used to wonder what it was about the dam that made me think of it at times and in places where I once thought of the Mindanao Trench, or of the stars wheeling in their courses, or of the words *As it was in the beginning, is now and ever shall be, world without end, amen.* Dams, after all, are commonplace: we have all seen one. This particular dam had existed as an idea in the world's mind for almost forty years before I saw it. Hoover Dam, showpiece of the Boulder Canyon project, the several million tons of concrete that made the Southwest plausible, the *fait accompli* that was to convey, in the innocent time of its construction, the notion that mankind's brightest promise lay in American engineering.

Of course the dam derives some of its emotional effect from precisely that aspect, that sense of being a monument to a faith since misplaced. 'They died to make the desert bloom,' reads a plaque dedicated to the 96 men who died building this first of the great high dams, and in context the worn phrase touches, suggests all of that trust in harnessing resources, in the meliorative power of the dynamo, so central to the early Thirties. Boulder City, built in 1931 as the construction town for the dam, retains the ambience of a model city, a new town, a toy triangular grid of green lawns and trim bungalows, all fanning out from the Reclamation building. The bronze sculptures at the dam itself evoke muscular citizens of a tomorrow that never came, sheaves of wheat clutched heavenward, thunderbolts defied. Winged Victories guard the flagpole. The flag whips in the canyon wind. An empty Pepsi-Cola can clatters across the terrazzo. The place is perfectly frozen in time.

But history does not explain it all, does not entirely suggest what makes that dam so affecting. Nor, even, does energy, the massive involvement with power and pressure and the transparent sexual overtones to that involvement. Once when I revisited the dam I walked through it with a man from the Bureau of Reclamation. For a while we trailed behind a guided tour, and then we went on, went into parts of the dam where visitors do not generally go. Once in a while he would explain something, usually in that recondite language having to do with 'peaking power', with 'outages' and 'dewatering', but on the whole we spent the afternoon in a world so alien, so complete and so beautiful unto itself that it was scarcely necessary to speak at all. We saw almost no one. Cranes moved above us as if under their own volition. Generators roared. Transformers hummed. The gratings on which we stood vibrated. We watched a hundred-ton steel shaft plunging down to that place where the water was. And finally we got down to that place where the water was, where the water sucked out of Lake Mead roared through thirty-foot penstocks and then into thirteen-foot penstocks and finally into the turbines themselves. 'Touch it,' the Reclamation said, and I did, and for a long time I just stood there with my hands on the turbine. It was a peculiar moment, but so explicit as to suggest nothing beyond itself.

There was something beyond all that, something beyond energy, beyond history, something I could not fix in my mind. When I came up from the dam that day the wind was blowing harder, through the canyon and all across the Mojave. Later, toward Henderson and Las Vegas, there would be dust blowing, blowing past the Country-Western Casino FRI & SAT NITES and blowing past the Shrine of Our Lady of Safe Journey STOP & PRAY, but out at the dam there was no dust, only the rock and the dam and a little greasewood and a few garbage cans, their tops chained, banging against a fence. I walked across the marble star map that traces a sidereal revolution of the equinox and fixes forever, the Reclamation man had told me, for all time and for all people who can read the stars, the date the dam was dedicated. The star map was, he had said, for when we were all gone and the dam was left. I had not thought much of it when he said it, but I thought of it then, with the wind whining and the sun dropping behind a mesa with the finality of a sunset in space. Of course that was the image I had seen always, seen it without quite realizing what I saw, a dynamo finally free of man, splendid at last in its absolute isolation, transmitting power and releasing water to a world where no one is.

(1970) *The White Album*, 1979

'The drive yourself car'

GERTRUDE STEIN

Thornton Wilder gave us his apartment it had two bedrooms and a sitting room dining room with a little kitchen and it had a nice way to see the Midway which was snowy and I liked to see it and I hired myself a drive yourself car a Ford car and it was surprisingly cheap to do this and I was to write four lectures and Alice Toklas was to keep house in Chicago and it was all to be very pleasant and it was.

The most exciting thing was the drive yourself car.

I had been driven a great deal since I was in America and now I was to drive myself. In Illinois there was no examination you just had to find the place to hire the car and we found it. There are so many cars in America so of course they could hire me one. It was some little distance away the place where we found it under the elevated and then in a street that was a little dreary and I said to the man but this garage is too far away, when I come home in the evening I would not want to come all this way to put it away. Why he said where are you living, in a little street off the Midway I said, well he said, well I said, well he said what is the matter with it, why nothing I said it is a nice quiet street, a friend has loaned us an apartment, well he said, what is it, well I said, yes he said, and I said you mean I can leave it there all night I said and he said why not and I said but dont I have to leave a light, why isn't the street lighted he said why yes very well lighted and he said well and I said all right. And we did we left it there all and every night. One morning when I woke up I always looked out to see if the car was still there but it had been snowing all night and the car was there and it was all covered with snow, I said to Alice Toklas what shall we do and she said she would telephone to the garage. She did. They said well what is it, and we said the car was covered with snow, well they said wouldn't it go and we said how could we tell if it was covered with snow and they said isn't there a janitor there and we said oh yes, well they said he could brush it off and we called him and he did and then we went off. Everything in America is just as easy as that.

It was a puzzle all the stolen cars so they said and yet nobody seemed to think about it you just left them in the street. We liked it.

When I was going to the lecture room one day one of the tires of the car had flattened, one of the boys said if you will give me your key and tell me the name of your garage I will have it ready for you and when I came out of course it was ready for me, once when we had gone into Chicago I always called it going into Chicago from the University once when we had gone in to do some shopping and we were lunching, a tire was flat and so I gave my key to the door-man and told him and told him to tell the garage I wished they would change the tire this time and when we came out there was a new car and with it newer tires and I said but that is not mine oh no said the door-man they took the other away and they left you this one and I never saw the other one again naturally not I had this one. I liked everything.

We did get lost in the park and at first we did get lost with the road signs. That is one of the things that is very interesting, the different way different countries tell you how to go along. In France it is all done by drawing in America mostly by words and most of them words of one syllable. No left U turns, that took me some time so much so that I did one. The policeman said where do you think you are going, I said I was turning, I guess you are a stranger he said and I said I was one and he said well go on but you will most likely get killed before you leave town.

Everybody's Autobiography, 1937, ch. 4

POEM,OR BEAUTY HURTS MR.VINAL

e. e. cummings

take it from me kiddo
believe me
my country, 'tis of

you,land of the Cluett
Shirt Boston Garter and Spearmint
Girl With The Wrigley Eyes(of you
land of the Arrow Ide
and Earl &
Wilson
Collars)of you i
sing:land of Abraham Lincoln and Lydia E. Pinkham,
land above all of Just Add Hot Water And Serve –
from every B.V.D.

let freedom ring

amen.   i do however protest,anent the un
-spontaneous and otherwise scented merde which
greets one(Everywhere Why)as divine poesy per
that and this radically defunct periodical.   i would

suggest that certain ideas gestures
rhymes,like Gillette Razor Blades
having been used and reused
to the mystical moment of dullness emphatically are
Not To Be Resharpened.   (Case in point

if we are to believe these gently O sweetly
melancholy trillers amid the thrillers
these crepuscular violinists among my and your
skyscrapers – Helen & Cleopatra were Just Too Lovely,
The Snail's On The Thorn enter Morn and God's
In His andsoforth

do you get me?)according
to such supposedly indigenous
throstles Art is O World O Life
a formula:example,Turn Your Shirttails Into
Drawers and If It Isn't An Eastman It Isn't A
Kodak therefore my friends let

us now sing each and all fortissimo A-
mer
i

ca,I
love,
You.   And there're a
hun-dred-mil-lion-oth-ers,like
all of you successfully if
delicately gelded(or spaded)
gentlemen(and ladies) – pretty

littleliverpill-
hearted-Nujolneeding-There's-A-Reason
americans(who tensetendoned and with
upward vacant eyes,painfully
perpetually crouched,quivering,upon the
sternly allotted sandpile
 – how silently
emit a tiny violetflavoured nuisance:Odor?

ono.
comes out like a ribbon lies flat on the brush

is 5, 1926

A Winter's Tale

SYLVIA PLATH

On Boston Common a red star
Gleams, wired to a tall Ulmus
Americana. Magi near
The domed State House.

Old Joseph holds an alpenstock.
Two waxen oxen flank the Child.
A black sheep leads the shepherds' flock.
Mary looks mild.

Angels – more feminine and douce
Than models from Bonwit's or Jay's,
Haloes lustrous as Sirius –
Gilt trumpets raise.

By S. S. Pierce, by S. S. Pierce,
The red-nosed, blue-caped women ring
For money. Lord, the crowds are fierce!
There's caroling

On Winter Street, on Temple Place.
Poodles are baking cookies in
Filene's show windows. Grant us grace,
Donner, Blitzen,

And all you Santa's deer who browse
By leave of the Park Commission
On grass that once fed Boston cows.
In unison

On Pinckney, Mount Vernon, Chestnut,
The wreathed doors open to the crowd.
Noel! Noel! No mouth is shut.
Off key and loud

The populace sings toward the sill
Of windows with odd violet panes.
O Little City on a Hill!
The cordial strains

Of bellringers and singers rouse
Frost-bitten pigeons, eddy forth
From Charles Street to the Custom House,
From South Station to North.

(1958) *Collected Poems*, 1981

On the Circuit

W. H. AUDEN

Among pelagian travelers,
Lost on their lewd conceited way
To Massachusetts, Michigan,
Miami or L.A.,

An airborne instrument I sit,
Predestined nightly to fulfill

Columbia-Giesen-Management's
Unfathomable will,

By whose election justified,
I bring my gospel of the Muse
To fundamentalists, to nuns,
To Gentiles and to Jews,

And daily, seven days a week,
Before a local sense has jelled,
From talking-site to talking-site
Am jet-or-prop-propelled.

Though warm my welcome everywhere,
I shift so frequently, so fast,
I cannot now say where I was
The evening before last,

Unless some singular event
Should intervene to save the place,
A truly asinine remark,
A soul-bewitching face,

Or blessed encounter, full of joy,
Unscheduled on the Giesen Plan,
With, here, an addict of Tolkien,
There, a Charles Williams fan.

Since Merit but a dunghill is,
I mount the rostrum unafraid:
Indeed, 'twere damnable to ask
If I am overpaid.

Spirit is willing to repeat
Without a qualm the same old talk,
But Flesh is homesick for our snug
Apartment in New York.

A sulky fifty-six, he finds
A change of mealtime utter hell,
Grown far too crotchety to like
A luxury hotel.

The Bible is a goodly book
I always can peruse with zest,

But really cannot say the same
For Hilton's *Be My Guest*,

Nor bear with equanimity
The radio in students' cars,
Muzak at breakfast, or – dear God! –
Girl-organists in bars.

Then, worst of all, the anxious thought,
Each time my plane begins to sink
And the No Smoking sign comes on:
What will there be to drink?

Is this a milieu where I must
How grahamgreeneish! How infra dig!
Snatch from the bottle in my bag
An analeptic swig?

Another morning comes: I see,
Dwindling below me on the plane,
The roofs of one more audience
I shall not see again.

God bless the lot of them, although
I don't remember which was which:
God bless the U.S.A., so large,
So friendly, and so rich.

About the House, 1966

Application for a Grant

ANTHONY HECHT

Noble executors of the munificent testament
Of the late John Simon Guggenheim, distinguished bunch
Of benefactors, there are certain kinds of men
Who set their hearts on being bartenders,
For whom a life upon duck-boards, among fifths,
Tapped kegs and lemon twists, crowded with lushes
Who can master neither their bladders nor consonants,
Is the only life, greatly to be desired.
There's the man who yearns for the White House, there to compose

Rhythmical lists of enemies, while someone else
Wants to be known to the *Tour d'Argent*'s head waiter.
As the Sibyl of Cumae said: It takes all kinds.
Nothing could bribe your Timon, your charter member
Of the Fraternal Order of Grizzly Bears to love
His fellow, whereas it's just the opposite
With interior decorators; that's what makes horse races.
One man may have a sharp nose for tax shelters,
Screwing the IRS with mirth and profit;
Another devote himself to his shell collection,
Deaf to his offspring, indifferent to the feast
With which his wife hopes to attract his notice.
Some at the Health Club sweating under bar bells
Labor away like grunting troglodytes,
Smelly and thick and inarticulate,
Their brains squeezed out through their pores by sheer exertion.
As for me, the prize for poets, the simple gift
For amphybrachs strewn by a kind Euterpe,
With perhaps a laurel crown of the evergreen
Imperishable of your fine endowment
Would supply my modest wants, who dream of nothing
But a pad on Eighth Street and your approbation.

(Freely from Horace)

The Venetian Vespers, 1979

The Almighty Dollar

W. H. AUDEN

Political and technological developments are rapidly obliterating all cultural differences and it is possible that, in a not remote future, it will be impossible to distinguish human beings living on one area of the earth's surface from those living on any other, but our different pasts have not yet been completely erased and cultural differences are still perceptible. The most striking difference between an American and a European is the difference in their attitudes towards money. Every European knows, as a matter of historical fact, that, in Europe, wealth could only be acquired at the expense of other human beings, either by conquering them or by exploiting their labor in factories. Further, even after the Industrial Revolution began, the number of persons who could rise from poverty to wealth was small;

the vast majority took it for granted that they would not be much richer nor poorer than their fathers. In consequence, no European associates wealth with personal merit or poverty with personal failure.

To a European, money means power, the freedom to do as he likes, which also means that, consciously or unconsciously, he says; 'I want to have as much money as possible myself and others to have as little money as possible.'

In the United States, wealth was also acquired by stealing, but the real exploited victim was not a human being but poor Mother Earth and her creatures who were ruthlessly plundered. It is true that the Indians were expropriated or exterminated, but this was not, as it had always been in Europe, a matter of the conqueror seizing the wealth of the conquered, for the Indian had never realized the potential riches of his country. It is also true that, in the Southern states, men lived on the labor of slaves, but slave labor did not make them fortunes; what made slavery in the South all the more inexcusable was that, in addition to being morally wicked, it didn't even pay off handsomely.

Thanks to the natural resources of the country, every American, until quite recently, could reasonably look forward to making more money than his father, so that, if he made less, the fault must be his; he was either lazy or inefficient. What an American values, therefore, is not the possession of money as such, but his power to make it as a proof of his manhood; once he has proved himself by making it, it has served its function and can be lost or given away. In no society in history have rich men given away so large a part of their fortunes. A poor American feels guilty at being poor, but less guilty than an American *rentier* who has inherited wealth but is doing nothing to increase it; what can the latter do but take to drink and psychoanalysis?

In the Fifth Circle on the Mount of Purgatory, I do not think that many Americans will be found among the Avaricious; but I suspect that the Prodigals may be almost an American colony. The great vice of Americans is not materialism but a lack of respect for matter.

The Dyer's Hand, 1963

Who Runs America?

ALLEN GINSBERG

Oil brown smog over Denver
Oil red dung colored smoke

level to level across the horizon
    blue tainted sky   above
Oil car smog gasoline
        hazing red Denver's day
          December bare trees
            sticking up from housetop streets
Plane lands rumbling, planes rise over
          radar wheels, black smoke
              drifts wobbly from tailfins

Oil millions of cars speeding the cracked plains
Oil from Texas, Bahrain, Venezuela Mexico
Oil that turns General Motors
        revs up Ford
    lights up General Electric, oil that crackles
thru International Business Machine computers,
        charges dynamos for ITT
     sparks Western Electric
         runs thru Amer Telephone & Telegraph
wires
Oil that flows thru Exxon New Jersey hoses,
rings in Mobil gas tank cranks, rumbles
         Chrysler engines
shoots thru Texaco pipelines,
     blackens ocean from broken Gulf tankers
spills onto Santa Barbara beaches from
        Standard of California derricks offshore.

Braniff Air, Denver-Dallas, December 3, 1974

Mind Breaths, 1977

EMPIRE

Don't tell me I am grown old and peevish and supercilious – name the geniuses of 1774, and I submit. The next Augustan age will dawn on the other side of the Atlantic. There will, perhaps, be a Thucydides at Boston, a Xenophon at New York, and, in time, a Virgil at Mexico, and a Newton at Peru. At last, some curious traveller from Lima will visit England and give a description of the ruins of St. Paul's, like the editions of Balbec and Palmyra; but am I not prophesying, contrary to my consummate prudence, and casting horoscopes of empires like Rousseau? Yes; well, I will go and dream of my visions.

Horace Walpole, to Sir Horace Mann, 24 November 1774

Verses on the Prospect of Planting Arts and Learning in America

GEORGE BERKELEY

The Muse, disgusted at an age and clime
    Barren of every glorious theme,
In distant lands now waits a better time,
    Producing subjects worthy fame;

In happy climes, where from the genial sun
    And virgin earth such scenes ensue,
The force of art by nature seems outdone,
    And fancied beauties by the true;

In happy climes, the seat of innocence,
    Where nature guides and virtue rules,
Where men shall not impose, for truth and sense,
    The pedantry of courts and schools:

There shall be sung another golden age,
    The rise of empire and of arts,
The good and great inspiring epic rage,
    The wisest heads and noblest hearts.

Not such as Europe breeds in her decay;
    Such as she bred when fresh and young,
When heavenly flame did animate her clay,
    By future poets shall be sung.

Westward the course of empire takes its way;
    The first four acts already past,
A fifth shall close the drama with the day:
    Time's noblest offspring is the last.

(1726) 1752

'Yelps for liberty'

SAMUEL JOHNSON

We are told, that the subjection of Americans may tend to the diminution of our own liberties: an event, which none but very perspicacious politicians are able to foresee. If slavery be thus fatally contagious, how is it that we hear the loudest yelps for liberty among the drivers of negroes?

But let us interrupt a while this dream of conquest, settlement, and supremacy. Let us remember that being to contend, according to one orator, with three millions of Whigs, and according to another, with ninety thousand patriots of Massachusets Bay, we may possibly be checked in our career of reduction. We may be reduced to peace upon equal terms, or driven from the western continent, and forbidden to violate a second time the happy borders of the land of liberty. The time is now perhaps at hand, which Sir Thomas Browne predicted between jest and earnest,

> When America shall no more send out her treasure,
> But spend it at home in American pleasure.

Taxation No Tyranny, 1775

'Worth fighting for'

EDMUND BURKE

I am sensible, sir, that all which I have asserted, in my detail, is admitted in the gross; but that quite a different conclusion is drawn from it. America, gentlemen say, is a noble object. It is an object well worth fighting for. Certainly it is, if fighting a people be the best way of gaining them. Gentlemen in this respect will be led to their choice of means by their complexions and their habits. Those who understand the military art, will of course have some predilection for it. Those who wield the thunder of the state, may have more confidence in the efficacy of arms. But I confess, possibly for want of this knowledge, my opinion is much more in favour of prudent management, than of force; considering force not as an odious, but a feeble instrument, for preserving people so numerous, so active, so growing, so spirited as this, in a profitable and subordinate connexion with us.

Speech on Conciliation with America, 1775

The Declaration of Independence

THOMAS JEFFERSON

THE UNANIMOUS DECLARATION OF THE THIRTEEN UNITED STATES OF AMERICA

In Congress, July 4, 1776.

When in the course of human events, it becomes necessary for one people to dissolve the political bands which have connected them with another, and to assume among the powers of the earth, the separate and equal station which the Laws of Nature and of Nature's God entitle them, a decent respect to the opinions of mankind requires that they should declare the causes which impel them to the separation.

We hold these truths to be self-evident, that all men are created equal, that they are endowed by their Creator with certain unalienable Rights, that among these are Life, Liberty and the pursuit of Happiness. That to secure these rights, governments are instituted among men, deriving their just powers from the consent of the governed. That whenever any form of government becomes destructive of these ends, it is the right of the people to alter or to abolish it, and to institute new government, laying its foundation on such principles and organizing its powers in such form, as to them shall seem most likely to effect their safety and happiness. Prudence, indeed, will dictate that governments long established should not be changed for light and transient causes; and accordingly all experience hath shown, that mankind are more disposed to suffer, while evils are sufferable, than to right themselves by abolishing the forms to which they are accustomed. But when a long train of abuses and usurpations, pursuing invariably the same object evinces a design to reduce them under absolute despotism, it is their right, it is their duty, to throw off such government, and to provide new guards for their future security. – Such has been the patient sufferance of these Colonies; and such is now the necessity which constrains them to alter their former systems of government. The history of the present King of Great Britain is a history of repeated injuries and usurpations, all having in direct object the establishment of an absolute tyranny over these States. To prove this, let facts be submitted to a candid world.

He has refused his assent to laws, the most wholesome and necessary for the public good.

He has forbidden his Governors to pass laws of immediate and pressing importance, unless suspended in their operation till his assent should be obtained; and when so suspended, he has utterly neglected to attend to them.

He has refused to pass other laws for the accommodation of large districts of people, unless those people would relinquish the right of representation in the legislature, a right inestimable to them and formidable to tyrants only.

He has called together legislative bodies at places unusual, uncomfortable, and distant from the depository of their public records, for the sole purpose of fatiguing them into compliance with his measures.

He has dissolved Representative Houses repeatedly, for opposing with manly firmness his invasions on the rights of the people.

He has refused for a long time, after such dissolutions, to cause others to be elected; whereby the legislative powers, incapable of annihilation, have returned to the people at large for their exercise; the state remaining in the mean time exposed to all the dangers of invasion from without, and convulsions within.

He has endeavoured to prevent the population of these States; for that purpose obstructing the laws for naturalization of foreigners; refusing to pass others to encourage their migration hither, and raising the conditions of new appropriations of lands.

He has obstructed the administration of justice, by refusing his assent to laws for establishing judiciary powers.

He has made judges dependent on his will alone, for the tenure of their offices, and the amount and payment of their salaries.

He has erected a multitude of new offices, and sent hither swarms of officers to harass our people, and eat out their substance.

He has kept among us, in times of peace, standing armies without the consent of our legislature.

He has affected to render the military independent of and superior to the civil power.

He has combined with others to subject us to a jurisdiction foreign to our constitution, and unacknowledged by our laws; giving his assent to their acts of pretended legislation:

For quartering large bodies of armed troops among us:

For protecting them, by a mock trial, from punishment for any murders which they should commit on the inhabitants of these states:

For cutting off our trade with all parts of the world:

For imposing taxes on us without our consent:

For depriving us in many cases, of the benefits of trial by jury:

For transporting us beyond seas to be tried for pretended offences:

For abolishing the free system of English laws in a neighbouring province, establishing therein an arbitrary government, and enlarging its boundaries so as to render it at once an example and fit instrument for introducing the same absolute rule into these Colonies:

For taking away our charters, abolishing our most valuable laws, and altering fundamentally the forms of our governments:

For suspending our own legislatures, and declaring themselves invested with power to legislate for us in all cases whatsoever.

He has abdicated government here, by declaring us out of his protection and waging war against us.

He has plundered our seas, ravaged our coasts, burnt our towns, and destroyed the lives of our people.

He is at this time transporting large armies of foreign mercenaries to complete the works of death, desolation and tyranny, already begun with circumstances of cruelty and perfidy scarcely paralleled in the most barbarous ages, and totally unworthy the head of a civilized nation.

He has constrained our fellow citizens taken captive on the high seas to bear arms against their country, to become the executioners of their friends and brethren, or to fall themselves by their hands.

He has excited domestic insurrections amongst us, and has endeavoured to bring on the inhabitants of our frontiers, the merciless Indian savages, whose known rule of warfare, is an undistinguished destruction of all ages, sexes and conditions.

In every stage of these oppressions we have petitioned for redress in the most humble terms: our repeated petitions have been answered only by repeated injury. A Prince, whose character is thus marked by every act which may define a tyrant, is unfit to be the ruler of a free people.

Nor have we been wanting in attention to our British brethren. We have warned them from time to time of attempts by their legislature to extend an unwarrantable jurisdiction over us. We have reminded them of the circumstances of our emigration and settlement here. We have appealed to their native justice and magnanimity, and we have conjured them by the ties of our common kindred to disavow these usurpations, which would inevitably interrupt our connections and correspondence. They too have been deaf to the voice of justice and of consanguinity. We must, therefore, acquiesce in the necessity, which denounces our separation, and hold them, as we hold the rest of mankind, enemies in war, in peace friends.

We, therefore, the Representatives of the united States of America, in general Congress, assembled, appealing to the Supreme Judge of the world for the rectitude of our intentions, do, in the name, and by authority of the good people of these Colonies, solemnly publish and declare, That these United Colonies are, and of right ought to be free and independent States; that they are absolved from all allegiance to the British Crown, and that all political connection between them and the State of Great Britain, is and ought to be totally dissolved; and that as free and independent States, they have full power to levy war, conclude peace, contract alliances, establish commerce, and to do all other acts and things which independent States may of right do. And for the support of this declaration, with a firm reliance on the protection of Divine Providence, we mutually pledge to each other our lives, our fortunes and our sacred honor.

1776

'Holding America'

EDMUND BURKE

I think I know America. If I do not, my ignorance is incurable, for I have spared no pains to understand it; and I do most solemnly assure those of my constituents who put any sort of confidence in my industry and integrity, that everything that has been done there has arisen from a total misconception of the object: that our means of originally holding America, that our means of reconciling with it after quarrel, of recovering it after separation, of keeping it after victory, did depend, and must depend in their several stages and periods, upon a total renunciation of that unconditional submission, which has taken such possession of the minds of violent men. The whole of those maxims, upon which we have made and continued this war, must be abandoned. Nothing indeed (for I would not deceive you) can place us in our former situation. That hope must be laid aside. But there is a difference between bad and the worst of all. Terms relative to the cause of the war ought to be offered by the authority of parliament. An arrangement at home promising some security for them ought to be made. By doing this, without the least impairing of our strength, we add to the credit of our moderation, which, in itself, is always strength more or less.

Letter to the Sheriffs of Bristol, 1777

'Freedom and slavery'

GEORGE GORDON, LORD BYRON

'I wish well', he used to say, 'to the United States of America: the government of that country is suitable to the people. The Americans profit very much by the emigration of artisans and mechanics, who carry with them, ready formed, that skill it has cost England vast sums of money to bring to perfection. They are children, who profit by the knowledge of their parents, but who are at the same time the victims of their prejudices. They have a fresh country to work on, and the civilization and knowledge of Europe to work with. They have carried with them, however, some of the worst vices of European society, and they have been heightened in the Southern States by a voluptuous climate, and by the facility the people once had of procuring slaves. Though I think the government of America good, because it is the government of the whole people, and adapted to their views, I have no love for America. It is not a country I should like to visit. The Americans, they say, are great egotists. I suppose all the people of young countries are so. Man must have something to be vain of, and when he has no ancestors in whose fame he may exult, he must talk and boast of himself. If we had as much communication with the natives of Owhyhee, or with the Indians of the Continent of America, as we have with the inhabitants of the United States, and if we understood their language, we should find them as vainglorious as the Americans. An Englishman does not boast of himself, because he can always boast of his country. For this he is called a patriot; but if he were to praise himself as much as he praises *his* institutions, he would be called an ass. He indulges his vanity, and gets credit for patriotism. Since it is found that the American government works well, in the political slang of the day, the Americans begin to boast of it. In a few years more, when they have produced a score or two of such men as Washington, Franklin, and Jefferson, when they can talk with pride of the antiquity of their institutions; when they can exult, perhaps, in some hundred victories, like that of New Orleans, selfishness and egotism will change their meaning, and be merged into a love of their country.

'On this account I have always thought the mode in which the Americans separated from Great Britain unfortunate for them. It made them despise or reject every thing English. They disinherited themselves of all the historical glory of England; there was nothing left for them to admire or venerate but their own immediate success, and they become egotists, like savages, from wanting a history. The spirit of jealousy and animosity, excited by the contests between England and America, is now subsiding. Should peace continue, prejudices on both sides will gradually decrease. Already the Americans are beginning, I think, to cultivate the antiquities of England, and as they extend their inquiries, they will find other objects of admiration besides themselves. It was of some importance, both for them and for us, that they did not reject our language with our government. Time, I should hope, would approximate the institutions of both countries to one another: and the use of the same language will do more to unite the two nations than if they both had only one king.

'I would not answer, indeed, for the continuance of the present system of government in America, should that country be involved in long and expensive wars. In any season of distress, the free and slave states will separate. Freedom and slavery cannot dwell under the same roof; to bind them together force is necessary, and nothing but an arbitrary master over both can keep them united.'

(1824) William Parry, *The Last Days of Lord Byron*, 1825

The United States

JOHANN WOLFGANG VON GOETHE

America, you are luckier
Than this old continent of ours;
You have no ruined castles
And no volcanic earth.
You do not suffer
In hours of intensity
From futile memories
And pointless battles.

Concentrate on the present joyfully!
And when your children write books
May a good destiny keep them
From knight, robber, and ghost-stories.

1827; trans. Robert Bly, 1966

To the President of the United States
[James Monroe]

THOMAS JEFFERSON

Monticello, October 24, 1823

Dear Sir, – The question presented by the letters you have sent me, is the most momentous which has ever been offered to my contemplation since that of Independence. That made us a nation, this sets our compass and points the course which we are to steer through the ocean of time opening on us. And never could we embark on it under circumstances more auspicious. Our first and fundamental maxim should be, never to entangle ourselves in the broils of Europe. Our second, never to suffer Europe to intermeddle with cis-Atlantic affairs. America, North and South, has a set of interests distinct from those of Europe, and peculiarly her own. She should therefore have a system of her own, separate and apart from that of Europe. While the last is laboring to become the domicil of despotism, our endeavor should surely be, to make our hemisphere that of freedom. One nation, most of all, could disturb us in this pursuit; she now offers to lead, aid, and accompany us in it. By acceding to her proposition, we detach her from the bands, bring her mighty weight into the scale of free government, and emancipate a continent at one stroke, which might otherwise linger long in doubt and difficulty. Great Britain is the nation which can do us the most harm of any one, or all on earth; and with her on our side we need not fear the whole world. With her then, we should most sedulously cherish a cordial friendship; and nothing would tend more to knit our affections than to be fighting once more, side by side, in the same cause. Not that I would purchase even her amity at the price of taking part in her wars. But the war in which the present proposition might engage us, should that be its consequence, is not her war, but ours. Its object is to introduce and establish the American system, of keeping out of our land all foreign powers, of never permitting those of Europe to intermeddle with the affairs of our nations. It is to maintain our own principle, not to depart from it. And if, to facilitate this, we can effect a division in the body of the European powers, and draw over to our side its most powerful member, surely we should do it. But I am clearly of Mr Canning's opinion, that it will prevent instead of provoking war. With Great Britain withdrawn from their scale and shifted into that of our two continents, all Europe combined would not undertake such a war. For how would they propose to get at either enemy without superior fleets? Nor is the occasion to be slighted which this proposition offers, of declaring our protest against the atrocious violations of the rights of nations, by the interference of any one in the internal affairs of another, so flagitiously begun by Bonaparte, and now continued by the equally lawless Alliance, calling itself Holy.

But we have first to ask ourselves a question. Do we wish to acquire to our own confederacy any one or more of the Spanish provinces? I candidly confess, that I have ever looked on Cuba as the most interesting addition which could ever be made to our system of States. The control which, with Florida Point, this island would give us over the Gulf of Mexico, and the countries and isthmus bordering on it, as well as all those whose waters flow into it, would fill up the measure of our political well-being. Yet, as I am sensible that this can never be obtained, even with her own consent, but by war; and its independence, which is our second interest, (and especially its independence of England,) can be secured without it, I have no hesitation in abandoning my first wish to future chances, and accepting its independence, with peace and the friendship of England, rather than its association, at the expense of war and her enmity.

I could honestly, therefore, join in the declaration proposed, that we aim not at the acquisition of any of those possessions, that we will not stand in the way of any amicable arrangement between them and the mother country; but that we will oppose, with all our means, the forcible interposition of any other power, as auxiliary, stipendiary, or under any other form or pretext, and most especially, their transfer to any power by conquest, cession, or acquisition in any other way. I should think it, therefore, advisable, that the Executive should encourage the British government to a continuance in the dispositions expressed in these letters, by an assurance of his concurrence with them as far as his authority goes; and that as it may lead to war, the declaration of which requires an act of Congress, the case shall be laid before them for consideration at their first meeting, and under the reasonable aspect in which it is seen by himself.

I have been so long weaned from political subjects, and have so long ceased to take any interest in them, that I am sensible I am not qualified to offer opinions on them worthy of any attention. But the question now proposed involved consequences so lasting, and effects so decisive of our future destinies, as to rekindle all the interest I have heretofore felt on such occasions, and to induce me to the hazard of opinions, which will prove only my wish to contribute still my mite towards anything which may be useful to our country. And praying you to accept it at only what it is worth, I add the assurance of my constant and affectionate friendship and respect.

To James Monroe, 24 October 1823

'The American Continents'

JAMES MONROE

Of events in that quarter of the globe, with which we have so much intercourse, and from which we derive our origin, we have always been anxious and interested spectators. The citizens of the United States cherish sentiments the most friendly in favour of the liberty and happiness of their fellow men, on that side of the Atlantic. In the wars of the European Powers, in matters relating to themselves, we have taken no part, nor does it comport with our policy to do so. It is only when our rights are invaded, or seriously menaced that we resent injuries, or make preparations for our defence.

With the movements in this hemisphere, we are, of necessity, more immediately connected, and by causes which must be obvious to all enlightened and impartial observers. The political system of the Allied Powers is essentially different, in this respect, from that of America. This difference proceeds from that which exists in their respective Governments. And to the defence of our own, which has been achieved by the loss of so much blood and treasure, and matured by the wisdom of their most enlightened citizens, and under which we have enjoyed unexampled felicity, this whole nation is devoted.

We owe it, therefore, to candour, and to the amicable relations existing between the United States and these Powers, to declare that we should consider any attempt on their part to extend their system to any portion of this hemisphere as dangerous to our peace and safety. With the existing colonies or dependencies of any European Power we have not interfered and shall not interfere.

But, with the Governments who have declared their independence and maintained it, and whose independence we have, on great consideration, and on just principles acknowledged, we could not view any interposition for the purpose of oppressing them, or controlling, in any other manner, their destiny, by any European Power, in any other light than as the manifestation of an unfriendly disposition towards the United States.

*

Our policy in regard to Europe, which was adopted at the early stage of the wars which have so long agitated that quarter of the globe, nevertheless remains the same, which is not to interfere in the internal concerns of any of its Powers; to consider the government *de facto* as the legitimate government for us; to cultivate friendly relations with it, and to preserve those relations by frank, firm and manly policy, meeting in all instances the just claims of every power; submitting to injuries from none.

But, in regard to these continents, circumstances are eminently and conspicuously different. It is impossible that the Allied Powers should extend their political system to any portion of either continent without endangering our peace and happiness; nor can anyone believe that our southern brethren, if left to themselves, would adopt it of their own accord.

It is equally impossible, therefore, that we should behold such interposition, in any form, with indifference.

Earlier on, in a reference to negotiations with Great Britain and Russia, about rights and interests on the northwest coast of America, the message declared: –

In the discussions to which this interest has given rise, and, in the arrangements by which they may terminate, the occasion has been judged proper, for asserting, as a principle in which the rights and interests of the United States are involved, that the American Continents, by the free and independent condition which they have assumed and maintain, are henceforth not to be considered as subjects for future colonization by any European Powers.

Federal Gazette, 3 December 1823

'The Russians and the Americans'

ALEXIS DE TOCQUEVILLE

There are at the present time two great nations in the world, which started from different points, but seem to tend towards the same end. I allude to the Russians and the Americans. Both of them have grown up unnoticed; and whilst the attention of mankind was directed elsewhere, they have suddenly placed themselves in the front rank among the nations, and the world learned their existence and their greatness at almost the same time.

All other nations seem to have nearly reached their natural limits, and they have only to maintain their power; but these are still in the act of growth.[1] All the others have stopped, or continue to advance with extreme difficulty; these alone are proceeding with ease and celerity along a path to which no limit can be perceived. The American struggles against the obstacles which nature opposes to him; the adversaries of the Russian are men. The former combats the wilderness and savage life; the latter, civilization with all its arms. The conquests of the American are therefore gained by the ploughshare; those of the Russian by the sword. The Anglo-American relies upon personal interest to accomplish his ends, and gives free scope to the unguided strength and common sense of the people; the Russian centres all the authority of society in a single arm. The principal instrument of the former is freedom; of the latter, servitude. Their starting-point is different, and their courses are not the same; yet each of them seems marked out by the will of Heaven to sway the destinies of half the globe.

1 The population of Russia increases more rapidly than that of any other country in the Old World.

Democracy in America, vol. 1, 1835, ch. 18, Conclusion,
trans. Henry Reeve; rev. Francis Bowen, 1862

'This modern Rome'

JOSE MARIA TORNEL Y MENDIVIL

For more than fifty years, that is, from the very period of their political infancy, the prevailing thought in the United States of America has been the
acquisition of the greater part of the territory that formerly belonged to
Spain, particularly that part which today belongs to the Mexican nation.
Democrats and Federalists, all their political parties, whatever their old or
new designations, have been in perfect accord upon one point, their desire
to extend the limits of the republic to the north, to the south, and to the
west, using for the purpose all the means at their command, guided by cunning, deceit, and bad faith. It has been neither an Alexander nor a Napoleon, desirous of conquest in order to extend his dominions or add to his
glory, who has inspired the proud Anglo-Saxon race in its desire, its frenzy
to usurp and gain control of that which rightfully belongs to its neighbors;
rather it has been the nation itself which, possessed of that roving spirit that
moved the barbarous hordes of a former age in a far remote north, has
swept away whatever has stood in the way of its aggrandizement.

*

Our continuous revolts made that country conceive the hope that we
would neglect or abandon our national and sacred charge, while the ill-
advised colonization laws and our still more imprudent and scandalous mismanagement of the public lands, so coveted and yet so freely and generously
distributed and given away, clearly showed that we knew neither how to
appreciate nor how to keep the precious heritage of the Spaniards. Unfor-
tunately they were not mistaken in their assumption, for at every step we
have displayed that candor, weakness, and inexperience so characteristic of
infant nations. Too late have we come to know the restless and enterprising
neighbor who set himself up as our mentor, holding up his institutions for
us to copy them, institutions which transplanted to our soil could not but
produce constant anarchy, and which, by draining our resources, perverting
our character, and weakening our vigor, have left us powerless against the
attacks and the invasions of this modern Rome. The example of an *ever increasing* prosperity was treacherously pointed out to us, and, attributing to
the written law the influence of habit and custom, we adopted the first without the steadying influence of the second. Thus we have chosen to live in
perpetual contradiction, in an anomalous state. How costly have been to us
the gifts of these new Greeks!

As a native of America I cannot regret the triumph of the Revolution of
1776, nor can I condemn the vast experiment in social welfare that has been

undertaken upon our continent. But that same Revolution which bore such happy results for the American people, – even though they may not be as extensive, as perfect, and as complete as its partisans would have us believe – brought many misfortunes to the human race when considered from other points of view.

*

The events of Madrid and Bayone in 1808, the subsequent uprising of the Spanish people against the hordes of Napoleon, the disordered state of the administration which naturally followed, the weakness of her revolutionary governments, barely able to maintain a precarious existence, all these circumstances united to favor the ambitious plans of the United States who now, ill-concealing their joy, threw off the hypocritical mask with which, for a time, they covered their true designs. The thinking men of the United States had clearly foreseen that their emancipation would be but the prelude to the emancipation of all the New World. They realized that sooner or later the important revelation that resistance to a remote and tyrannical power could be crowned with complete victory would not be disregarded by the Spanish colonies. Nor were they ignorant of the fact that their early independent existence, their progress in civilization, and the experience gained through their own administration would assure them a preeminent position of power and influence in determining the fate of the new nations when they became established. To cooperate in this great enterprise was to safeguard their own existence by the most effective means. In spite of the advantageous position of the United States, of their growing maritime power, of the war-like disposition of their inhabitants, of the determination displayed in their struggles, of the abundant resources of their soil and the bright prospects of their industry, they could not aspire to a superior rank among the nations of the world, as long as they had to compete with the old and powerful countries of Europe. The setting changed, however, with the appearance of other independent nations in the New World. It was, therefore, to the essential interest of the United States to encourage by their example, their counsel, and their material help the insurrection of Spanish America. Here they saw the realization of their ulterior motives enhanced by the sympathy created for themselves and the inherent weakness of the ephemeral governments of the new nations. Egoism is an inseparable vice of the genius of the Anglo-Saxon race. If they proclaim or sustain the august rights of liberty and independence, it is not because of the noble sympathy felt for a just and sacred cause; rather it is out of regard for their interests, it is their own improvement which they seek with indefatigable zeal. The time that has elapsed since our fortunate emancipation, a time so rich in disappointments, has removed the band that inexperience placed over our eyes. Who is ignorant today of the real cause, the prime motive behind the decision taken by the United States in favor of the independence of the Spanish colonies?

*

It cannot be denied that the immense majority of the American people participated in our melancholic tragedies for the purpose of weakening the power of Spain and out of a desire to exercise a direct influence, inevitable as a result of the vigor of a people full of life and dynamic activity, upon the fate of poorly educated peoples who would in the end destroy themselves by their excesses and the horrors of continuous civil war. Nothing could withstand the popularity of the Anglo-American system of government. The influence of Spain seemed to end at the Pillars of Hercules. The newborn star of the nations that rose upon the ruins of a decrepit monarchy shined fitfully and with a reddish glow.

The Americans decided to fan the spirit of insurrection in the Spanish colonies during the darkest hour of the conflict for their former ally and benefactor, taking advantage of the critical situation, and aware of the ultimate success which they foresaw. Companies which rendered direct services to the rebels were organized in Baltimore, expeditions were outfitted in New York; money, munitions, and armament were liberally furnished in New Orleans to carry on the struggle against Spain, to destroy and banish her commerce. It was thus that the plans to weaken more and more the power of a friendly nation were put into execution in order to snatch from her, immediately after, her most valuable possessions.

> (1835) *The Mexican Side of the Texas Revolution*;
> trans. Carlos E. Castaneda, 1956

'The boundaries of nations'

JUAN BAUTISTA VIGIL

The speech which you [General Kearny, of the US Army] have just delivered, in which you announce that you have taken possession of this great country in the name of the United States of America, gives us some idea of the wonderful future that awaits us. It is not for us to determine the boundaries of nations. The cabinets of Mexico and Washington will arrange these differences. It is for us to obey and respect the established authorities, no matter what may be our private opinions.

The inhabitants of this territory humbly and honorably present their loyalty and allegiance to the government of North America. No one in this world can successfully resist the power of him who is stronger.

Do not find it strange if there is no manifestation of joy and enthusiasm in seeing this city [Santa Fe] occupied by your military forces. To us the power of the Mexican Republic is dead. No matter what the condition, she was our mother. What child will not shed abundant tears at the tomb of his parents? I might indicate some of the causes of her misfortunes, but family problems should not be made public. Let it suffice to say that civil war is the cursed source of the deadly poison that has stifled one of the noblest and greatest countries that was ever created. Today we belong to a great and wonderful nation; its flag, with its stars and stripes covers the horizon of New Mexico, and its brilliant light shall grow in our soil like good seed well cultivated. We recognize your kindness, your courtesy, and that of your accommodating officers, and the strict discipline of your troops; we know we belong to the Republic that owes its origins to the immortal Washington, whom all civilized nations admire and respect. How different would be our situation had we been invaded by European nations! We are aware of the unfortunate condition of the Poles.

In the name, then, of the entire land, I swear obedience to the Northern Republic, and I tender my respect to its laws and authority.

1846; archives of the State of New Mexico, trans. Stan Steiner in *Aztlan*,
ed. Luis Valdez and Stan Steiner, 1972

England and America, 1

J. K. STEPHEN

Republic of the West,
     Enlightened, free, sublime,
Unquestionably best
     Production of our time.

The telephone is thine,
     And thine the Pullman Car,
The caucus, the divine
     Intense electric star.

To thee we likewise owe
     The venerable names
Of Edgar Allan Poe,
     And Mr Henry James.

In short it's due to thee,
    Thou kind of Western star,
That we have come to be
    Precisely what we are.

But every now and then,
    It cannot be denied,
You breed a kind of men
    Who are not dignified,

Or courteous or refined,
    Benevolent or wise,
Or gifted with a mind
    Beyond the common size,

Or notable for tact,
    Agreeable to me,
Or anything, in fact,
    That people ought to be.

Lapsus Calami, 1891

'Independence to the people of Cuba'

CHARLES ELIOT NORTON

There are, indeed, many among us who find justification of the present war in the plea that its motive is to give independence to the people of Cuba, long burdened by the oppressive and corrupt rule of Spain, and especially to relieve the suffering of multitudes deprived of their homes and of means of subsistence by the cruel policy of the general who exercised for a time a practical dictatorship over the island. The plea so far as it is genuine deserves the respect due to every humane sentiment. But independence secured for Cuba by forcible overthrow of the Spanish rule means either practical anarchy or the substitution of the authority of the United States for that of Spain. Either alternative might well give us pause. And as for the relief of suffering, surely it is a strange procedure to begin by inflicting worse suffering still. It is fighting the devil with his own arms. That the end justifies the means is a dangerous doctrine, and no wise man will advise doing evil for the sake of an uncertain good. But the plea that the better government of Cuba and the relief of the reconcentrados could only be secured by war is the plea either of ignorance or of hypocrisy.

But the war is declared; and on all hands we hear the cry that he is no

patriot who fails to shout for it, and to urge the youth of the country to enlist, and to rejoice that they are called to the service of their native land. The
sober counsels that were appropriate before the war was entered upon must
give way to blind enthusiasm, and the voice of condemnation must be si-
lenced by the thunders of the guns and the hurrahs of the crowd. Stop! A
declaration of war does not change the moral law. 'The ten commandments
will not budge' at a joint resolve of Congress. Was James Russell Lowell
aught but a good patriot when during the Mexican war he sent the stinging
shafts of his matchless satire at the heart of the monstrous iniquity, or
when, years afterward, he declared, that he thought at the time and that he
still thought the Mexican war was a national crime? Did John Bright ever
render greater service to his country than when, during the Crimean war,
he denounced the Administration which had plunged England into it, and
employed his magnificent power of earnest and incisive speech in the endeavour to repress the evil spirit which it evoked in the heart of the nation?
No! the voice of protest, of warning, of appeal is never more needed than
when the clamour of fife and drum, echoed by the press and too often by
the pulpit, is bidding all men fall in and keep step and obey in silence the
tyrannous word of command. Then, more than ever, it is the duty of the
good citizen not to be silent, and spite of obloquy, misrepresentation and
abuse, to insist on being heard, and with sober counsel to maintain the everlasting validity of the principles of the moral law.

So confused are men by false teaching in regard to national honour and
the duty of the citizen that it is easy to fall into the error of holding a declaration of war, however brought about, as a sacred decision of the national
will, and to fancy that a call to arms from the Administration has the force
of a call from the lips of the country, of the America to whom all her sons
are ready to pay the full measure of devotion. This is indeed a natural and
for many a youth not a discreditable error. But if the nominal, though
authorized, representatives of the country have brought us into a war that
might and should have been avoided, and which consequently is an unright-
eous war, then, so long as the safety of the State is not at risk, the duty of
the good citizen is plain. He is to help to provide the Administration responsible for the conduct of the war with every means that may serve to bring
it to the speediest end. He is to do this alike that the immediate evils of the
war may be as brief and as few as possible, and also that its miserable train
of after evils may be diminished and the vicious passions excited by it be
the sooner allayed. Men, money, must be abundantly supplied. But must
he himself enlist or quicken the ardent youth to enter service in such a
cause? The need is not yet. The country is in no peril. There is always in
a vast population like ours an immense, a sufficient supply of material of
a fighting order, often of a heroic courage, ready and eager for the excite-

ment of battle, filled with the old notion that patriotism is best expressed in readiness to fight for our country, be she right or wrong. Better the paying of bounties to such men to fill the ranks than that they should be filled by those whose higher duty is to fit themselves for the service of their country in the patriotic labours of peace. We mourn the deaths of our noble youth fallen in the cause of their country when she stands for the right; but we may mourn with a deeper sadness for those who have fallen in a cause which their generous hearts mistook for one worthy of the last sacrifice.

Speech, 'True Patriotism' (1898) in *Letters*, 1913

On an Invitation to the United States

THOMAS HARDY

I

My ardours for emprize nigh lost
Since Life has bared its bones to me,
I shrink to seek a modern coast
Whose riper times have yet to be;
Where the new regions claim them free
From that long drip of human tears
Which peoples old in tragedy
Have left upon the centuried years.

II

For, wonning in these ancient lands,
Enchased and lettered as a tomb,
And scored with prints of perished hands,
And chronicled with dates of doom,
Though my own Being bear no bloom
I trace the lives such scenes enshrine,
Give past exemplars present room,
And their experience count as mine.

Poems of the Past and the Present, 1901

Over There

GEORGE M. COHAN

Johnnie get your gun, get your gun, get your gun,
Take it on the run, on the run, on the run,
Hear them calling you and me,
Ev'ry son of liberty.
Hurry right away, no delay, go today,
Make your daddy glad to have had such a lad,
Tell your sweetheart not to pine,
To be proud her boy's in line.

CHORUS
Over there, over there,
Send the word over there
That the Yanks are coming,
The drums rum tumming ev'rywhere,
So prepare, say a prayer,
Send the word to beware,
We'll be over, we're coming over
And we won't come back till it's over,
Over there, over there.

Johnnie get your gun, get your gun, get your gun,
Johnnie, show the Hun you're a son of a gun,
Hoist the flag and let her fly,
Yankee Doodle do or die.
Pack your kit, show your grit, do your bit,
Yankees to the ranks from the towns and the tanks,
Make your mother proud of you
And the Red, White and Blue.

1917

'The germans'

GERTRUDE STEIN

Gertrude Stein used to get furious when the english all talked about german organisation. She used to insist that the germans had no organisation. Don't you understand the difference, she used to say angrily, any two americans, any twenty americans, any millions of americans can organise themselves to do something but germans cannot organise themselves to do anything, they can formulate a method and this method can be put upon them but that isn't organisation. The germans, she used to insist, are not modern, they are a backward people who have made a method of what we conceive as organisation, can't you see. They cannot therefore possibly win this war because they are not modern.

Then another thing that used to annoy us dreadfully was the english statement that the germans in America would turn America against the allies. Don't be silly, Gertrude Stein used to say to any and all of them, if you do not realise that the fundamental sympathy in America is with France and England and could never be with a mediaeval country like Germany, you cannot understand America. We are republican, she used to say with energy, profoundly intensely and completely a republic and a republic can have everything in common with France and a great deal in common with England but whatever its form of government nothing in common with Germany. How often I have heard her then and since explain that americans are republicans living in a republic which is so much a republic that it could never be anything else.

The Autobiography of Alice B. Toklas, 1933, ch. 6

The Evening Land

D. H. LAWRENCE

Oh, America,
The sun sets in you.
Are you the grave of our day?

Shall I come to you, the open tomb of my race?

I would come, if I felt my hour had struck.
I would rather you came to me.

For that matter
Mahomet never went to any mountain
Save it had first approached him and cajoled his soul.

You have cajoled the souls of millions of us,
America,
Why won't you cajole my soul?
I wish you would.

I confess I am afraid of you.

The catastrophe of your exaggerate love,
You who never find yourself in love
But only lose yourself further, decomposing.

You who never recover from out of the orgasm of loving
Your pristine, isolate integrity, lost æons ago.
Your singleness within the universe.

You who in loving break down
And break further and further down
Your bounds of isolation,
But who never rise, resurrected, from this grave of mingling,
In a new proud singleness, America.

Your more-than-European idealism,
Like a be-aureoled bleached skeleton hovering
Its cage-ribs in the social heaven, beneficent.

And then your single resurrection
Into machine-uprisen perfect man.

Even the winged skeleton of your bleached ideal
Is not so frightening as that clean smooth
Automaton of your uprisen self,
Machine American.

Do you wonder that I am afraid to come
And answer the first machine-cut question from the lips of your iron
    men?
Put the first cents into metallic fingers of your officers
And sit beside the steel-straight arms of your fair women,
American?

This may be a withering tree, this Europe,
But here, even a customs-official is still vulnerable.

I am so terrified, America,
Of the iron click of your human contact.
And after this
The winding-sheet of your self-less ideal love.
Boundless love
Like a poison gas.

Does no one realise that love should be intense, individual,
Not boundless.
This boundless love is like the bad smell
Of something gone wrong in the middle.
All this philanthropy and benevolence on other people's behalf
Just a bad smell.

Yet, America,
Your elvishness,
Your New England uncanniness,
Your western brutal faery quality.

My soul is half-cajoled, half-cajoled.

Something in you which carries me beyond,
Yankee, Yankee,
What we call human.
Carries me where I want to be carried . . .
Or don't I?

What does it matter
What we call human, and what we don't call human?
The rose would smell as sweet.
And to be limited by a mere word is to be less than a hopping flea,
    which hops over such an obstruction at first jump.

Your horrible, skeleton, aureoled ideal,
Your weird bright motor-productive mechanism,
Two spectres.

But moreover
A dark, unfathomed will, that is not un-Jewish;
A set, stoic endurance, non-European;
An ultimate desperateness, un-African;
A deliberate generosity, non-Oriental.
The strange, unaccustomed geste of your demonish New World nature
Glimpsed now and then.

Nobody knows you.
You don't know yourself.
And I, who am half in love with you,
What am I in love with?
My own imaginings?
Say it is not so.

Say, through the branches
America, America
Of all your machines.
Say, in the deep sockets of your idealistic skull,
Dark, aboriginal eyes
Stoic, able to wait through ages
Glancing.

Say, in the sound of all your machines
And white words, white-wash American,
Deep pulsing of a strange heart
New throb, like a stirring under the false dawn that precedes the real.

Nascent American
Demonish, lurking among the undergrowth
Of many-stemmed machines and chimneys that smoke like pine-trees.

Dark, elvish,
Modern, unissued, uncanny America,
Your nascent demon people
Lurking among the deeps of your industrial thicket
Allure me till I am beside myself,
A nympholepht,

'These States!' as Whitman said,
Whatever he meant.

Birds, Beasts and Flowers, 1923

Rank

LINCOLN KIRSTEIN

Differences between rich and poor, king and queen,
Cat and dog, hot and cold, day and night, now and then,
Are less clearly distinct than all those between
Officers and us: enlisted men.

Not by brass may you guess nor their private latrine
Since distinctions obtain in any real well-run war;
It's when off duty, drunk, one acts nice or mean
In a sawdust-strewn bistro-type bar.

Ours was on a short street near the small market square;
Farmers dropped by for some beer or oftener to tease
The Gargantuan bartender Jean-Pierre
About his sweet wife, Marie-Louise.

GI's got the habit who liked French movies or books,
Tried to talk French or were happy to be left alone;
It was our kinda club; we played chess in nooks
With the farmers. We made it our own.

To this haven one night came an officer bold;
Crocked and ugly, he'd had it in five bars before.
A lurid luster glazed his eye which foretold
He'd better stay out of our shut door,

But did not. He barged in, slung his cap on the zinc:
'Dewbelle veesky,' knowing well there was little but beer.
Jean-Pierre showed the list of what one could drink:
'What sorta jerk joint you running here?'

Jean-Pierre had wine but no whisky to sell.
Wine loves the soul. Hard liquor hots up bloody fun,
And it's our rule noncommissioned personnel
Must keep by them their piece called a gun.

As well we are taught, enlisted soldiers may never
Ever surrender this piece – M1, carbine or rifle –
With which no mere officer whomsoever
May freely or foolishly trifle.

A porcelain stove glowed in its niche, white and warm.
Jean-Pierre made jokes with us French-speaking boys.
Marie-Louise lay warm in bed far from harm;
Upstairs, snored through the ensuing noise.

This captain swilled beer with minimal grace. He began:
'Shit. What you-all are drinkin's not liquor. It's piss.'
Two privates (first class) now consider some plan
To avoid what may result from this.

Captain Stearnes is an Old Army joe. Eighteen years
In the ranks, man and boy; bad luck, small promotion;
Without brains or cash, not the cream of careers.
Frustration makes plenty emotion.

'Now, Mac,' Stearnes grins (Buster's name is not Mac; it is Jack),
'Toss me your gun an' I'll show you an old army trick;
At forty feet, with one hand, I'll crack that stove, smack.'
'Let's not,' drawls Jack back, scared of this prick.

'You young punk,' Stearnes now storms, growing moody but mean,
'Do you dream I daren't pull my superior rank?'
His hand snatches Jack's light clean bright carbine.
What riddles the roof is no blank.

The rifle is loaded as combat zones ever require.
His arm kicks back without hurt to a porcelain stove.
Steel drilling plaster and plank, thin paths of fire
Plug Marie-Louise sleeping above.

Formal enquiry subsequent to this shootin'
Had truth and justice separately demanded.
Was Stearnes found guilty? You are darned tootin':
Fined, demoted. More: reprimanded.

The charge was not murder, mayhem, mischief malicious,
Yet something worse, and this they brought out time and again:
Clearly criminal and caddishly vicious
Was his: Drinking With Enlisted Men.

I'm serious. It's what the Judge Advocate said:
Strict maintenance of rank or our system is sunk.
Stearnes saluted. Jean-Pierre wept his dead.
Jack and I got see-double drunk.

Rhymes of a PFC, 1964

'Total war'

GARRY WILLS

America in the early 1940's fell in love with total war; and no wonder. The war was the best thing that had happened to this country in a long time. It did what the New Deal never really accomplished – carried us fully out of the Great Depression, and restored us to the boom-expansiveness of our Gilded Age. It did this by renegotiating the close relationship between business and the federal government – and in the process it expanded the federal government much farther and faster than the New Deal ever did. The nation stretched and rearranged itself – blacks moved North to new jobs, women went into the work market, laboratories and universities and factories expanded with federal money and war programs. By virtue of our brains and effort, we made ourselves the most formidable industrial and military power in the history of the world. Even the secret of the universe's own structure – the atom – served our national goals, which were mankind's and the world's goals.

Americans need to find morality at work behind material success. Money is justified on Horatio Alger grounds, as the reward of virtue and effort. We never doubted our right to use absolute instruments of destruction in World War II – artificially created fire storms, saturation bombing, napalm flamethrowers, both our atom bombs – to enforce our demand for unconditional surrender. Our victory *must* be total, because we were fighting total evil. Winston Churchill piously rumbled that the Germans 'must bleed and burn, they must be crushed into a mass of smoldering ruins' – and, of the Japanese, that 'we shall wipe them out, every one of them, men, women and children.'

We achieved that most refined of pleasures, a virtuous hate. Killing for an idea is the worst kind of killing, ideological killing. Better to hate a person, the assailant of one's family or home, than to hate an idea. What if the idea hides behind an otherwise law-abiding and unmenacing exterior? Then one must steel oneself against all normal amenities and personal attraction. Then one launches a crusade – to be followed by an inquisition.

It is hard to climb back down from a self-righteous 'high' of hatred. The arrogance of victory has been a commonplace at least since Aeschylus's time. And our hate had been given the stunning late justification of Buchenwald and Belsen, the stunning last paroxysms of Hiroshima and Nagasaki. Who could doubt that ours was the purest and most complete victory ever? If power corrupts, we came closer to absolute power, over the world and over our own people's outlook, than any other nation had ever come. Why did we expect to pay no price for this? But when we set about ruling the world we had saved, liberals like Henry Steele Commager chided those who felt there could be anything impure about America's use of its power. He wrote, at the peak of the Cold War: 'The record is perhaps unique in the history of power: the organization of the United Nations, the Truman Doctrine, the Marshall Plan, the Berlin airlift, the organization of NATO, the defense of Korea, the development of atomic power for peaceful purposes, Point Four – these prodigious gestures are so wise and so enlightened that they point the way to a new concept of the use of power.' Now power purified – and the saints are free of many restrictions imposed on those without proper doctrine.

An essential ingredient of our wartime euphoria had been the concentration of our energies upon a total enemy. In 1946 there was a reluctance to surrender that focusing device. Return to peacetime was looked at warily – wartime had become 'normal', preferable to the prewar drift and sluggishness. So we maintained the draft, while Truman fought very hard to impose universal military training on all young males. The OSS was loath to go out of existence. The FBI, expanded to new kinds of power against espionage at home and throughout South America, did not want to give up its new powers. Atomic research continued at full speed and in secret, keeping the issue of security checks alive into peacetime. Crusaders slow to take their armor off get itchy under it, and start to look ridiculous. What could put the moral shine back on that armor but the discovery, off on the horizon, of another Total Enemy? The reluctance of our demobilization in late 1945 explains the rush of glee at our remobilization in early 1947. The liberal second lieutenants and intelligence officers were back in business, and business looked liberal again. We had a world still to save, with just those plans – from NATO to the Korean War – that Professor Commager called 'so wise and so enlightened'. A thousand wartime ties, relaxed slightly in 1946 to moans of economic and psychic discontent, twanged back tight again and gave America its tonic.

Ideology played its part – give the Red-baiters their due: America has never loved socialism. So did economic interest – give Coolidge his due: America's business never gets far away from Business. But so did psychology – give Aeschylus his due: wars take their toll, especially total wars, and especially a total war against a doctrine won by history's greatest military-scientific breakthrough. As Miss Hellman points out, Americans feared 'Bolshies' from 1917 on, but they did not have the instruments for a large-scale investigation or purge. The notorious Palmer Raids had to rely on a small force of federal marshals and an uncooperative Labor Department. But after World War II we had a bloated and ideologized FBI, the congressional committees, an internal security program, a worldwide intelligence operation, and the will to make our Truth prevail. Our postwar world began, instead of ending, with a bang, and we did not intend to whimper. Instead, we bullied.

Bullied, for a start, our own citizenry. But that is part of any crusade. Eleventh-century crusaders first 'cleaned out' European ghettos, before getting to the Holy Land. We began World War I by throwing men like Karl Muck into detention, and World War II by imprisoning the Nisei. In 1947 we began what James Burnham wanted to call World War III by throwing Gerhard Eisler, a German Communist visitor to this country, into a detention camp at Ellis Island. In 1947, by proclamation of the President, we were back at war, and even liberals had long been telling Americans that war obliges them to hate the alien doctrine. We obliged. Communism became exactly what Fascism had been. Our propaganda effort had to be turned against the second enemy just as it had been against the first – Congressman Nixon must 'encourage' Hollywood to make anti-Russia movies.

One reason the World War enmities could be so quickly revived, with a new focus on Russia, was the depth of America's understanding of herself as always at odds with alien doctrine. We boast that the nation was brought into being by dedication to a *proposition*, in Lincoln's phrase. We date the country's inception not from the actual inauguration of constitutional government but from the declaration of our principles thirteen years earlier. An element in America's sense of mission has always been the belief that close foreign ties might sully the purity of republican doctrine, a fear expressed by Jefferson himself. It was not enough to be American in citizenship or residence – one must be American in one's thoughts. There was such a thing as Americanism. And lack of right thinking could make an American citizen un-American. The test was ideological. That is why we had such a thing as an Un-American Activities Committee in the first place. Other countries do not think in terms of, say, Un-British Activities as a political category. But ours was the first of the modern ideological countries, born of revolutionary doctrine, and it has maintained a belief that return to doctrinal purity is the secret of national strength for us.

It is typical that the very term 'un-American activities' was first advanced by a liberal, Representative Samuel Dickstein, who proposed in 1934 that a permanent committee be established to look into the pro-German sympathies of the German-American Bund. It is also typical that in 1938, when the Committee was finally brought into being, it was the result of a compromise with those who wanted to investigate radicals and socialists as well as Fascists. Liberals in America have often elaborated an ideological test which the right wing applies more broadly and ferociously than the liberals originally intended. That is the story of Truman's loyalty program and purge of the State Department in 1947. These moves are sometimes made with a hope that they will obviate more repressive acts by the right; but instead they legitimate the later, harsher measures. All later excesses arise from the first principle of ideological self-testing. If it is not enough to possess citizenship and obey the laws, if one must also subscribe to the propositions of Americanism, then we create two classes of citizens – those loyal and pure in doctrine, and those who, without actually breaking any law, are considered un-American, insufficient in their Americanism. These latter can be harassed, spied on, forced to register, deprived of governmental jobs and other kinds of work.

It is easy to explain in this way the FBI's harassment, going far beyond enforcement of the law, of the Ku Klux Klan. After all, our country was conceived in liberty and dedicated to the proposition that all men are created equal. Since the Klan did not believe in the proposition, it was not fully American, even when it was not breaking the law. But once you set up such a division within the citizenry, you open a Pandora's box. How are we to know what others think about the doctrines of Americanism unless we investigate their thoughts, make them profess their loyalty, train children up in the government's orthodoxy? Aren't we always at war with error, both at home and abroad – and aren't wartime measures always justifiable? Aren't we all insufficiently dedicated to our self-constituting doctrine, and so must test ourselves, make demands on ourselves, train ourselves to fuller Americanism? We are not merely a country. We are an Ism. And truth must spread without limit; it cannot countenance error. So John F. Kennedy orated: 'In the election of 1860 Abraham Lincoln said the question was whether this nation could exist half-slave or half-free. In the election of 1960, and with the world around us, the question is whether the world will exist half-slave or half-free.' In the war of minds, anyone not fully committed to the propositions of freedom is an enemy. The reign of the Committee had long historical forces to draw on, explaining its power.

Introduction to Lillian Hellman's *Scoundrel Time*, 1976

Why Are We in Vietnam?

NORMAN MAILER

He knew the arguments for the war, and against the war – finally they bored him. The arguments in support of the war were founded on basic assumptions which had not been examined and were endlessly repeated – the arguments to withdraw never pursued the consequences.

He thought we were in the war as the culmination to a long sequence of events which had begun in some unrecorded fashion toward the end of World War II. A consensus of the most powerful middle-aged and elderly Wasps in America – statesmen, corporation executives, generals, admirals, newspaper editors, and legislators – had pledged an intellectual troth: they had sworn with a faith worthy of medieval knights that Communism was the deadly foe of Christian culture. If it were not resisted in the post-war world, Christianity itself would perish. So had begun a Cold War with intervals of overt war, mixed with periods of modest collaboration. As Communist China grew in strength, and her antagonisms with the Soviet Union quickened their pace, the old troth of the Wasp knights had grown sophisticated and abstract. It was now a part of the technology of foreign affairs, a thesis to be called upon when needed. The latest focus of this thesis was of course to be found in Vietnam. The arguments presented by the parties of war suggested that if Vietnam fell to the Communists, soon then would Southeast Asia, Indonesia, the Philippines, Australia, Japan, and India fall also to the Chinese Communists. Since these Chinese Communists were in the act of developing a nuclear striking force, America would face eventually a united Asia (and Africa?) ready to engage America (and Russia?) in a suicidal atomic war which might level the earth, a condition to the advantage of the Chinese Communists, since their low level of subsistence would make it easier for them to recover from the near to unendurable privations of the post-atomic world.

Like most simple political theses, this fear of a total nuclear war was not uttered aloud by American statesmen, for the intimations of such a thesis are invariably more powerful than the thesis itself. It was sufficient that a paralysis of thought occurred in the average American at the covert question: should we therefore bomb the nuclear installations of the Chinese now? Obviously, public discussion preferred to move over to the intricate complexities of Vietnam. Of course, that was an ugly unattractive sometimes disgraceful war, murmured the superior apologists for the Hawks, perhaps the unhappiest war America had ever fought, but it was one of the most necessary, for (1) it demonstrated to China that she could not advance her guerrilla activities into Asia without paying a severe price; (2) it rallied the small Asian powers to confidence in America; (3) it underlined the depth of our promise to defend small nations; (4) it was an inexpensive means of containing a great power, far more inexpensive than fighting the power itself; and (5) it was probably superior to starting a nuclear war on China.

In answer, the debaters best armed for the Doves would reply that it was certainly an ugly disgraceful unattractive war but not necessary to our defense. If South Vietnam fell to the Vietcong, Communism would be then not 12,000 miles from our shores, but 11,000 miles. Moreover, we had not necessarily succeeded in demonstrating to China that guerrilla wars exacted too severe a price from the Communists. On the contrary, a few more guerrilla wars could certainly bankrupt America, since we now had 500,000 troops in South Vietnam to the 50,000 of the North Vietnamese, and our costs for this one small war had mounted to a figure between $25,000,000,000 and $30,000,000,000 a year, not so small an amount if one is reminded that the Second World War cost a total of $300,000,000,000 over four years, or less than three times as much on an average year as Vietnam! (Of course, there has been inflation since, but still! What incredible expense for so small a war – what scandals of procurement yet to be uncovered. How many more such inexpensive wars could the economy take?)

The Doves picked at the seed of each argument. Yes, they said, by fulfilling our commitments to South Vietnam, we have certainly inspired confidence in the other small Asian powers. But who has this confidence? Why the most reactionary profiteers of the small Asian nations now have the confidence; so the small Asian nations are polarized, for the best of their patriots, foreseeing a future plunder of Asia by Asian Capitalists under America's protection, are forced over to the Communists.

Yes, the Doves would answer, it is better to have a war in Vietnam than to bomb China, but then the war in Vietnam may serve as the only possible pretext to attack China. Besides the question of Chinese aggression has been begged. China is not, by its record, an aggressive nation, but a timid one, and suffers from internal contradictions which will leave her incapable for years of even conceiving of a major war.

This was not the least of the arguments of the Doves: they could go on to point out that North Vietnam had been occupied for centuries by China, and therefore was as hostile to China as Ireland was to England – our intervention had succeeded therefore in bringing North Vietnam and China closer together. This must eventually weaken the resistance of other small Asian powers to China.

Besides, said the Doves, part of the real damage of Vietnam takes place in America where civil rights have deteriorated into city riots, and an extraordinary number of the best and most talented students in America are exploring the frontiers of nihilism and drugs.

The Doves seemed to have arguments more powerful than the Hawks. So the majority of people in America, while formidably patriotic were also undecided and tended to shift in their opinion like the weather. Yet the Hawks seemed never too concerned. They held every power securely but one, a dependable consensus of public opinion. Still this weakness left them unperturbed – their most powerful argument remained inviolate. There, the Doves never approached. The most powerful argument remained: what if we leave Vietnam, and all Asia eventually goes Communist? all of Southeast Asia, Indonesia, the Philippines, Australia, Japan, and India?

Well, one could laugh at the thought of Australia going Communist. The Hawks were nothing if not humorless. If Communist China had not been able to build a navy to cross the Straits of Formosa and capture Taiwan, one did not see them invading Australia in the next century. No, any decent Asian Communist would probably shudder at the thought of engaging the Anzacs, descendants of the men who fought at Gallipoli. Yes, the Hawks were humorless, and Lyndon Johnson was shameless. He even invoked the defense of Australia.

But could the Dove give bona fides that our withdrawal from Vietnam would produce no wave of Communism through Asia? Well, the Dove was resourceful in answers, and gave many. The Dove talked of the specific character of each nation, and the liberal alternatives of supporting the most advanced liberal elements in these nations, the Dove returned again and again to the profound weaknesses of China, the extraordinary timidity of Chinese foreign policy since the Korean war, spoke of the possibility of enclaves, and the resources of adroit, well-managed economic war in Asia.

Yet the Doves, finally, had no answer to the Hawks. For the Doves were divided. Some of them, a firm minority, secretly desired Asia to go Communist, their sympathies were indeed with Asian peasants, not American corporations, they wanted what was good for the peasant, and in private they believed Communism was probably better suited than Capitalism to introduce the technological society to the peasant. But they did not consider it expedient to grant this point, so they talked around it. The others, the majority of the Doves, simply refused to face the possibility. They were liberals. To explore the dimensions of the question, might have exploded the foundation of their liberalism, for they would have had to admit they were willing to advocate policies which would conceivably end in major advances of Asian Communism, and this admission might oblige them to move over to the Hawks.

Mailer was bored with such arguments. The Hawks were smug and self-righteous, the Doves were evasive of the real question.

Excerpt, *The Armies of the Night*, 1968, book 1, part 4, section 7

Projected Scenario of a Performance to Be Given Before the UN

LAWSON FUSAO INADA

I am a mad mother-
fucker, or in other
words, a very irate
citizen – that's what
you call the black
and white of it all.
(general applause)
But that's an over-
simplification – how
about other colors?
(scattered applause)
And I'm supposed to
be yellow as butter

or expensive spread?
Call me a very irate
fatherhugger, that's
what we Asians have
to be, making these
various variations.
But, you fine folks
sitting there behind
smiles and earphones,
don't you know that
Yellow is now in THE
majority, according
to THE latest census?
Wake up – we are king
kong over this world.
And that's why I've
retired as uncrowned
undefeated Japanese
American myopic fast
draw $1.98 stickless
temporary press poet.
Nobody listened but
a listless literati.
I got better things
to do. Lot quicker.
Quicker than trivial
treaties or ass-pats
and some minor dying.
Nothing shaping up.
That's why I shaped
this up like a comb –
so turn it sideways –
isn't that the way
we write and screw?
(applause from Jap
and Chink delegates)
That's why I already
shipped this c.o.d.
hotline to all your
prexies and diplomats
and right about NOW
they're stroking at

that funky-butt hair
and splitting right
quick from multiple
yellow monosodium A-
sian flu and nuclear
mongoloid jaundice –
whoo whee yeah, man.
(very loud applause
from slanty sections,
plus ahsos and gongs,
what else but gongs)
I tried to make this
in Confucius' shape
so it could puff up
and fly way out and
he could snipe your
ass off – but that'd
take too much time.
Get the doors, Boys –
Numbers 5 to 18 Sons –
it's what's written,
it's all over, we're
taking over, taking
back fortune cookies,
eye operations, bug
juice. Taking over
Hollywood *and* EBONY.
Taking over your old
calendar. Last year
was Year of the Wasp.
And everybody's got
to eat noodley food
with pipe cleaners.
Toss me that kimono,
Boys, and my thongs.
Make sure it's Jap
slapped on the soles.
Everybody up, y'all.
Madame Butterfly Rag.
So all together now,
sing! Think Yellow!
Bonsai! Viva Banzai!

> Top Bonanza! You're
> in the yellow misce-
> genation, number one
> like a chinaman could
> with liberty or chop-
> sticks for all – Bong!

Before the War, 1971

The Laws

MAXINE HONG KINGSTON

The United States of America and the Emperor of China cordially recognize the inherent and inalienable right of man to change his home and allegiance, and also the mutual advantage of the free migration and emigration of their citizens and subjects respectively from the one country to the other for purposes of curiosity, of trade, or as permanent residents. Article V of the Burlingame Treaty, signed in Washington, D.C., July 28, 1868, and in Peking, November 23, 1869

The First Years: 1868, the year of the Burlingame Treaty, was the year 40,000 miners of Chinese ancestry were Driven Out. The Fourteenth Amendment, adopted in that same year, said that naturalized Americans have the same rights as native-born Americans, but in 1870 the Nationality Act specified that only 'free whites' and 'African aliens' were allowed to apply for naturalization. Chinese were not white; this had been established legally in 1854 when Chan Young unsuccessfully applied for citizenship in Federal District Court in San Francisco and was turned down on grounds of race. (He would have been illegal one way or another anyway; the Emperor of China did not give permission for any of his subjects to leave China until 1859.) Debating the Nationality Act, Congressmen declared that America would be a nation of 'Nordic fiber'.

1878: California held a Constitutional Convention to settle 'the Chinese problem'. Of the 152 delegates, 35 were not American citizens but Europeans. The resulting constitution, voted into existence by a majority party of Working Men and Grangers, prohibited Chinese from entering California. New state laws empowered cities and counties to confine them within specified areas or to throw them out completely. Shipowners and captains were to be fined and jailed for hiring or transporting them. (This provision was so little respected that the American merchant marine relied heavily on Chinese seamen from the Civil War years to World War I.) 'Mongolians, Indians, and Negroes' were barred from attending public schools. The only California fishermen forced to pay fishing and shellfish taxes were the Chinese, who had brought shrimp nets from China and started the shrimp, abalone, and lobster industries. (The taxes were payable monthly.) Those Chinese over eighteen who were not already paying a miner's tax had to pay a 'police tax', to cover the extra policing their presence required. Though the Chinese were filling and leveeing the San Joaquin Delta for thirteen cents a square yard, building the richest agricultural land in the world, they were prohibited from owning land or real estate. They could not apply for business licenses. Employers could be fined and jailed for hiring them. No Chinese could be hired by state, county, or municipal governments for public works. No 'Chinese or Mongolian or Indian' could testify in court 'either for or against a white man'.

At this time San Francisco supplemented the anti-Chinese state laws with some of its own: a queue tax, a 'cubic air ordinance' requiring that every residence have so many cubic feet of air per inhabitant, a pole law prohibiting the use of carrying baskets on poles, cigar taxes, shoe taxes, and laundry taxes.

Federal courts declared some of the state and city laws unconstitutional, and occasionally citizens of a county or city repealed an especially punitive ordinance on the grounds that it was wrong to invite the Chinese to come to the United States and then deny them a livelihood. The repealed laws were often reenacted in another form.

1880: The Burlingame Treaty was modified. Instead of being free, the immigration of Chinese laborers to the United States would be 'reasonably limited'. In return (so as not to bring about limits on American entry into China), the American government promised to protect Chinese from lynchings.

1881: The Burlingame Treaty was suspended for a period of twenty years. (Since 1881 there has been no freedom of travel between China and the United States.) In protest against this suspension and against the refusal to admit Chinese boys to US Army and Naval academies, China ordered scholars studying in the United States to return home. The act suspending the treaty did have two favorable provisions: all Chinese already resident in the United States in 1882 could stay; and they were permitted to leave and reenter with a Certificate of Return.

1882: Encouraged by fanatical lobbying from California, the US Congress passed the first Chinese Exclusion Act. It banned the entrance of Chinese laborers, both skilled and unskilled, for ten years. Anyone unqualified for citizenship could not come in – and by the terms of the Nationality Act of

1870, Chinese were not qualified for citizenship. Some merchants and scholars were granted temporary visas.

1884: Congress refined the Exclusion Act with An Act to Amend an Act. This raised fines and sentences and further defined 'merchants' to exclude 'hucksters, peddlers, or those engaged in taking, draying, or otherwise preserving shell or other fish for home consumption or exportation'.

1888: The Scott Act, passed by Congress, again forbade the entry of Chinese laborers. It also declared that Certificates of Return were void. Twenty thousand Chinese were trapped outside the United States with now-useless re-entry permits. Six hundred returning travelers were turned back at American ports. A Chinese ambassador, humiliated by immigration officers, killed himself. The law decreed that Certificates of Residence had to be shown on demand; any Chinese caught without one was deported.

1889: Chinese pooled money to fight the various Exclusion Acts in the courts. They rarely won. In *Chae Chan Ping* v. *The United States*, Chae Chan Ping argued for the validity of his Certificate of Return. The Supreme Court ruled against him, saying that 'regardless of the existence of a prior treaty', a race 'that will not assimilate with us' could be excluded when deemed 'dangerous to . . . peace and security . . . It matters not in what form aggression and encroachment come, whether from the foreign nation acting in its national character or from vast hordes of its people crowding in upon us.' Moreover, said the Court, 'sojourners' should not 'claim surprise' that any Certificates of Return obtained prior to 1882 were 'held at the will of the government, revocable at any time, at its pleasure'.

1892: The Geary Act extended the 1882 Exclusion Act for another ten years. It also decreed that Chinese caught illegally in the United States be deported after one year of hard labor.

Chinese Americans formed the Equal Rights League and the Native Sons of the Golden State in order to fight disenfranchisement bills. Chinese Americans demanded the right to have their citizenship confirmed before traveling abroad.

1893: In *Yue Ting* v. *The United States*, the US Supreme Court ruled that Congress had the right to expel members of a race who 'continue to be aliens, having taken no steps toward becoming citizens, and incapable of becoming such under the naturalization laws'. This applied only to Chinese; no other race or nationality was excluded from applying for citizenship.

1896: A victory. In *Yick Wo* v. *Hopkins*, the US Supreme Court overturned San Francisco safety ordinances, saying that they were indeed designed to harass laundrymen of Chinese ancestry.

1898: Another victory. The Supreme Court decision in *The United States* v. *Wong Kim Ark* stated that a person born in the United States to Chinese parents is an American. This decision has never been reversed or changed, and it is the law on which most Americans of Chinese ancestry base their citizenship today.

1900: Deciding *The United States* v. *Mrs Cue Lim*, the Supreme Court ruled that wives and children of treaty merchants – citizens of China, aliens traveling on visas – were allowed to come to the United States.

1904: The Chinese Exclusion Acts were extended indefinitely, and made to cover Hawai'i and the Philippines as well as the continental United States. The question of exclusion was not debated in Congress; instead, the measure passed as a rider on a routine appropriations bill. China boycotted American goods in protest.

1906: The San Francisco Board of Education ordered that all Chinese, Japanese, and Korean children be segregated in an Oriental school. President Roosevelt, responding to a protest from the Japanese government, persuaded the Board of Education to allow Japanese to attend white schools.

1917: Congress voted that immigrants over sixteen years of age be required to pass an English reading test.

1924: An Immigration Act passed by Congress specifically excluded 'Chinese women, wives, and prostitutes'. Any American who married a Chinese woman lost his citizenship; any Chinese man who married an American woman caused her to lose her citizenship. Many states had also instituted antimiscegenation laws. A Supreme Court case called *Chang Chan et al.* v. *John D. Nagle* tested the law against wives. Chang Chan et al. lost. For the first time, the 1924 Immigration Act distinguished between two kinds of 'aliens': 'immigrants' were admitted as permanent residents with the opportunity to become citizens eventually; the rest – scholars, merchants, ministers, and tourists – were admitted on a temporary basis and were not eligible for citizenship. The number of persons allowed in the category of immigrant was set by law at one-sixth of one percent of the total population of that ancestry in the United States as of the 1920 census. The 1920 census had the lowest count of ethnic Chinese in this country since 1860. As a result, only 105 Chinese immigrants were permitted each year.

In *Cheuno Sumchee* v. *Nagle*, the Supreme Court once again confirmed the right of treaty merchants to bring their wives to the United States. This was a right that continued to be denied to Chinese Americans.

1938: A Presidential proclamation lifted restriction on immigration for Chinese and nationals of a few other Asian countries. The Chinese were still ineligible for citizenship, and the quota was '100'.

1943: The United States and China signed a treaty of alliance against the Japanese, and Congress repealed the Exclusion Act of 1882. Immigration continued to be limited to the 1924 quota of 105, however, and the Immigration and Nationalization Service claimed to be unable to find even that many qualified Chinese. A 'Chinese' was defined as anyone with more than

50 percent Chinese blood, regardless of citizenship or country of residence. At this time Japanese invaders were killing Chinese civilians in vast numbers; it is estimated that more than 10 million died. Chinese immigration into the United States did not rise.

1946: Congress passed the War Bride Act, enabling soldiers to bring Japanese and European wives home, then enacted a separate law allowing the wives and children of Chinese Americans to apply for entry as 'non-quota immigrants'. Only now did the ethnic Chinese population in the United States begin to approach the level of seventy years previous. (When the first Exclusion Act was passed in 1882, there were some 107,000 Chinese here; the Acts and the Driving Out steadily reduced the number to fewer than 70,000 in the 1920s.)

1948: The Refugee Act passed by Congress this year applied only to Europeans. A separate Displaced Persons Act provided that for a limited time – 1948 to 1954 – ethnic Chinese already living in the United States could apply for citizenship. During the postwar period, about 10,000 Chinese were permitted to enter the country under individual private bills passed by Congress. Confidence men, like the Citizenship Judges of old, defrauded hopeful Chinese by promising to acquire one of these bills for $1,500.

1950: After the Chinese Communist government took over in 1949, the United States passed a series of Refugee Relief Acts and a Refugee Escapee Act expanding the number of 'non-quota immigrants' allowed in. As a condition of entry, the Internal Security Act provided that these refugees swear they were not Communists. (Several hundred 'subversives or anarchists' of various races were subsequently deported; some were naturalized citizens who were 'denaturalized' beforehand.)

1952: The Immigration and Nationality Act denied admission to 'subversive and undesirable aliens' and made it simpler to deport 'those already in the country'. Another provision of this act was that for the first time Chinese women were allowed to immigrate under the same conditions as men.

1954: Ruling on *Mao* v. *Brownell*, the Supreme Court upheld laws forbidding Chinese Americans to send money to relatives in China. Before the Communist Revolution, there were no such restrictions in effect; Chinese Americans sent $70 million during World War II. Nor could they send money or gifts through CARE, UNESCO, or church organizations, which provided only for non-Communist countries.

1957: The Refugee Relief Act of 1953 expired in 1956 and was followed by the Act of 1957, which provided for the distribution of 18,000 visas that had remained unused.

1959: Close relatives, including parents, were allowed to enter.

1960: A 'Fair Share Refugee Act' allowed certain refugees from Communist and Middle Eastern countries to enter. Close to 20,000 people who were 'persecuted because of race, religion, or political beliefs' immigrated before this act was repealed in 1965, when a new act allowed the conditional entry of 10,200 refugees annually.

1962: A Presidential directive allowed several thousand 'parolees' to enter the United States from Hong Kong. Relatives of citizens and resident aliens were eligible. President Kennedy gave Congress a special message on immigration, saying, 'It is time to correct the mistakes of the past.'

1965: A new Immigration and Nationality Act changed the old quota system so that 'national origin' no longer means 'race' but 'country of birth'. Instead of being based on a percentage of existing ethnic populations in the United States, quotas were reallocated to countries – 20,000 each. But this did not mean that 20,000 Chinese immediately could or did come to the United States. Most prospective immigrants were in Hong Kong, a British colony. Colonies received 1 percent of the mother country's allotment: only 200. 'Immediate relatives', the children, spouses, and parents of citizens, however, could enter without numerical limitations. Also not reckoned within the quota limitations were legal residents returning from a visit abroad.

1968: Amendments to the Immigration and Nationality Act provided that immigrants not be allocated by race or nation but by hemispheres, with 120,000 permitted to enter from the Western Hemisphere and 170,000 from the Eastern Hemisphere. This act limits immigration from the Western Hemisphere for the first time in history. The 20,000-per-country quota remained in effect for the Eastern Hemisphere, no per-country limitation for the Western Hemisphere.

1976: The Immigration and Nationality Act Amendments, also called the Western Hemisphere Bill, equalized the provisions of law regulating immigration from the two hemispheres. The House Committee on the Judiciary in its report on this legislation stated, 'This constitutes an essential first step in a projected long-term reform of US Immigration law.' The 20,000-per-country limit was extended to the Western Hemisphere. The limitation on colonies was raised from 200 to 600.

1978: The separate quotas for the two hemispheres were replaced by a worldwide numerical limitation on immigration of 290,000 annually. On the basis of the 'immediate relatives' clause, about 22,000 Chinese enter legally each year, and the rate is increasing. There are also special quotas in effect for Southeast Asian refugees, most of whom are of Chinese ancestry. In the last decade, the ethnic Chinese population of the United States has doubled. The 1980 census may show a million or more.

China Men, 1980

ENVOI

The One Thing That Can Save America

JOHN ASHBERY

Is anything central?
Orchards flung out on the land,
Urban forests, rustic plantations, knee-high hills?
Are place names central?
Elm Grove, Adcock Corner, Story Book Farm?
As they concur with a rush at eye level
Beating themselves into eyes which have had enough
Thank you, no more thank you.
And they come on like scenery mingled with darkness
The damp plains, overgrown suburbs,
Places of known civic pride, of civil obscurity.

These are connected to my version of America
But the juice is elsewhere.
This morning as I walked out of your room
After breakfast crosshatched with
Backward and forward glances, backward into light,
Forward into unfamiliar light,
Was it our doing, and was it
The material, the lumber of life, or of lives
We were measuring, counting?
A mood soon to be forgotten
In crossed girders of light, cool downtown shadow
In this morning that has seized us again?

I know that I braid too much my own
Snapped-off perceptions of things as they come to me.
They are private and always will be.
Where then are the private turns of event
Destined to boom later like golden chimes
Released over a city from a highest tower?
The quirky things that happen to me, and I tell you,
And you instantly know what I mean?
What remote orchard reached by winding roads
Hides them? Where are these roots?

It is the lumps and trials
That tell us whether we shall be known
And whether our fate can be exemplary, like a star.

All the rest is waiting
For a letter that never arrives,
Day after day, the exasperation
Until finally you have ripped it open not knowing what it is
The two envelope halves lying on a plate.
The message was wise, and seemingly
Dictated a long time ago.
Its truth is timeless, but its time has still
Not arrived, telling of danger, and the mostly limited
Steps that can be taken against danger
Now and in the future, in cool yards,
In quiet small houses in the country,
Our country, in fenced areas, in cool shady streets.

Self-Portrait in a Convex Mirror, 1975

ACKNOWLEDGMENTS

We are grateful for permission to reprint copyright material by the following authors:

ROGER ANGELL, from *Five Seasons*, copyright 1972, 1973, 1974, 1975, 1976, 1977 by Roger Angell; reprinted by permission of Simon & Schuster and of ICM.

MARY ANTIN, from *The Promised Land*; by permission of Arno Press.

JOHN ASHBERY, from *Self-Portrait in a Convex Mirror*; by permission of Carcanet Press Ltd. 'The One Thing That Can Save America', copyright © 1975 by John Ashbery, from *Self-Portrait in a Convex Mirror*; used by permission of Viking Penguin, a division of Penguin Books USA, Inc.

W. H. AUDEN, from *Collected Poems* (ed. Edward Mendelson), and from *The Dyer's Hand*, by permission of Faber and Faber. 'American Poetry' and 'Postscript: The Almighty Dollar' from *The Dyer's Hand and Other Essays*, copyright © 1956 and 1962 by W. H. Auden; reprinted by permission of Random House, Inc. 'New Year Letter', 'Marginalia', and 'On the Circuit', copyright © 1941 and renewed 1969, 1966, and 1966 by W. H. Auden; reprinted by permission of Random House, Inc.

STEPHEN VINCENT BENÉT, 'American Names', from *The Selected Works of Stephen Vincent Benet*, Holt, Rinehart & Winston, Inc., copyright 1927, renewed © 1955; reprinted by permission of Brandt & Brandt Literary Agents, Inc.

ELIZABETH BISHOP, 'Florida', from *The Complete Poems, 1927–1979*, copyright © 1979, 1983, by Alice Helen Methfessel; reprinted by permission of Farrar, Straus & Giroux, Inc.

BLACK ELK, reprinted from *Black Elk Speaks*, by John G. Neihardt, by permission of University of Nebraska Press; copyright 1932, 1959, 1972, by John G. Neihardt; copyright © 1961 by the John G. Neihardt Trust.

ROBERT BLY, 'The United States', from *Forty Poems on Recent American History*; by permission of Robert Bly.

BERTOLT BRECHT, translated by Frank Jellinek, reprinted from *Bertolt Brecht: Poems 1913–1956*, copyright © 1976 by Eyre Methuen Ltd.; reprinted by permission of Methuen London and of the publisher Routledge, Chapman and Hall, Inc.

C. CASTANEDA (translator), from *The Mexican Side of the Texas Revolution*; by permission of Arno Press.

WILLA CATHER, from *Death Comes for the Archbishop*, copyright 1929 by Willa Cather and renewed 1957 by Edith Lewis and The City Bank Farmers Trust Co.; reprinted by permission of Virago Press and Alfred A. Knopf, Inc. From *My Antonia*, copyright 1918, © renewed 1946 by Willa Sibert Cather, copyright © renewed 1977 by Bertha Handlan; reprinted by permission of Houghton Mifflin Company; all rights reserved.

ELDRIDGE CLEAVER, from *Soul on Ice*, copyright © 1968; by permission of McGraw-Hill, Inc.

ALISTAIR COOKE, from *One Man's America*, copyright 1952 by Alistair Cooke; reprinted by permission of Alfred A. Knopf, Inc.

E. E. CUMMINGS, reprinted from *IS 5*, edited by George James Firmage, from *The Complete Poems 1913–62*, published by MacGibbon & Kee, an imprint of Harper-Collins Publishers Limited, and also by permission of Liveright Publishing Corporation. Copyright © 1985 by E. E. Cummings Trust. Copyright 1926 by Horace

reprinted by permission of the publisher. 'Theme for English B', copyright 1951 by Langston Hughes, renewed 1979 by George Houston Bass; by permission of Harold Ober Associates Incorporated.

LAWSON FUSAO INADA, 'Projected Scenario' from *Before the War*; copyright © 1971 by Lawson Fusao Inada; by permission of William Morrow & Co., Inc.

CHRISTOPHER ISHERWOOD, from *Exhumations*; reprinted by permission of Methuen London and of Donadia & Ashworth, Inc.

JACK KEROUAC, from *On the Road*; by permission of Andre Deutsch Ltd., and of the estate of the late Jack Kerouac by courtesy of A. M. Heath & Company Ltd.

MARTIN LUTHER KING, JR, from *A Testament of Hope*; by permission of Joan Daves Agency; copyright 1963 by Martin Luther King, Jr., renewed by Coretta Scott King in 1991.

MAXINE HONG KINGSTON, from *China Men*, copyright © 1977, 1978, 1979, 1980 by Maxine Hong Kingston; reprinted by permission of A. M. Heath & Company Ltd and of Alfred A. Knopf, Inc.

LINCOLN KIRSTEIN, from *Rhymes of a PFC*; by permission of Lincoln Kirstein.

WENDY LESSER, from *His Other Half: Men Looking at Women through Art*, copyright © 1991 by Wendy Lesser; by permission of Harvard University Press.

SINCLAIR LEWIS, from *Babbitt*; by permission of Jonathan Cape. Excerpt from *Babbitt*, copyright 1922 by Harcourt Brace Jovanovich, Inc. and renewed 1950 by Sinclair Lewis, reprinted by permission of the publisher.

ROBERT LOWELL, from *For the Union Dead*, by permission of Faber and Faber. 'For the Union Dead', from *For the Union Dead*; copyright © 1960, 1964 by Robert Lowell; reprinted by permission of Farrar, Straus & Giroux, Inc.

NORMAN MAILER, from *The Armies of the Night*; reprinted by permission of the author and the author's agents, Scott Meredith Literary Agency, Inc., 845 Third Avenue, New York, New York 10022; copyright © 1968 by Norman Mailer; used by permission of New American Library, a division of Penguin Books USA, Inc.

MALCOLM X, from *The Autobiography of Malcolm X*; by permission of Hutchinson.

MARY MCCARTHY, from *On the Contrary*; by permission of the Estate of the late Mary McCarthy and William Heinemann Ltd. by courtesy of A. M. Heath & Company Ltd., and of Margo Viscusi and Eve Stwertka.

H. L. MENCKEN, from *Prejudices*, copyright 1927 by Alfred A. Knopf, Inc., and renewed 1955 by H. L. Mencken; reprinted by permission of the publisher.

JAMES MICHIE, from *Possible Laughter*; by permission of James Michie.

MARIANNE MOORE, from *Complete Poems*; by permission of Faber and Faber. 'Baseball and Writing', copyright © 1961 Marianne Moore, © renewed 1989 by Lawrence E. Brinn and Louise Crane, Executors of the Estate of Marianne Moore, from *The Complete Poems of Marianne Moore*; used by permission of Viking Penguin, a division of Penguin Books USA, Inc. 'New York', reprinted by permission of Macmillan Publishing Company from *Collected Poems of Marianne Moore*; copyright 1935 by Marianne Moore, renewed 1963 by Marianne Moore and T. S. Eliot.

MERRILL MOORE, from *M*; by permission of Mrs Merrill Moore.

OGDEN NASH, from *Verses from 1929 On*, copyright 1935 by Ogden Nash; first appeared in the *Saturday Evening Post*; by permission of Little, Brown & Co. From *I Wouldn't Have Missed It*, by permission of Andre Deutsch Ltd.

FRANK O'HARA, from *Robert Motherwell*, © The Museum of Modern Art, 1965; reprinted by permission of the Museum of Modern Art. 'To the Film Industry in Crisis', from *Meditations in an Emergency*, copyright © 1957 by Frank O'Hara; used by permission of Grove Press, Inc.

SYLVIA PLATH, from *Collected Poems* (ed. Ted Hughes), by permission of Faber and

INDEX

Inclusions in the anthology are indicated by bold type.